Wittgenstein's
VIENNA

Gustav Klimt, from *Ver Sacrum*

Wittgenstein's VIENNA

Allan Janik and Stephen Toulmin

Elephant Paperbacks
Ivan R. Dee, Publisher, Chicago

This edition of *Wittgenstein's Vienna* corrects a number of minor errors, typographical and otherwise, that were part of the first edition. We are grateful to all those friends and critics who were kind enough to help us identify them, and especially to Marcel Faust and Reinhard Merkel, who carefully corrected the text in the course of preparing a German translation.
—THE AUTHORS

First ELEPHANT PAPERBACK edition published 1996 by Ivan R. Dee, Inc., 1332 North Halsted Street, Chicago 60622. Manufactured in the United States of America and printed on acid-free paper.

Library of Congress Cataloging-in-Publication Data:
Janik, Allan.
    Wittgenstein's Vienna / Allan Janik and Stephen Toulmin. — 1st Elephant pbk. ed.
        p.   cm.
    ''Elephant paperbacks.''
    Originally published: New York: Simon and Schuster, 1973.
    Includes bibliographical references and index.
    ISBN 1-56663-132-7 (alk. paper)
    1. Wittgenstein, Ludwig, 1889–1951. 2. Vienna (Austria)—Intellectual life. 3. Logical positivism.   I. Toulmin, Stephen Edelston.   II. Title.
B3376.W564J36 1996
943.6'13044—dc20   96-24766

Contents

Contents

Contents

Preface

Ludwig Wittgenstein is best known for his two major philosophical books, the *Tractatus Logico-Philosophicus,* published just after World War I, and the *Philosophical Investigations,* on which he was still working at the time of his death in 1951.

Yet, quite apart from his published writings, Wittgenstein was also a remarkable man who grew up in a remarkable milieu. He spent his childhood and youth in a family and a house that formed one of the cultural foci of Viennese life in the years between 1895 and 1914, one of the most fertile, original and creative periods in art and architecture, music, literature and psychology, as well as in philosophy. And anyone who had the chance of knowing Wittgenstein personally soon found that he had first-hand interests and knowledge in all those fields and more. So, in this book we have tried to paint a picture of late Habsburg Vienna and its cultural life; we believe that in presenting this picture we shall have helped to make Wittgenstein's own intellectual preoccupations and achievements more intelligible.

At the same time, we must make it clear at the outset that this book is in no sense a biography of Wittgenstein, either personal or intellectual. Instead, we are concerned here with one specific problem, which is defined at the end of the first chapter, and with a hypothetical solution to that problem which, if well-founded, will serve to re-establish the significance of links between Wittgenstein and the Viennese, German-language thought and art of his time that have been obscured as a result of his later associations with the English-speaking philosophers of, for example, Cambridge and Cornell. In order to deal with this problem effectively, we were compelled—in the nature of the case—to assemble a substantial body of circumstantial evidence, especially about such comparatively unfamiliar figures as Karl Kraus and Fritz Mauthner. Rather than sacrifice too much of the resulting detail so as to keep the focus on Wittgenstein alone, we have decided to present the whole of our picture, in all its richness and complexity, in a way that makes Wittgenstein a crucial figure, but not the only man on stage. Apart from anything else, it seemed to us, this had the makings of a good story!

A few explanatory remarks should be added about the structure of the book and the nature of the claims we would make for its argument. In the first place, then, Chapter 2 is not intended as a formal history of the late Habsburg scene. (For that, someone with the talents and experience of a Carl Schorske would be required.) Rather, it represents a collection of sample episodes and items chosen to set the scene for the analysis that follows. It is based, in part, on autobiographical reminiscences of such eyewitnesses as Bruno Walter and Stefan Zweig, and on the writings of such contemporary authors as Robert Musil; in part, on conversations with a great range of friends and acquaintances in Vienna and elsewhere; in part, on standard historical authorities. For anyone who knows his Musil or Schorske it will contain no surprises. On the contrary, one of the most striking things we found, in preparing this chapter, was the unanimity—often, down to the very adjectives—of the reports and descriptions of the different writers and speakers on whom we relied.

The chapter on Karl Kraus is another matter. Hitherto, scholarly studies of Kraus have been chiefly literary (e.g., those of Zohn and Iggers) or historical (e.g., that of Frank Field). Though our own discussion does not seriously contradict or supersede those studies, it does go beyond them, in placing a novel philosophical and ethical interpretation on Kraus's writings and opinions. The central importance we have given to Kraus as a representative ethical spokesman for his milieu is one point over which this book makes new claims and must be judged as such. To some extent, the same is true of the manner in which we have juxtaposed Ludwig Wittgenstein and Fritz Mauthner. Although Wittgenstein explicitly contrasts his own philosophical approach to that of Mauthner at one central point in the *Tractatus,* we have no further evidence that the *Tractatus* itself was actually intended as a reply to Mauthner's earlier "critique of language"; so our view of the relations between Mauthner and Wittgenstein is, in this respect, frankly conjectural.

A word about our division of labor: the main work involved in the preparation of Chapters 2, 3, 4 and 5 was undertaken by A.S.J., that for Chapters 1, 7, 8 and 9 by S.E.T., while that for

Chapter 6 was shared. Both of us, however, have worked over the entire book and have agreed on the final text. Given the unorthodoxy of the central view here presented, and the great differences in our respective backgrounds and directions of approach, it has been a surprise and a delight to discover how quickly and how easily we were in fact able to reach agreement on all substantial points. Specifically, S.E.T. knew Wittgenstein personally, and studied under him at Cambridge in 1941 and again in 1946–47, coming to his work primarily from the standpoints of physics, philosophy of science and philosophical psychology. A.S.J. came to Wittgenstein's work much later, with a previous preparation in ethics, general philosophy and intellectual history, writing an M.A. thesis at Villanova University on the parallels between Schopenhauer and Wittgenstein, and a doctoral dissertation at Brandeis University, much of which is incorporated in the present book. Despite these differences, we have had no difficulty in arriving at a common view of Wittgenstein's work and its significance, which diverges markedly from the "received interpretation"—as represented in the commentaries of, for example, Max Black and Elizabeth Anscombe—that is based almost exclusively on Wittgenstein's association with the logicians Gottlob Frege and Bertrand Russell. In this, we have had some encouragement from conversations with Professor G. H. von Wright and others, whose familiarity with the German-language physics, philosophy and literature of the period has made them aware how necessary it is to consider Wittgenstein not just as a logician and philosopher of language, but also as a Viennese and a student of theoretical physics and engineering.

Many friends and colleagues in the United States, Austria and elsewhere have helped us in our work. Michael Slattery, of Villanova, first introduced A.S.J. to the subject, and he has remained a valued onlooker and critic; Harry Zohn, of Brandeis, has unstintingly given advice and help from his vast knowledge of the late Habsburg period. Some of the preparatory work for the book was included in an article by S.E.T. for *Encounter* and in a paper given before the Boston Colloquium for Philosophy of Science in January 1969. In Vienna, A.S.J. had extensive conversations with many people; among those who went particularly out of their way to help were Marcel Faust, Raoul Kneucker, Rudolf Koder and Dr. and Mrs. Paul Schick. The same was true, in Innsbruck, of Walter Methlagl, of the *Brenner Archiv*. In addition, the reference staff of the Österreichische Nationalbiblio-thek and the Wiener Universitätsbibliothek were most helpful at every stage.

Above all, we are happy to express our warmest thanks to all those members of Ludwig Wittgenstein's family who gave us so much information and so vivid a picture about Wittgenstein the man, his family background and the milieu into which he grew up, notably, to his nephew Thomas Stonborough, without whose willing and generous collaboration all our work would have been so much harder. The "all-pervading atmosphere of humanity and culture" which Bruno Walter found among the Wittgensteins at the turn of the century has not been diminished in the least with the passage of time.

ALLAN S. JANIK
STEPHEN E. TOULMIN

1

Introduction:

PROBLEMS AND METHODS

Our subject is a fourfold one—a book and its meaning; a man and his ideas; a culture and its preoccupations; a society and its problems. The society is Kakania*—in other words, Habsburg Vienna during the last twenty-five or thirty years of the Austro-Hungarian Empire, as captured with such perceptive irony by Robert Musil in the first documentary volume of his novel *The Man Without Qualities*. The culture is, or appears at first sight to be, our own twentieth-century culture in its infancy; the "modernism" of the early 1900s, represented by such men as Sigmund Freud, Arnold Schönberg, Adolf Loos, Oskar Kokoschka and Ernst Mach. The man is Ludwig Wittgenstein; the youngest son of Vienna's leading steel magnate and patron of the arts, who set aside his necktie and his family fortune in favor of a life of Tolstoyan simplicity and austerity. The book is Wittgenstein's *Tractatus Logico-Philosophicus*, or *Logisch-philosophische Abhandlung*,[1] a highly condensed and aphoristic text on the philosophy of language which claimed to present, "on all essential points, the final solution of the problems of philosophy"[2] and was recognized from the outset as being one of the key works of its age,[3] yet remains even today one of the least self-explanatory books ever published—an enigma, or *roman à clef*, to which the reader can bring any of a dozen different interpretations.

* This name was invented by Robert Musil, and combines two senses on different levels. On the surface, it is a coinage from the initials K.K. or K. u. K., standing for "Imperial-Royal" or "Imperial and Royal," which distinguished all the major institutions of the Habsburg Empire. (For this, see the quotation from Musil below, in Chapter 2, page 36.) But to anyone familiar with German nursery language, it carries also the secondary sense of "Excrementia" or "Shitland."

13

Our aim is, by academic standards, a radical one: to use each of our four topics as a mirror in which to reflect and to study all the others. If we are right, the central weaknesses manifested in the decline and fall of the Habsburg Empire struck deep into the lives and experiences of its citizens, shaping and conditioning the central and common preoccupations of artists and writers in all fields of thought and culture, even the most abstract: while, in return, the cultural products of the Kakanian milieu shared certain characteristic features, which speak of, and can throw light on, the social, political and ethical context of their production. These features, we shall argue, are epitomized most concisely in Wittgenstein's *Tractatus*.

In putting forward such a thesis, one must immediately be aware of the opposition it will provoke, merely on account of its *form,* and also of the serious problems of intellectual method and proof which are necessarily involved in making out a case in its defense.[4] So let us begin here by indicating straightaway why, in our opinion, every one of our four chosen topics presents special problems and paradoxes to orthodox scholarly analysis and calls for hypotheses of a special, and specifically interdisciplinary, kind.

Our tentative solutions to these Kakanian paradoxes will have nothing particularly mystifying or high-flown about them. Far from producing some *Zeitgeist* or similar historical *virtus dormitiva* as the unenlightening key to our explanatory analysis, we shall simply draw attention to ("assemble reminders about") a large number of well-attested facts about the social and cultural situation in the last years of Habsburg Vienna. And we shall add, as the "missing premises" in our argument, a severely limited number of supplementary hypotheses, several of which are at once open to indirect support and confirmation.

The residual problems on which we shall be concentrating arise in the following way. Suppose we approach the last days of the Austro-Hungarian Empire—or, as Karl Kraus ironically called them, *Die Letzten Tage der Menschheit*[5]—with absolute respect for the accepted subdivision of the academic enterprise into separate "fields of study," each with its own independent set of "established" methods and questions. The result will be that, even before we begin our specific discussion of the four topics in turn, we shall have abstracted and separated both the problems that we are allowed to pose and the considerations we are permitted to advance.

The political and constitutional history of the Habsburg regime is (on this assumption) a subject to be discussed entirely on its own. A narrative account of its fortunes and misfortunes in the years between 1890 and 1919 should presumably be constructed around the actions and motives of the Emperor Francis Joseph and the Archduke Francis Ferdinand, the conversations of Aehrenthal and Izvolski, the attitudes of all the varied parties and nationalities, the corrosive effects of the 1909 Zagreb treason trials and the associated Friedjung Affair, and the rising star of Thomas Masaryk. The origins of Schönberg's twelve-tone system of musical composition are something quite else. The historian of music must presumably focus his attention, in that case, on the technical problems posed by the apparent exhaustion of the older diatonic system in Wagner, Richard Strauss, and the earlier works of Schönberg himself. (It would not immediately occur to him that Schönberg's relations with a journalist like Kraus had any direct significance for an understanding of his musical theories.) Likewise with the artistic breakaway by which the painters of the Secession separated themselves from the established activities of orthodox academic art; likewise, again, with the beginnings of "legal positivism" in the jurisprudence of Hans Kelsen; with the literary ambitions and fortunes of Rilke and Hofmannsthal; with the analytical methods of Boltzmann's statistical thermodynamics, the parts played by Adolf Loos and Otto Wagner as precursors of the Bauhaus school of architecture, and the philosophical program of the *Wiener Kreis*. In each case, the orthodox first step is to treat the developments in question as episodes in a more or less self-contained history of, say, painting or legal theory, architectural design or epistemology. Any suggestion that their cross-interactions might have been as significant as their own internal evolutions will be considered only grudgingly, after all internal factors have been demonstrably exhausted.

As for the life and character of a man like Ludwig Wittgenstein, who became notorious—even legendary—for personal idiosyncrasies and quirks of temperament, it would seem at first glance quite indispensable to leave these on one side when assessing his direct intellectual contributions to the philosophical debate.[6] Meanwhile, when considering the *Tractatus* from the point of view of historians of logic or philosophers of language, it seems that we can hardly do anything else than begin from Gottlob Frege and Bertrand Russell, who were the explicit objects of Wittgenstein's admiration, and ask how far Wittgenstein's own formal and conceptual innovations enabled him to overcome the logical and philosophical obstacles left unsolved by Russell and Frege.

That, one must say, *would* in each case be the course to adopt, *on the assumption* that the Viennese situation truly lent itself to a complete understanding, in terms of the orthodox modes of academic inquiry. Our present account, by contrast, rests—methodologically speaking—on the contrary assumption: namely, that the distinctive features of the social and cultural situation in the Vienna of the early 1900s require us for once to question the initial abstractions involved in the orthodox separation of powers of, for example, constitutional history, musical composition, physical theory, political journalism and philosophical logic. For, so long as we treat the validity of those abstractions as absolute, some of the most striking things about Ludwig Wittgenstein the man and his first philosophical masterpiece, about Viennese modernism and its Habsburg background will remain not just unexplained but inexplicable. On the other hand, these very same features can become wholly intelligible and lose their paradox, on one condition: namely, that we look at the cross-interactions among (1) social and political development, (2) the general aims and preoccupations in different fields of contemporary art and science, (3) Wittgenstein's personal attitude toward questions of morality and value, and (4) the problems of philosophy, as these problems were understood in the Vienna of 1900 and as Wittgenstein himself presumably conceived them when he embarked on the inquiries of which the *Tractatus* was the end product.

For example, by the standards of the late nineteenth century, Austria-Hungary, or the Dual Monarchy, or the House of Habsburg—to refer to it by only three of its many alternative designations—was one of the acknowledged "superpowers," having a vast territory, a well-established power structure, and a long record of apparent constitutional stability. In 1918, the political work of centuries collapsed like a card castle. Whereas in 1945 the imperial house of Japan retained enough mandate to bow before the consequences of military defeat without dynastic disaster, and whereas after 1918 Wilhelmine Germany preserved the political unity imposed on it by Bismarck even though losing its royal head, in the Habsburg superpower military defeat was followed at once by the crumbling-away not just of the monarchy's authority, but of all the pre-existing political bonds holding the Empire together. For centuries the existence of the House of Habsburg was a dominant political fact—perhaps, even, *the* dominant political fact—throughout its ancestral territories. Yet, leaving aside the architectural style of castles and town halls, and the German-speaking communities of, say, Transylvania and the Banat, the Balkans today show scarcely any sign that the Habsburg Empire ever existed. It has vanished leaving little more trace than the Hitlerian occupation of 1938–44, or the Japanese Co-Prosperity Sphere of 1941–45. Even its great rival, the Ottoman Empire, has left a more enduring mark on Balkan life and customs, as one soon discovers in areas like Macedonia and South Serbia, where many towns and villages retain their mosques and the Turkish language is still an accepted medium of communication among Greek- and Vlach- and Slavic- and Albanian-speaking villages.[7]

After reading the standard political histories of the Dual Monarchy, however, one is left in some bewilderment that the First World War had quite so catastrophic an effect on Habsburg power and influence. After riding out the revolutionary storms of 1848, military defeat by Prussia, and a whole sequence of nationalist movements among Magyars and Czechs, Rumanians and South Slavs, why did it then collapse so finally and completely? Even as comprehensive and magisterial a work as C. A. Macartney's *The Habsburg Empire, 1790–1918,* leaves one much better informed about the trees, yet almost as much in the dark about the wood as before. But, after all, there is no reason for surprise in this. Given all the rules of the scholarly game, it is the prime task of such works to add to our detailed knowledge of all the political conversations, maneuvers, concordats, conferences and decrees through which the constitutional history of the chosen period and regime worked itself out; and this tends only to distract us from the larger framework of scientific, artistic and philosophical ideas, ethical and social attitudes, personal and communal aspirations, within which all those political moves took place, and on whose character they were necessarily dependent for their leverage and long-term effect. It is only rarely that these ideas and attitudes have the direct relevance to the immediate course of social and political change that we shall find them having in turn-of-the-century Austria.

Similarly, if we look on early-twentieth-century Viennese architecture and art, journalism and jurisprudence, philosophy and poetry, music, drama and sculpture as so many parallel and independent activities which just happened to be going on in the same place at the same time, we shall once again end by accumulating vast amounts of detailed technical information in each separate field, while shutting our eyes to the most significant fact about all of them—namely, that they *were* all going on in this same place at this same time. In this respect, we can easily be misled by the profound differences between late Habsburg Vienna—where artistic and cultural life was the concern of a tightly knit group of artists, musicians and writers who were accustomed to meeting and arguing almost every day and had little sense of the need for professional specialization—and present-day Britain or America, say, where academic and artistic specialization is taken for granted and the various fields of creative activity are cultivated in substantial independence of one another. If Viennese culture in the 1900s did us the favor of mirroring our own current specializations, the separation of (for example) art-history and literature might indeed be legitimate and relevant. As it is, we overlook the interdependence of the different Viennese arts and sciences at our peril.

Was it an absolute coincidence that the beginnings of twelve-tone music, "modern" architecture, legal and logical positivism, nonrepresentational painting and psychoanalysis—not to mention the revival of interest in Schopenhauer and Kierkegaard—were all taking place simultaneously and were so largely concentrated in Vienna? Was it merely a curious biographical fact that the young conductor Bruno Walter should regularly have accompanied Gustav Mahler to the Wittgenstein family mansion in Vienna and should have discovered in conversation that shared interest in Kantian philosophy which led Mahler to present Walter at Christmas, 1894, with the collected works of Schopenhauer?[8] And was it no more than a personal tribute to the individual versatility of Arnold Schönberg that he turned out a striking series of paintings and some highly distinguished essays, on top of his revolutionary activities as a composer and musical theorist? This may seem to be so, until we find Schönberg presenting a copy of his great musical textbook on *Harmonie-lehre* to the journalist and writer Karl Kraus, with the inscription, ''I have learned more from you, perhaps, than a man should learn, if he wants to remain independent.''[9]

If, by contrast, we are prepared to take Schönberg's own practice and testimony at their face value, we shall have to change our methods of inquiry. Why does it seem paradoxical to us today that Schönberg, the musician, should have recognized a profound debt to a journalist such as Kraus? And why—more generally—did artistic and intellectual methods which, up to the late 1880s, had kept their place in so many fields almost without challenge come under critical attack and find themselves displaced by the modernism which was the wonder or horror of our grandfathers, all at the same moment? We shall never succeed in answering these questions, if we confine our attentions narrowly to, say, the novel principles of twelve-tone composition, the stylistic innovations of Klimt, or the extent of Freud's indebtedness to Meynert and Breuer. Still less, shall we then be able to broaden our social view and recognize how that same Vienna, which prided itself on its image as the City of Dreams, could at the same time be described by its own most penetrating social critic as the ''Proving-Ground for World Destruction.''[10]

Similar paradoxes and inconsistencies distort our view of Ludwig Wittgenstein, both as a man and as a philosopher. As has often been remarked, one of the gravest misfortunes that can affect a writer of great intellectual seriousness and strong ethical passions is to have his ideas ''naturalized'' by the English. All the moral indignation, political barbs and social vitriol of George Bernard Shaw were robbed of their power the moment the English public for which he wrote pigeonholed him securely as an Irish wag and a comic playwright. And something of this same fate has shaped the current reputation of Ludwig Wittgenstein—at any rate, as he is seen by most professional English-speaking philosophers in Britain and America.

When, at Frege's suggestion, Wittgenstein first made contact with Russell and was drawn into the charmed circle of Cambridge intellectuals who so influenced his life both before 1914 and again from 1929 on, he was entering into a cultural situation and a group of active, opinionated and self-willed men having well-marked preoccupations and a very definite history.[11] Russell, in particular, was charmed, intrigued and impressed; it was gratifying and flattering to find this brilliant young foreigner paying so much attention to his work on logic and apparently ready to take up his own unsolved problems just at the point where Russell left off.[12] So it is understandable that Russell himself thought of Wittgenstein as a highly talented friend and pupil, and viewed his comments and writings entirely with an eye to his own problems in symbolic logic and epistemology; and it is pardonable, also, that Wittgenstein's later abandonment of formal, quasi-mathematical methods and problems in favor of a more discursive, "natural-history" approach to human language, should have struck Russell as a heresy, and even as a defection.[13] Yet, the very fact that Wittgenstein was introduced to the other Cambridge philosophers—and so to the whole network of English-speaking academic philosophers—through Bertrand Russell has given the whole subsequent interpretation of Wittgenstein's ideas a Cambridge-orientated stamp. As a by-product of this fact, a gulf has opened up between our views of the academic Wittgenstein and Wittgenstein the man. Surely (his Cambridge colleagues agreed) he was a curious, touchy and eccentric figure, with un-English habits of dress and social opinions, and a quite unfamiliar moral earnestness and intensity. Yet they were ready to ignore these foreign oddities and idiosyncrasies on account of the unique contribution he was apparently making to the development of English philosophy.

When Wittgenstein submitted the *Tractatus* as his doctoral dissertation, G. E. Moore is reputed to have sent in an examiner's report including the words, "It is my personal opinion that Mr. Wittgenstein's thesis is a work of genius; but, be that as it may, it is certainly well up to the standard required for the Cambridge degree of Doctor of Philosophy."[14] And a "genius" was what he remained to the end, in the eyes of his English-speaking colleagues and successors. By labeling Wittgenstein as a foreigner of odd personal habits, with an extraordinary, phenomenal, possibly unique, talent for philosophical invention, the English thus defused the impact of his personality and moral passion as completely as they had earlier neutralized Shaw's social and political teachings. It scarcely seems to have occurred to them that there might be more than a chance connection between the man who rejected all his traditional privileges as a fellow of Trinity College, Cambridge, who was never seen around the town except wearing an open-necked shirt and one or two zipper-fastened parkas, and who insisted passionately—as a point of ethics rather than aesthetics—that the only kind of movies worth seeing were Westerns, and (on the other hand) the philosopher whose brilliant variations on the theories of Frege, Russell and G. E. Moore were doing so much to carry forward the English philosophical argument. No doubt, something in his family background and upbringing would explain his personal peculiarities—"Viennese, you know; Freud and all that . . ."—but, meanwhile, we must concentrate our professional attentions on the propositions advanced by Wittgenstein the formal logician and philosopher of language.

This was the point of view from which Wittgenstein's students at Cambridge still saw him during his final years in the Chair of Philosophy at Cambridge, to which he was appointed after Moore's retirement.[15] Those of us who attended his lectures during the Second World War or during his last two years of teaching there, in 1946 and 1947, still found ourselves looking upon his ideas, his methods of argument and his very topics of discussion as something totally original and his own. Viewed against the English background, indeed, his later teachings appeared unique and extraordinary, just as the *Tractatus* had earlier appeared to Moore. For our own part, we struck Wittgenstein as intolerably stupid. He would denounce us to our faces as unteachable, and at times he despaired of getting us to recognize what sort of point he was trying to get across to us. For we had come to his sparsely furnished eagle's-nest of a room at the top of the Whewell's Court tower with philosophical problems of our own; and we were happy enough to lap up the examples and fables which comprised so large a part of his lectures and bring them to bear on those preconceived, Anglo-American questions. His denunciations we ignored. At best we treated them as jokes; at worst they seemed to us at the time one more manifestation of the intellectual arrogance that had led him to speak of "the *truth* of the thoughts" set out in the *Tractatus* as "unassailable and definitive" and as "the final solution" to the problems of philosophy.[16]

Yet the question needs now to be raised, in retrospect, whether, after all, the mutual incomprehension between Wittgenstein and his Cambridge pupils was not *genuine*—indeed, whether it was not as complete and thoroughgoing as he himself evidently believed.

If the story we shall be telling in the present book has any validity, one of its implications will be that the preconceptions with which his English hearers approached him debarred them almost entirely from understanding the point of what he was saying. We saw him as a divided man, as an English-speaking philosopher with a uniquely original technical genius, who just happened also to adhere personally to an extreme moral individualism and egalitarianism. We would have done better to see him as an integral and authentically Viennese genius who exercised his talents and personality on philosophy among other things, and just happened to be living and working in England. At the time, Wittgenstein appeared to be spinning the whole substance of his later philosophy out of his own head, like some intellectually creative spider; in fact, much of his material had origins that his English audiences knew next-to-nothing about, and many of the problems he chose to concentrate on had been under discussion among German-speaking philosophers and psychologists since before the First World War. If there was an intellectual gulf between us and him, it was not because his philosophical methods, style of exposition and subject matter were (as we supposed) unique and unparalleled. It was a sign, rather, of a culture clash: the clash between a Viennese thinker whose intellectual problems and personal attitudes alike had been formed in the neo-Kantian environment of pre-1914, in which logic and ethics were essentially bound up with each other and with the critique of language (*Sprachkritik*), and an audience of students whose philosophical questions had been shaped by the neo-Humean (and so pre-Kantian) empiricism of Moore, Russell and their colleagues.

In our present argument, we shall not say anything to cast doubt on either the importance or the originality of Wittgenstein's actual contributions to philosophy; on the contrary, once his arguments are put back into context and the sources of his problems are identified, the true novelty and significance of his ideas becomes all the more apparent. But we shall be having to insist, in due course, that Wittgenstein the moral individualist and Wittgenstein the technical philosopher of "truth tables" and "language games" were quite as much alternative aspects of a single consistent personality as, say, Leonardo the anatomist and draftsman, or Arnold Schönberg the painter and essayist, musical theorist and admirer of Karl Kraus.

The need to look afresh at the relation between Wittgenstein

Introduction

the man and Wittgenstein the philosopher is confirmed, when we turn to the fourth outstanding set of unresolved paradoxes and problems. These are the ones that arise directly in the interpretation of the *Tractatus Logico-Philosophicus* itself. As we have remarked, Wittgenstein's writings have commonly been viewed as contributions to the development of either twentieth-century mathematical logic or British analytical philosophy. His personal associations with Russell and Frege, G. E. Moore and John Wisdom, have overshadowed everything else in his cultural origins and intellectual concerns. He has been applauded or attacked as the coauthor of the "method of truth tables," as the dominant influence on the positivism of the interwar years, as the critic of "private languages," "ostensive definitions" and "sense data," as the analyst of "intellectual cramps," "language games" and "forms of life"—in short, as a man who took the ideas and methods of Bertrand Russell and G. E. Moore, and refined them far beyond anything their first authors had imagined. Yet, if we see the publication of the *Tractatus* exclusively as an episode in the history of philosophical logic, one significant feature of the book remains totally mysterious. After some seventy pages apparently devoted to nothing but logic, theory of language and the philosophy of mathematics or natural science, we are suddenly faced by five concluding pages (propositions 6.4 on) in which our heads are seemingly wrenched around and we are faced with a string of dogmatic theses about solipsism, death and "the sense of the world" which "must lie outside the world." Given the sheer disproportion in the space allotted respectively to the logico-philosophical preliminaries and these last moral-theological aphorisms, the temptation has been to dismiss the final propositions as *obiter dicta*—like the casual afterthoughts which are put in for effect at the end of some legal judgment and have no subsequent binding force, since they have no juridical bearing on the case in hand.[17]

Yet is this reading of the *Tractatus* really justified? Were these last reflections about ethics, value and "the problems of life" mere claptraps, makeweights, or private afterthoughts? Or do they have some integral connection with the main text, which the familiar interpretation overlooks? So long as one remains in the professional technical world of English-language philosophy, this doubt is, perhaps, no more than academic. But it becomes an active one, when one makes the geographical shift from Cambridge to Austria and finds that the *Tractatus* is usually viewed as an ethical treatise. Those Austrians who were closest to Wittgenstein insist that whenever he concerned himself with anything, it was from the ethical point of view; in this sense he reminded one of them directly of Kierkegaard.[18] The *Tractatus* was more than merely a book on ethics in the eyes of his family and friends; it was an ethical *deed*, which *showed* the nature of ethics. And this impression is only reinforced by the recent *Memoir*, published along with Paul Engelmann's collection of *Letters from Ludwig Wittgenstein*, as well as by his correspondence with Ludwig Ficker.[19] For Engelmann, with whom Wittgenstein discussed the *Tractatus* more than he did with any of the other people who have since written about it, the point of the book was deeply ethical. Engelmann characterized Wittgenstein's basic idea as that of separating ethics from any sort of intellectual underpinning. Ethics was a matter of "wordless faith"; and Wittgenstein's other concerns were viewed as arising, predominantly, out of this fundamental notion.

We accordingly find a direct conflict between the established English-language literature, which treats the *Tractatus* as an essay about logic and the theory of language, and the tradition, still current in Viennese intellectual circles, which takes a very different view of what Wittgenstein was doing. Ever since Bertrand Russell wrote his introductory essay to the *Tractatus,* English-speaking philosophers have almost universally assumed that the fundamental concern of the *Tractatus* was with technical problems in philosophical logic and with the relation of language to the world. The fact that Wittgenstein initially rejected Russell's introductory essay as misleading, even to the point of wondering whether he should withdraw the book from publication,[20] they have construed as indicating only that Russell had misrepresented certain limited aspects of the work; basically, they have continued to consider it an investigation of the logic of language, with certain curious implications about values. This interpretation has gathered weight from the fact that logical positivists, such as Carnap and Ayer, clutched the work to their bosoms and treated it as an empiricist bible. And, although somebody as close to Wittgenstein as Elizabeth Anscombe has dismissed the views of the positivists as irrelevant to a proper understanding of the *Tractatus,* her own alternative claim is simply that too little attention has been paid to Frege as Wittgenstein's most important precursor—so keeping the spotlight firmly focused on logic.[21]

Anyone who tries to understand the *Tractatus* is, therefore, confronted with two contrasting views about the very subject matter of the book. These may be referred to, for convenience, as the "ethical" and the "logical" interpretations. Both views have reputable support. Both explain certain aspects of the *Tractatus*, yet neither suffices as a complete explanation. Our own analysis in this book will, once again, have the effect of reversing the balance in the current English and American view. We shall be arguing here that, in order to understand the book in a way which coincides with Wittgenstein's own intentions, one must accept the primacy of the "ethical" interpretation. Quite apart from all the circumstantial evidence that we shall be assembling in the following chapters, there are two immediate reasons for doing so. In the first place, Wittgenstein himself objected to every interpretation given to the work during his lifetime; and most subsequent interpretations have differed from those published during his lifetime only in detail. In the second place, Paul Engelmann's firsthand testimony must be regarded as more authoritative than the subsequent inferences of those who have approached the *Tractatus* with "logical" presuppositions and orientations. After all, Engelmann was in close contact with Wittgenstein during the very period when the book was written, and the two men had frequent opportunities for discussing the work.

The most important suggestion that Engelmann has to offer about the interpretation of the *Tractatus* is that the book should be considered as emerging from a particular cultural milieu. Engelmann identifies this milieu with the Vienna in which Wittgenstein grew to maturity and in particular with a current in that milieu represented most strikingly in the works of Karl Kraus and Adolf Loos.[22] Unfortunately, Engelmann himself provides very little information about the Vienna of Kraus and Loos— only the bare bones of the cultural scene in *fin-de-siècle* Vienna. And one of the main purposes of the present book is to pursue further the area of investigation that Engelmann has opened up: namely, the historical dimension of Wittgenstein's early work.

A very few writers have offered other, complementary insights into Wittgenstein's historical background. His friend and pupil Maurice Drury has reported that Wittgenstein regarded Kierkegaard as the most important thinker of the nineteenth century;[23] Miss Anscombe has suggested that his work is seen properly only in relation to that of Frege;[24] several writers have noticed similarities and parallels between the views of Wittgenstein and those of Schopenhauer;[25] Erich Heller and Werner Kraft have emphasized the relation of the *Tractatus* to writings about the nature of language by other Central European thinkers of the same time, such as Kraus, Mauthner and Landauer;[26] while Erik Stenius and Morris Engel have pointed to Kantian elements both in the *Tractatus,* and in Wittgenstein's later philosophy.[27] Yet much more than this needs to be done to bring to light the essential character of the Viennese cultural scene, if one is to resolve entirely the central paradox about the *Tractatus*— namely, how one is to reconcile the "ethical" Wittgenstein with the "logical" Wittgenstein and so heal over the incision that subsequent academic surgery has made in our views both of the man and of his work.

In this preliminary discussion of method, our argument has been that an orthodox, scholarly analysis imposes on our picture of Wittgenstein's Vienna, and of Wittgenstein himself, abstractions which are in point of fact irrelevant and inapplicable. There are two reasons for this irrelevance, one general, the other peculiar to philosophy. In the first place, all the abstractions in question take for granted—and are themselves products of—an intellectual and artistic specialization which was unknown in the cultural life of late Habsburg Vienna and has become entrenched only in the subsequent fifty years. In the second place, they reflect more particularly a conception of philosophy as an autonomous, professionalized academic discipline—a conception that has become dominant in the universities of Britain and the United States only since the Second World War and is uniquely irrelevant to pre-1914 Austria. In Wittgenstein's Vienna, everyone in the educated world discussed philosophy and regarded the central issues in post-Kantian thought as bearing directly on his own interests, whether artistic or scientific, legal or political. Far from being the specialized concern of an autonomous and self-contained discipline, philosophy for them was multifaceted and interrelated with all other aspects of contemporary culture.

Given this contrast, one further question arises. After 1920 the *Tractatus* itself became a foundation stone of the new "professionalized" philosophy. Within the resulting discipline, the attempt was made to separate "technical" issues of philosophy from their larger cultural matrix and to set these theoretical analyses on an independent basis, as free from extraneous commitments as the problems and theorems of, say, pure mathematics.[28] Yet was this (we must now ask) in any way part of Wittgenstein's own intention? And can we hope to understand the *Tractatus* aright if we see it primarily as an element in the academic traditions which other men subsequently built upon it? That too is a question which we shall answer in our own way, in the light of our present investigations. For the moment, it is enough to point out one thing only. Wittgenstein himself did nothing to cut himself off from the wider literary and cultural traditions with which he was familiar in his youth. His comparative ignorance of the older philosophical classics was counterbalanced by a rich and varied familiarity with the main figures on the German and Austrian scene. And the mottoes he chose for his two chief books were taken from authors who could hardly have been more typically Viennese—Kürnberger for the *Tractatus*, Nestroy for the *Investigations*.

George Santayana used to insist that those who are ignorant of the history of thought are destined to re-enact it. To this, we shall here add a corollary: that those who are ignorant of the context of ideas are, similarly, destined to misunderstand them. In a very few self-contained theoretical disciplines—for example, the purest parts of mathematics—one can perhaps detach concepts and arguments from the historico-cultural milieus in which they were introduced and used, and consider their merits or defects in isolation from those milieus. (So it was possible for a self-taught Ramanujan, living alone in India, to master the theory of numbers to such a point that he could make serious contributions to European mathematics.) Elsewhere, the situation is different, and in philosophy that difference is probably inescapable. Despite the valiant efforts of the positivists to purify philosophy of historical dross and reframe its questions in the kind of abstract, general form already familiar in mathematics, the philosophical problems and ideas of actual men—the young Ludwig Wittgenstein, as much as anyone—confront us like geological specimens *in situ;* and, in the process of chipping them free from their original locations, we can too easily forget the historical and cultural matrix in which they took shape, and end by imposing on them a sculptural form which reflects the preoccupations, not of their author, but of ourselves.

How is this to be avoided? In the case of Wittgenstein, we can do so by keeping one key question in the center of our minds. That question is: What philosophical problems did Wittgenstein himself already have in mind, *before* he ever got in touch with Frege and Russell? Even now, in the 1970s, authoritative and scholarly books about Wittgenstein and the *Tractatus* still invite us to assume that his philosophical interests and preoccupations date from *after* those meetings; that his concern with philosophy was awakened by his contact with the mathematical logic of Frege and Russell, and subsequently with the epistemology and linguistic analysis of Russell and Moore. (David Pears's recent essay on Wittgenstein is a perfect illustration of this tendency.)[29] Yet there is, surely, a strong presumption *against* this point of view. For all Wittgenstein's later indebtedness to "the great works of Frege and the writings of my friend Mr. Bertrand Russell,"[30] we must remember that he himself took the initiative in approaching the two men. Far from his becoming interested in philosophy only after those contacts, it appears that he *already* had a well-formed set of philosophical problems in mind and hoped to find a solution for them, using the logical methods of Russell and Frege. As for the origin of these problems themselves, he presumably encountered them in the course of his Viennese upbringing and education.

Certainly there is something generally implausible about any picture of Wittgenstein as a philosophical "pupil" or "follower" of Frege, Russell and Moore. We know that Frege was quite at a loss to understand Wittgenstein's questions and passed him on to Russell in the hopes that he could do better; but, to judge from Wittgenstein's reaction to Russell's *Tractatus* introduction, the cross-purposes in that case were no less complete. We shall do much better to treat him as an entirely independent philosopher and see whether we cannot identify the issues which occupied the center of his mind by looking, rather, at the ideas and writers he was already familiar with, before he ever turned to Frege for help and advice. That is what Engelmann's *Memoir* encourages us to do, and it is also in line with a remark which Wittgenstein's own friend and literary executor, Professor G. H. von Wright, once made to us—that the two most important facts to remember about Wittgenstein were, firstly, that he was a

Viennese and, secondly, that he was an engineer with a thorough knowledge of physics.[31]

And—in the absence of more direct evidence—we can hope to answer the question, What philosophical problems did Wittgenstein originally have in mind?, only if we are prepared to look first at the situation into which he grew up. Given a brilliant young man of great sensitivity, born into the very individual surroundings of Wittgenstein's family—at the focus of not just the industrial wealth, but also the culture, especially the musical culture, of late Habsburg Vienna—and exposed to a rigorous training in the mathematics and physical theory of men like Heinrich Hertz and Ludwig Boltzmann, what group of problems might reasonably be expected to present themselves to him as *the* problems of philosophy and as problems to which the techniques of Russell's logic might enable us to give an unassailable and definitive and, so, final solution?

In answering that question, we must forget about the ideas and methods that Wittgenstein picked up subsequently from Frege and the Cambridge analytical philosophers, and put to use for his own philosophical purposes. Instead, we must look directly at the Vienna of Wittgenstein's childhood—at its social and political problems, its cultural preoccupations, and above all at that general philosophical framework which was the common possession of musicians, writers, lawyers and thinkers of all kinds, quite as much as of academic philosophers. And, to the extent that the *Tractatus* is a key book for understanding the period from which it came, we can hope that this investigation will cast light in both directions, so that, in reappraising our view of Ludwig Wittgenstein and his ideas about language, we shall come to see more clearly also the character of the Viennese environment which was the cradle for so much in mid-twentieth-century art and thought.

Having stated the key question about Wittgenstein which it will be our central purpose to answer, we must now set it to one side. For the first step toward answering it must (if we are right) be to engage in a complex, cross-disciplinary study—namely, to set the political and social, cultural and philosophical preoccupations of Austria alongside one another and see them as framed and reflected in one another. If one is interested only in the historical origins of Wittgenstein's *logical methods,* there is, of course, no need to question the prime importance of Gottlob

Frege and Bertrand Russell. Yet the historical origins of his *philosophical ideas* will prove to be something quite else; those we can recognize only by attempting a hypothetical reconstruction of Wittgenstein's background and education, based in the first place on our independent knowledge of the broader Austrian context.

In the first section of this book, accordingly, we shall be studying the political and social character of "gay Vienna" in the last decades of the Habsburg monarchy. In it we shall see a superpower plagued by problems of rapid economic change and turbulent racial minorities, a power whose established constitutional structure was, at essential points, incapable of adapting itself to the novel demands of its changing historical situation. Next we shall be focusing on the common themes and problems which, within this late Habsburg milieu, engaged the attention of writers, thinkers and artists in all fields, and of which Karl Kraus was the acknowledged, and most articulate spokesman. This was a society in which all established media, or means of expression—from the language of politics across the board to the principles of architectural design—had seemingly lost touch with their intended "messages," and had been robbed of all capacity to perform their proper functions.

When Kraus called for a critique of language, as the crucial instrument of thought, he did so with a moral hatred for that slovenliness in thought and expression which is the enemy of individual integrity, and leaves one defenseless against the political deceptions of corrupt and hypocritical men. But Kraus's one-man crusade to restore the honesty of social debate had wider implications also. Very soon it woke echoes in other fields of intellectual and artistic activity, and broadened into the demand for a critique of the means of expression used in all fields —for example, for a stripping-away of all that conventional and meaningless decoration with which sentimentality had encumbered the creative arts, so as to restore the expressive capacities they needed in order to fulfill their original and proper functions once again. How could any "medium" be adequate to any "message"? How could anything whatever serve as a means of expressing or symbolizing anything else? All over the artistic and intellectual field, we find men taking up this same critique. In what sense if any could music (for example), or painting, or architecture, or everyday language, be regarded as a "representation," or *Darstellung?* And what alternative "symbolic function" could it be said to have? All those issues which Marshall McLuhan has popularized in the last few years were debated with far greater seriousness and rigor in the Vienna of Kraus and Boltzmann, Loos and Schönberg.

Far from originating in Wittgenstein's *Tractatus,* as we shall see, the idea of regarding language, symbolisms and media of expression of all kinds as giving us "representations" (*Darstellungen*) or "pictures" (*Bilder*) had by 1910 become a commonplace in all fields of Viennese cultural debate. Among scientists, this notion had been in circulation at least since the time of Hertz, who had characterized physical theories as providing just such a *Bild* or *Darstellung* of natural phenomena.[32] At the other extreme, it was equally familiar among artists and musicians; Arnold Schönberg, for instance, wrote an essay on musical thought, with the title, *Der Musikalische Gedanke und die Logik, Technik, und Kunst seiner Darstellung.*[33] By the time Wittgenstein came on the scene, this debate had been going on for some fifteen or twenty years in the drawing rooms of Vienna, often in terms drawn from the Kantian tradition, notably from the "antiphilosopher," Arthur Schopenhauer. Wittgenstein's achievement, we shall argue, was not to initiate this discussion, but to draw the threads finally together by providing a completely general and definitive analysis of the issues involved. And the way in which he did this had one further advantage for him personally: it enabled him to undercut some pressing intellectual problems about his own ethical position—not by equipping that position with intellectual foundations, to be sure, but by giving seemingly unanswerable support to his own Kierkegaardian view that, over moral issues, no question of intellectual foundations can properly arise.

So far, we have only stated our agenda for the chapters which follow, and said a little about the character and method of our inquiries. Even so, we cannot expect academic, or professional, philosophers to be happy with our explanation. Still, any picture of Wittgenstein as one of the first generation of twentieth-century professional philosophers appears defensible only so long as we view him against the background of English-language philosophy. (How much of a revolutionary he then appears.) Once we see him in his native surroundings, by contrast, the inadequacy of that picture is quite clear. For, in addition to the paradoxes that arise from divorcing the logico-linguistic Witt-genstein from the ethical Wittgenstein, we shall then be confronted with a further puzzle—namely, the fact that, in carrying further the program of linguistic analysis inaugurated by Russell and Moore, Wittgenstein happened, quite coincidentally, to resolve a general problem about representation which had been vexing all his Viennese contemporaries; and he happened to do so, using the very same terminology that they had used themselves!

To sum up: the historical arguments put forward in this book are designed to throw light not so much on Wittgenstein's *beliefs,* as on his *problems.* A thinker of Wittgenstein's profundity, independence and originality, does not adopt his characteristic intellectual and moral beliefs, simply on account of the historical influence of some stronger-minded predecessor or contemporary; to that extent, we must let his arguments stand on their own feet, and see how he set out to provide an unassailable and definitive justification for those beliefs. But, when it comes to understanding the problems which gave those arguments and beliefs their significance for him, we can no longer make so clean a separation between his ideas, on the one hand, and the historico-cultural context of their exposition, on the other. Regarded as documents in logic and the philosophy of language, the *Tractatus* and the *Philosophical Investigations* stand—and will continue to stand—on their own feet. Regarded as solutions to intellectual problems, by contrast, the arguments of Ludwig Wittgenstein, like those of any other philosopher, are, and will remain, fully intelligible only when related to those elements in their historical and cultural background which formed integral parts of their original *Problemstellung.*

2

Habsburg Vienna:

CITY OF PARADOXES

Ah, Vienna, City of Dreams!
There's no place like Vienna!

Madman in Robert Musil's
The Man Without Qualities,
Vol. III, Ch. 33

In the popular imagination, the name "Vienna" is synonymous with Strauss waltzes, charming cafés, tantalizing pastries, and a certain carefree, all-embracing hedonism. To anyone who has scratched this surface even slightly, a very different picture emerges. For all those things that went to make up the myth of Vienna, the City of Dreams, were simultaneously facets of another, darker side of Viennese life.

The best-known of Strauss's waltzes, *The Blue Danube,* was written a few weeks after the military defeat of Austria-Hungary by Prussia at Sadowa, which ended Habsburg claims to hegemony in the German-speaking world.[1] The rapidity with which Francis Joseph's army was dispatched by that of Bismarck made it clear that the Dual Monarchy had become, at best, a second-rate power. Similarly, the most successful of Strauss's operettas, *Die Fledermaus,* had the effect of taking the minds of the Viennese burghers off the disastrous stock-market crash of May 9, 1873, a date subsequently referred to by the Austrians as Black Friday.[2]

The waltz has always been the symbol of Viennese *joie de vivre;* yet it, too, had its other face. One visitor from Germany described Strauss and his waltzes as providing an escape into the demonic:

African and hot-blooded, crazy with life . . . restless, unbeautiful, passionate . . . he exorcises the wicked devils from our bodies and he does it with waltzes, which are the modern exorcism . . . capturing our senses in a sweet trance. Typically African is the way he conducts his dances; his own limbs no longer belong to him when the thunderstorm of his waltz is let loose; his fiddle-bow dances with his arms . . . the tempo animates his feet; the melody waves champagne-glasses in his face and the devil is abroad. . . . A dangerous power has been given into the hands of this dark man; he may regard it as his good fortune that to music one may think all kinds of thoughts, that no censorship can have anything to do with waltzes, that music stimulates our emotions directly, and not through the channel of thought . . . Bacchantically the couples waltz . . . lust let loose. No God inhibits them.[3]

This is but one of many reports in which contemporary observers spoke of the Viennese passion for the dance as pathological and as reflecting their need to escape the harsh realities of daily life in the City of Dreams.

The delightful cafés lining the streets of Vienna, where one can sit the whole day with a single cup of coffee or glass of wine, reading newspapers and magazines from all over the world, formed an essential part of the Viennese way of life; and they have always struck tourists as the embodiment of a relaxed, carefree existence. But, as with Viennese music and dancing, there was another side to this institution. Throughout the nineteenth century and right up to the present, Vienna has had a grave housing shortage. Viennese working-class housing has always been inadequate, both in quality and in quantity. Its apartments were dreary and impossible to heat adequately, so there has always been a need to escape these dingy and cold living quarters, and it was satisfied by the warmth and cheer of the ubiquitous cafés. Once again, the charm of the cafés was the other face of the hard realities of life as most Viennese knew it; and similar ambiguities characterized many aspects of Viennese life.[4]

Few cities have been as unkind as Vienna, during their lifetimes, to those men whom it proclaimed cultural heroes after their deaths. In music alone, one can cite Franz Schubert, Hugo Wolf and Arnold Schönberg; but the case of Gustav Mahler is a particularly illuminating instance of this duplicity. For, at one and the same time, Mahler was lionized as the greatest of conductors, who had raised the Imperial Opera to a hitherto-unequaled pre-eminence, yet denounced as a degenerate (because Semitic) composer.[5] In music as in painting the voice of mediocrity, personified in Hanslick and Makart, was able to dictate to Viennese society as a whole critical standards and judgments that were for the most part sterile and academic. And Hanslick too was himself a part of the Austrian paradox: in an enthusiastic review of *Tannhäuser* in 1846, this champion of Brahms had been among the very first to sing the praises of Richard Wagner, whose archenemy he later became.[6] In a city that prided itself as a matrix of cultural creation, life was thus made as difficult as possible for real innovators.

At the turn of the century, likewise, Vienna was the medical center of the world. America owes its pre-eminence in the medical sciences of our own time, in no small part, to the thousands of medical students who traveled to Vienna at a time when the standards of American medicine were scandalously low, in order to study with such luminaries as Hebra, Skoda, Krafft-Ebing and Billroth.[7] Yet, in their own home city the pioneering work of Freud in psychoanalysis and of Semmelweis on infection went unrecognized, because their contemporaries did not have sufficient breadth of vision to recognize the significance of their work. The case of Freud is too well known to warrant repeating here. Semmelweis, who discovered that the dirty fingernails of midwives and obstetricians can cause fatal infection to mother and child alike, found it impossible to propagate his discovery in Vienna because doctors with political influence who were opposed to his findings saw to it that he was excluded from positions where he might implement those findings, and professionally discredited him. Semmelweis died in a mental institution some fifteen years after his life-saving discovery, unable to cope with the ridicule that had been heaped upon him and his life's work.[8]

The implications of Freud's views about the role of sexuality in human life offended the sensibilities of middle-class Viennese, while the satires and polemics of Karl Kraus attacked their hypocrisy and sham in a brilliant, witty and masterful prose style. The Viennese, in return, so feared to discuss the issues that Freud and Kraus had raised that they would never publicly mention their names in writing—so tacitly conceding the truth of their assertions. The resulting conspiracy of silence (*Totschweigentaktik*) did not prevent the works of Freud from becoming known in translation; but, in the case of Kraus, his highly idiomatic, punning, colloquial, and consequently untranslatable German has prevented him from becoming widely known. That penetrating and impartial onlooker, Robert Musil—whose novel, *The Man Without Qualities,* has captured the atmosphere of *fin-de-siècle* Vienna better than any other historical or literary work —expressed the feelings of many Austrians when he remarked, "There are two things one can't fight against, because they are too long, too fat, and have neither head nor foot—Karl Kraus and psychoanalysis."[9] Intellectual and cultural center she might be: all the same, Vienna was quite incapable of coping with her own critics.

Social and political movements as opposed as Nazism and German anti-Semitism on the one hand and Zionism on the other had their origins in Old Vienna, as did some of the central elements in modern Catholic social thought and the original adaptation of Marx known as "Austro-Marxism." Not least among the ambiguities and paradoxes of Old Vienna was the fact that this city, which had been the Habsburg capital for hundreds of years, was the capital of a realm that had *no accepted name!* As always, Musil is the best commentator:

It was *kaiserlich-königlich* (imperial-royal) and it was *kaiserlich und königlich* (imperial and royal) to every thing and person; but esoteric lore was nevertheless required to be sure of distinguishing which institutions and persons were to be referred to as *k.k.,* and which as *k. u. k.* On paper, it called itself the Austro-Hungarian Monarchy; in speaking, however, one referred to it as "Austria"—that is to say, it was known by a name which it had, as a state, solemnly renounced by oath while preserving it in all matters of sentiment, as a sign that feelings are just as important as constitutional law, and that regulations are not the really serious thing in life. By its constitution it was liberal, but its system of government was clerical. The system of government was clerical, but the general attitude to life was liberal. Before the law all citizens were equal: not everyone, of course, was a citizen. There was a parliament which made such vigorous use of its liberty that it was usually kept shut; but there was also an Emergency Powers Act, by means of which it was possible to manage without Parliament. And, each time that everyone was just beginning to rejoice in absolutism, the Crown decreed that there must now again be a return to parliamentary government.[10]

The constitutional and social paradoxes embodied in the Habsburg monarchy and its capital could scarcely be put more succinctly. The sensuous worldly splendor and glory apparent on its surface were, at a deeper level, the very same things that were its misery. The stability of its society, with its delight in pomp and circumstance, was one expression of a petrified formality which was barely capable of disguising the cultural chaos that lay beneath it. On closer scrutiny, all its surface glories turned to their opposite; this is the fundamental truth about all aspects of life in the Dual Monarchy. These same paradoxes were reflected equally in its politics and its mores, its music and its press, its Imperial aristocracy and its workers.

The central factor responsible for this state of affairs was, without serious doubt, the unshakable commitment of the ruling dynasty to the Habsburg concept of *Hausmacht*—the idea that the Habsburgs were the instruments of God on Earth. The destiny of Austria-Hungary in Europe, and even the very physical structure of its capital city, were to a great extent determined by the penultimate incarnation of that idea, the Emperor Francis Joseph. Through the persons of Francis Joseph himself, his grandfather Francis I, and Metternich, who was the obedient executor of the Emperor Francis' will during the thirteen-year reign of the imbecile Emperor Ferdinand from 1835 to 1848—the so-called *Vormärz,* or "Pre-March"—the Habsburg idea shaped the policy of the Empire for a total of one hundred and twenty-four years. The most infamous manifestation of this policy was the Emperor Francis' so-called "Metternich System," which was the means of excluding revolution and revolutionary ideas from the Habsburg domain. (Metternich not only did not devise the system, he was not even in agreement with all the policies it encompassed.)[11] Yet even this did not satisfy Francis, who was opposed to all change per se. He was so afraid of change, indeed, that he refused to replace civil servants appointed by his predecessor, the "revolutionary" Emperor, Joseph II, even though they were opposed to his policies, insisting that the status quo be preserved in the most literal sense.[12]

Francis' goal was *Ruhe und Ordnung*—the "law and order" of a police state. Censorship was strict and universal. The construction of a railroad system was forbidden, on the grounds that it might become a vehicle of revolution.[13] Protestant seminaries were founded, so that ordinands need not leave the country for their education, and risk picking up new and presumably sub-

versive ideas.[14] All change was a threat to the Habsburg idea—
"My realm," Francis remarked, "resembles a worm-eaten
house. If one part is removed, one cannot tell how much will
fall."[15] As Metternich summed it up on another occasion, *"J'ai
gouverné l'Europe quelquefois, l'Autriche jamais."*[16] Even after
Francis' death, Metternich continued as the executor of his
policy. The net result of fifty-six years of this system was the
1848 Revolution.

The 1848 upheaval brought the eighteen-year-old Francis
Joseph to the Imperial throne; and the failure of that upheaval
brought in its train, on the part of the new Emperor, a whole
series of policies which, in the course of his sixty-eight-year reign,
became the more and more revolutionary-seeming means toward
consistently reactionary ends.[17] The very length of Francis
Joseph's reign gave the monarchy an illusory stability. The most
radical of his moves—on the face of it—was the introduction into
the western part of the monarchy, in 1907, of universal manhood
suffrage; but this seemingly liberal move was, in fact, designed to protect the Emperor's control over the Army against
those in Hungary who wanted to create a separate Hungarian
army.[18] Despite such palliative measures, the old system survived; and the continuity from Metternich to Francis Joseph becomes—thanks to hindsight—increasingly apparent, from the
appointment of Taaffe as "Kaiserminister above party" to the
resignation of Koerber at the end of 1904. By this time, it had
become apparent that "Austria could still be governed, but only
by non-parliamentary methods, which could, of course, only be
applied as long as she possessed a sufficient number of disciplined
servants willing and able to carry them through."[19] But this did
not seem to the Emperor to matter, so long as his control of the
military was unchallenged.

As this cumbrous structure entered the twentieth century, both
the Emperor's tenacity and the conflict of nationalities, which
made the Empire so difficult to govern, were growing by leaps
and bounds. Even to sketch the highlights in the development of
this nationalism is far beyond the scope of the present volume,
since it would involve tracing a hundred years in the histories of
all the multinational state's eleven constituent peoples, in all
their labyrinthine interrelations. Still, two facets of the problem
are worth mentioning. Paradoxically, it was the modernizing reforms of Joseph II that roused the national consciousness slum-

bering in the Empire.[20] At first, this consciousness manifested it-self merely in the revival of vernacular literature and philology: the first vernacular poetry in Hungarian was produced among the sons of the Hungarian nobility at the leading Habsburg *Gymnasium,* the *Theresianum.*[21] By the middle of the nineteenth century, however, this national consciousness had become trans-formed into the brand of particularist politics which ultimately led to a war which was to destroy the Habsburg regime and with it everything the Habsburgs stood for in Central Europe.

Another revealing incident is the so-called "Cilli Affair,"[22] which indicates the proportions to which the problem had devel-oped even before the end of the nineteenth century. Already, in 1895, the question as to what language of instruction should be used in the schools of this Styrian town had become significant enough to bring down a government. This was truly "a question which in itself revealed all the maladies of Austria, and all the tangles of national controversy."[23] The Slovenes, who lived chiefly in the Styrian countryside, desired a *Gymnasium* in which their language would be the language of instruction. The Germans, who were a majority in the town and in the Styrian Diet, consistently refused on the grounds that, as a result, Ger-man and Germans would disappear from Cilli. The Slovenes had thus to take their case to the Reichsrat, where it was decided to establish such a school; and, when the Germans in the ruling coalition heard of this decision, they left the government, which consequently fell from power. Nationalism had taken its toll. The Cilli Affair helped to make the Southern Slavs and the Czechs aware of the rise of German nationalism, which was the basis of their common plight. Before long, fist fights and flying inkwells were replacing debate between the different national factions in the Reichsrat. It is surely no accident that Hans Kohn, the leading historian of nationalism, should have been a native of this "realm without a name."

After studying nineteenth-century Habsburg history, one can hardly deny the charm of Hegelian dialectic, as a mode of histori-cal explanation; for in it one continually sees situations begetting their own opposites. The effort to introduce German in place of Latin, so as to streamline Imperial administration, begat Hun-garian and Czech cultural nationalism by reaction, and this in due course developed into a political nationalism. Slav national-ism in the politics and economics in turn begat German economic and political nationalism; and this in its turn begat anti-Semitism, with Zionism as a natural Jewish reaction. All in all, it is enough to cause one's head to spin. The idea of the Habsburg *Hausmacht* centered around absolute Imperial control of the military and its financing[24]—"One spent tremendous sums on the army," writes Musil, "but only just enough to assure one of remaining the second-weakest among the Great Powers"[25]—and Habsburg intransigence over this issue begat further intransigence in the Hungarian nationalists, who insisted that the only Hungary they could conceive was a "greater Hungary." Was not Hungary identical with the lands of the Crown of St. Stephen?

At times, Francis Joseph could more or less admit this claim. Especially during the years when wheat was at a premium in Europe, the abundance of the Hungarian harvests served to replenish the overtaxed Imperial Treasury, whose poverty helped to account for the Empire's "second-weakest" status. Thus, he could accept the 1867 compromise as a cruel blow necessitated by the coincidence of a precarious economic position and a major military setback. But the *Hausmacht* could not withstand further competition from the Crown of St. Wenceslas, which was the goal of the aspiring Czech nationalists. So, while Francis Joseph faithfully and tenaciously respected his commitment to Hungary —which the Hungarians themselves regarded as no more than the first step toward a purely personal union of the Kingdoms of Austria and Hungary—he could not budge in the face of demands for the recognition of similar claims by the Czechs or the Southern Slavs.[26] For these communities had not so much to offer as Hungary, and their claims posed a threat to the sovereign's conception of the role ordained by God for him and for the dynasty.

In the end, the monarchy's affairs assumed a formalism behind which there existed nothing but vacuousness and chaos. At the best of times, Francis Joseph was mediocre and shallow, relying always on ceremonial for insulation, which more and more became a cover both for his own personal failings and for his ungovernable mélange of Germans, Ruthenes, Italians, Slovaks, Rumanians, Czechs, Poles, Magyars, Slovenes, Croats, Transylvanian Saxons and Serbs. The general attitude of the nationalities toward their emperor was not unlike that common among the intellectuals in the last years of the Habsburg superpower:

The Emperor and King of Kakania was a legendary old gentleman. Since that time a great many books have been written about him and one knows exactly what he did, prevented or left undone; but then, in the last decade of his and Kakania's life, younger people who were familiar with the current state of the arts and sciences were sometimes overtaken by doubt whether he existed at all. The number of portraits one saw of him was almost as great as the number of inhabitants of his realms; on his birthday there was as much eating and drinking as on that of the Saviour; on the mountains the bonfires blazed, and the voices of millions of people were heard vowing that they loved him like a father. Finally, an anthem resounding in his honour was the only work of poetry and music of which every Kakanian knew at least one line. But this popularity and publicity was so overconvincing that it might easily have been the case that believing in his existence was rather like still seeing certain stars, although they ceased to exist thousands of years ago.[27]

Yet for all this—for the middle classes, at least—the existence of the Emperor "simply was surprisingly real,"[28] as was the City of Dreams.

In all of the Habsburg lands, Vienna was unique in one important respect. Here was at least partially achieved that supranational, cosmopolitan consciousness which was the dynasty's only hope for survival. The external splendors of *fin-de-siècle* Vienna were, after all, largely due to Francis Joseph in person. Between 1858 and 1888 he rebuilt the city, as though to efface 1848 and everything it represented.[29] Where the city walls had previously been, the city was encircled by a magnificent, sixty-foot-wide, tree-lined boulevard, the celebrated Ringstrasse. Where the Turks had camped during the siege of Vienna, a fine new city hall was erected. But this was only a beginning. He constructed also a new Imperial Palace, with two new museums opposite it, a new Reichstag building, and a controversial new Imperial Opera House and, as the final touch, a new Imperial Theater where the Viennese could satisfy their passion for drama. Twice during Francis Joseph's reign, the city limits were extended. It abounded with parks and fine statuary. But the extension of the city limits from the *Gürtel* to their present boundaries in 1890, on completion of this great urban renewal, coincided with the last of the concessions which the aging Emperor could make to the modern world. He eschewed the telephone, the automobile, and the typewriter, as well as the electric light. (To the end of his reign, the *Hofburg* was lit by kerosene lamps.) As for the "primitive toilet facilities in the palace," Arthur May reports that these "so irritated Stephanie, Francis Joseph's daughter-in-law, that she had two bathrooms installed at her own expense."[30] Yet, on the entire continent of Europe, Francis Joseph's Vienna could be compared as a city only to Paris. This was the physical setting of a Vienna that rapidly became not just a city, but the symbol of a way of life.

As the Good Old Days drew to a close, Vienna was above all a city of the bourgeoisie. Most of her leading figures in all fields came from a bourgeois background. Though Vienna had been a commercial center from time immemorial and had been the center of large-scale public administration since the reign of Maria Theresa, the Viennese bourgeoisie acquired its individual character during the third quarter of the nineteenth century. This was the period of industrial expansion, when vast fortunes were made and lost by the investor, the industrial organizer, or the man with an innovative manufacturing technique—the *Gründerzeit,* which created the material fortunes on which the next generation depended for leisure in which to cultivate the arts. Financial success was the basis for a patriarchal society. Bourgeois marriages were arranged as if they were first and foremost business mergers rather than affairs of the heart.[31] In Old Vienna, one could truly say, with Marx, that "the bourgeoisie has torn away from the family its sentimental veil, and has reduced the family relation to a mere money relation."[32]

For the would-be tycoon, a "good marriage" was essential. The values which this society cherished were reason, order and progress, perseverance, self-reliance and disciplined conformity to the standards of good taste and action. The irrational, the passionate and the chaotic were to be avoided at all costs. By following these rules, one would be rewarded with a good name and whatever measure of success was regarded as commensurate with individual talent. This success was made visible in the property that a man possessed. As Max Stirner was wont to put it, a man expressed himself in what he *owned.*

In such a society, with a profound commitment to the order and traditions of the past, it is not surprising that stability had a high place in the list of virtues. The concrete embodiment of these ideas was a man's home, which in this period was truly (and often literally) his castle. In this microcosm of the monarchy, the father of the household was the guarantor of order and security and, as such, possessed absolute authority. And the significance of the home did not end in its being the reflection of a man's success. It was also a refuge from the world outside, a place where the tedious details of the workaday world were not permitted entry. For one who was not of that era, it is difficult to imagine just what it was like to be born and grow into maturity in such an isolated environment, with all the cares of life so punctiliously circumvented. Stefan Zweig, who grew up in just such a house, remarked wistfully:

Whenever, in conversation with a younger friend, I relate some episode of the times before the first war, I notice from their astonished questions how much that is still obvious reality to me has already become historical and incomprehensible to them. And some secret instinct tells me that they are right. All the bridges between our today and our yesteryears have been burnt.[33]

The significance of Zweig's *World of Yesterday*, to those who formed its last and crowning generation, can be measured only by their sense of loss. For the war destroyed that insulation from reality which the bourgeois home had been created to provide, and it left its inhabitants confronting aspects of reality with whose cruelties they were simply unprepared to deal.

The artificiality of this bourgeois view of life is manifest at every point. If the home was more than a mere *machine à vivre*, so too the objects that filled it had a symbolic value as much as a function. At the time, conservative critics saw the influence of the nineteenth century as a disaster permeating all aspects of life. Nowhere was the true nature of the era more apparent than in the lack of style which marked its design. Having no style of their own, the bourgeois could only imitate the past; so they filled their homes with imitations of the art of past eras. Every room was cluttered with garish *objets d'art* in differing styles. Again and again, the complex was preferred to the simple, the decorative to the useful, resulting in rooms that were vulgar to look at and barely habitable. If fashion dictated that one's home must be furnished in the styles of former ages and other cultures, its dictates were not to be disputed. Musil's ironic eye saw to the heart of the matter:

The *nouveau riche* class, on the other hand, in love with the imposing and grandiose eras of their predecessors, had involuntarily made a fastidious and refined selection. Wherever a castle had passed into bourgeois possession, it was not merely provided with modern conveniences, like an heirloom chandelier with electric wiring run through it; but, in the furnishing of it, too, what was less good had been cleared out and things of value had been added, either according to personal choice, or on the infallible advice of experts. Incidentally, this process of refinement was demonstrated most impressively not in the castles but in the town houses, which had been furnished in keeping with the times, with all the impersonal luxury of an ocean liner; but which—in this country of refined social ambition—still in an ineffable breadth, in a scarcely perceptible widening of the distance between pieces of furniture, or in the dominating position of a picture on a wall, preserved the delicately clear reflected glint of a great glory that had passed away.[34]

So, in the very furnishings of the homes that were their castles, the rising bourgeoisie expressed their own imperfect emulation of the Habsburg monarchy's ancient Catholic aristocracy.

Once inside his castle, the paterfamilias could devote himself to enjoying the fruit of his labors—to the art, the music and the literature which were at once the "natural" humanizing outlet for all of his passions and the source for him of metaphysical truth. In due time, as the desire to imitate the aristocracy became more widespread, patronage of the arts was transmuted into a symbol of wealth and status, and was pursued with ulterior motives. Once the castle and refuge had become a reflection of the man in the market place, the polish and grace acquired from the arts became desirable for something other than their intrinsic worth. A man proved that he was someone by devoting his free time to the arts as wholeheartedly as he did his working time to his business. Viennese of the generation that reached maturity at the turn of the century were raised, indeed, in an atmosphere so saturated with, and devoted to, "aesthetic" values that they were scarcely able to comprehend that any other values existed at all.

An eminent historian of Viennese culture in this era has contrasted Austrian aestheticism with its French and English counterparts:

In brief, the Austrian aesthetes were neither as alienated from their society as their French soulmates, nor as engaged in it as their English ones. They lacked the bitter anti-bourgeois spirit of the first, and the warm melioristic thrust of the second. Neither *dégagé* nor *engagé*, the Austrian aesthetes were alienated, not from their class, but with it from a society that defeated its expectations and rejected its values.[35]

Traditionally, the bourgeois had found in art an instrument of instruction in metaphysical and moral truth. During the *Gründerzeit,* this notion was so far extended that man's aesthetic taste was a barometer of his social and economic status. For the following generation, Art became a way of life. If the generation of the *Gründer* held that "Business is Business" and art is essentially the ornamentation of (business) life, their sons, for whom art was essentially something creative, retorted that "Art is Art" and business is a tedious distraction diverting one from (artistic) creation. The generation of the *Gründer* valued an art that was oriented toward the values of the past; they were collectors, or curators of those museums which they referred to as their homes. The art of the younger generation, by contrast, was forward-looking and innovative, and it formed the center of their lives.

This was the background to the circle of young poets, focused around Arthur Schnitzler and Hermann Bahr, who met at the Café Griensteidl and were known as *Jung Wien:* the most distinguished of them being Hugo von Hofmannsthal and Stefan Zweig. They had been raised in a society that thought it quite natural to center its life upon the theater, which formed the standards of speech, dress and mores;[36] and in a city in which the standards of journalism were exceptionally high. Indeed, the *Neue Freie Presse* was a contender for the title of the best paper in Europe. "In Vienna," Zweig wrote, from his aestheticist point of view,

there was really only one journal of high grade, the *Neue Freie Presse,* which, because of its dignified principles, its cultural endeavors and its political prestige, assumed in the Austro-Hungarian monarchy a role not unlike the *Times* in England or the *Temps* in France.[37]

That which they (and indeed their fathers) considered to be the *ne plus ultra* in the paper was the literary or cultural essay, the "feuilleton"—

The feuilleton writer, an artist in vignettes, worked with those discrete details and episodes so appealing to the nineteenth century's taste for the concrete. But he sought to endow his material with color drawn from his imagination. The subjective response of the reporter or critic to an experience, his feeling-tone, acquired clear primacy over the matter of his discourse. To render a state of feeling became the mode of formulating a judgment. Accordingly, in the feuilleton writer's style, the adjectives engulfed the nouns, the personal tint virtually obliterated the contours of the object of discourse.[38]

It is clear from Zweig's autobiography that to have an essay accepted by Theodor Herzl, the feuilleton editor of the *Neue Freie Presse,* was to have "arrived" on the Austrian literary scene.

The status that the fathers had purchased by their business labors meant little to the sons. For these devotees of *l'art pour l'art,* the only worthy task was to nurture the fledgling poet within. To the fathers, it seemed immoral that the sons should reject the values of the society in which they themselves had struggled to obtain an identity. Once having succeeded in establishing themselves in the old order, the fathers were its stanchest defenders, and they did their utmost to curb the innovating natures of the younger generation. So, at least, the young aesthetes saw the educational system, whose diet of learning unrelated to life filled them with a constant weariness and boredom. To escape the world where "business is business," they fled to the coffeehouses frequented by artists, where they found a vitality and spontaneity of self-expression completely lacking in their rote education. Given such a system of regimentation, in which the teacher's word was law and there were no such things as students' rights, it is hardly curious (Zweig commented) that it should have produced the man who discovered the significance of "inferiority feelings" in the explanation of human behavior— Alfred Adler.[39] So repressive was the system, in Zweig's view, that any thought or activity not in explicit conformity with traditional authority became, for many, a source of guilt.

Zweig did not explicitly identify the origins of Freudian psychoanalysis—with its emphasis on the frustration springing from repressed sexual desire as the key to an understanding of neuroses and of human behavior in general—with the fact that Freud too was a Viennese; yet he emphasized that this was a society completely preoccupied with the thought of sex. The very fact that sex was never to be discussed openly insured that it was always upon one's mind.[40] Sexual taboos, far from promoting "purity" of thought and deed, served to make people sex-conscious to the extreme. Whether the bourgeois Viennese of the time were more or were less preoccupied with sex than their opposite numbers in Paris, London or Berlin is an open question; but it is at least certain that there was no socially accepted channel for expressing this preoccupation. The older generation viewed it as an anarchical force which must be completely regulated by society. There must not be the slightest public admission that such an urge actually exists, let alone that it is fundamental to human nature or that its frustration can have disastrous consequences. This conspiracy of silence about sex had two results: on the one hand, an overt inhibition and ignorance of sexual matters; on the other, a covert emphasis on sex.

In a society so thoroughly patriarchal, the women were bound to suffer most. Every part of the feminine anatomy had to be concealed by clothing so cumbersome that it was impossible to dress oneself without assistance.[41] This cumbrous clothing necessitated in turn a totally artificial manner of movement on women's part. The code of conduct required of women was equally artificial—on top of which, society did not permit women to be educated beyond what was essential to "good breeding." Finally, the very fact that middle-class marriage was first and foremost a business contract rather than a personal union[42] helps to explain why so many of Freud's patients were middle-aged bourgeois women and also some of the limitations to the scope of Freudian analysis. In short, the whole design of the society was such as to frustrate women. Zweig remarks:

This is how the society of those days wished young girls to be: silly and untaught, well-educated and ignorant, curious and shy, uncertain and unprotected and predisposed by this education, without knowledge of the world from the beginning, to be led and formed by a man in marriage without any will of their own.[43]

The man's problem was different, but none the less disturbing. Since a middle-class marriage presupposed the gentleman in question to be established both financially and socially—that is, thoroughly committed to the *status quo*—it was necessary for men to remain unmarried up to the age of twenty-five or twenty-six; social manhood was thus recognized only six to ten years after actual manhood. If a man was to find a sexual outlet, therefore, he had to turn to prostitutes, for sexual relations with a girl of "good breeding" were entirely out of the question. Hence (Zweig asserts), prostitution "constituted a dark underground vault over which rose the gorgeous structure of middle-class society with its faultless, radiant façade."[44]

While women were required to submit to the frustrations of

celibacy, men could find an outlet—but at a high price, since they always risked venereal disease. The only alternative was to shun this world for the artist's life of the coffeehouses, and this was to label oneself a decadent, immoral aesthete.

If any single factor can be singled out to account for the special character of Vienna's bourgeois society—if, indeed, this is itself simple enough to be called a single factor—it is the failure of liberalism in the political sphere. It is, perhaps, hardly surprising that in the Habsburg monarchy liberalism should have been stillborn, for the liberals came to power only as a result of the debacle at Sadowa, at the hands of Bismarck. Carl Schorske tells the story in a single paragraph:

Austrian liberalism, like that of most other European nations, had its heroic age in the struggle against aristocracy and baroque absolutism. This ended in the stunning defeat of 1848. The chastened liberals came to power and established a constitutional regime in the 1860's almost by default. Not their own internal strength, but the defeats of the old order at the hands of foreign enemies brought the liberals to the helm of the state. From the first they had to share their power with the aristocracy and the imperial bureaucracy. Even during their two decades of rule, the liberals' social base remained weak, confined to the middle-class Germans and German Jews of the urban centers. Increasingly identified with capitalism, they maintained parliamentary power by the undemocratic device of the restricted franchise.[45]

The middle classes in general were never ready to assume political power. Given so small a base—made even smaller by the scandals which followed the Crash of 1873—liberalism was spent by the 1890s and was supplanted by the rise of the new mass parties which came to dominate Viennese politics. For a middle class which, try though it might, had never entirely succeeded in becoming a part of the Old Order, aestheticism became the only alternative to immersion in business affairs. So art, which had earlier been the decoration adorning middle-class success in business, became for the younger generation an avenue of escape. (This explains how Schorske can refer to the Austrian aesthetes as alienated *"with* their class" rather than *from* it.) At the turn of the century, accordingly, Viennese aestheticism and the mass political movements emerged alongside each other, but independently, as the twin orphans of liberalism.

The goals which the liberals had aspired to realize once they came into power were, firstly, the transformation of the Habsburg Empire into a genuine constitutional monarchy in which they, the entrepreneurs, would replace the aristocracy as the ruling class; secondly, the establishment of a strong central administration through parliamentary channels; and thirdly, the replacement of superstitious feudal Catholicism with modern scientific rationalism (i.e., *laissez-faire*) as the official state philosophy.[46] All of this was to be brought about by the national group with the deepest cultural roots: the German *Volk*. In the minds of the German-speaking population, then, liberal nationalism had always been based upon cultural facts. What Slovak poets were there to compare with Goethe and Hölderlin? What composers of the rank of Mozart, Gluck and Beethoven, not to mention Wagner? The Italians alone could compare with the Germans, but they were never interested in anything but a complete separation from the Habsburg domains. Ruthene, Slovene and Slovak culture had become literate only recently. Czech and Hungarian literary and musical culture were barely a century old. Surely, thought the liberals, there could be little doubt in anyone's minds that no other nation could lay claim to cultural equality with the Germans, let alone hegemony over them. Yet these arguments had by then lost the wider force and appeal they had possessed in the days of Joseph II's attempts at reform. By 1848, indeed, the cultural nationalism evoked in response to Joseph's Germanization of the imperial bureaucracy had become a political nationalism. By the nineties, it had become mass-based and, by the dialectical pattern of Habsburg history, had elicited its regular counterreactions among the Germans in Vienna.

In 1848, the three major cities in the Empire—Prague, Vienna and Budapest—were all of them German cities; indeed, the overwhelming majority of towns possessed largely German populations.[47] (It is easy for outsiders to forget that Prague, for example, was a German cathedral city long before Vienna.)[48] This state of affairs was largely changed by the *Grundungsfieber* of the fifties and sixties, with Vienna as the most notable exception. She, of course, had the advantage of an immediate countryside populated by Germans; nevertheless, by the time World War One rolled around, her population of two million already included 200,000 Czechs.[49] Drawn away from the countryside by the agrarian depressions of the late-nineteenth century, which affected the entire Empire except for Hungary and Transylvania, the movement into the cities of these minority groups transformed their composition and their politics.

The failure of Habsburg liberalism to appeal to these new groups in no small part sealed its fate. Thus, by the turn of the century, the most thriving political groups in Vienna were working-class movements captained by defectors from liberalism. Viktor Adler, the organizing spirit behind Austrian Social Democracy; Karl Lueger, the Christian Social demagogue; Georg Ritter von Schönerer, the fanatical Pan-German; and even Theodor Herzl, the prophet of Zionism—each began his political career as a liberal. The defection of these men from liberalism resulted from the traditional liberals' incapacity to come to grips with the problems of urban growth and industrialization, with Adler and the Social Democrats seeking to continue the constructive work of the liberal tradition, while in Lueger and Schönerer—and, by reaction, Herzl—the politics of reason was transformed into a politics of fantasy, built upon the social blight of anti-Semitism.

Adler and Schönerer had been associated with the radical wing of the liberal party which drafted the Linz Program in 1882.[50] (By 1884, Lueger too had publicly endorsed one of its main points.) The Program combined social reforms that were contrary to *laissez-faire* with a nationalism that was openly, but not rabidly, anti-Semitic. Insofar as the liberals were unable and unwilling to carry through such reforms, they fertilized the soil for the mass movements which were to displace moderate middle-class liberalism so completely, both from the right and from the left.

The housing crisis, alluded to earlier, was but one of the grave problems facing the industrial proletariat in Vienna.[51] Vienna had always had a housing shortage, and the rapid growth of its population (from 476,220 in 1857 to 2,031,420 in 1910) merely aggravated a long-standing problem. By 1910, the average Viennese dwelling housed 4.4 persons, with an average of 1.24 per room (including kitchens, bathrooms and front halls); "a considerable number of persons" were even reduced to "living in caves dug in railway embankments, in boats, in hiding places under the bridges, and in other emergency refuges." The situation in Budapest (the fastest-growing capital city in nineteenth-century Europe) was even worse: in 1905, thirty-five persons were found to be nesting in the trees of its public parks.[52] Yet the Viennese situation was critical. Many people were forced not only to let all their spare rooms, but also to rent bed space to *Bettgeher,* who enjoyed no privileges whatsoever in the apartment, not even the use of any closet space that might exist. Young girls sometimes turned to prostitution, simply in order to have a place to sleep. In 1910 there were but 5,734 single-family homes, housing a mere 1.2 percent of the total Viennese population. Only 7 percent of the buildings used exclusively as dwellings were equipped with bathrooms and toilets, while a scant 22 percent had indoor toilets. On the average, rent took one quarter of a worker's wages. Admittedly, the workers did not face the same slum problem as their counterparts in, say, Naples or Glasgow, but theirs was far from a pleasant lot.

As late as the eighties, Viennese workers faced a seven-day, seventy-hour week, tempered by a customary absenteeism on Mondays, to sleep off Sunday night's hangover.[53] Many factories employed women and children alongside men. The women received considerably smaller wages than the men, and they had no alternative second source of income except "the oldest profession." After 1883, employers were required to see that children were allowed Sunday—or at least one whole day per week—off work; children were also allowed to rest for an hour, after eleven hours' work, but their wages were, of course, not the wages of an adult. (Even so, not all of the industrial workers had moved to the factories because they had been displaced by machinery in the agricultural areas; despite the fact that the very best industrial wages were kept at a bare minimum, some were actually attracted by the pay!)

The average worker's diet too reflected the conditions under which he lived. He had a breakfast of coffee and a roll, a midmorning snack of bread and butter, a main meal of soup, vegetable(s), bread, and perhaps coffee or beer; in the afternoon, he had a snack of bread, and an evening meal which was basically bread, with the occasional sausage. His table carried beef, horsemeat and fish only on festive occasions. In such circumstances, workers formed benevolent organizations, which developed into trade unions. By 1870 these had won the right to collective bargaining, and the industrial workers finally found effective political expression, with the reorganization of the Social Democratic party, in December of 1888.

Before that date, the history of Austrian Social Democracy had been one of internecine strife over ideological theory and strategy. This theoretical struggle ensured that the party remained leaderless. The transformation which, within twenty-two years, brought the Social Democrats from insignificance to being the largest party in the Reichsrat, while holding together a political spectrum ranging from anarchists to monarchists, was the work of one man, Viktor Adler. The charisma of Adler, like that of Lueger, Schönerer and Herzl, virtually established and sustained his party. In each case, the story of the man is the story of the party, and to understand the man is to comprehend the social forces that he personified.

Like so many of the dramatis personae of his age, Adler was of Jewish ancestry, though he had accepted Christian baptism and had liberal, even nationalist, leanings.[54] His early nationalism was cultural, and he was for a time a vehement Wagnerite. But his experiences as a physician treating the poor made him aware of the conditions of the proletariat, in a city whose cost of living was the highest in Europe and comparable with that in the United States. He thereupon embraced the Marxian solution to the problem of modern society, with the same boundless enthusiasm he had previously displayed for the works of Wagner. This enthusiasm was matched only by his capacity to communicate it to those who surrounded him. Although he professed the "revolutionary and antiliberal" Marxism of the German Social Democrats, he did not formulate policy any more than his German counterparts. Instead, he stressed that the most important thing for Socialists was unity. His powerful and moving oratory, as well as his personal philanthropy, help to explain how he was able to provide the leadership required. While he insisted upon the primacy of the economic order and the inevitability of revolution, he oriented his life and practical policies around the values of reason, justice and nonviolent opposition to capitalism.

Adler's evolutionary approach was based upon the premise that the main concern of the party ought to be preparedness—that is, that the party must make its members ready to assume power when the time came. He therefore initiated adult-education programs, established libraries, discussion groups for workers of all ages, and Social Democratic organizations of every sort. Two first-rank publications were founded: the daily *Arbeiter Zeitung,* and the monthly *Der Kampf.* His central aim was to better the whole life of the entire community. Thus, while his socialism transcended the limitations of liberalism by extending its goals, it displayed continuity with the ideals of reason and progress to which the liberals had subscribed. So, while liberalism failed as a political movement, it would be false to say that it died; right up to the very last days of the Empire, the majority of middle- and upper-middle-class Viennese professed to be "liberals." Nor was Viennese liberalism sterile. Its theorists still rank high in the history of economics; for instance, Menger's Marginal Utility Theory—so characteristically Viennese in its emphasis upon the psychological and subjective factors which underlie value—is still a central tenet of many modern economists.[55] Last but not least, liberalism's legacy to Adler's socialism was just that continuity which distinguished Adler and the party he created from the rival movements inspired by Lueger, Schönerer and Herzl.

If Adler dedicated his charismatic energies to humanistic and rational goals, Karl Lueger, the leader of the Christian Social party, lent his to demagoguery and opportunism.[56] As mayor of Vienna, Lueger possessed these qualities more abundantly than any of his contemporaries. "Handsome Karl" had an eloquent command of the charming Viennese dialect, and a sense of occasion at baptisms, weddings, anniversaries and suchlike, which endeared him to the *petit bourgeois* artisans, clerks and municipal servants, who made him the most powerful elected official in the Dual Monarchy. Just as Adler harnessed and channeled the political aspirations of the proletariat, Lueger did likewise for those "little men" who felt that they were gradually being squeezed out of existence between big business and organized labor.

Lueger came to the Christian Social movement in 1888, the same year that Adler began his reorganization of the Social Democrats at Hainfeld. Catholic political thought in the Empire had previously been based on an antiliberal, feudal aristocracy. It contrasted the idealized personal character of the "relations of production" in the precapitalist era to the dehumanizing plight inflicted on the proletariat by capitalist industrialization. Its chief sponsors were the Princes Alois and Alfred Liechtenstein, while the ideologue of the movement was a Prussian convert who had emigrated to the Empire, Karl von Vogelsang. (Vogelsang can also be credited with the basic social ideas of Pope Leo XIII's encyclical *Rerum Novarum,* which makes him the father—or grandfather—of modern Catholic social thought.)[57] All of this Lueger used for his own purposes. The son of a concierge at the Vienna Technical Institute, he had risen by his own labors to become a lawyer and a member of the Municipal Council, and was a man whom the "little men" could easily respect. Lueger made his reputation in the Municipal Council, where he was known for his relentless exposure of the corruption of "Jewish capitalists." He enhanced his popularity by his advocacy of franchise reform and, as mayor, by a vast program of public works.

Nowhere in liberal capitalism was the Jewish element more prominent than in the Habsburg Empire. Those who sought scapegoats during the twenty-three years of depression which followed the Bourse crash of 1873 found obvious candidates in the Jews and in the corruption of many liberal deputies, which had involved so many Jewish financiers and businessmen. One historian has written that "anti-Semitism rose as the stock market fell."[58] As a young left-wing liberal, Lueger had already been exposing corruption, mismanagement and profiteering in municipal affairs in the mid-seventies, and he constantly railed against the corrupting influence of big business. But his anti-Semitism was more opportunistic and propagandist than fanatical or doctrinaire—social and economic, rather than racialist or religious. The shopkeeper could respond to this because his competition so often came from "the Jew down the street."

Once securely established in power—having been elected mayor five times before the Emperor, who found his rabble-rousing techniques disgraceful and unbecoming in a public servant, finally agreed to confirm his appointment—Lueger's attacks on the "Judaeo-Magyars" grew fewer and fewer, and less and less vehement. Throughout his career, indeed, he rarely declined invitations to dine at the tables of the Jewish capitalists whom he excoriated in his speeches. This attitude is best summed up in his infamous remark, *"Wer ein Jud ist, bestimme ich."* When the circumstances were appropriate, he could in fact bring himself to say something not unpleasant, at least about the Viennese Jews:

I dislike the Hungarian Jews even more than I do the Hungarians, but I am no enemy of our Viennese Jews; they are not so bad and we cannot do without them. My Viennese always want to have a good rest; the Jews are the only ones who always want to be active.[59]

Lueger's redeeming characteristic was the fact that, despite being a demagogue, he did give his whole energy to the cause of the "little men," and he left the lot of the *petit bourgeois*, and the city in general, substantially improved. In the political sphere, he championed electoral reform, after the gross injustices of the system of "electoral geometry" devised by Schmerling. The vast public-works projects which he initiated included the formation of a native gas company to replace the British company that had hitherto supplied Vienna, improved public transportation, a new water system, improved bridges, the establishment of orphanages and hospitals, the construction of canals, enlarged park and playground space, more schools, free lunches for poor children, and many similar social services. So it is unjust to condemn Lueger out of hand, as some have tended to do, just because Hitler considered Lueger's policies models for his own public-works programs. It is fairer to recall, instead, that the fine statue adorning the Luegerplatz was put up after World War One by a Social Democratic administration. In his own way, Lueger is as difficult a character to appraise as the Emperor who so despised him. Both men had certain genuinely commendable traits, and our judgment is easily warped by the complexity both of the events in which they participated and of those subsequent developments which they affected.

No such complexity surrounds Lueger's counterpart in the German Nationalist movement in the Habsburg Empire, Georg Ritter von Schönerer.[60] His infamous legacy was the explicit rejection of the ideals of reason and progress, and their replacement by the politics of the will to power. Of the four figures who most reflect the atmosphere on the political scene in Vienna before World War One, Schönerer was the least charismatic and the only one who never achieved a mass following. His effect was, rather, to introduce the politics of violence into the city; the characteristic marks of his brand of political nihilism were violent rhetoric and street fighting. He was the son of a wealthy parvenu nobleman and was known as the Knight of the Rosenau, after his father's estate; and he became increasingly hot-tempered, romantically "Germanic," and fanatically anti-Semitic as he grew older. Schönerer began his political career by representing the interests of the neighboring farmers, who recognized him as an "improving landlord." Like Lueger and Adler, he at first associated himself with the left democrats among the liberals in the Reichstag. As with so many among their number, he feared that Taaffe's "Iron Ring" was destined to produce an encirclement of the culturally superior and enlightened Germans by the inferior and barbarous Slavs. This would be especially damaging to the Germans of Bohemia and would orient foreign policy toward the Tsar and away from Schönerer's ideal of Germanic superiority, Bismarck. (Incidentally, German nationalism, like all ideologies, was abhorrent to the pragmatic Bismarck.)

Schönerer's fear of Slav encirclement, combined with a feeling for social questions, led him to collaborate with Adler, Friedjung and others, in drafting the Linz Program in 1882. (Curiously, the *Statthalter* would not permit Schönerer's group to convene at Linz, so the program could not be adopted there.[61]) In 1885 a twelfth point was added, pledging that the nationalist faction of the Liberal party would work for "the removal of Jewish influence from all sections of public life . . . indispensable for carrying out the reforms aimed at it."[62] From this point forward, Schönerer's fanatical nationalism and doctrinaire anti-Semitism began to displace his concern for social justice. In 1884, Lueger joined him in denouncing a proposal to renew the Rothschild concession for the Northern Railroad linking Vienna with the industrial areas of northern Bohemia, as carrying further the corrupting influence of the Jews on public life. As early as 1878, Schönerer had shocked and astounded even his fellow German nationalists, when he shouted out in Parliament, "If only we already belonged to the German Empire!"[63] Some ten years later, on March 8, 1888, the Knight of Rosenau gave his concept of nationalism a thorough practical demonstration, when he and his companions wrought havoc in the offices of the *Neues Wiener Tageblatt,* breaking up the presses and beating up the staff.

Schönerer paid a high price for this exploit: a jail term, loss of political rights for five years, and cancellation of his patent of nobility. Up to this point, his following had consisted largely of university students, professors and other professionals, who felt threatened by competition from Jews; together with artisans, small businessmen and minor officials sharing similar fears. Yet he won these followers with a self-contradictory ideology, well described by Schorske as a mélange of "aristocratic élitism and enlightened despotism, anti-Semitism and democracy, 1848 *grossdeutsch* democracy and Bismarckian nationalism, medieval chivalry and anti-Catholicism, guild restrictions and state ownership of public utilities."[64] With these ideals, he could attract people to himself, but his fanaticism and intransigence prevented him from carrying his ideas through to fruition. Consequently, he lost the city's artisans and clerks to Lueger; his inability to accomplish anything effective, reinforced by his anti-Catholic and anti-Habsburg rantings, finally made him repulsive to that class of men, while his personal authoritarianism led inevitably to a fragmentation of his following.

After the *Neues Wiener Tageblatt* fiasco, when Lueger had displaced him, Schönerer turned away from the capital to seek a following elsewhere, in the industrial areas of northern Bohemia. Andrew Whiteside has meticulously described the nationalism which developed among the German working class, as they met competition from Czechs who were willing to work in poorer conditions for less pay.[65] Both Czechs and Germans considered that the Social Democratic party, with its emphasis upon gradualism and reconciliation, was selling them out. As a result, each group formed its own working-class party in opposition to the internationalist and prodynastic policies of Adler. It did not take very long for the Germans to lay the blame for the failure, as they saw it, of the Social Democrats in Bohemia. Were not their ranks Jew-ridden? (As August Bebel was reported to have said; anti-Semitism was "the socialism of the dunce.")[66] In Bohemia in the late 1890s, however, this was but one aspect of the all-pervasive nationalities question. The Badeni Ordinances of 1897 stipulated that both German and Czech were to be languages of the inner service in Bohemia, and provoked a violent reaction both there and in Vienna. To the Germans, this was tantamount to recreating the Iron Ring, since few Germans bothered to learn Czech. To the Czechs, it was their long-awaited due. To Badeni, it guaranteed Czech support in the decennial negotiation with Hungary over the economic treaty. To Schönerer, it was an opportunity, such as had not before offered itself, to practice the politics of the will.

In the capital, in Graz and in Salzburg, as well as in Bohemia, rioting broke out on a scale that could be compared only to the events of 1848. But there was this important difference: 1848 had witnessed the outcry of hungry mobs for parliamentary representation, while 1897 witnessed the radicalization of the otherwise highly respectable law-and-order bourgeoisie. Mass nationalism, initiation to that mysterious entity the *Volk* by street violence and a baptism of blood, had arrived in the Habsburg monarchy and was there to stay. Badeni himself suffered a slight wound in a duel with Schönerer's fellow nationalist Karl Wolff. The matter became serious enough to affect the Viennese restaurants, where Germans refused to serve Czech customers. Though Schönerer's greatest political success was to come only in 1901, when twenty-one members of his Pan-German Union were elected to the Reichstag, within twelve months of the 1901 elections the Pan-German Union had splintered, and his true legacy to the politics of the Empire was his role in the 1897 demonstrations. His conception of violence as a political means was to leave a deep impression on the minds of those to whom German nationalism came as a messianic message. These included the failed painter and would-be artist from Linz, Adolf Hitler, whose admiration for Lueger was eclipsed only by his sympathy for the dedication and idealism which, as he saw it, the Knight of the Rosenau brought to his noble cause. As late as 1928, Oscar Jászi could write his *Dissolution of the Habsburg Monarchy* without referring to Schönerer. The style of his nationalism, which rejected the values upon which European civilization had been raised, had not yet become the pattern of political praxis. But the time was soon to come when a frustrated man from Braunau was to spell out in gross detail the practical implications of Schönerer's nihilism.

Perhaps the strangest paradox of Viennese life is the fact that the politics of both the Nazis' Final Solution and the Zionists' Jewish State not only sprang up there, but had strikingly similar origins.[67] True, Zionism already had a long history before Herzl discovered that he was not only a Jew but the leader of the new Exodus. But it was only when this extraordinary man became converted to the Zionist movement that it became a political force to be reckoned with. Herzl's path to Zionism is so curious that it is well worth following out here; his personal story is itself an essential element in the collapse of the City of Dreams.

Herzl was not a native Viennese. He was born in Budapest, but not long after his arrival in Vienna in 1878 he, like so many other immigrants, had become, so to say, more Viennese than the Danube. His family was assimilated Jewish: politically liberal and culturally German. The exclusion of all but a very few Jews from the aristocracy led them to compensate by entering the cultural élite. For the purpose of the official census, which used language as the criterion of nationality, Yiddish was treated as a German dialect, so the Jews had for years been counted as Germans. So it need be no surprise that the Jews of Vienna should have turned to German culture to create an aesthetic aristocracy, and so escape (as Herzl saw it) from the lives of trade for which middle-class Jews were otherwise destined. Many a Jew found himself an enthusiastic Wagnerite, like Viktor Adler, while Herzl was not alone among his race in responding affirmatively to his first encounter with German nationalism.

A considerable number of Viennese Jews had long ceased to practice Judaism and had accepted baptism, usually as Lutherans. Many of them had actually forgotten that their families were Jewish. Viktor Adler and Heinrich Friedjung, the liberal historian, both belonged to this class of converts; as a young man, Herzl himself was ready to accept baptism, apart from his fear of offending his parents. Although the prosperous apostate and assimilated Jews were the most prominent of their race, there were Jews in every class save the high aristocracy, from which they were fully excluded. By 1910, indeed, they constituted ten percent of the city's population and made up the largest segment of the legal, medical and journalistic professions. The Leopoldstadt in the second district, across the Danube Canal, meanwhile housed large numbers of immigrant Orthodox "Ostjuden" from Galicia, who were the very antithesis of their capitalist coreligionists in the fashionable upper-middle class. Taking the number of people of Jewish descent into account would drive the figures considerably higher, for even the ranks of the anti-Semites included many apostate Jews, who displayed a public anti-Semitism as a sign that they had renounced their past.

Herein lies the shocking element in Herzl's career. His Zionism was, in a sense, the result of a most curious kind of anti-Semitism and his failure to escape, as he sorely desired, from his own Judaism. Herzl was first, last and always a dandy; his insistence that frock coats be worn at the first Zionist International Conference in Basel is but one instance of that affectation which was one of his primary characteristics. His manner of dress and his aspirations to the aristocracy were functions of his dandyism, and his greatest fear was social rejection; he never got over his rejection by the Albia fraternity at the university, when his defense of Judaism caused his exclusion. Naturally enough, he was drawn to the medium of the feuilleton, which required of its practitioners a certain degree of narcissism in order to "subjectify the objective" to the necessary degree. By 1891, Herzl's facility in the form had procured him the prestigious position of Paris correspondent for the *Neue Freie Presse,* and his experiences there transformed the dandy into a Zionist. Early in life, Herzl had digested Dühring's arguments for the revocation of Jewish emancipation—he had agreed that the businessman-Jew, who was lacking in culture and nobility, ought to be excluded from Europe. In Paris, he now came into contact with the writings of Drumont, and these confirmed in him the idea that the Jew did not "belong" in Europe, and had no roots there. During this period, Herzl covered two trials, each of which was to have an impact upon his Zionism. The first was that of the anarchist Ravachol, who deeply impressed him with his fanatical will to power. The other was the Dreyfus Affair, which confirmed all that he had read in Dühring and Drumont. When Dreyfus was condemned, France, the cradle of liberty, had rejected him too. Only socialism could save the Jew, but what was there in socialism of the aristocratic or aesthetic? Nothing. Failing any solution in rational politics, Herzl turned, like his contemporaries Barrès, D'Annunzio and George, to romantic solutions. The first was that Jewish honor must be established by dueling; Herzl himself would challenge a prominent Viennese anti-Semite, such as Lueger or Prince Alois Liechtenstein, and if he were killed he would become a martyr to his cause and excite world opinion in its favor. If, on the other hand, he killed his opponent, he would stage a spectacular, moving defense, exposing the evils of anti-Semitism; as a result, he would be freed, and the world would be set aright. His alternative plan was, if anything, even more of an adolescent fantasy: he would enlist the support of the Pope against the enemies of the Children of Israel; and in return he would see to it that the Jews of the monarchy would present their youth in St. Stephen's Cathedral for mass conversion.

But it is to Herzl's "experience" of Wagner's *Tannhäuser* that we directly owe his advocacy of the Jewish state. During a performance of that opera, the truth of irrational *Völkisch* politics became clear to him, in a flash of intuition. The only answer lay in a state where Jews would not be guests or intruders, but would truly have roots. For Herzl, this involved translating Wagner's *Gesamtkunstwerk* from the sphere of art into that of politics. How could such a Jewish state be realized? Herzl's answer was characteristically Viennese: "If you wish it, it is no fairy tale," and "If you don't wish it, it is a fairy tale."[68] Thus, the origin of modern Zionism was yet another Viennese response to the problems of alienation in modern mass society, which were first generally recognized in Europe only after World War One. Like Schönerer, Herzl sought to lead his people in founding a new society, within which Truth would not be compromised by a degenerate aristocracy, a materialistic middle-class, or an ignoble proletariat: rather, it would be enshrined in a spiritual elite, whose collective will alone would bring it into existence.

Such were the dreams that were dreamed by those who knew Vienna best. This was the bitter pill that lay beneath the sugar-coating of hedonistic aestheticism and *Sachertorte*. Yet the middle-class, and above all the young middle-class, Viennese hardly recognized the seriousness of the situation that was developing before their very eyes. Zweig reports that, when he and his friends read the newspapers, they passed over the Boer War, the Russo-Japanese War, and the Balkan crises, in much the same way that they disregarded the sports page.[69] Before the final cataclysm of 1914, almost their only inkling that the Habsburg stability disguised an essential cleavage between appearance and reality came from the Redl Affair.

In May 1913, it was discovered that the deputy director of the Imperial-and-Royal Army Intelligence, Alfred Redl, was a traitor, and that he had become one in order to finance a life of homosexual debauchery.[70] Which was the more shocking and disgraceful crime in the bourgeois eyes of the City of Dreams, the treason or the homosexuality, is a moot question. What is certain is that the Redl Affair opened the closet door and displayed the skeletons that had hitherto been concealed within it. Redl, who was the son of a poor railway clerk in Lemberg (Lvov), had risen to prominence in the Empire's military machine, by an exceptional capacity to conceal his true opinions and attitudes, an uncanny knack for saying just what his superiors wanted him to say, and for doing just what was expected in any situation. As with so many boys of his generation, his sexual awakening came during his days in Cadet School. (Musil's own partly autobiographical novel, *Young Törless,* centers on just such a situation and was received as nothing short of scandalous.) Redl cleverly hid the truth about his homosexuality as successfully as he had hidden everything about himself. He was a man with but one goal: the status which accompanied success in the military. He sacrificed everything and everyone to this end, proving that anything was possible in the Empire for a man who did not quibble over means, so long as he kept up appearances.

To Vienna, he was the ideal officer—temperate, clever, charming, even masculine. He had taken great care to cast just such an image, putting on the façade of a loyal, obedient officer, quick to size up a situation. His generosity endeared him to his colleagues and subordinates, while his elegant, extravagant tastes were those that the Viennese cherished most. When the news reached Stefan Zweig in Paris that the General Staff colonel whom he had known by sight was a double agent in the pay of the Tsar, he confessed himself terror-stricken. For the Redl case illustrated the deceptive aspect of everything in the monarchy.[71] This officer, who had been commended by the Emperor, was a traitor. War, the last thing conceivable to the bourgeois mind, was by no means out of the question. Evidence of homosexuality high in the military—though, in fact, it was rare—struck at the very core of bourgeois morality. Yet the most important aspect of the Redl Affair was not immediately obvious. Here was the case of a man who had succeeded *precisely because* he could assume a mask that completely veiled his real personality. In Habsburg society as a whole, artificiality and pretense were by now the rule rather than the exception, and in every aspect of life the proper appearances and adornments were all that mattered.

No one knew this, or portrayed it in his work, better than Arthur Schnitzler. This physician's son, himself a physician turned playwright, brought his unique talents to bear in a masterful diagnosis of the "Last Days of Vienna."[72] Like his eminent contemporaries, Sigmund Freud and Viktor Adler, Schnitzler was a bourgeois Jewish doctor, and had worked as an assistant in Meynert's clinic, where he specialized in the techniques of hypnosis.[73] When he turned from a typical middle-class career to writing, Schnitzler was thus intimately familiar with the course of bourgeois life. In so doing, however, he did not reject his past but rather turned his abiding interest in the psyche into new channels. Literature had been his first love and he had set it aside at his father's insistence, while pursuing a more conventional and respectable bourgeois occupation. Schnitzler's extraordinary capacity to diagnose the plight of his society, in literary form, was thus the result of the fact that, as physician and poet, he straddled two vastly different generations with vastly different sets of values. And this dual background provided Schnitzler with a theme that pervaded all of his work—namely, the problem of communication.

Schnitzler rightly saw that the problem of communication has two aspects: one personal, the other social. The meaninglessness of sex reflected the identity crisis of the individual, while anti-Semitism was its social embodiment. While the sexual elements in Schnitzler's world have long been in the public eye, his concern with anti-Semitism is anything but insignificant. He considered it to be one manifestation of the human condition, a symptom of a universal spiritual malaise, rather than some sort of social paranoia. In his novel *Der Weg ins Freie* he portrays the essential insolubility of the Jewish problem, and is critical of his friend Herzl's all-too-facile solution. His play *Professor Bernhardi* is an attempt to classify and analyze anti-Semitism in its various guises: by the end, *Bernhardi* is a morphology not only of anti-Semitism, but of all the destructive and dehumanizing forces at work in society. In his portrayal of his hero, Schnitzler remains true to his class, his profession, and his race. (In Schnitzler's pathological universe of decadence and egoism, the medical profession is one of the few bright spots.) Egoism lies at the root of all of men's problems. They cannot communicate, because they encapsulate themselves hopelessly within social roles which satisfy their immediate desires, and thereby rob themselves of all hope of more lasting fulfillment.

His *Reigen*—familiar in English translation, as *Hands Around, Ring Around the Rosey* and *La Ronde*—is a penetrating glance at the whole spectrum of social types, epitomizing the dynamics of human relationships reduced to a single common denominator, in the desire for immediate sexual gratification. *Reigen* depicts ten characters—rich and poor, mighty and humble, crass and sensitive—in the context of sexual relations of both kinds with others of the ten, and unfolds like a dance of death. It is a sequence of character studies by a master literary psychoanalyst, whom Freud could hail as a "colleague." The characters include a soldier who cannot wait to be satisfied by one woman, so that he may rush on to the next—reflecting Schnitzler's low view of the military, especially the officer class, whom he portrays as shallow, intolerant, self-indulgent and forceful devotees of an anachronistic code of honor. His Count, like the rest of the declining aristocracy, is treated with a sympathetic irony; at the opposite end of the social ladder is the streetwalker, society's victim, who is none the less capable of a spark of kindness toward the embarrassed, unsure Count.

Eroticism thus becomes a principle of social dynamics, and sexuality is the only kind of personal contact of which Schnitzler's characters are capable. This is the very point of the "dance" motif: sex without love is a meaningless, mechanical ritual. As in Strauss and Lehár, society gleams and glitters on the outside, but within there is only hedonistic egoism. One half of society is incapable of opening itself to another, one half refuses to make the effort. In Musil's words, "the notion that people who live like that could ever get together for the rationally planned navigation of their intellectual and spiritual destiny was simply unrealistic; it was preposterous."[74] A coating of waltzes and whipped cream was the surface covering to a despair-ridden society in which Felix Salten could be denounced for the "Jewish babble" of the rabbits in *Bambi*,[75] and police extorted protection money from women forced into prostitution by meager wages.[76] In the process, all proportion between appearances and realities had disappeared.

Near the beginning of his classic study of suicide, published in 1897, Émile Durkheim remarks how timely such a study is:

At any given moment the moral constitution of society established the contingent of voluntary deaths. There is, therefore, for each people a collective force of a definite amount of energy, impelling man to self-destruction. The victim's acts, which at first seem to express only his personal temperament, are really the supplement and prolongation of a social condition which they express externally.[77]

Subsequent thought has done much to reinforce Durkheim's views. If the Habsburg Empire's national, racial, social, diplomatic and sexual problems were as grave as we have suggested, the Empire's suicide rate should have been correspondingly high. The list of prominent Austrians who were to die by their own hands is, in fact, both long and distinguished. It includes Ludwig Boltzmann, the father of statistical thermodynamics; Otto Mahler, the brother of the composer, who was not lacking in musical talent himself; Georg Trakl, a lyric poet whose talents have been rarely surpassed in the German language; Otto Weininger, whose book *Sex and Character* had made him a *cause célèbre*, only a few months before his suicide in the house where Beethoven died; Eduard van der Nüll, who was unable to bear the criticism that was leveled upon the Imperial Opera House he designed; Alfred Redl, whose story has already been told; and no less than three of Ludwig Wittgenstein's own elder brothers. Perhaps the most bizarre case is that of General Baron Franz von Uchatius, the designer of the 8-cm. and 9-cm. cannon. His crowning achievement was to have been the gigantic 28-cm. field piece; but, when the weapon was tested, the barrel split, and a few days later Uchatius was found dead in his arsenal, having cut his own throat. Even the Imperial-and-Royal House had not been spared. In 1889, at his lodge in Mayerling, Crown Prince Rudolf took his life and that of the woman he loved, Baroness Maria Vetsera, in circumstances that were more lurid than romantic. These were a few of the men for whom Vienna, the City of Dreams, had become a city of nightmares past further bearing.

The problems of identity and communication plagued Viennese society at every level—political and social, individual and even international. The international problems followed fast upon the exclusion of the Habsburg realm from the young strong German Reich that had been fashioned by Bismarck. The political problems are too vast to be discussed adequately in a single volume, let alone a chapter or paragraph; they can at best be hinted at by considering the case of the Czechs, who were probably the best-placed of the Empire's subject peoples—that is, of the nationalities other than the Germans, Magyars, Italians and Poles. By 1907, when universal manhood suffrage was introduced into the western half of the monarchy, the Czechs would no longer communicate with the Germans, because the Germans failed to recognize the Czech language. As with all the minorities, this was their means of identifying themselves within the Empire; language was the basis of social as well as political identity in the bitter struggles for civil rights which marked the final years of Habsburg rule before the cataclysm of 1914.

In a different but by no means unrelated manner, the generation of aesthetes—typified by *Jung Wien*—sought in their poetry a more "authentic" language, one that would allow them to escape from the straitjacket of bourgeois society. And the remainder of our story has to do with the ways in which such geniuses as Kraus and Schönberg, Loos and Wittgenstein, recognized that the escapism of the aesthetes was no more than a narcissistic pseudo-solution to the problem. Whereas Musil considered that "everyday language, in which words are not defined, is a medium in which nobody can express himself unequivocally," and that unambiguous expression would be possible only in some private, nonfunctional, as yet unknown—and perhaps impossible —"holiday language,"[78] based directly on Machian "sense-impressions," Kraus, Schönberg, Loos and Wittgenstein found the key to a solution of all these problems in a fundamental, but essentially positive critique of the accepted means of expression. Since all these men took a cue from the life and work of Karl Kraus, it is to him that we must now turn.

3

Language and Society:

KARL KRAUS AND THE LAST DAYS OF VIENNA

Nur in der Wonne sprachliche Zeugung
wird aus dem Chaos eine Welt

—KRAUS, *Pro Domo et Mundo*

For Karl Kraus, Vienna was a "proving ground for world destruction,"[1] just as for the author of *Mein Kampf* it was "the hardest, but the most thorough school."[2] If anything, Kraus was even more acutely aware than Schnitzler and Musil of the dehumanizing forces operating in Vienna; but, unlike them, he was not satisfied with diagnosis, and he believed that major surgery alone could save the society. Like the ancient Hebrews, the Viennese had wandered from the path of righteousness, and Kraus was the Jeremiah sent to reprimand them for their waywardness. The weapons of this prophet, "the most Viennese of Viennese writers,"[3] were polemic and satire. To the Viennese nothing was more important than the arts, especially literature, theater and music, and their very tastes in these matters reflected (in Kraus's view) the moral duplicity which existed throughout the society. So it was precisely through literature and music that he would lay bare the hypocrisy underlying life in the City of Dreams.

Like so many of his eminent contemporaries, Kraus came from a well-to-do Jewish family.[4] His father was a merchant who had emigrated from Bohemia when Karl was a very young child. So he was eminently qualified for the task which he chose for himself when, at the age of twenty-four, he began publication of his satirical fortnightly, *Die Fackel,* in 1899. Kraus's talents for satire were such that Moritz Benedikt, the editor of the *Neue Freie Presse,* had in the previous year offered him a position as the paper's chief satirist, a position which had been vacant for five years, apparently because no one could be found good enough to replace the talented Daniel Spitzer. There can thus be no doubt of Kraus's extraordinary satirical talent; indeed, his very mastery of language accounts for the effectiveness of his polemics at the time, and also for the fact that many of his works are simply untranslatable. Everything in his style was deliberate; he was known to fret for hours over the position of a comma. He played games, not only with the words of the German language in his puns, but also with the very style of those whom he sought to discredit. The fallacies in a man's logic as well as the defects of his character, he maintained, are reflected in his style of writing and in the very structure of his sentences. In a negative as well as a positive sense, *le style, c'est l'homme même;* it was just a matter of seeing it in the right light.

Die Fackel, Kraus's "antipaper," was modeled after Maximilian Harden's *Die Zukunft* in Germany and was the instrument Kraus used to expose corruption wherever he found it. From 1899 right up to 1936, 922 issues of the little red booklet delighted and infuriated the Viennese public, with its attacks and parodies on Hermann Bahr and the aesthetes, Hofmannsthal, the operettas of Franz Lehár, Franz Werfel, Kraus's own prototype Harden, and innumerable other writers; with its attacks on the corruption of the police, the Zionism of Herzl, and the brutishness and futility of World War One; and, last but by no means least, with its criticisms of the *Neue Freie Presse,* the very paper which had earlier employed him and offered him such a prestigious post. During the first twelve years of publication, Kraus included also pieces by Peter Altenberg, Houston Stewart Chamberlain, Richard Dehmel, Egon Friedell, Else Lasker-Schüler, Wilhelm Liebknecht, Detlev von Liliencron, Adolf Loos, Heinrich Mann, Arnold Schönberg, Frank Wedekind, Franz Werfel and Hugo Wolf. But, from November 1911, he wrote the whole of each issue himself, with the exception of one issue in 1912 which contained a contribution by August Strindberg.

Rarely has there been such a complete identity of a writer and his work. Kraus lived for his writings and ordered his life around his work: no personal sacrifices were too great for it. He himself referred to it as "an inverted way of life,"[5] sleeping by day and working all night. That such satirical activity could be physically dangerous was indicated in the *Fackel's* first quarterly "statement of accounts," which included the following ironical entry:

anonymous reviling letters	236
anonymous threatening letters	83
assaults[6]	1

Only a man with a personality far out of the ordinary could spend nearly forty years of his life in such a manner. It was not for nothing that Theodor Haecker in his 1913 monograph, *Søren Kierkegaard und die Philosophie der Innerlichkeit,* should have likened Kraus to Kierkegaard himself.[7]

A superficial acquaintance with Kraus and his work might give the impression that he was simply a crank, with many axes to grind. He at first strikes one as being obsessed with hatreds—for the feminist movement and women in general, for Zionism, for the press, for successful innovative writers and for psychoanalysis. Here is a man whose wrath seems to be meted out in an absolutely arbitrary manner. He could poke fun at Hermann Bahr for changing his political and aesthetic positions in the way most men changed their shirts, since Bahr had been successively a moderate socialist, an atheist, a Pan-German, a realist, an Impressionist, a liberal, and finally a monarchist Catholic. Yet Kraus himself had supported at one time or another, a liberal, a conservative, a socialist, and a clerical position. He entered the Catholic Church, but identified himself with the Church publicly only when he left it in 1922, twenty-three years after similarly renouncing Judaism.

To judge by first appearances alone, the personal attacks that Kraus leveled at everyone around him, including many former friends, such as Harden, can be explained only as the acts of a jealous, if witty, cynic. Yet what on the face of them are attacks against *bêtes noires* are, in fact, much more than that; they are rooted in a general view that judges artistic honesty and truth to be the most important factors in life. To understand Kraus, one must comprehend the integrating factor which made his life and work a consistent, coherent unity and proved him to be at once anything but a crank, and much more than a run-of-the-mill journalist. In Kraus's hands, polemic and satire became weapons with which to direct men away from everything superficial, corrupt and dehumanizing in human thought and action, back to the "origin" of all values, and so, in effect, to accomplish a regeneration of culture as a whole. His aphorisms bit at the hypocrisy that passed in Old Vienna for morality, and at the twaddle that passed for art. In his hands, scathing wit—in the form of polemics, satires and aphorisms—were instruments of civic and cultural education. Though he ridiculed politicians, his critique of society was never merely political; for Kraus, the sphere of politics was concerned only with surface problems, while the roots of the contemporary crisis lay in a spiritual malaise.

Consider, for example, Kraus's attitude toward prostitution. Stefan Zweig has emphasized the social role of prostitutes in the Vienna of his youth. Prior to a late marriage—and sometimes afterward as well, since marriage was so often merely a business merger—prostitutes provided the only sexual outlet for the young Viennese bourgeois. Yet this prostitution was simultaneously immoral and a social necessity, illegal and protected by the police, though at a price. Meanwhile, the prostitutes themselves faced ubiquitous disease, as well as exploitation by the madames and pimps. Kraus found this situation not only intolerable in itself, but a prime symptom of the inherent duplicity of current bourgeois Judaeo-Christian morality. So he rallied to the support of the prostitutes, whom he considered more heroic than soldiers. The latter served the existing social order by facing injury, disease and death; the former did likewise, but were subject in addition to social and legal penalties. In Kraus's eyes, legal action taken against a prostitute marked the transition from private immorality, on the part of her hypocritical accusers, to public immorality, on the part of the hypocritical laws against prostitution.

He railed against both this evil and the depraved society that institutionalized such hypocrisy in its legal system. In such essays as "Sittlichkeit und Kriminalität," Kraus ridiculed the legal system and defended the rights of this persecuted minority, just as he did those of that other, more persecuted sexual minority, the homosexuals. As to them, Kraus argued that a person's sexual activities were his affair and his alone, just so long as they did no one any harm. The real perverts and agents of a perverted society were the police and the scandalmongers who hounded these groups in the press and elsewhere.

Kraus's defense of the prostitute and the homosexual was, however, more broadly based, being rooted in his general conception of feminine sexuality. As Kraus saw her, woman is a totally sexual being: everything a woman does emanates from the sexuality which is her essence—*operatio sequitur esse.* In this respect, the woman differs from the man: the man *has* sexual urges, the woman *is* sexuality itself. Woman is emotion, irrationality and sexuality incarnate. She only appears to be of the same race as the man, for he, being at least potentially rational, has a capacity, which she lacks, for controlling his sexual nature. Hence, it makes no sense to hold a woman rationally accountable for her conduct, since it is in fact determined by the unconscious sensuality which is her very nature. Kraus viewed it as a fundamental indication of respectable sanctimoniousness that Viennese society recognized and demanded from mistresses precisely that which it resolutely denied to wives, and so privately encouraged that which it legally and socially forbade.

This Krausian conception of womanhood—which grew out of a debate familiar also to Freud and his other Viennese contemporaries—should be understood alongside, and in contrast with, the work of the enigmatic Otto Weininger, which Kraus both admired and reacted against at the same time. Weininger twice shocked Vienna in 1903: first, by the publication of his chief book, *Sex and Character,* which had the marks of genius; and secondly by his suicide in the house where Beethoven had died, which elevated him further into a full-fledged Romantic hero.[8] Anti-Semitic writers later asserted that Weininger was the wisest of Jews: when he realized the impossibility both of assimilation and of continuing to live as a Jew in non-Jewish society, he chose the only reasonable solution to his dilemma; believing as he did that the Jewish character was by nature the lowest, most depraved type of character—the lowest form of "womanhood" —and that all character was eternal and immutable, he had no alternative.

The intellectual origins of Weininger's characterology lay, he claimed, in Plato, Kant and Schopenhauer;[9] in Aristophanes' speech in the *Symposium;* in the individual's "intelligible character" outside of time, as discussed in Kant's *Idea of a Universal*

History (the character which, if accessible, would enable us to predict his actions with complete accuracy and so determine every historical act); and in Schopenhauer's "Metaphysics of Sexual Love." But there was also much of Weininger himself in that scandalous work; and, as in the case of Freud, not a little of the scandal lay precisely in what it reflected of the ways in which the Viennese saw themselves.

Weininger's views were based upon the notion that the concepts *masculine* and *feminine* represent, primarily, psychological ideal types or variations on Platonic ideas, and are embodied only secondarily in actual human beings.[10] The ideal types do not and cannot, according to Weininger, exist in a pure form; but they do provide a basis for explaining human behavior—even if a poor basis, since they allow for explanation only after the event. The "masculine idea" is that of perfect rationality and creativity. The "feminine idea" is the antithesis of the masculine —that is, a purely wanton urge to sexual gratification, an urge that is in principle unsatisfiable. The essence of womanhood is expressed in the ancient myths of the *magna mater*—universal, inchoate fecundity, the source of all irrationality and chaos in the world. Just as the sexual organ is at the center of the female body, so the sexual idea is the self-thinking thought which constitutes her psyche.

All the men and women who actually exist are androgynous, as Aristophanes had argued in Plato's *Symposium*. In them, the two ideal types are found mixed together in varying proportions, each individual possessing psychological counterparts to the anatomical vestiges of the opposite sex. The ideal human relationship then occurs when, for example, the femininity of the man exactly counterbalances the masculinity of the woman, so that

$$\text{male } (m\tfrac{3}{4} + f\tfrac{1}{4}) + \text{female } (f\tfrac{3}{4} + m\tfrac{1}{4}) = 1 \text{ male } \& 1 \text{ female}$$

and the constituents taken together add up to the two ideal types. In proportion as two actually existing individuals vary from this equation, they will be unhappy together, since they will not (literally) fulfill one another. On this theory, the homosexual is then a male who is psychologically more than 50 percent feminine; and it is this fact that explains his "depraved" state.[11]

All the positive achievements in human history, Weininger argued, are due to the masculine principle. All art, literature, legal institutions, and so on, flow from this masculine principle. The "eternal feminine," far from drawing us onward and upward, is responsible for all the destructive, nihilistic events and tendencies in history. The Aryan race is the embodiment of the masculine-creative principle of being, while the feminine-chaotic principle of nonbeing is embodied in the Jewish race and, above all, in Jewish culture.[12] On his own principles, Weininger's final act of despair was the inevitable verification of his own theory. He thereby made himself a prime example of that curious, but by no means rare, phenomenon which Theodor Lessing has described as "Jewish self-hatred" (*Judischer Selbsthass*).[13]

In his monograph on *Otto Weininger und scin Werk* published in 1912, Carl Dallago, a fellow-Austrian and a member of the Brenner Circle (which formed around Ludwig Ficker in Innsbruck and included also such notables as Theodor Haecker and Georg Trakl) praised Weininger's "spiritual honesty,"[14] an attitude toward Weininger shared by Kraus and many others. For Dallago, Weininger was a Nietzschean character who philosophized, not by reading books and writing learned articles, but from within the depths of his own personal experience of life. This was the correct way to carry on the philosophical enterprise, even though Weininger had cast off in the wrong direction and overstated his own case, through confusing the power of women *over him* with the power of "the feminine," purely and simply.[15] In his dualism, Weininger had been too much of an intellectual, too much of a rationalist; and this, according to Dallago, caused him to miss the true significance of love in human life. In Dallago's view, Weininger had many of the right categories, but failed to understand that the "nothingness" essential to woman is one aspect of the Kierkegaardian abyss, into which one must leap in order to find truth—that is, that the "nothingness" which woman is, is precisely the "origin" where Kraus located the source of all values.[16]

Kraus shared both Dallago's view of Weininger's significance and his critique of Weininger's position. Indeed, one can scarcely penetrate to Kraus's fundamental ideas without a prior knowledge of Weininger's work. Kraus accepted the premise that there is a vast difference between masculine and feminine sexuality, that "male" and "female" are distinct characterological categories. He further maintained, with Weininger, that "rationality" is the distinguishing characteristic and exclusive property of the masculine, and "emotion" that of the feminine. Yet there the comparison ends. Kraus was anything but the same kind of rationalist as Weininger. He did not exalt the rational element, but rather considered it as having a purely instrumental function in putting order into our activities. It is doubtful whether Kraus was familiar with the biological-instrumentalist theories of knowledge which became commonplace with the popularization of Darwin's discoveries, or with their simultaneous distortion by such people as Ernst Haeckel. Kraus himself was no philosopher, still less a scientist. If Kraus's views have a philosophical ancestry, this comes most assuredly from Schopenhauer; for, alone among the great philosophers, Schopenhauer was a kindred spirit, a man of philosophical profundity, with a strong talent for polemic and aphorism, a literary as well as a philosophical genius.

Schopenhauer (with Kierkegaard) was the only philosopher who appealed to Kraus. Schopenhauer's views on the essential nature of masculinity and femininity had influenced Weininger, though in the final analysis they remain opposed to the view Kraus accepted, particularly in their negative attitude toward the essence of the feminine. Kraus's conception of the feminine is more like that of Dallago. The emotional essence of woman is not wanton or nihilistic, but is rather a tender *fantasy,* which serves as the unconscious origin of all that has any worth in human experience. Herein lies the source of all inspiration and creativity.[17] Reason itself is merely a technique, a means by which men obtain what they desire. In itself it is neither good nor evil, it is merely effective or ineffective. Reason must be supplied with proper goals from outside; it must be given direction of a moral or aesthetic type. The feminine fantasy fecundates the masculine reason and gives it this direction. The source of moral and aesthetic truth is, thus, the unity between feeling and reason; these two are complementary sides of one and the same coin. Yet fantasy remains the guiding element since, without proper feelings, without a sense of the value of things, reason becomes an instrument which makes the evil man only more effective in his malefactions. Kraus's point, then, is that the feminine is the source of all that is civilizing in society. So the feminist movement became a threat from the other side. The feminist picture of woman as man's equal was, in its own way, as distorted as Weininger's; it attempted to eradicate the very wellsprings of civilization. This is what made Kraus an implacable enemy of woman's rights. The goal of human life was to find one's way to this origin:

> *Two runners run the track of time,*
> *Reckless the one, the other strides in awe.*
> *The one from nowhere, wins his goal; the other—*
> *The origin his start—dies on the way.*
> *And he from nowhere, he that won, yields place*
> *To him who ever strides in awe and e'er*
> *Has reached his terminus: the origin.*[18]

Fantasy—the "eternal feminine" which, as Goethe put it in the concluding line of *Faust, Part II,* "draws us on"—is under attack on all sides in the modern world. It is threatened by such diverse, seemingly unrelated forces as a corrupt press, the feminist movement, aestheticism, bourgeois morality, psychoanalysis, Zionism, and, of course, the misunderstanding and misuse of sex itself. For Kraus, the encounter between man and woman was the "origin" by which reason was fecundated from the wellspring of fantasy. The product of this encounter was an artistic creativity and a moral integrity, which expressed itself in everything that the person does. This is the central notion from which Kraus's whole life and work assumes its unity. A systematic analysis of his polemic bears this out.

Among those few of Kraus's aphorisms which have become known outside his native land is the much-quoted remark, "Psychoanalysis is that spiritual disease of which it considers itself to be the cure."[19] His attacks on psychoanalysis at first appear to have a personal basis; but they were, in fact, leveled against the distorted picture of human nature which Freud and his immediate coterie were propounding. For Kraus, Freud and his circle were simply replacing the traditional Judaeo-Christian bourgeois myths about sexuality with another in the form of psychoanalysis. The immediate occasion for this onslaught was an "analysis" of his own "case" by Fritz Wittels, a man who had been an admirer of Kraus, but had recently taken to Freudianism with enthusiasm. In a paper given before the Vienna Psychoanalytical Society, Wittels—a *terrible simplificateur*—attempted to locate the source of Kraus's polemics in his Oedipal frustration.[20] Briefly, in attacking Moritz Benedikt and the *Neue Freie Presse,* Kraus was endeavoring to attack his own father, with whom, in fact, his relations had not actually been strained. Wittels placed great weight on the fact that Kraus's father was called Jacob, the Hebrew for "blessed"; and this, of course, was the equivalent of the Latin *benedictus,* the root of Benedikt's name. Kraus's attacks in *Die Fackel* were construed as an attempt to prove to his father (Moritz Benedikt-Jacob Kraus) that his own little organ (*Die Fackel*) was every bit as effective as his father's great big organ (the *Neue Freie Presse)!* This was taking psychoanalysis too far even for its founder. In the subsequent discussion, the ever-skeptical Freud made it clear that he considered such wild speculations as unfounded and unscientific, but this attack on his own work made Kraus pay attention to the dangers inherent in the psychoanalytical picture of human nature.

For Freud, the unconscious was the exact antithesis of Kraus's conception. Freud's id was a seething mass of irrational, egocentric, antisocial impulses which could at best be held at bay by reason. Aesthetic and moral values were the result of frustration, which was an essential concomitant of the socialization of these impulses. To Kraus, this was tantamount to severing all ties with the creative fantasy which is the source of all that is healthy in the individual and society. Thus, the new myth was no better than the one it sought to displace and was itself one more manifestation of the illness it sought to cure. Psychoanalysis was in fact a further complication, rather than a solution, of the psychological problems that afflicted the Viennese middle class.

Not the least of these problems was hysteria, a physical ailment that appeared to have no physiological cause. Kraus saw that the actual root of this problem, so common among bourgeois *Wienerinnen,* lay in the business character of bourgeois marriage. Marriages designed to create financial dynasties, regardless of the personal fulfillment of the partners, guaranteed frustration, especially for women in so straitlaced a society. For the husbands, incompatibility meant recourse to prostitutes, or to affairs of the sort that Schnitzler was so adept at recreating in his stories and plays. For the wives, the problem was more complicated, since it was instilled in them early on that only lascivious, depraved women could actually desire or enjoy sexual gratification. No wonder if, when they discovered that sex was pleasant after all, they came to think of themselves in those terms; extramarital sex, which was a challenging game for the husbands, necessarily generated deep-seated feelings of guilt in the wives.

Kraus firmly believed that a change in social mores would bring about the end of the hysterical Viennese wife. Once men and women looked on marriage as a life partnership that ought to be entered into totally—within which sexual and spiritual fulfillment were opposite sides of a single coin—married life would become an arena where reason and fantasy could interact without hindrance, and this would lead to cultural as well as personal dividends. Hysteria would cease to be "the running milk of motherhood"[21]—that is, part and parcel of the "maturation" of so many middle-class Viennese women.

Kraus's barbs against psychoanalysis accordingly reflected much more than a personal dislike. Psychoanalysis, in his view, aimed at a further distortion of the balance between the masculine and the feminine, reason and fantasy, the conscious and the unconscious. This could lead only to a deepening crisis in society, as it carried men farther away from the "origin," away from the fantasy. "I would rather go back to childhood with Jean Paul than with Sigmund Freud,"[22] Kraus insisted. For Jean Paul, childhood was that time of life when fantasy vivifies all that we do, while for Freud it is nothing but a series of crises that issue in frustration. Kraus feared that the psychoanalytic approach to life, with its emphasis on adjustment to society, threatened the artist:

Nerve doctors who ruin genius for us by calling it pathological should have their skulls bashed in by the genius' collected works. . . . One should grind one's heel into the faces of all rationalistic helpers of "normal humanity" who give reassurance to people unable to appreciate works of wit and fantasy.[23]

Herein lay the reason for Kraus's wholehearted opposition, not just to psychoanalysis but also, curiously enough, to the press.

Kraus could have endorsed the views of an English historian that the papers created opinion in accord with political and economic interests. His main complaint was that the press assumed a role far beyond its proper function of objectively reporting the news, even when it actually succeeded in being objective. This deviation was a threat to civilization, since it too threatened the life of fantasy. Thus, he founded *Die Fackel* as an "antipress"; in the words of one Kraus scholar, in order "to fight the press, to undermine public confidence in it, and to undo the damage it was currently doing."[24] It was typical of Kraus that he should choose to concentrate the brunt of his attack on the illustrious *Neue Freie Presse,* which was without doubt the foremost paper in the Empire and possibly the one with the highest journalistic standards in the world. (Wickham Steed, the Vienna correspondent of the London *Times,* reported—as much in truth as in jest—that Francis Joseph was the most powerful man in the Dual Monarchy, except for its editor, Benedikt.)[25] And it was precisely the pre-eminence of the paper that caused Kraus to focus his barrage upon it.

Once again, Kraus's jibes at the press appeared to many the rantings of a malcontent, for everyone knew the immense international reputation of Vienna's *Neue Freie Presse.* Yet certainly his polemic was not the result of any frustration of his own journalistic ambitions, nor was it occasioned by any prior attack upon him. What provoked his diatribes was, more, the exalted role that the press has assumed for itself in bourgeois society. And the *Neue Freie Presse* was a special object of his wrath, precisely because its high journalistic standards were allied to a point of view and presentation which were anything but objective. Fear of official censorship, in fact, made the paper the covert mouthpiece of the regime, while its elegant reporting was always slanted toward industrial interests. In Kraus's view, therefore, claims to journalistic excellence included, above all, a claim to excellence in deceit. It was the most deserving of attack, because it exemplified all the things that other newspapers sought to emulate and was the ideal to which every other publisher aspired.

Industrial interests infiltrated the whole press; even the Socialist press regularly carried heavy capitalist advertising.[26] Kraus shared the recently deceased Wilhelm Liebknecht's low opinion of the press which he printed in the *Fackel* in 1900:

There is no baseness which the press would not be ready to falsify and pass off as a magnanimous deed; there is no crook on whose head it would not place the laurels of glory or the oak-wreath of citizenly virtue, whenever that served its purposes.[27]

No institution more opposed the "social blight" of prostitution, or was more indignant to discover that "depraved and perverted" homosexuals walked the streets of Vienna; yet the very same press contained, in its classified section, innumerable advertisements for "masseur" services and "companions."[28] Evidently the proprietors were not above accepting money for the back pages from the very people whom they reviled on the front pages. Was there not collusion here with the police, who extorted money from the prostitutes by guaranteeing them protection within their specified territories? For Kraus, there was no doubt about it. In his extreme moments, Kraus considered the strictest censorship preferable to such a press.

What roused Kraus's resentment toward current journalism to particular heights was the mingling of opinion and fact involved in presenting news slanted by political interest. The hypocrisy of the press was also a function of greed; it prostituted itself before the interests of industry, distorting facts for money. But the situation was even more complicated than this. The whole society was completely imbued with hypocrisy; and, as a result, it was the aesthetic side of the press which Kraus found most offensive of all. The cultural essay, or feuilleton, was for many the most important section of the whole paper. If the class standpoint of the paper resulted in a general distortion of the news, it was specifically distorted in the free mingling of fact and opinion, rational objectivity and subjective reaction, that was the deliberate aim of the feuilleton. As Carl Schorske describes it in a passage cited earlier,[29] the feuilleton called for a species of vignette, in which a situation was described with all the color the author could muster; it was a subjective response to an objective state of affairs, intended to be conveyed in language which was laden with adverbs and especially adjectives; so much so, that the objective situation was lost in the shuffle. Objective facts were thus viewed through the prismlike emotions of the writer. Success in this essay form was open only to those narcissistic enough to regard their own emotional responses as having a universal perceptiveness and quality.

For the bourgeois Viennese, with their passion for the arts, the feuilleton was the high point of all journalism, and the dream of every would-be man of letters was to be published in the *Neue Freie Presse*. To Kraus, however, the feuilleton destroyed both the objectivity of the situation described and the creative fantasy of the writer, since, while distorting the news as facts, it prevented the writer from coming to terms with the depths of his own personality by demanding a response to a ready-made situation. So it both reduced the essayist's creativity to the level of word-manipulating and prevented the reader from making any rational assessment of the facts of the case. Here, then, was the ideal medium for those who believed in art for art's sake, the perfect journalistic form for the aesthete. Its narcissism made it a denial of all that Kraus held sacred—that is, the notion that fantasy fecundates reason in the encounter between man and woman. So it need not be surprising that Kraus leveled an all-out attack against everyone having any connection with the feuilleton—writers, editors, and reading public alike. Their joint conspiracy of egotism was, Kraus believed, a supreme manifestation of the duplicity characteristic of bourgeois society. Thus Kraus's attitude toward the feuilleton was both a reflection of his ideas about the origin of creativity and the point at which his views on language and art made direct contact with his polemics against the hypocrisy of the society in which he lived.

Such a literary form as the feuilleton could only have assumed the cultural significance it did in *fin-de-siècle* Vienna, in a society in which decadent aestheticism was the rule rather than the exception—in which (to paraphrase Carl Schorske)[30] artists were not alienated *from,* but rather alienated *with* their whole class. Such, indeed, was Kraus's own view of the art and the society to which he himself in so many ways belonged. Bahr, Schnitzler, Salten, and the whole *Jung Wien* group were, in his view, the foremost exponents of the inverted view of the world that characterized the Habsburg capital. Just as, for the preceding generation of liberal *laissez-faire* and economic positivism, "Business is business" had been a motto and a credo, and the classical economic laws of the market a metaphysics, so now the generation of the aesthetes were literary positivists, for whom the motto was "Art for art's sake," and a technical perfection of form was the chief end of literature. This conception of the artist as the consummate stylist was the exact opposite of Kraus's own, and *Die Fackel* rarely passed up an opportunity to poke fun at the perpetrators of such "works of art."

It is a central fact about Karl Kraus that the man and his work are unclassifiable. None of the standard literary or artistic categories—Impressionist, Expressionist, Social Realist, and so on—is applicable to him. To Kraus, this was a triumph, for he desired precisely to be unique. Both for Kraus and for those who saw themselves as extending his achievement in their own work, uniqueness was the distinguishing characteristic of the true artist; the quality which can be acquired only by the man who has found the "origin," and in whom true "fantasy" is therefore operative. The distinguishing characteristic of all that is moral and artistic, for Kraus, is *integrity*. Integrity is what Kraus found lacking in so many of his contemporaries, and this lack made them deserving of his attack.

This emphasis on integrity explains why Kraus could be fond even of such early feuilleton writers as Spitzer, Kürnberger, and Speidel, while being nevertheless vehemently opposed to the form itself.[31] It explains also how the ever-widening circle of writers whom he considered to be leading society into barbarism could include both impressionists and expressionists; why his barbs were cast impartially at Bahr, Hofmannsthal, Reinhardt, Werfel, and Lehár—to mention only the best-known. Kraus did not pit one school against the other, as critics so often do. Rather he concerned himself with the integrity of the individual writer. It was not a matter of ideology or literary schools; it was always a question of the unity of form and personality. So, in every case, Kraus's polemics were inevitably *personal*. He viewed a man's art as intimately connected with his moral character. To criticize a work of art was to determine whether or not it was a true expression of the artist. On this conception of art, there was no room for sensationalism or for crowd pleasing; these were betrayals of the nature of art, rooted in character defects. His polemics therefore aimed at bringing out the moral defects in the character of the writer, corresponding to the aesthetic defects in his work—hence his critical assaults on Bahr, Lehár, and others.

Kraus's opposition to Bahr and *Jung Wien* was based not so much on their philosophy of literature as on their personal attitudes toward their work. Bahr had sought a philosophical basis for impressionism in the psychology of Ernst Mach, particularly in the notion that all knowledge is an ordering of "sense impressions" according to the simplest mathematical formula. What Bahr found significant here was the notion that sensory data— that is, subjective states—are the basis for all knowledge. From this, he concluded that the impressionst's effort to describe his subjective experiences in the most colorful manner was not only warranted, but in some sense necessary, since on Mach's view these experiences alone are "real." Kraus's dispute was not with this abstract view of literature, but with the majority of its actual practitioners. This is indicated, for example, by his respect and admiration for the vignettes of Peter Altenberg, which, for all their unique qualities, fitted Bahr's general description of art.

The differences between Bahr and Altenberg lay in the fact that, for Bahr, writing was an occupation, not an organic extension of his personality. Bahr the writer and Bahr the man were not identical; Bahr was an opportunistic character, who wrote what he thought his public wanted. Altenberg, on the other hand, was an integral man. The man and his work were at all times one. In Vienna, artistic life centered in the coffeehouses, where its exponents met and talked and then went home; all except Altenberg, for he *lived* in the Café Central. There was no part of Altenberg's life that was not, at the same time, a part of his work. In less than a page of print he could convey the charm of some typical scene or personal encounter on the street or in a park or hotel or café of Old Vienna, just because he was himself so much a part of that ambience. With his sandals, slouch hat and walking stick, "P.A." was a proto-Hippie and could capture what was unique and charming in Viennese life, precisely because of what he was.

The case of Max Reinhardt also throws light on Kraus's views about the nature of art. Strictly speaking, Kraus's polemic against Reinhardt, his collaborator Hofmannsthal and the Salzburg Festival belong to a period later than that which we are concerned with here; but the underlying conflict of aesthetic principles had its origins before 1914. Kraus considered Reinhardt's theatrical techniques a kind of glorified sleight of hand, an extravaganza intended to divert the audience from the quality of the drama. In Reinhardt's hands, a theatrical production became a mere spectacle and an exercise in deception, for all the embellishments served only to distract the audience from what they had come to see—actors creating the realm of fantasy before their very eyes. "In earlier times, the decorations were made of cardboard and the actors were genuine. Now," Kraus lamented, "the decorations are beyond any doubt real, and the actors are made of cardboard."[32]

In Reinhardt's "theater of spectacle," all was external. It followed that such a theater could achieve no more than superficiality. Kraus desired to replace it with a "theater of poetry," which he attempted to realize in his dramatic readings. Here, there was nothing but the text and its interpreter—no costumes, no scenery, not even action. Given Kraus's view of the functions of the theater and acting, nothing more was required. If the drama had any real worth and the actors had any genuine proficiency, anything else could only interfere with the drama.

He was no more lenient with Reinhardt's playwrights, such as Hugo von Hofmannsthal. Hofmannsthal was very much under the influence of Wagner when he turned to the stage. What struck him as of paramount importance in Wagner was the concept of the *Gesamtkunstwerk*,[33] that artistic vehicle which would combine all the performing arts—poetry, music, and theater—into a unity that would produce the same essential effect as the ancient drama. The aim of Hofmannsthal's plays was to evoke in the audience a new type of catharsis. Wagner conceived a music-drama which should revivify the German *Volk*, by presenting the great Germanic virtues as exemplified in old Norse myths. His theory of art was in fact a social philosophy, and his drama was a means toward implementing that philosophy. Hofmannsthal assimilated this conception and applied it, first by imitating ancient Greek plays, as in his *Elektra*, then by adapting it to certain medieval and baroque conceptions, to yield the new Christian drama of the Festival Plays and such operas as *Die Frau ohne Schatten*. In this way, Hofmannsthal hoped to regenerate the society in which he lived, as a response to the experience his art would evoke in those who beheld it. In the very process of attending these productions they would participate in the action, and their characters would undergo a consequent transformation. By experiencing the disastrous results of their own selfishness, they would be converted and committed to a Christian *agape* which would lead to a transformation of society.

Like Wagner, Hofmannsthal thought that spectacular theatrical effects were capable of producing equally spectacular effects in those who beheld them, and this belief inspired his collaboration both with Reinhardt and with Richard Strauss. Strauss's curious sense of theatrical authenticity has been well described by Barbara Tuchman in her *Proud Tower*, as "freaks of realism"—for example, his demand that Clytemnestra's sacrifice in *Elektra* should involve live sheep and bulls.[34] Kraus, by contrast, was convinced that nothing did more to destroy and distract from the experience of theater than such "effects." Hofmannsthal was endeavoring to recapture the baroque by imitating it and by enhancing its style and plots with the effects that a Max Reinhardt could provide. But the attempt to influence politics and society by these curious anachronistic pageants was totally absurd—all the more so after World War One. To suppose that lighting, noise, and the spectacle of a reconstituted baroque, could directly change the world was for Kraus sheer illusion. Here was yet another "cure" which was merely "part of the disease."

Kraus was especially sensitive to the folly of Hofmannsthal's schemes, not because the very idea of a social and political function for the theater struck him as essentially ridiculous, but because he himself was deeply committed to the role of the theater as an important force for morality within society. Hofmannsthal infuriated him, because his conception of drama was so banal. Hofmannsthal did indeed have a sense of the role that fantasy ought to play in life, but he was unaware of the extent to which it must be mediated by reason. Kraus rightly saw that by producing works of art so obviously based upon uncontrolled fantasy, one reduced it to the level of the commonplace and so betrayed it.

To complete our picture of Kraus the polemicist, as a background to what might be called the "philosophical underpinnings" of his life and work, let us consider finally the reasons which led him to attack Lehár, as one of the most degenerate artists of his day. Franz Lehár, composer of such operettas as *The Merry Widow* and *The Count of Luxemburg,* was a cynical crowd pleaser who wrote his operas simply to make money and was consequently an enemy of all that was authentic in contemporary culture.[35] The success of Lehár's operettas was likewise, in Kraus's eyes, a barometer of the moral degeneration of Viennese life. By catering to their basest instincts, Lehár made himself, more than any other figure, responsible for the poor taste of the Viennese populace. He gave them a new "realism" in the operettas, with an explicit treatment of sexual themes which titillated rather than edified his audience. The very success of this deliberate titillation enraged Kraus—"An inartistic truth about an evil is itself an evil. Truth must be valuable in and of itself. Then it becomes reconciled to evil and its grief over the fact that there is evil."[36]

For Kraus, "immoral art" was the negation of art, just as "ugly truth" was falsity. Society was in a sad enough state before Lehár came on the scene; he merely encouraged the forces of decadence by portraying it with such "charm" in his musicals. As with the *Neue Freie Presse,* Lehár became a special object of Kraus's wrath, because he was so good at carrying through and popularizing this decadent art. For Lehár, sex was basically something egocentric and common; in Kraus's opinion, this "realistic" or plausible treatment of sexual matters divested the relations between man and woman of their mysterious poetic element and completely distorted their creative power.

In this, Lehár was the antithesis of Jacques Offenbach, whom Kraus admired so much that he actually translated *La Perichole* into German, and sang it in a sort of *Sprechgesang.* Alban Berg, who was an admirer of Kraus, reported that, although Kraus possessed very little vocal talent, his profound feeling for Offenbach in these recitals conveyed an extraordinary sense of Offenbach's music.

Kraus's admiration for Offenbach was an expression of something very central to his conception of art. For Kraus, operetta was "the fulfillment of the true meaning of the theater,"[37] because it was most capable of forming the character of its audience; its very essence was to teach moral values of aesthetic experience. Through this vehicle—at least, in the conception of romantic operetta which he considered alone authentic—the audience was put directly into contact with the world of fantasy. Offenbach carried this out better than any other composer; in his opera buffa an "inverted world" was stood on its feet again. If Offenbach succeeded where Kraus's contemporaries failed so miserably, this was because the imaginary settings and the implausibilities of his plots enabled the audience to detach itself from the banalities of everyday life and be transported into a magical world where they experienced before their very eyes the triumph of good over evil. This was the only sort of theater which was naturally musical, one in which music was an essential part of the drama, and not merely an additional source of effects.[38]

This attachment to a theater which evoked moral discipline by the power of poetry linked Kraus not only to Offenbach, but to a main current in traditional Austrian theater. Mozart's *Magic Flute* is the best-known example of the Austrian "magic farce," a kind of fairy-tale pantomime which was at the same time a pedagogic instrument.[39] Nineteenth-century Austrian drama had been deeply rooted in this traditional popular theater. It was a purely romantic theater, where fantasy reigned supreme, and where good and evil were always clearly defined and always in combat. It was, above all, an instrument of social criticism that enshrined moral values. Before the 1848 revolution, it dominated the Viennese theatrical scene, in the plays of Raimund, and it found its perfect realization in the works of Nestroy.

Johann Nepomuk Nestroy would perhaps have passed into oblivion had it not been for the efforts of Kraus. Nestroy was considered by the Viennese public—with its penchant for missing the point—as no more than a very witty actor, in the sense in which it found Kraus's most devastating satires "witty." Nestroy was his own director, writer and stage manager, as well as starring actor. As a writer, he transformed the plots of French social satires into sparkling parodies of Viennese life. (The musical show *Hello, Dolly!* is, in fact, an up-dated version of an adaptation by Thornton Wilder of one such Nestroy play!) The basis of Nestroy's humor lay in his amazing feeling for the nuances of ordinary spoken language. His was not the stately drama of the Imperial Theater, but rather a highly individual slapstick, written for common folk, with roots reaching as far back as Shakespeare's comedies, now transposed into the idiomatic language of the Austrian aristocrats, bourgeois and peasants. His sensitivity to Viennese idiom and dialect made his work so untranslatable that he remains unknown outside the German-speaking world.

Nestroy's real tool was, of course, German, the language he truly mastered as a virtuoso. He combined Viennese idiom and High German into similes, metaphors, mixed-up proverbs, and gyrating figures of speech. His word-creations may have been primitive or ingenuous, but they were never an end in themselves.[40]

During the short-lived success of the 1848 uprising, Nestroy tried his own hand at writing political plays; but, with the counterrevolution, they were suppressed by the censor. This led him to write dialogue which was in itself inoffensive but which, when delivered by Nestroy the actor with a wink or a shrug of the shoulders, changed its meaning completely and resulted in frequent jail sentences for him. Nestroy's tongue-twisting songs, with their parodies of German multisyllabic words, combined to make his a unique form of music drama. To the majority, who did not penetrate his subtlety, Nestroy provided a coarse, earthy humor; to the Habsburg censor, he was a dangerous nihilist; yet to a few who saw the full depths of his work, Nestroy was, in the words of Egon Friedell, "the greatest, in fact the only, Austrian philosopher." Friedell characterized him as a Socratic dialectician and a Kantian analyzer, a Shakespeareanly strug-gling soul that, with a truly cosmic fancy, distorted the metric of human things, in order thereby to let them appear for the first time in their true dimension.[41]

Here, in the plays of Nestroy, one can understand the Krausian notion that the *language* of the satirist attains the "origin," as it lays bare the moral character of the person who speaks. In this type of linguistic art, the writer and his work are fused into such a unity that the writer has no identity apart from his work. In short, the man and his work were so perfectly integrated that he expressed his character through the very nuances of the gram-mar that he used to expose the foibles and hypocrisies of society. This was the task which Kraus saw himself as continuing.

Throughout his life, Kraus's efforts to carry on the work of Nestroy involved him in litigation. The differences in their re-spective methods—the fact that for Kraus battle took place largely in print, for Nestroy on the stage—were rooted in the integrity of the individuals. Each was a consummate artist who turned his artistry into the most effective weapon he pos-sessed, in the battle against the deterioration of values in society. When personal integrity is the measure of virtue, imitation is the chief vice. (That is why Kraus's immediate followers resembled him, integrity apart, in so few respects.) In the struggle against a bourgeois morality based on "good breeding" and doing what "one does," the authentically moral man uses the gifts which he himself possesses to the best of his particular talents. So the Krausian can engage in a critique of culture only indirectly— that is, by maintaining what Paul Engelmann referred to as a "creative separation" between reason and fantasy, between the sphere of "facts" and the sphere of "values."[42] This explains why those who view the resulting work only superficially easily misunderstand it, as has certainly been the case with the two most eminent Krausians, Ludwig Wittgenstein and Arnold Schönberg. For, like Kraus and Nestroy before him, the Kraus-ian will be appreciated by some for the wrong reasons and con-demned as a nihilist by others on equally mistaken grounds, both sets of critics having somehow stopped short of the Krausian "origin."

The central notion that unifies the life and work of Karl Kraus is, then, the "creative separation" of the two spheres of factual discourse and literary artistry. It followed from this separation that Kraus was never *doctrinaire* in his polemics; only a man who has an excessive faith in the efficacy of ideas in forming people's character and actions can afford to be doctrinaire. This was, as we have seen, the exact opposite of Kraus's view (that reason is morally neutral), which formed the basis for the personal nature of his polemic. Men, not ideas, are moral or immoral. Hence his critique of, say, expressionism was directed against those writers who merely sought after novel effects to make their points; it did not extend to such outstanding expressionists as the poet Georg Trakl and the playwright Frank Wedekind. Men of integrity, brilliant writers with character, might belong to any movement, for they really had no choice in the matter. What Kraus said of himself also applied to any authentic writer—"I command the language of others. Mine does what it wants with me."[43]

The writer who manipulated words was immoral in proportion to his talents, because he lacked integrity; the man and his work were not one and the same. The paradigm of such an author was Heinrich Heine. It was he who introduced the French feuilleton form into German, a language for which it was unsuited; and the very fact that Heine was a master of the technique made his example all the more disastrous. Technique, in the Krausian view, was a product of reason and calculation and so must always be a means. Heine had converted it into an end in itself.

As Kraus saw it, even technical competence, or "virtuosity," cannot be attained by those whose only interest in writing is financial success or renown. To prove that this was the case with the *Neue Freie Presse*, he was in the habit of submitting pseudonymous letters to the editor, comprising sheer nonsense couched in mock scholarly language. It was necessary for him to submit these under an alias, because the Viennese newspapers' way of handling Kraus's attacks was from the beginning the *Totschweigentaktik*—no matter what he did, his name was never to be mentioned in the paper. (The *Neue Freie Presse* would not report the funeral of Peter Altenberg, for example, because this would have compelled it to mention Kraus, who had read at graveside.)[44] One of his most celebrated nonsense letters described an earthquake from the point of view of a mining engineer. It included fictitious distinctions between "cosmic" and "telluric" tremors, and in the course of his description the

mythical engineer related how the mysterious *Grubenhund* beast
became restless and began to bellow.[45] Kraus delighted in such
escapades; any competent editor with average intelligence ought
to be able to see through his little jokes. As a further aggrava-
tion, he wrote a letter to the press protesting the treatment at the
hands of the Munich government of Ernst Toller, the playwright-
president of the short-lived Bavarian Socialist Republic, and
signed it with the names of Hofmannsthal, Bahr, and five other
notables. The "signatories" were somewhat embarrassed when
they publicly thanked the anonymous author of the letter for doing something that they should have done themselves in the first
place.[46]

When Heine failed to distinguish the boundaries of factual discourse that separate it from artistic and moral discourse, he had
opened a Pandora's box. The failure to make this "creative
separation," Kraus declared, leads to a falsification of the factual, and a debasement or distortion of the aesthetic and moral.

Adolf Loos and I—he literally and I grammatically—have done nothing
more than show that there is a distinction between an urn and a chamber
pot and that it is this distinction above all that provides culture with
elbow room. The others, those who fail to make this distinction, are divided into those who use the urn as a chamber pot and those who use the
chamber pot as urn.[47]

Kraus here expresses his deep conviction that the sphere of
values is altogether distinct from the sphere of facts. The evil
effects of mingling the two are most evident, firstly, in the feuilleton, in which imagination runs riot with the facts, and secondly, in the concept of "moral legislation" (for example, the
laws against prostitution), in which morality is represented as
something that can be deduced from "natural moral laws"—
than which nothing could be more unnatural.

Kraus's insistence that he is trying to effect, by a polemical
analysis of grammar and language, the same "creative separation" between the sphere of reason (or fact) and that of fantasy
(or value) as Adolf Loos was doing in his critique of bourgeois
Viennese taste, by distinguishing merely functional artifacts
from genuine objects of art, should be taken quite literally. From
the very beginning of Kraus's career, he identified absolutely the
aesthetic form and the moral content of a literary work, seeing
its moral and aesthetic worth as reflected in its language. As time
passed, he became more and more convinced of this truth.

Gradually, after 1905, it is borne in upon him that language—that is, the way a statement is made—bears within itself *all* the signs he needs to understand the moral and ethical quality of that statement and of him who made it. Conversely, it is necessary to read a statement in a way that is supremely sensitive to all its linguistic qualities, in order to discover the truth.[48]

Kraus's analytical and polemical commentary on such a statement did not add anything new to it, but merely showed more clearly what lay hidden within it. Any writer who lacked integrity was like the man of whom Lichtenberg—whom Kraus greatly admired—had said, "He can't hold his ink; and when he feels a desire to befoul someone, he usually befouls himself most."[49] This description applied particularly to the press; it determined his method for showing the world how corrupt the press was, and a fortiori how corrupt the society was. Kraus's critique of the way people used language *in* his society was, thus, an implied criticism *of* that society.

Kraus's attitude toward language has been described as a sort of "erotic mysticism," having affinities to the Hasidism which Martin Buber was in the process of discovering,[50] and which inspired the writer of the ninth *Duino Elegy* to sing of "the heaviness and long experience of love" as "unutterable."[51] His assertion that his language "does what it wants with him" is an expression of this attitude. Accordingly, less and less effort was required to expose the duplicity in the language of the corrupt; often, it was enough to quote that person's own words in *Die Fackel* without comment, and the context was enough to reveal the truth about its author. In his monumental satire on World War One, *Die Letzten Tage der Menschheit,* Kraus used this technique with great success. It is a seven-hundred-page play, with a thirteen-page cast of characters, and records Kraus's reactions to the war minutely, incorporating whole speeches and editorials directly from the newspapers as they stood, in a way reminiscent of the more recent play *Oh, What a Lovely War!*

This language mysticism may be taken to imply that the perfect satire is a work which in no way changes the statements that are being satirized, but simply shows them in a light which illuminates their inherent hypocrisy. Like no other writer, except possibly Nestroy, Kraus believed that his mission was to show the world how every statement had an unspoken moral dimension, by virtue of what might be termed its "pre-established harmony'' with morality. Even the complex jokes, of which he and Nestroy were so fond, could thus lead one to a moral insight. Kraus's critique of Viennese society was therefore rooted, partly in language mysticism, partly in the unflinching steadfastness with which he maintained his supreme principle of creative integrity—''If I must choose the lesser of two evils, I will choose neither.''[52]

This saying became the motto for a whole generation of Viennese who emulated Kraus in a wide range of different fields and pursuits. We shall turn next to consider a few of the most important of these ''Krausians.''

4

Culture and Critique:

SOCIAL CRITICISM AND THE LIMITS OF ARTISTIC EXPRESSION

*Modern morality consists in accepting
the standards of one's age.*

—OSCAR WILDE

It is not easy today, especially for a younger American, to recognize just how small and tightly knit were the cultural circles of the Habsburg monarchy. We are accustomed to living in a society in which there are many different cultural centers and a great many diverse cultural attitudes. Mass education makes it difficult, likewise, to conceive of a country of fifty million in which the cultural elite forms a tiny minority, and that strongly oriented towards an imperial capital. So it is difficult now to understand exactly how central Vienna was to the Empire's entire cultural life. (The position of Paris in French culture is, perhaps, the only comparable present-day phenomenon.) Thus it comes as a slight shock to discover that Anton Bruckner gave piano lessons to Ludwig Boltzmann;[1] that Gustav Mahler would bring his psychological problems to Dr. Freud;[2] that Breuer was Brentano's physician;[3] that the young Freud fought a duel with the young Viktor Adler, who had attended the same high school as both the last of the Habsburgs, Charles I, and Arthur Seyss-Inquart, later the Nazi Commissioner of Holland;[4] and that Adler himself, like Schnitzler and Freud, had been an assistant in Meynert's clinic.[5] In short, in late Habsburg Vienna, any of the city's cultural leaders could make the acquaintance of any other without difficulty, and many of them were in fact close friends despite working in quite distinct fields of art, thought and public affairs.

This factor needs to be borne in mind when we discover that a whole range of intellectual and artistic creations, ranging from the music of Arnold Schönberg to the architecture of Adolf Loos —and including even, in its own way, Ludwig Wittgenstein's *Tractatus Logico-Philosophicus*—were intimately and consciously related to, and even extensions of, the critique of language and society conducted by Karl Kraus. Each of these men acknowledged the inspiration of Kraus and could be said to be a Krausian; but the integrity of a Krausian demanded in each case that the struggle against moral and aesthetic corruption be carried on by a critique of that particular area of human experience in which the individual artist or writer was himself most at home. For Loos, this was architecture and design; for Schönberg, it was music; for Wittgenstein, philosophy.

In the last chapter we saw Kraus identifying his task with that of Loos; so that Kraus considered himself as doing for language what Loos was doing in the sphere of design—making people *morally* aware of the essential distinction between the chamber pot and an urn! This, indeed, was the central idea behind everything Loos did—distinguishing articles for use from *objets d'art*. Just as Kraus had declared war upon the feuilleton, for obliterating the distinctions between reason and fantasy, Loos waged a similar war against the "art" which consisted in ornamenting articles for daily use, on the grounds that the very notion of "applied art" obliterated a similar distinction between a utensil and an art object. Loos desired to eliminate all forms of decoration from functional items—"Cultural evolution is equivalent to the removal of ornament from articles in daily use."[6] He put this notion into effect himself by designing buildings that entirely lacked the conventional elaborate façade. According to Loos, the architect like any other craftsman should follow the plumber as his model, not the sculptor.

Loos did not put these aesthetic theories forth in a vacuum. If we need to understand the background of Viennese letters and journalism in order to comprehend the life work of Karl Kraus, we must similarly look at developments in the plastic arts, and at the late-nineteenth-century canons of popular taste, in order to grasp the significance of Loos's program for art and architecture. In the mid-1890s, naturalism and academicism were supreme in the most admired painting of Austria-Hungary. In order to study painting, one had to attend the Imperial Academy, and the arbiter of good taste there was Professor Hans Makart, whose paintings have been described as "huge academic machines," and as "decorative works of vast dimensions and glowing colors."[7] (One famous example is his portrait of the celebrated actress Charlotte Wolter.) Makart's art was ornate, drawing heavily on mythological subjects; and this was the paradigm which all aspiring painters were required to follow slavishly. The Academy was a state institution in a conservative state, so it is not surprising that a rigid formalism was the order of the day, or that, instead of favoring innovation in the arts, it imposed upon its students the bourgeois prejudices of an earlier generation. Nor is it any wonder that the students at the Academy finally rebelled against their master, of whom one eminent historian of the monarchy has said, "His drawing was defective, his execution careless, his material of inferior quality, and he was guilty of glaring anachronisms."[8]

In 1897, Gustav Klimt led nineteen students in withdrawing from the Academy, and forming "the Secession." Klimt and his followers insisted that the artistic revolution initiated by the French Impressionists, twenty-three years before, had at last come to Austria to stay. The days when imitation of past forms could be the goal of the painter were past; the twentieth century must have its own style. Thus the motto of the movement was, *Der Zeit ihre Kunst, der Kunst ihre Freiheit* ("To the era its proper art, to art its proper freedom"). Klimt provided the movement with a guiding spirit rather than with any fixed views of what painting ought to be. This nondoctrinaire approach was essential to the freedom these artists sought, and to that "new art" which would be the reflection of the spirit of the new century. Thus, precious few common characteristics can be found in the paintings of those artists whose works are commonly referred to as *Secessionstil*.

As a movement, the work of the nineteen around Klimt was not unrelated to the parallel Berlin Secession, which had begun in 1892 but did not exhibit till 1898, and which is called *Jugendstil*.[9] The inspiration for the movement in Germany, which can be detected also in the work of Klimt, was the *art nouveau* of Odilon Redon and Puvis de Chavannes, heavily influenced by the symbolist poets. These painters and poets were concerned to discover all the possibilities latent in the medium they utilized. They were anxious to escape from the shackles of popular taste and develop the finer subtleties of their media. Nothing was to be clearly spelled out—only suggested, hinted at, by means of the nuances of the medium. In *art nouveau* nothing was explicit, just as in the art of Makart everything was explicit. For some, like the Impressionists, color was to replace line; for others, line was to dominate over color, as it did in the paintings of Egon Schiele. The decorous bunches of grapes flanking huge masses of languishing female flesh, in Makart and his like, were to be banished forever. The history of the resulting movement is the history of Austrian Expressionism, which begins with Klimt in the 1890s and ends with Kokoschka after World War One—a story requiring a book of its own. However, it is worthwhile here to look at Klimt's achievement in particular, since this shows us, simultaneously, the break with tradition and the transition from Impressionism to Expressionism.

Klimt's paintings were highly personal creations, which were much admired both by his colleagues and by the public, but he evoked no imitations. When we look at many of his paintings, we are struck by their monumentality and sensuality. Klimt's large-scale use of gold and silver makes some of his works look like modern ikons, as does his weakening of the representational, and his use of a nonrepresentational ornamentation. Klimt's art was meant to reflect a transformation of the everyday by the artist's imagination. By his lavish use of ornamentation, he sought what Henry van de Velde has termed "a logical structure of products, uncompromising logic in the use of materials."[10] Few of the other artists influenced by *art nouveau* were capable of using ornament with the same success as Klimt; for too many of them, ornamentation of a fantastic kind became an *idée fixe,* in a way that it never became for Klimt. These artists merely exchanged the popular type of decoration for ornamentation of a more esoteric type; for them, there was no real escape from tradition, only a flight. Klimt's achievement lay in his complete mastery of technique and in the utter charm of his imagination, which "sold" the public a form of art that was neither mythological, historical, nor naturalistic. By proving that innovation was not *ipso facto* change for the worse, he thus accomplished an important feat of aesthetic education.

(So immediately successful were Klimt and the Secession on the surface that by 1900—only three years after the rebellion at the Academy—the movement was officially represented at the Paris International Exhibition. This is an indication of the extraordinary capacity that the old Empire appeared to possess to reconcile itself with, and draw the teeth of, its critics just so long as they did not threaten the *Hausmacht* or the central values of the society. Or maybe there was some sort of "elective affinity" between the glitter and dazzle of Klimt's ornamentation, and the superficial splendor of Habsburg institutions and social life!)

The architects and designers of the Secession embraced Klimt's style of ornamentation with an enthusiasm paralleled only by those who were later to make a dogma of the purely functional. Foremost among the architects was Otto Wagner, a former professor of architecture at the Academy, who joined the Secession in 1899.[11] In his earliest days, Wagner had designed Renaissance-style buildings and had been an advocate of an historical style, but he now came to realize that contemporary social life and culture should be the springs of contemporary design. His *Moderne Architektur,* in which he expounded his views, was highly influential in shaping the minds of young architects. With their pastel-colored, smooth façades, his buildings emphasized the rectangular rather than the curve. Even where he employed the curve, as in his controversial subway station on Karlsplatz, the rectangle still appears dominant. The equally controversial Post Office Savings Bank buildings also displayed Wagner's monumental imagination; but, in terms of ornamentation, it could not be compared to Josef-Maria Olbrich's Secession building with its golden cabbage atop. So, in architecture as in paintings, bizarre decoration was replacing conventional ornament. The same was true of the artifacts that Kolo Moser, Josef Hoffmann and their circle were producing in the Wiener Werkstätte, founded in 1903. As with the work of Klimt, the products of these men are still significant today, as the transition to a truly "modern" style of design.

Egon Friedell has described the homes of the bourgeois Viennese in his *Cultural History of the Modern Age,* in a way which makes absolutely clear the necessity for the Secession in the field of design. The house which he describes as typical of contemporary "good taste" inspires horror in the reader today:

Theirs were not living-rooms, but pawnshops and curiosity shops . . . [There was] a craze for totally meaningless articles of decoration . . . a craze for satin-like surfaces: for silk, satin and shining leather; for gilt frames, gilt stucco, and gilt edges; for tortoise shell, ivory, and mother-of-pearl, as also for totally meaningless articles of decoration, such as Rococo mirrors in several pieces, multi-colored Venetian glass, fat-bellied Old German pots, a skin rug on the floor complete with terrifying jaws, and in the hall a life-sized wooden Negro.

Everything was mixed, too, without rhyme or reason; in the boudoir a set of Buhl, in the drawing-room an Empire suite, next door a Cinquecento dining-room, and next to that a Gothic bedroom. Through it all a flavor of polychrome made itself felt. The more twists and scrolls and arabesques there were in the designs, the louder and cruder the color, the greater the success. In this connection, there was a conspicuous absence of any idea of usefulness or purpose; it was all purely for show. We note with astonishment that the best situated, most comfortable and airy room in the house—the "best room"—was not intended to be lived in at all, but was only there to be exhibited to friends.[12]

Passion for ornament turned into a delight in the unreal, with every artifact having a quite distinct "appearance" and "reality"—

Every material used tries to look like more than it is. Whitewashed tin masquerades as marble, papier mâché as rosewood, plaster as gleaming alabaster, glass as costly onyx . . . The butter knife is a Turkish dagger, the ash tray a Prussian helmet, the umbrella stand a knight in armor, and the thermometer a pistol.[13]

Under no circumstances should an object reveal its purpose by its shape—if, indeed, the object served any function at all. Ornament thus became a way of distorting things, an end in itself rather than an embellishment. Nothing was immune. Funerals themselves became extravaganzas, not unlike circus parades, as the very design of artifacts came to reflect the elaborate emptiness of social life and politics in the last days of Habsburg rule.

In a society for which "good taste" was the first among values, to challenge popular and academic taste radically was to question the very foundations of society. This was the task that the nineteen members of the Secession had begun; but their efforts to bring art closer to life fell far short of the mark. Their aestheticism succeeded merely in transforming the contemporary views about ornamentation; they cured the symptoms, not the disease. Like *Jung Wien,* the members of the Secession were so much a part of the society that even their rebellion from it was carried through in its terms and was therefore radically incomplete and ineffective. So, just as Kraus had taken it upon himself to expose the superficiality of *Jung Wien*'s values, it was left to Loos to drive home the sad fact about the Secession—that its ideals were unrealizable, because its members were too much a part of the established society.

Art, like *belles-lettres,* could be reformed only by an artist who assumed the role of an Old Testament prophet. This is precisely what Loos did. He declared war on all forms of ornamentation in architecture and design. His essay "Ornament and Crime," which won the status of Scripture among Dada artists, condemned all forms of decoration on articles of use. The degeneracy of his contemporaries could be read in the fact that modern Europeans actually bore tattoo marks on their bodies. Tattooing had a significant place in Papuan culture, but in Habsburg culture, Loos insisted, "those who have been tattooed and are not in custody are latent criminals or degenerate aristocrats."[14] They could be classed only with the creators of *graffiti*—"You can measure the culture of a country by the extent to which its lavatory walls are scribbled on."[15] Loos claimed that there was a definite link between the antisocial tendencies of criminals and the fact that so many of them sported tattoos; while the "good taste" of the middle class in the Habsburg monarchy marked them, in his view, as no better than sophisticated barbarians. He went so far as to date the political decay of the Dual Monarchy from the establishment of a government-subsidized Academy for Applied Art. Only a society which no longer desired to see things as they really are could possibly be so enamored of ornament; in the healthier Anglo-Saxon world, he declared, use was primary, and decoration mere embellishment.[16]

Where beauty and use were sufficiently distinguished, so that one could still distinguish art from artifact and the one did not engulf and pervert the other, decoration could still be meaningful. Ornament could genuinely embellish American and British artifacts; but, in Austria, "ornament is no longer organically related to our culture, it is no longer the expression of our culture."[17] It had become a Frankenstein monster and was smothering the artisan's creativity. The ornate utensils adorning bourgeois Viennese homes in imitation of every previous age and the decoration of functional objects according to the principles of the "new art" were equally the objects of Loos's diatribe; both of them obliterated the essential distinction between the artist and the artisan. Like Kraus, but in contrast to Gropius and the Bauhaus, Loos was not doctrinaire, nor did he attack ornamentation as such, since he did believe that it could be acceptable as long as it was organically related to cultural life. Rather, his attack was mounted against the fetish of ornamentation, both among the well-to-do classes in Vienna and among the rebellious representatives of "new art."

In the sphere of design, Loos battled against the notion of applied art, in the same way that Kraus fought the feuilleton. As with the feuilleton the very notion of applied art involved a contradiction in terms. The products of the applied artist were not more useful or functional artifacts, but simply heavily embellished utensils. Decoration was "applied" from outside to everything from beer mugs to doorknobs. In this, Loos perceived a mixture of fact and fantasy which was highly detrimental to both. The principles for designing objects for use should be purely factual and determined by the functions that the objects are to serve. Such artifacts ought to be as simple and serviceable as possible. Their design ought to be so "rational" that any two artisans faced with the same task would produce identical objects. Since the utensil was to be designed for use in a particular place, and at a particular time, its design was always determined by the context—that is, the mode of life—current in that particular milieu:

I assert that use [is] the form of culture, the form which makes objects ... We do not sit in such-and-such a way, because a carpenter has built a chair in such-and-such a way; rather the carpenter makes the chair as he does, because someone wants to sit that way.[18]

The form of objects for use is thus a reflection of life in a society, and the only justified changes in the former are those which arise from changes in the latter. This is the meaning of Loos's assertion that he was "against revolution." It was not that he was a counterrevolutionary, but that his was a revolution *against* revolutions in design which are not rooted in the demands of social life.

According to Loos, *objets d'art* were quite the opposite of artifacts; their function was indeed revolutionary. Art is great when it is atemporal and revolutionary. The artisan produces objects for use here and now, the artist for all men everywhere. The ancient Greeks understood this. Their utensils and architecture were built for their own purposes, in the attempt to perfect the environment in which they lived; their tragedy, on the other hand, depicted the universal human condition. Art aims at edifying men's minds by refocusing their attentions from the dullness and drudgery of everyday life into the sphere of fantasy and spiritual values. In this sense, art is always revolutionary; it aims at transforming a man's vision of the world and his attitudes toward his fellow men.

Loos's critique of the society extended to all matters of taste, ranging across the board from hair styles, dress and table manners, to design and architecture; but it was in this last field that he himself put his ideas into practice. His attitude toward building is aptly summed up as follows:

The house has to please everyone. To distinguish it from art that does not have to please anyone. Art is a private matter for the artist. Not so with the house. The work of art is set forth in the world without any necessity for its being used for anything. The house serves a purpose. The art work is not answerable to anyone, the house is to everyone. The work of art wants to tear men from their comfort [*complaisance*]. The house has to serve their comfort. The art work is revolutionary, the house is conservative. . . . *Has the house nothing to do with art, and is architecture not one of the arts? That is the truth.*[19]

All the buildings which Loos designed bear witness to his credo. His identification of culture with simplicity of design is nowhere more evident than in the building which he erected on the Michaelerplatz, opposite the Imperial Palace in Vienna. It is a perfectly unadorned building, lacking even a decorative surround to the windows, a simplification that Loos pioneered. When the building was completed, its very simplicity and functionality were regarded as an intentional insult to the Emperor, by virtue of its contrast with the incredibly ornate domed entrance to the Imperial Palace, which it appeared to defy.[20] With its smooth, plain façade the modern commercial building appeared to be admonishing Habsburg society that its ornamental conception of good taste was perverted and perverting.

The very objects which were intended to serve man had thus come to enslave him. Both the middle classes, who subscribed to

the accepted aesthetic canons, and the craftsmen, who designed
and produced the resulting objects, had come to be the servants
of ideas gone wild. The relation of their work to social life had
become inverted; they were determining how men ought to live
by building as they did, rather than building to suit the contemporary form of life. By his polemic, Loos hoped to drive home
this criticism both to the public and to the artisans; while, by his
buildings, he aimed to show the way toward re-establishing the
proper relationship between design and life. In the hope of elim-
inating the reign of terror imposed on social life and art alike by
the demands of "style," he drew a radical distinction between
them. And, in his effort to get art seen in its proper perspective,
he was soon joined by the controversial and self-taught painter
Oskar Kokoschka.

Kokoschka's independence and genius expressed itself from
the start in a whole range of forms, of which drawing and painting were but two. With his *Murder, Hope of Women* (1907)
Kokoschka has been acclaimed as the founder of antigrammatical
expressionist drama, for in it he "radically distorted" the rules
of German word order; while his corpus also includes a number
of poems and essays on art.[21] Loos introduced Kokoschka to
many of his friends and acquaintances, including Kraus and Altenberg and the art historians Hans and Erica Tietze, whom
Kokoschka sketched and painted many times. The paintings
Kokoschka produced during this period are done in the darkest
of values, and emphasize the flatness of surface. The artist has
referred to them as his "black" paintings.

My early black portraits arise in Vienna before the World War; the
people lived in security, yet they were all afraid. I felt this through their
cultivated form of living, which was still derived from the baroque; I
painted them in their anxiety and pain.[22]

Kokoschka clearly saw in their faces the spiritual vacuum that
filled the lives of so many Viennese, and he painted what he saw.
Like Klimt, he desired to bring out this spiritual element; but,
unlike Klimt, he sought the spiritual within the intensely individual faces he painted, rather than attempt to surround them with
a decorous air of "spirituality." Klimt's portraits always emphasize the static nature of the subject, while Kokoschka's bring
out the reflection of a man's character dynamically in his face,
especially his eyes, and in his hands. Face and hands, between

them, convey sheer terror in the presence of reality. In short, Kokoschka subscribed to the doctrine that the artist must never shout what he is trying to depict, but must let it suggest itself. Klimt does this by the external setting; Kokoschka does it by delineating the spiritual behind the physical, in such a way that the individuality of the subject achieves universality precisely because he is so individual. In Loos's eyes, Kokoschka was the master of decoration and ornament, because he used it with exactitude to express the inner character of the subject. Kokoschka's art thus laid hold of the sphere of fantasy and depicted its role in men's lives on their very faces, laying bare the eternal which was latent within the temporal and so "showing" things about a man that are almost impossible to state.

The lifework of Arnold Schönberg attests to the manner in which the cultural critique inspired by Karl Kraus could be, and was, extended into yet another sphere—that of music. Schönberg has identified his aims with those of Kraus, even more dramatically than Kraus himself did his with those of Loos. On the flyleaf of Kraus's presentation copy of the *Theory of Harmony*, as we remarked earlier, Schönberg wrote the inscription, "I have learned more from you, perhaps, than a man should learn, if he wants to remain independent."[23] Like Kokoschka, Schönberg was a many-sided and self-taught genius. Quite aside from his music and music theory, he was also a first-rate painter and a member of the *Blaue Reiter* group of Expressionists; his essay "On the Relation to the Text" first appeared in their catalogue in 1912, along with two of his drawings.[24] His talent for painting won praise from Klee and Kandinsky, another member of the *Blaue Reiter*.[25] His style of writing too was highly individual, with a penchant for puns and a truly Krausian feeling for the nuances of language. This is respected in the very title of *Die glückliche Hand,* as well as in its text and in many of his other works. Schönberg's music and painting, like the buildings of Loos and the polemics of Kraus, were yet another element in the common all-embracing critique of contemporary society and culture; but, since it is by his music that he made his reputation, we shall here expound the fundamental views which he shared with Kraus and Loos with special reference to his music.

Schönberg saw clearly that Viennese society was as stifling to the composer's fantasy as it was to the painter's. Conformity to conventional tastes, elaboration of orchestration, emphasis upon the effects which the music produced in the listener, were considerations no composer who hoped to be successful could dare to ignore. So, as a background both to his compositions and to the theory which they were intended to illustrate, we must look closely at Viennese tastes in music in the period before World War I; and there is no better guide to this subject than the essays of Edward Hanslick, the founder of modern music criticism and of music appreciation as an academic subject.

In the latter half of the nineteenth century, the music-loving public had been sharply divided between those who were avidly enthusiastic for Richard Wagner's "music of the future" and those who championed with equal zeal the more traditional approach of Brahms. It was not possible to be at all interested in music, without taking sides in this dispute. The most famous and acid pro-Wagner critic was George Bernard Shaw; foremost among the advocates of Brahms was Edward Hanslick, professor of music at the University of Vienna.[26] This was no novel debate; it had roots as far back as the feud between Piccinni and Gluck in Paris, in 1778. The central question was whether music was "self-sufficient"—that is, merely a coherent assemblage of sounds, and a language unto itself—or whether it was essential for it to express ideas or feelings—that is to symbolize something other than the musical. Among the supporters of the former view was the Austrian poet, Franz Grillparzer; among the latter, composers of the stature of Rameau and Rousseau.[27] Whether Hanslick was an illuminating and penetrating thinker who made a genuine contribution to this discussion or merely the mouthpiece of the musical establishment, a pedantic mediocrity blindly opposing all innovation, is still an open question. The truth probably lies somewhere between these extremes. The former opinion is supported by his exceptionally thorough approach to criticism;[28] he never reviewed a performance of a work that he had not played through for himself beforehand. The latter is supported by statements like those reported by Henry Pleasants, in the biographical essay which introduces a collection of Hanslick's reviews:

He once confessed that he would rather see the complete works of Heinrich Schütz destroyed than Brahms' *Ein Deutsches Requiem,* the complete works of Palestrina than Mendelssohn's, all the concertos and sonatas of Bach than the quartets of Schumann and Brahms, and all of Gluck than

Don Giovanni, Fidelio, or *Der Freischütz.* "A shocking confession," he added, "but an honest one!"[29]

Hanslick's curious blend of perspicacity and narrow-mindedness helped to justify the attention of friends and foes alike. The Wagnerites wrote him off as yet another "Jew in music" (it is worth recalling that Wagner used racial categories to describe types of music); but, in doing so, they forgot that Hanslick himself was among the earliest supporters of *Tannhäuser,* which he always praised. The same Hanslick whom they followed their master in reviling could still bring himself to recognize Wagner's achievement, while deploring their own slavish adulation.

I know very well that Wagner is the greatest living opera composer, and the only one in Germany worth talking about in a historical sense. He is the only German composer since Weber and Meyerbeer whom one cannot disregard in the history of dramatic music. Even Mendelssohn and Schumann—not to speak of Rubenstein and the newer ones—can be ignored without leaving a gap in the history of opera. But between this admission and the repulsive idolatry which has grown up in connection with Wagner, and which he has encouraged, there is an infinite chasm.[30]

Wagner was offensive to Hanslick because, in personal as well as musical matters, he was always the conjurer, always the entertainer, never serious or morally responsible in what he did. The cult that surrounded him bore witness to that. Decoration and tone painting were his *forte,* but his was thoroughly unnatural music.

The natural relationship has been reversed. The orchestra is the singer, bearing the guiding thoughts; the singers are merely complementary.[31]

(The "guiding thoughts" referred to here are, of course, the "leitmotifs" by which Wagner aimed to depict specific events, objects and persons within the opera.)

So the spiritual unity which Wagner sought in the *Gesamtkunstwerk* of his "music-drama" ended by producing something that was an aberration, both as music and as drama. To Hanslick, it was more the music of the past—that is, an exaggerated romanticism—than the "music of the future," and he could only deplore the way in which such composers as Bruckner and Richard Strauss had been "taken in" by it.

Hanslick had pointed out the fallacies involved in this view of music as early as 1854, in the first edition of his treatise *On the Beautiful in Music,* which subsequently went into nine German editions, as well as into English, Italian, French and Russian translations. The position he takes in this essay is that music is, properly speaking, not a language of feelings as the romantics assert, but a logic of sound in motion. The same tune, he argues, can with equal ease be made to express joy or sadness, the sublime or the ridiculous. He admits that music does in practice evoke an emotional response in the listener, but this is only a secondary feature, which music possesses in common with every other art.

Every real work of art appeals to our emotional faculty in some way, but none in any exclusive way. No canon peculiar to musical aesthetics alone can be deduced from the fact that there is a certain connection between music and the emotions.[32]

Those who opposed him on this point for the most part singled out vocal or operatic pieces. Hanslick was quick to reply that this was where the root of their fallacy lay.

In vocal or operatic music, it is impossible to draw so nice a distinction between the effect of the music, and that of the words, that an exact definition of the share which each has had in the production of the whole becomes practicable.[33]

Only instrumental music is music *simpliciter*, so,

if we wish to decide the question whether music possesses the character of definiteness, what are its nature and properties, and what its limits and tendencies, no other than instrumental music can be taken into consideration.

Literary subjects are in no way subjects for music composition; they merely provide the composer with "suggestions."

What, then, is the *subject* of a musical composition? Hanslick replies that it has no subject other than the "musical idea" itself: "The theme, or themes, are the real subject of a piece of music."[34] Composition consists in articulating themes according to "certain elementary laws, which govern both the human organism and the phenomena of sound."[35] The foremost of these is the "primordial law of harmonic progression"[36] by means of which themes are developed and transformed. It supplies the logical basis of composition. The composer is thus a kind of logician whose operations are not adequately expressible in any metalanguage. By the very nature of music itself, any attempt to *describe* in words what he *produces* must fail.

All the fantastic descriptions, characterizations and periphrases are either metaphorical or false. What in any other art is still descriptive is in music already figurative. Of music it is impossible to form any but a musical conception, and it can be comprehended and enjoyed only in and for itself.[37]

One who desires to know what a piece of music is "about" can discover the answer to his question only by hearing it played, by an aesthetic analysis of the harmonic structure of the melodies which the work contains. The composer is not responsible for the "pre-established harmony" which permits his audience to identify his themes with certain feelings.

One of the curiosities of Viennese cultural history is the fact that the theories by which Arnold Schönberg created a revolution in composition are so strikingly in accord with those of the conservative critic Hanslick. A comparison of their respective attitudes to Wagner's music will help us here, not only to contrast their views on music theory, but also to evaluate Hanslick's place in the history of criticism and to introduce Schönberg's views on the nature of music. Schönberg, like Hanslick, was well acquainted with the works of Wagner, and he recognized Wagner's talents. His admiration led him, indeed, to compose such early works as *Erwartung* and notably the *Gurrelieder* in the style of Wagner. Yet he resembled Hanslick also in detesting all composition which aimed at effects of a kind other than musical; both Hanslick and Schönberg felt only scorn for Wagner's racist romanticism, and for the personal cult with which Wagner surrounded himself.

Still, Schönberg did not overlook the fact that, by his use of the leitmotif, Wagner himself had made a significant contribution to the very "logic of composition" which Hanslick considered the essence of music. (Hanslick had dismissed the leitmotif as an unnecessary embellishment, noteworthy only for its occasional charm in breaking up the monotony of the vocal declamation taking place on the stage.) "In music," Schönberg wrote, "there is no form without logic, there is no logic without unity";[38] and he considered that Wagner was performing a great service to music in making the first conscious attempt to unify opera *from within* the musical score, independently of the action on the stage. Mozart and other great opera composers had done this unconsciously, but Wagner's was the first explicit effort to formulate a principle by which it might be accomplished. If Hanslick was unable to see this, it proved only that he did not recognize the full implications of the ideas that he championed. Schönberg also agreed with Hanslick that, in composers like Wagner, Bruckner and Richard Strauss, harmony had got out of hand; this fact was closely linked with their concern for effects, whereas the structure of a composition should properly be musical alone. Yet Schönberg looked further than Hanslick. In his view, the true cure for this disease was nothing less than a radically new theory of harmony. In Hanslick's terms, it was the "logic of composition" that stood in need of revision.

Schönberg himself referred to this task as "breaking through the limits of a bygone aesthetic."[39] He approached the task in the same spirit as De Morgan and Boole, who had been subjecting Aristotelian logic to a similar scathing critique and insisting that a new view of logic was required—thus "breaking through the limits of a bygone logic," so to speak. One can, indeed, draw a close analogy between Schönberg's *Harmonielehre* and Whitehead and Russell's *Principia Mathematica,* as compendious expositions of a new logic. In 1932, Schönberg wrote, in a letter:

I believe that meaningful advantage can be derived from this art of composition when it is based upon knowledge and realization that comes from musical logic; and that is also the reason why I do not teach my students "twelve-tone composition" but "composition," in the sense of musical logic; the rest will then come sooner or later.[40]

Where was this musical logic to be found? Bach and Mozart and Beethoven were its foremost exponents, Brahms and Wagner also possessed an unconscious understanding of it, as did Schubert and Mahler and even Max Reger. All these composers understood the nature and articulation of musical ideas.

Schönberg's method of teaching, by a very rigorous analysis of the structure of musical ideas, disappointed many students, who came to him seeking rather to master the *technique* of composition with "twelve-tone rows." But Schönberg was adamant in his insistence that the only way to learn to write music was by a thoroughgoing study of the older masters:

Scholarship is concerned with presenting its ideas exhaustively and in such a way that no question remains unanswered. Art, on the other hand, contents itself with a many-sided presentation, in which the idea appears unambiguously without having to be directly stated as such. Thus a window remains open through which from the viewpoint of knowledge surmise may enter.

In Counterpoint, it is not so much a matter of the combination itself (that is, it is not an end in itself) as of such a many-sided presentation of the idea. The theme is so constructed that it already contains within itself these many figures, through which the many-sided presentation of the idea is made possible.[41]

Strict adherence to rules of composition is, paradoxically, the source of the composer's freedom. He wished to teach them *how to express themselves,* a task which he conceived could only be accomplished by a thorough knowledge of the master's articulation of musical ideas; not by teaching them directly "how to compose," but only by indirectly teaching them the language of music in which they could come to express themselves. The twelve-tone row was thus, for Schönberg, a principle of organization. It was a more rigorous and reformed method for an age of slovenly composition. In this respect, Schönberg saw himself as a modern Monteverdi, simplifying the tortuously complex harmonies of a Richard Strauss, a Reger or a Mahler, just as Monteverdi had simplified Renaissance polyphony.

Modern composers were thoroughly lacking in discipline, and the twelve-tone row was far more rigorous than the seven. It was therefore, *one way* of obtaining the requisite discipline: "My works are twelve-tone *compositions,* not *twelve-tone* compositions. Here again I am confused with Hauer, to whom composition is only secondary."[42] (Joseph Matthias Hauer was the eccentric composer who introduced the twelve-tone technique, but did so with intentions very different from Schönberg's.)[43]

In the latter half of the nineteenth century, romanticism had made composition a matter of "inspiration," and as a result composers had neglected discipline. Undisciplinedly "inspired" composers had produced cumbrous works which required simplification. This was the function of the twelve-tone row: "The row, thus, is contained a priori as a melodic element in the musical inspiration."[44]

Thus, working from principles quite similar to those of Hanslick's treatise *On the Beautiful in Music,* Schönberg ushered in a revolution, not only in music theory, but in musical composition as well. Still, just as in painting a Klimt was required before a Kokoschka was even possible, and in architecture an Otto Wagner before a Loos—a transition figure, in whom ornamentation served the fantasy instead of stifling it—the Vienna which Schönberg made his home already contained just such a transitional composer, in the person of Gustav Mahler. Schönberg's esteem for Mahler is well summed up in the dedication of the *Harmonielehre:*

This book is dedicated to the memory of Gustav Mahler. The dedication was intended to give him some small pleasure while he still lived. It was also meant to express reverence for his immortal compositions, and to show that these works, which academic musicians pass by with a shrug of the shoulders, indeed with contempt, are worshiped by someone who is perhaps not entirely ignorant either. Gustav Mahler was denied greater joys than my dedication was meant to provide. This martyr, this saint, had to pass on, before he had even seen his work through to the point where he could safely hand it over to his friends. To give him pleasure would have been enough for me. But now he is dead, I want my book to win me respect, so that nobody can pass by when I say, "That was one of the truly great men!"[45]

As director of the Imperial Opera, Mahler was identified with everything progressive in music. He was largely responsible for the rapidly growing popularity of Wagner and Mozart; and he was therefore greatly admired as an impresario and conductor. As a composer, however, the fickle Viennese considered him a nihilist, as they did Schönberg. At first sight, Mahler's enormous symphonic pieces requiring a large orchestra, chorus and solo vocalists appear the complete antithesis of Schönberg's mature works. Yet Schönberg was deeply impressed by the integrity which totally informed each of Mahler's works, from the *Songs of a Wayfarer* to the *Song of the Earth.* These huge romantic symphonies and song cycles, with their alternating exhilaration and despair in the face of existence, were the perfect expressions of a romantic hero isolated within his society—"as a Bohemian among Austrians, as an Austrian among Germans, as a Jew throughout the world."[46] Each day in the life of this successful *fin-de-siècle* artist alternated between exhilaration and despair at existence. Mahler everywhere sought answers to the ultimate questions:

How dark is the foundation upon which our life rests? Whence do we come? Whither does our road take us? Have I really willed this life, as Schopenhauer thinks, before I ever was conceived? Why am I made to feel that I am free, while yet I am constrained within my character as in a prison? What is the object of toil and sorrow? How am I to understand the cruelty and malice in the creations of a kind God? Will the meaning of life finally be revealed by death?[47]

He sought the answers to these questions wherever he might find them—in the music of Mozart and Wagner, and in that of Anton Bruckner; in poetry, and also in science; in the philosophy of Kant, and in that of Schopenhauer. His music was an attempt to express his experience of life in sensuous and ornate music; and, thanks to his all-embracing integrity, he succeeded in an individual way which, like Klimt's, was forever closed to others.

Mahler's legacy to Schönberg lay in the dominance of "authenticity" over "convention" in matters of sound; one did not compose in order to produce pleasant sounds, but in order to express one's personality. Schönberg embraced this idea wholeheartedly, but he insisted that future composers would have this way open to them only if they subjected *themselves* to the most rigorous discipline. To Mahler, self-expression and self-discipline alike came naturally and spontaneously; therein is the explanation of his exceptional life's work. As with all authentic music, his innovative fantasy was the source of his musical ideas—

Music is not merely another kind of amusement, but a musical poet's, a musical thinker's representation of musical ideas; these musical ideas must correspond to the laws of human logic.[48]

At the root of Schönberg's concept of music, accordingly, lies the Krausian ideas of fantasy; and this is also the explanation of Berg's comment about Kraus having the capacity to express Offenbach's musical ideas by virtue of his spiritual kinship with Offenbach. Fantasy produces the themes, the musical ideas; musical logic, the theory of harmony, provides the laws of its development. Both are essential to good music. Fantasy is the *fons et origo* of creativity, it is primary; but that is not to say that the discipline is any less required. Style, which Schönberg defines as "the quality of a work," is based upon "natural conditions expressing him who produced it."[49] It is an expression of the integrity of the composer, and an index of the authenticity of its aesthetic qualities.

Schönberg expressed his basic conception of musical creativity in an essay entitled "Style and Idea." In this essay, as in our own present discussion of Schönberg, nothing is said about *sound* itself. This is because Schönberg, unlike Hanslick, considered the question, how a composition sounds, as having no importance.

Only the authenticity of the musical idea and its articulation according to musical logic matter to him. For this reason, he could praise so unlikely a composer as George Gershwin for the authenticity of his music;[50] and we may add that Hanslick himself praised Sir Arthur Sullivan on similar grounds.[51] Schönberg used to defend his so-called "atonal" music—while disavowing the term—against those who attacked it for its dissonance, by reminding them that the musically untutored had similarly attacked all the classical Viennese composers, whom they considered to be writing dissonant monstrosities. But Haydn and Mozart did not write for the untutored, and never aimed at "sounding good." The audiences for which they composed were made up of such nobles as Esterhazy and the Prince-Archbishop of Salzburg, who were themselves amateur musicians and, so, aware of the subtleties of the compositions they had commissioned and capable of appreciating their technical aspects. Schönberg then turns the argument against modern "music lovers," who do not understand anything about music but "know what they like."

To be musical means to have an ear in the *musical* sense, not in the *natural* sense. A musical ear must have assimilated the tempered scale. And a singer who produces natural pitches is unmusical, just as someone who acts "naturally" in the street may be immoral.[52]

Viewed from this perspective, all of Schönberg's compositions represent attacks on the pseudo-sophistication of bourgeois aestheticism. His work as a composer becomes, simultaneously, a critique of society, somewhat as Loos's architecture did. In the latter half of the nineteenth century, composers had "copped out." They had deliberately written music that their audiences would find pleasing, and thus they reversed the true order of things. All groups alike were at fault, and all must be chastised. This is the negative aspect of his revolution in music, which we can now see in its true perspective as one further attempt at a "creative separation" of all dramatic or poetical ornament from the musical idea itself and its presentation according to the laws of musical logic. So the "beautiful" in music is, for Schönberg, a by-product of the composer's integrity, a function of his search for truth—"the artist attains the beauty without willing it, for he is only striving after truthfulness."[53] This is what qualified him for partnership in the enterprise that Kraus was carrying on in letters, and Loos in design. So Schönberg's lifework illustrates, along with that of Kraus and Loos, how a critique of the mores of contemporary Viennese society with its artificiality and aestheticism quite naturally assumed the form of a critique of aesthetic expression.

The fact that this awareness of the central problems of "communication," and of moral "authenticity," was not the exclusive property of Kraus and his allies is indicated by the case of Hugo von Hofmannsthal. In the year 1891, Schnitzler and the rest of *Jung Wien* were electrified by the poetry of a mysterious character going by the name of Loris. Not since Goethe and Hölderlin had such exquisite lyrics been penned. Perfect form of expression was united with an insightful power to capture and condense the abiding in the ephemeral. In short, the lyrics of Loris were paradigms of aesthetic perfection. It is difficult to describe their astonishment at the discovery that Loris was a seventeen-year-old high-school student. Schnitzler could find no better words to express it than to speak of "the miracle of Hofmannsthal."

The young Hofmannsthal's cosmopolitan background penetrated everything that he was to write. His immediate background was a bourgeois one; the noble *von* had been awarded to his father. The family, of Jewish origins, had Italian and German connections, and they had embraced Roman Catholicism. Hofmannsthal's early education in Italy and his own Italian heritage made this young Austrian unique among the aesthetes of his day; unlike so many of them, he never felt any conflict between the "dark serious, deeply moral Teutonic ideal" and the "sprightly, festive Latin aestheticism." Similarly, he never experienced the generation gap. Although his father was a successful businessman, the orthodox mentality of "Business is business, and art is art" was quite foreign to his house. Hofmannsthal never felt the same need to rebel as, say, a Schnitzler, whose home was one in which one could profitably search for Oedipus complexes.

These factors helped to shape Hofmannsthal's artistic activity and explain some of the distinctive characteristics of his work. Aesthetes throughout Europe were committed to the principle that the essence of art is the creation of beauty through form alone. The only duty of the artist is to produce works of formal perfection. As Oscar Wilde wittily put it, punning on the word *artificial,* "The first duty in life is to be as artificial as possible. What the second duty is no one has yet discovered." Aesthetes everywhere likewise considered this maxim as universally opposed to the bourgeois "Protestant Ethic." Thus Gide and D'Annunzio, as well as Wilde, saw a universal opposition between life and art, an opposition that Hofmannsthal only partly shared.

For Hofmannsthal, the goal of poetry was the creation of unity between the self and the world. This element always remained central to his conception of the artist's vocation, even after he had radically altered his view of art in other respects. The young Loris sought to unify the self and the world at the point where they interacted: his impressions. Poetry was a recording, an articulation, of these impressions and images. "I am a poet," says Loris, "because my experience is pictorial";[54] in these images, objective content and subjective form become one. Like so many other Viennese aesthetes, Hofmannsthal found in the philosopher Ernst Mach a theory of knowledge that appeared to confirm his poetic experience completely. "The world consists only of our sensations," Mach asserted, "in which case, we have knowledge *only* of sensations";[55] Mach went on to argue that physics was a shorthand method of relating and correlating these sense data, with the help of mathematics. Hofmannsthal, like his contemporary Hermann Bahr, considered Mach so significant that he actually attended his lectures at the university. It seemed to Hofmannsthal—as to Bahr and others—that if Mach was correct, the poet was surely expressing more of "reality" in his verses than the scientist could do. The scientist stood at one remove from sensations, because he described them in a nonverbal way, by means of mathematics. The poet endeavored to express his sensations directly, in as thoroughgoing and precise a manner as possible.

What is it about reality that enables objectivity and subjectivity to coincide in the sensuous image? This question perplexed the young Hofmannsthal above all others. As he grappled with this problem, the answer that appealed most to him was the old Platonic thesis of "pre-existence." In that state, all souls, all minds are one; and one with the stuff of the universe. As in Plato, knowing comes to be identified with remembering. The very function of the lyric is, then, to "touch strings and strike harmonies which have been asleep in us without our knowledge, so that we look into the depths of wondrous mysteries as if a new meaning of life were opened to us.''[56]

Hofmannsthal's early plays, such as the fragment, *The Death of Titian,* and *Death and the Fool,* and his poems such as the famous ''Manche freilich müssen drunten sterben,'' reflect this preoccupation with the ideas of death and pre-existence. And it was this youthful concern with death that led him to his eventual recognition of the limits of language and to a rejection of aestheticism.

For the young Hofmannsthal, the meaning of life presented no problems; in his utter passivity, he could somehow become one with all Creation and attain a state in which the self shrank to an extensionless point. In the depths of this aesthetic mysticism, his feeling of exultation issued in poetry, poetry written with a command of language rarely equaled in German literature, and from the depths of a self-knowledge hitherto regarded as inconceivable in one so young. His poetry appeared to flow freely from some infinite source. He did not need to think about writing, he simply wrote—that is, until his twenty-fifth year. At that time, he experienced a crisis which compelled him to reject all that had gone before. The first inklings of what was to come were in *Death and the Fool,* where the aesthete realizes, too late, that he has dissipated himself in egoism. Hofmannsthal's *Tale of the Six Hundred and Seventy-Second Night* contains a fuller expression of the aesthete's fear that the world may crumble around him. He had begun to reconsider the question whether language as such was capable of expressing *anything* of the meaning of life. The daemon that had taken hold of Loris had left him; he could no longer write poetry.

His literary apologia for giving up the medium of poetry came in his story *The Letter of Lord Chandos,* published in 1902. (This *Letter* is written in magnificent and detailed German of a kind appropriate to a courtier writing—ostensibly—to Francis Bacon, Lord Verulam.) There he wrote, ''I have lost completely the ability to speak or to think of anything coherently.''[57] The rare gifts which he had possessed as a youth, the capacity to compose spontaneously, seemed to vanish as he grew in consciousness, as though his very attempts to understand himself had dried up the springs of his creativity. The poet of whom it was said that if only he had died at the age of twenty-five he would have been guaranteed immediate entry to the Hall of the Immortals, could no longer write a line:

I experience in and around me a blissful never-ending interplay, and among the objects playing against one another there is not one into which I cannot flow. To me, then, it is as though my body consists of nought but ciphers which give me the key to everything; or as if we could enter into a new and hopeful relationship with the whole of existence, if only we began to think with the heart. As soon, however, as this strong enchantment falls from me, I find myself confused; wherein this harmony transcending me and the entire world consisted, and how it made itself known to me, I could present in sensible words as little as I could say anything precise about the inner movements of my intestines or a congestion of my blood.[58]

Hofmannsthal's problem here is quite explicitly one of *language*. He clearly states that he perceives the world and its meaning just as before, but can no longer even begin to put that meaning into words.

Gerhard Masur has written that "his earlier belief in the redemption of the world through the medium of the poetic word—his own medium, that is—had been shattered; and without faith in this tool he found it beyond his power to create."[59] It must be emphasized that this in no way implies that Hofmannsthal had nothing to say: it was rather that language, or at least *his* language, simply could not express those things which were most important in life. Nor was it implied that language cannot express anything at all, for the very existence of the *Chandos Letter* contradicts this interpretation; it is only the things that are of greatest significance— the meaning of life, the ultimate values —that are inexpressible.

The difficulty of Lord Chandos raises the problem, "Where can the aesthete turn when he has lost faith in his medium, when it dawns on him that perfection of form alone is insufficient, and there is something to the external claims of morality after all?" How is he to regain entry to this all-important realm, when he cut himself off from it at the very start? For Hofmannsthal, the answer clearly lay in rejection of aestheticism itself. So he began to search for a method by which to teach men "to think with the heart." Now that the old medium had failed him, he required a new way to convey his message. This search was to lead him to his collaboration with Richard Strauss, in *Rosenkavalier, Elektra, Arabella, Die Frau ohne Schatten,* and other works; and also to the rediscovery of the Spanish Baroque and Calderón, which culminated in the Salzburg Festival Plays and his collaboration with Max Reinhardt.

What, then, was the root of Lord Chandos' crisis? It would be fair to say that, in the course of his appraisal of the nature of poetry, Hofmannsthal came to realize that the self-centeredness of the young aesthete Loris was in fact a distortion of the world, since his impressionist lyrics pictured the world as lacking a moral dimension. His awareness of the shortcomings of the lyric, the aesthete's medium par excellence, grew in direct proportion to his inability to write in that form. His new task was to discover a medium that would permit him to draw men to a consideration of values and of the meaning of life, on an existential plane. In one sense, the experience of Lord Chandos itself implies a critique of Mach's sensationalism; in a nutshell, Hofmannsthal's message is that such a theory of knowledge—which locates the foundation of knowledge in sensuous images—is radically deficient, because the most pressing questions about life and society are unanswerable, and cannot even be represented, in terms of sense impressions alone. Wolfram Mauser puts his finger on the root of Hofmannsthal's problem, when he says,

Images and concepts only lead back to themselves. They do not open any way to the nature of things and to individual life. They are a roundelay, similar to a circle in which everything is in tune, everything is in a state of harmony and beauty, but they are "eyeless statues" which surround him, forms without genuine relation to existence.[60]

Concepts and images cannot convey the subjectivity of truth; only experiences which could affect the innermost being, the very way of life of the audience would accomplish this.

The artistic vehicle that Hofmannsthal finally settled upon was the *Gesamtkunstwerk*, a theater which sought to emulate that of ancient Greece by unifying all the arts. Poetry, drama and music would fuse to produce in its audience an experience which was at once social and religious. Hofmannsthal thus turned away from the attempt to capture the world in aesthetically perfect pictures (*Bilder*), and endeavored instead to convey an actual experience of life (*Gebärde*) as it ought to be. He gave up attempting to convey impressions of the world, in favor of the attempt to convey the very essence of the human and the moral, employing a medium which aimed not merely at communicating ideas, but in transforming the way in which men conducted their lives. This task could not be accomplished by words alone, but might be attained by an operatic allegory. Fittingly enough, his first major effort in this genre, and the first fruit of his collaboration with Richard Strauss, was his adaptation of Sophocles' *Elektra*. Hofmannsthal was ultimately to produce six operas with Strauss, with Max Reinhardt often staging them. He also produced a version of *Everyman* for the Salzburg Festival, an adaptation of Calderón, in *The Tower*, and a fairy tale of resurrection, in *The Woman without a Shadow*. These are all stories of man's existential condition—his encapsulation within his ego, and his redemption from egoism, the source of all that is antisocial in him, through Christian *agape*.

Hofmannsthal's solution to the problems of life lay in a radical reassertion of the older values of the Habsburg baroque heritage, in which he saw the basis of a universal, humanistic culture. The Habsburgs had fallen upon evil times because they had come under the sway of brutish Prussian ideas, which were foreign to the true spirit of Austria; but when that spirit was revitalized (by his works) it would lead the world to see the folly of the war which was (in 1917) raging throughout Europe. The poet had become a prophet, who sought to humanize the irrational in man, to transform hatred and greed into love and cooperation, using the *Gesamtkunstwerk* to produce a socializing catharsis and so solve the problems of modern society. Hofmannsthal's view of art, as the cure for the human ills of industrial society, shared something with the views of Kraus, Loos and Schönberg. Although Kraus attacked and ridiculed him as being naïve about the ways of the world—since truth is existential rather than abstract, a matter of actions rather than beliefs —for both men theater was the primary instrument for propagating moral values. Kraus was, we may say, so violently opposed to Hofmannsthal, precisely because he was close and yet at the same time so far away from the ideal of Nestroy.

We have spotlighted the problem of language in Hofmannsthal, because this serves to introduce and illustrate our own central hypothesis about Viennese culture—namely, that to be a *fin-de-siècle* Viennese artist or intellectual, conscious of the social realities of Kakania, one had to face the problem of *the nature and limits of language, expression and communication*. Half a dozen other illustrations might have served our purpose equally well. We might have discussed the Rilke of the autobiographical *Notebooks of Malte Laurids Brigge,* or the Kafka of the fragmentary *Description of a Struggle.* Both men certainly formulated the problem of existence in terms of the limits of language, and the encapsulation of the self. Though they wrote these works before the First World War, their despair at the irrationality of existence essentially spoke to the postwar world; here one can only survive silently, because society itself has crumbled. (Kraus himself seems eventually to have sensed this. As the Third Reich was establishing itself, it became more and more apparent to him that the weapons he had used before and during the war were increasingly powerless, though he never for a moment ceased to struggle against the inhuman forces in the world wherever he met them.) In the last days of the Habsburg monarchy, where Rilke and Kafka first saw the light of day —and especially in *fin-de-siècle* Prague, which merits a study in itself—one could at least catch a glimpse of what Europe was to become after World War One, before it was remotely conceivable as a political fact.

Musil, who was not from Prague, shared with Rilke and Kafka a prewar concern with the incapability of language to explain men's innermost being to others. He brought this out explicitly in his autobiographical story of life in a military high school, *Young Törless* (1906). At the time, his novel had a shock effect, since Musil spoke openly for the first time of the homosexuality which was widespread in such schools. But this was by no means the point of the novel. The *dénouement* comes when Törless has to explain his intense feelings to the authorities and finds that this is impossible.[61] Once again, language cannot express what is most real; this is something which remains forever private in the depths of the person's subjectivity. This problem remained to the very end unresolved for Musil, both in his life and in his writings.

Here it is worth pointing out that Musil too was an admirer of Mach; yet he was a "Machian" in a more significant sense than Bahr or Hofmannsthal, since he had been trained both as an engineer and as an academic philosopher.[62] Musil's doctoral dissertation for the philosophy faculty in Berlin was in fact on Mach; and he gave up a promising career in philosophy only with the success of *Törless* in 1906, when he turned down academic appointments at M̶

academic philosophy, Musil

lems raised by philosophy, psy

could not be solved. So he aband

Broch, who had a similar background,

way, therefore, *The Man Without Qual*

"philosopher's novel," and deserves specia

dents of twentieth-century philosophy, for m

sons that *Tristram Shandy* does for students of

seventeenth century.

To sum up: by the year 1900, the linked problems of c

cation, authenticity and symbolic expression had been fac

parallel in all the major fields of thought and art—by Kraus a

Schönberg, Loos and Hofmannsthal, Rilke and Musil. So the

stage was set for a *philosophical* critique of language, given in

completely general terms. The next item on our agenda is to look

and see how this task presented itself to thinkers and writers

brought up in the Viennese milieu of the 1890s and 1900s—espe-

cially, when it was viewed in the light of the three philosophical

traditions with which they were most familiar. These were (1)

the neoempiricism of Ernst Mach, with its emphasis on "sense

impressions" and natural science; (2) the Kantian analysis of

"representation" and the "schemata," regarded as determining

the forms of experience and judgment, and its continuation by

the antiphilosopher Arthur Schopenhauer; and (3) the anti-in-

tellectualist approach to moral and aesthetic issues put forward

by that other antiphilosopher, Søren Kierkegaard, and echoed

in the novels and essays of Leo Tolstoy.

We shall begin this philosophical reconstruction by looking at

the views of the first modern European writer to consider *lan-

guage itself* as the central and crucial topic for philosophical ex-

amination. Given the outcome of our investigations to date, it

will come as no surprise that this first attempt to give such a

completely general critique of language, from the philosophical

point of view, was made by a Bohemian apostate Jew who, as a

drama critic in Berlin, straddled in his own person the frontiers

between philosophy and literature. The man was Fritz Mauthner,

a writer whose *Sprachkritik* Wittgenstein himself referred to

later in the *Tractatus,* and whose skeptical aims and discursive

methods he explicitly contrasted with his own more formal and

rigorous approach to the philosophy of language.

ꞵunich and Berlin. Given the state of
decided that the fundamental prob-
ꞵhology and modern logic simply
ꞵed it for literature, just as
was to do later. In its own
ꞵies is pre-eminently a
ꞵ attention from stu-
ꞵch the same rea-
ꞵocke and the
ꞵd
ꞵommuni-
ꞵed in
ꞵd

ɔn

n,

, by Mauthner

Philosophers have always been concerned with problems relating to language. From Plato and Aristotle to Petrus Hispanus and Thomas of Erfurt, from John Locke to Maurice Merleau-Ponty, questions about symbolism, meaning and prediction have always been live issues, while, in their efforts to explain the relations between mind and reality, thought and being, philosophers have been continually impressed by the importance of problems relating to language. Yet, until the latter part of the nineteenth century, problems in the philosophy of language remained essentially secondary to issues of other kinds.

Nobody did more to change this situation, in the long run, than Immanuel Kant. During the hundred years following the publication of his *Critique of Pure Reason,* the implications of his "critical" program gradually came to dominate German philosophy and natural science; and, as a result, the problems of language were brought into the center of the philosophical picture. Previously, the primary topics for any philosophical theory of knowledge had been "sense perception" and "thought"; these have been regarded as prior and independent elements in experience, with language as a secondary instrument or means by which knowledge, once formed, was given public expression.

Kant's emphasis on the role of the "forms of judgment" in giving a "structure" to knowledge implicitly challenged the subsidiary role hitherto allotted to language and grammar. According to his account, the logical or linguistic forms of judgment were the forms, also, of any genuine "experience." Knowledge involves not just the conceptual interpretation of formless, preconceptual sensory inputs, or impressions. Our very sense experiences present themselves to us with an epistemic structure; this structure can be characterized only in terms of the forms of judgment, and these forms themselves can be expressed only in terms of the standard forms of logical grammar. So, instead of beginning our philosophical analysis of knowledge with raw sense impressions—as the empiricists have done—we must now treat the basic data of experience as comprising structured sensory "representations," or *Vorstellungen.* The common forms of language and thought were built into our sense experience, or representations, from the very start; and the limits or boundaries of the "reason" were thus, implicitly, the limits or boundaries of representation and language also. We shall see in this chapter how, between 1800 and 1920, the problem of defining the essential scope and limits of the *reason* was twice transformed: first, into the problem of defining the essential scope and limits of representation and, subsequently, into that of doing the same for language.

By profession, Fritz Mauthner was a journalist rather than a philosopher. But his experience as a journalist and observer of political ideas drove him into a position of extreme philosophical nominalism, which he attempted to carry through in such a way as to yield a complete and consistent nominalist theory of knowledge. (One is reminded of Thomas Hobbes's *Leviathan,* with its similar alliance of epistemology and political philosophy.) The immediate stimulus to Mauthner's nominalist "critique of language" was his reaction against the political witchcraft he saw being exercised all around him by the use of such grandiose abstract terms as *Volk* and *Geist.* Like Bertrand Russell—whose ideas about the "logical construction" of abstract terms out of simpler, more concrete ones were similarly spurred on, in part, by his early interest in socialism and his suspicion of large political abstractions like "the state"—Mauthner came to epistemology and the theory of language through marrying a liberal, antiauthoritarian position in politics to a Machian empiricism in philosophy.

In his efforts to maintain a thoroughgoing nominalism, Mauthner was led to the conclusion that all philosophical problems are, in fact, problems about language. For the strict nominalist, "concepts" are nothing more than words which are adopted to name or otherwise describe collections of "individuals"; general terms are thus names or descriptions of aggregates of individuals, rather than of genuine "entities." Mauthner considered that concepts must be identical with words and speech, and consequently, identical with thought, since it was clearly impossible even to imagine something without being able to *say* what that something is. To the end of his days, he was aware that this was anything but an iron-clad argument, but it seemed a far more reasonable position than the contrary view, that thought and language, concepts and words, are not identical. Mauthner's difficulties grew largely out of the fact that no such connection between thought and language could be proven in brain physiology; Gershon Weiler's recent study *Mauthner's Critique of Language* contains an excellent discussion of the subtle relationship between the scientific and the philosophical sides of Mauthner's ideas.

Hence, beginning from a traditional starting point, Mauthner drew radical conclusions as to just what the program of philosophy ought to be—

Philosophy is theory of knowledge. Theory of knowledge is critique of language [*Sprachkritik*]. Critique of language, however, is labor on behalf of the liberating thought, that men can never succeed in getting beyond a metaphorical description [*bildliche Darstellung*] of the world utilizing either everyday language or philosophical language.[1]

Philosophical language was merely a refinement of ordinary language, and was every bit as metaphorical as it. Like all rigorous nominalists, he was skeptical about our capacity to know the world. Nominalists have traditionally tried to argue that names are the exact correlatives of sense experiences, and so the only sound foundations for knowledge. Mauthner, as we shall see, went one better in asserting, on the basis of his theory of meaning, that names are at best *metaphors* for what the senses perceive. The resulting variation on Humean skepticism led him to the task, which he considered a "Kantian" one, of determining the nature and limits of language.

What disturbed Mauthner, above all, was the tendency ordinary people have to attribute reality to abstract and general terms. This natural tendency to reify abstractions he regarded as the origin not just of speculative confusion, but also of practical injustice and evil in the world. Reification—to use a Machian phrase—begets all sorts of "conceptual monsters." In science, these include such misleading notions as force, laws of nature, matter, atoms and energy; in philosophy, substance, objects and the absolute; among religious ideas, God, the devil and natural law; in political and social affairs, obsession with notions like the Race, the Culture, and the Language, and with their purity or profanation. In all such cases, reification involves assuming the existence of entities which are "metaphysical." So Mauthner considered metaphysics and dogmatism to be two faces of a single coin, which was also the fountainhead of intolerance and injustice.

Such were the considerations which led him to undertake his critique of language. It was a Kantian effort, inasmuch as it was antimetaphysical and directed toward setting limits to the "sayable"; but its roots lay more in British than in German thought. Kant had been right in the task that he had set for himself, but his Germanic heritage blinded him to the prejudice in favor of the abstract inherent in the German language—the feature which Leibniz and Wolff had erroneously considered to be the glory of German, qualifying it eminently for scientific expression. Mauthner viewed his own work, by contrast, as belonging to the British tradition of nominalism and empiricism. He considered Locke to have been the pioneer of language critique with his theory of meaning in the *Essay Concerning Human Understanding*. (That essay Mauthner believed would have been more appropriately called *A Grammatical Essay*, or *A Treatise on Words*, or simply *Language*.) Likewise, he identified as his immediate predecessor Arthur Schopenhauer, who had been conspicuous among leading nineteenth-century German philosophers as an intellectual Anglophile.

Mauthner also claimed to take his point of departure in philosophy from Schopenhauer. It was Schopenhauer's formulation of the epistemological question, in his dissertation *On the Fourfold Root of the Principle of Sufficient Reason*, that made Mauthner aware of just what philosophy is all about. Indeed, he said, Schopenhauer's impact on him was so great that he had difficulty in extricating himself from Schopenhauer's system. In *The Fourfold Root,* Schopenhauer had attempted to solve the age-old problem of the relation between reason and nature in a Kantian manner by maintaining that nature is, in fact, a product of reason. The essential function of reason was to contribute the a priori elements—that is, the necessary connections between our representations of experience, which make a systematic (and consequently scientific) knowledge of nature possible. In itself, of course, this did not represent an advance beyond the critical philosophy of Immanuel Kant; but Schopenhauer himself—as we shall see shortly—was a Kantian revisionist, not merely an expositor of the master. He maintained that the complexities of the Analytic were unnecessary; that the Categories of the Understanding were superfluous, because all that Kant really needed to justify was Causality—that is, the necessary connection between phenomena—and that it was the very nature of reason to provide such a "causal nexus." The purpose of *The Fourfold Root* was, then, to explain how the four classes of judgments which comprise all our knowledge—whether of nature, logic and mathematics, physical science, or the behavioral sciences—are based upon one and the same causal nexus as it applies to different classes of phenomena; and, further, how these four classes of judgments are distinct and must remain so.

Mauthner was deeply impressed by the elegance and clarity with which Schopenhauer executed his revision of Kant's first critique. Schopenhauer's identification of reason and language (and his citing of a similar equation between *ratio* and *oratio* in Cicero's *De officiis*) made this achievement seem all the more startling, especially to one already interested in the philosophical problem of language. As Mauthner saw it, *The Fourfold Root* construed the order in nature as a priori, contrary to Aristotle and the Scholastics; and the a priori was identical with language, the true *logos*. Yet, for all its profundity, this position was not beyond Mauthner's criticism. Schopenhauer too had fallen victim to the ever-present temptation to reify abstract words. While his epistemology constituted a major breakthrough, his philosophy of the world as will contained a residual element of Scholasticism. In his notion of will, Schopenhauer remained subject to what Mauthner refers to as "word superstitions" (*Wortaberglauben*), asserting that they are existing objects corresponding to words.

Mauthner argues that the notion of will arises from experience of our various perceptions as pleasant or unpleasant. Schopenhauer distinguishes the experience of like or dislike from the perception that accompanies it: so arises his distinction between "knowing" and "willing." But Mauthner maintains that this distinction is not legitimate, since like or dislike is itself a perception—a representation of a feeling (*Gefühlsvorstellung*), but a representation nevertheless, not something entirely distinct from our other perceptions. And, if Schopenhauer were entitled to make the sort of distinction he attempts here, even then the will could not legitimately be *spoken* of, for the only language we possess is one which describes our representations. Moreover, Schopenhauer had failed to distinguish between the will considered as an entity (*Wille*) and the deliberate actions (*Handlungen*) which are the practical expressions of "willing." In Mauthner's view, when Schopenhauer thought that he was being metaphysical, he was actually being metaphorical. Actually, Schopenhauer's metaphysical will is only a metaphorical expression of the *appearance* of human self-consciousness. Thus, Schopenhauer too had committed the fallacy of reification in attempting to reach beyond the word *will* to a real entity—namely, the Will.

Mauthner's analysis of Schopenhauer's notion of will is typical of the whole program of the *Dictionary of Philosophy* which he published in 1910. His aim in the *Dictionary* was to analyze a hundred and one crucial words in the philosophical vocabulary, in much the same manner as he had dealt with Schopenhauer's will; and the methodology of the book is a reflection of his theory of knowledge. He begins by explaining the "psychological origin" of each term—that is, the sort of sense data it arises from. He then proceeds to explain how a term that originally functioned as, say, an adjective is transformed into a noun—that is, how the process of reification applies to the given term. Finally, he relates these changes in usage to the history of philosophy. His goal was to demonstrate to metaphysicians that all the issues to which they address themselves are based on an illicit move, an assertion that there are "objects" which correspond to the "properties" that we alone can perceive. Furthermore, the contingent nature (*Zufallssinn*) of our sensory apparatus guarantees that necessary truth—that is, knowledge which is "true for all time"—is an impossibility for us.

As Weiler has pointed out, the notion of the contingency of the senses is Mauthner's most original, as well as his central, philosophical conception. It determines his attitude to science and logic, as well as his view that critique of language is a "learned ignorance," because it shows that there can be no eternal truths, even within the critique itself. His method, then, is psychological and historical; as such, it is similar to Mach's "historical and critical" exposition of the physical sciences. Indeed, it would not be inaccurate to assert that where Mach had executed a critique of the language of physics, Mauthner was attempting a critique of language in general. Just as Mach based his critique on the analysis of sensations, Mauthner's critique was rooted in his psychology; yet even here his skepticism complicated matters, for he insisted that "mind" is unknowable, owing to the fact that the senses are oriented to the physical, or "external," rather than to the psychical, or "internal." Consequently, even psychology cannot really be a science. Thus, while sharing his spirit, Mauthner was even more thoroughly skeptical than Mach. Both men were vigorous positivists, denouncing the idolatrous obfuscations of the metaphysicians. For Mach, the prime enemies were the scientists of an earlier, more theological, era; for Mauthner, they were scholastic theologians, materialistic scientists, and those Platonizing, racist nationalists who had invented the Germanic ideology. Those were the opponents Mauthner had sought to refute in his earlier book *Contributions to a Critique of Language,* which first appeared in 1901.

At first glance, the most startling aspect of Mauthner's critique is, perhaps, his insistence that there is no such "thing" as *language,* but only individual human beings who use language. His own nominalism, that is, compelled him to include language itself as a reified abstraction. For Mauthner, then, language is an activity, not some sort of entity. However, the crucial point is that language is a human activity and, as such, a purposeful one. It orders human life in the way that a rule orders a game. "Language is only a convention, like a rule of a game: the more participants, the more compelling it will be. However, it is neither going to grasp nor alter the real world."[2]

Thus, we can understand language properly only in terms of a specific language which is part of a specific social complex. Language is a social phenomenon, to be grasped along with other associated customs of the individuals who use it. (At this point, Mauthner's position was very much influenced by the *Völkerpsychologie* of Lazarus and Steinthal.) A given culture distinguishes itself from all other cultures by the means by which it organizes itself, and the most distinctive of such means is its language. A culture's language is part of its operating equipment—specifically, it is the communal memory, since it contains within its vocabulary the verbal expression of its traditional customs and practices. Hence Mauthner continually refers to language as the "common sensorium" of a culture. Conversely, however, the customs and practices of a culture are the source of the meaning of its language; and in this duality lies the source of one of the many tensions in Mauthner's thought.

Like the British empiricists, Mauthner wanted to root all knowledge firmly in the sensations of the individual; however, he also wished to retain the viewpoint of *Völkerpsychologie*—that is, the insight that language is a social phenomenon. Sensations, as such, can never partake of the social character of language; while language, as such, can never partake of the private character of sensations. While insisting to the last that there exists a perceptual basis upon which the edifice of language is raised, Mauthner resolved this dilemma (to the degree to which he ever did resolve it) by appealing to the pragmatic nature of language. Sensory impressions *simpliciter* cannot be the basis of meaning, since that would give rise to inescapable difficulties. For how, in that case, could any two people know that they had both given the "right" name to the "right" impression? How could men have ever come together to name sense impressions? Would they not have had to possess a language to begin with? Clearly, the public aspects of language can never be accounted for purely and simply in terms of an origin in private sense experience. However, if one considered language as a part of man's biological equipment and, so, as an instrument of survival—a view which Mach had made fashionable at that time—one can see a way clear of these difficulties. If the original purpose of words was to insure the survival of a group of men in a situation where a single individual could not survive, it made little difference whether or no the same sensory image was before different men's minds when a word was used, just so long as they all knew how to react, what was expected of them, when such a word was used. What really matters, what really has *meaning,* is not the image a word or sentence conjures up, but the action that it suggests or commands, warns from or prohibits.

Thus, Mauthner surmounted his difficulty by considering language primarily as a necessary condition for the survival of the human species, and consequently as a necessary basis for community living. At the same time, as a philosophical empiricist, he did not deny the perceptual basis of the radically differing images occurring in the minds of different individuals on hearing the same word. On the contrary, Mauthner's pragmatic theory of language at once explained another phenomenon which he considered to be essential to language: the phenomenon of *mis*understanding. Just because language is a mediator between men when they *act,* it can similarly become a barrier when they desire to *know.* Just as an ocean simultaneously separates and joins continents, so too language is at one and the same time a bridge and a barrier between men—"Language is not a possession of the solitary individual, because it only exists between men. However, language is not common to two men, because plainly two men never conceive the same thing by the words."[3]

This is so because language is essentially metaphorical. As such, it is by its very nature ambiguous; no one can ever be certain, either that he understands what another is saying, or that he is himself understood. Furthermore, "words are always *in statu nascendi.*"[4] Not only language, but the whole of culture as well, is continually in a state of transformation. Nothing stands still.

In the practical affairs of everyday life, the inescapable ambiguity of language permits sufficient clarity to establish a pragmatic unity of purpose but, as an instrument for coming to know and understand the world, language is of very little value. Even if human beings had some way of attaining objectivity in knowledge, language itself is too ambiguous to convey it. (Mauthner illustrates the point by analyzing the first two lines of Goethe's poem *An den Mond*—eight words in all.[5] Before he has exhausted the possible meanings of the words individually, and the varied ways in which they may be construed in combination, his discussion has run to sixteen pages.) From this inherent ambiguity, Mauthner infers that language is nonetheless eminently qualified to mediate subjective states between individuals—that is, to convey emotions. Precisely because it is essentially metaphorical, language is well adapted to poetry, but ill adapted to science and philosophy.

It is impossible to arrest the conceptual content of words permanently. Therefore knowledge of the world through language is impossible. It is possible to arrest the motive content of words. Therefore art is possible through language, verbal art, poetry.[6]

The metaphorical nature of language precludes all univocity and thereby makes any sort of precise scientific knowledge impossible. Science too is, at best, poetry.

The laws of the natural sciences and the moral sciences then turn into social phenomena, the natural rules of the party game of human cognition. They are the poetics of the *fable convenue* of learning.[7]

Mauthner's *Critique* thus appeared to have dire results for science. Yet the actual existence and success of logic, mathematics and the natural sciences, far from contradicting his concept of the contingency of the senses, did not perturb Mauthner in the least. His analysis of these subjects followed lines similar to those of Mill's empiricism. Being consistent with the views of Mach and to some extent those of Kirchhoff, they consequently possessed some scientific reputability among his contemporaries. Thus, Mauthner considered hypotheses to be good guesses—successful "shots in the dark," so to say. The foundation of all science is exceptionally good inductions; the so-called laws of nature are nothing more than historical generalizations, and Mauthner spared no effort to explain the historical origin of the notion that physical laws are inexorable. He considers that the term "law of nature" is a metaphor left over from the bygone days of mythological explanation, when Nature was personified in the endeavor to comprehend it. He traces the origins of the notion back to Plato and Aristotle, and particularly to Lucretius, who first used the phrase explicitly. In the Middle Ages, the notion became incorporated into theology as the "natural law" of God, the divine providential ordering of the universe. With Spinoza's *Deus sive Natura* it became secularized, along with much else that had earlier belonged exclusively to the sphere of theology. Thus did the myth of the "laws of nature" pass down to the present time; the phrase began as a metaphor and later became reified and universally adopted by scientists. In fact, says Mauthner, there are no "laws" anywhere, only chance phenomena. Modern physical science had fallen victim to the same sort of mythologizing as took place when the followers of Darwin transformed "evolution" from a principle of explanation into a metaphysics of nature.

Mauthner's analysis of logic clearly resembles that of Mill. He too rejects the claim that the syllogism can extend knowledge. The only "necessity" in logic is the necessity of identity, which is incapable of extending our knowledge: all substantive syllogisms fall into either the class of *non sequitur* or that of *petitio principii* argument. Mauthner's critique in fact reduced logic to the psychology of thinking, and, a fortiori, to the psychology of language. Logic was identical with that part of social psychology (*Völkerpsychologie*) which related the observances, usages and other activities of a people to their language. As such, it had no value in the search for knowledge.

Thus I want to say that our faith in logic, our faith that our knowledge of the world will be increased through logical operations, is a theological faith.[8]

The idea that there exists such a *thing* as logic, in the sense of something universal and immanent in all languages, is another illegitimate reification. Belief in such a *thing,* even though it appears to comprise a body of knowledge, is superstition. "Everything about thinking is psychological," Mauthner insists; "only the pattern [*Schema*] of our thinking is logical."[9] However, the pattern of a man's thinking—and of his speaking, which is the same thing—is determined by, and reciprocally determines, the culture in which he lives, as both develop simultaneously; it is not something pre-existing which can be derived from "immutable laws of thought."

Sound human understanding would necessarily have to learn that henceforth there are as many logics as there are languages with different structures.[10]

Logic is thus transformed into a matter for cultural anthropology, since there is no common structure or cultural pattern necessarily underlying all languages. He thus ends up in a thoroughgoing cultural relativism.

Mauthner the relativist pokes fun at the absolute of the theologians and metaphysicians:

Even the most certain truth is only more or less true. Real Truth is a metaphysical concept. Men attained to the concept of Truth just as they did the concept of God—without any experience. In this sense one may certainly assert: God is Truth.[11]

Indeed, Mauthner's attempt to set the limits of language has led him to the self-deprecatory truth of Nicholas of Cusa's "unlearned knowing," and the learned ignorance of the ironic Socrates, whom the Oracle praised as the wisest among men for his awareness of his own ignorance. In Mauthner's view, the negative conclusion of the skeptic is as near as one can get to the truth.

Faust is a philosopher not because, besides jurisprudence, medicine, and (alas!) theology, he has thoroughly studied philosophy: rather, because he sees that one cannot know anything and because this makes his heart burn with concern.[12]

Mauthner sighs that philosophy must hark back to its Pythagorean origins and resign itself to a love of wisdom and a striving after truth, rather than claim the possession of it. The very conception of a "critique of language" confronts the difficulty that such a critique must itself be undertaken in and with words. It is born in contradiction and ends in silence, in what Mauthner has termed the "suicide" of language.

That would truly be the redeeming act, if Critique could be carried on with the quietly despairing suicide of thought or language, if Critique did not have to be carried on with words possessing a semblance of life.[13]

The end of the way through the critique of language is Maeterlinck's holy silence—"As soon as we really have something to say, we are forced to be silent."[14] However, this silence is of far greater value than all that is verbally expressible. This is the end of Mauthner's road; with this belief, he takes a place beside Eckhardt and Cusanus. He shares their notion of the ultimate, that unspeakable feeling of mystical unity with the universe. This clarifies the assertion in the Introduction to Mauthner's *Dictionary*, which we touched on earlier—the assertion to which Wittgenstein himself was to allude shortly afterward in the *Tractatus*—that he would be pleased

if an intelligent reader has to affirm, when all is said and done, that skeptical resignation, insight into the incomprehensibility of reality, is not merely another negation among others. It is our best knowledge. Philosophy is theory of knowledge. Theory of knowledge is critique of language. Critique of language, however, is effort on the behalf of the liberating thought that man can never succeed in getting beyond a metaphorical description of the world utilizing either everyday language or philosophical language.[15]

Again and again in the history of philosophy, assertions of epistemological skepticism—that is, the thesis that knowledge is impossible—have generated, by reaction, an epistemological "transcendentalism," which takes the possibility of knowledge as indisputable and asks, instead, how and on what conditions it is possible. So here, with Mauthner's three linked claims—that "men can never succeed in getting beyond a metaphorical description of the world"; that true knowledge is impossible either in science or philosophy; and that the so-called laws of nature are no more than "social phenomena," or *fables convenues*— these assertions at once invited a counterdemonstration that systematic knowledge is indeed possible in logic and science alike and that these subjects do enable us, on certain assumptions, to get a genuine grasp of the real world. And, in due course, we shall find the young mechanical-engineer-turned-philosopher Ludwig Wittgenstein basing his *Tractatus Logico-Philosophicus* on the conception of a *bildliche Darstellung* of the world about which Mauthner himself had written. For Wittgenstein, however, this phrase will have a radically different meaning from the "metaphorical description" of Mauthner; for Wittgenstein they will refer, rather, to a "representation" of the world having the form of a "mathematical model," in the sense in which Heinrich Hertz had analyzed the theoretical representations of the physical sciences.

But this is to run ahead. During the last decades of the nineteenth century, the status and validity of scientific knowledge had been discussed at length by a great many German-speaking scientists and philosophers of science, including such distinguished men as Gustav Kirchhoff, Hermann von Helmholtz and Ernst Mach, Heinrich Hertz and Ludwig Boltzmann. The term "representation," which played a large part in this debate, had been put into circulation by Kant and Schopenhauer. This term dovetailed two connected notions, which were not clearly distinguished at the time and are frequently confused to this day. In one sense, the term had a "sensory" or "perceptual" use— as in the physiological optics of Helmholtz and the psychology of Mach—which linked it back to the empiricist philosophies of Locke and Hume. In the other sense, it had a more "public" or "linguistic" use—as in the mechanics of Hertz—similar to that of the phrase "graphical representation" in physics today. On the whole, the "sensory" use was associated with the German word *Vorstellung*, the "public" use with the word *Darstellung;* the former word is, for instance, the standard German translation for the Lockean term "idea." But there are important exceptions to this generalization—for example, Mauthner himself —and the accounts given in nineteenth-century German philosophy of the status of scientific knowledge were deeply affected by the resulting ambiguities. So, at this point in our reconstruction, we must turn and look more closely at that debate in the philosophy of science, beginning with the dominant figure of Mach.

Seldom has a scientist exerted such an influence upon his culture as has Ernst Mach. As we have already seen, his psychology had a direct impact on the aesthetic views of *Jung Wien;* Hofmannsthal himself attended Mach's university lectures and recognized Mach's problems 'as somehow similar to his own, while Robert Musil was very much in Mach's debt.[16] In addition, through their influence on Hans Kelsen and his positivist theory of law, Mach's ideas played a significant role in the drafting of the postwar Austrian constitution, for which Kelsen was in no small part responsible.[17] Mach's ideas were embraced with enthusiasm by Austrian revisionist Marxists.[18] The Machist version of Marxism penetrated Russian socialism through the agency of Bogdanov, and achieved a position from which it could challenge Leninism as a theoretical exposition of socialism. (Lenin's reply to Bogdanov, *Materialism and Empirio-Criticism,* was thus occasioned by Mach's ideas or certain applications of them.)[19] In the twenties, the prominent Austrian social scientist Otto Neurath founded the Ernst Mach Verein, a forerunner of the Vienna Circle.[20] From poetry to philosophy of law, from physics to social theory, Mach's influence was all-pervasive in Austria and elsewhere. Not the least of those who came under Mach's spell was the young physicist Albert Einstein, who acknowledged Mach's "profound influence" upon him in his youth.[21] It has further been brought to light that Einstein's early career was modeled on Mach's view of the nature of the scientific enterprise.[22] After meeting Mach, a dazzled William James could only refer to him as a "pure intellectual genius," who read and discussed absolutely everything.[23]

Mach's reduction of all knowledge to sensation forms the base on which all of his thinking is founded. The task of all scientific endeavor is to describe sense data in the simplest or most economical manner. Mach actually prefers to designate sense data by the more neutral and noncommittal term "elements"; it is the feature of simplicity or economy which is distinctively scientific. So Mach's point of view is that of a thoroughgoing phenomenalist; the world is the sum total of what appears to the senses. So, dreams constitute "elements" in the world just as much as any other class of elements, for "inner" experience is *experience* quite as much as "outer" experience is. Abstract conceptions, ideas, representations, are similarly reduced to sense data, by being identified as species concepts which enable us to deal with groups of "elements" efficiently.

As a positivist, Mach was absolutely opposed to any sort of metaphysical speculation. He equated metaphysics with mysticism and consequently with obfuscation in science. In psychology he was a relentless opponent of all those who posited the "ego" as an entity; he rejected any position which smacked of the slightest hint of dualism, for he said that all dualism culminates in metaphysics. Indeed, as an ardent positivist, he did not recognize philosophy to have any legitimacy apart from science, and he continually insisted that he was not a philosopher. David Hume, the destroyer of all metaphysical claims to truth, and Georg Christoph Lichtenberg, the enemy of all pseudo science, were his philosophical heroes. Mach was, in fact, the first man to draw attention to the philosophical significance of Lichtenberg, whose writings soon became popular and influential in the artistic and intellectual circles of Vienna.

Mach conceived the problem of science to be threefold.

We learn very soon to distinguish our presentations from our sensations (perceptions). Now the problem of science can be split into three parts:
1. The determination of the connexion of presentations. This is psychology.
2. The discovery of the laws of the connexion of sensations (perceptions). This is physics.
3. The clear establishment of the laws of the connexion of sensations and presentations. This is psychophysics.[24]

For his conception of "psychophysics," Mach was indebted to Gustav Theodor Fechner. Fundamentally, psychophysics is a monistic philosophy which attempts to explain how the psychical and the physical are two aspects of one and the same reality.

However, the most successful attempt to unite physics and psychology into one science was that of Richard Avenarius, whom Mach recognized as a colleague.

As to the views of Avenarius, the affinity between them and my own is as great as can possibly be imagined where two writers have undergone a different process of development, work in different fields, and are completely independent of one another.[25]

In his "critique of pure experience," Avenarius sought to avoid the Scylla and Charybdis of materialism and idealism by recourse to a naïve realism having affinities with the philosophies of G. E. Moore and Edmund Husserl. Like Moore, he sought to avoid the conundrums of the metaphysicians by appealing to common-sense realism. To the question, "How do I know that here are two hands?" Moore responded by holding first one and then the other up before him and saying, "Because here is one and here is the other";[26] and Avenarius would have appreciated the force of this sort of explanation. Like Husserl, Avenarius believed that the task of philosophy is to *describe* the world as we meet it in ordinary experience—"The important thing for experience is how it is characterized, not what exists without it."[27] Thus Avenarius "brackets" the question of the existence of the objects of consciousness, as does Husserl with his concept of the *epoche*.[28] The two thinkers agree that there is no pure "consciousness," that consciousness is "known" only inasmuch as it is *consciousness of* some object.

That, however, is as far as the similarity between them extends. Avenarius insists that the perspective of "pure experience" is the meeting place of realism and solipsism, because it makes no difference to his phenomenalistic description of experience whether or not other minds exist. The objects of pure experience are *facts,* not perceptions—". . . by pure experience we shall mean experience as the immediate cognition of fact, which facts may be things or relations, thoughts, feelings, convictions, or uncertainty."[29] Avenarius' goal is the systematization of all our experience into a central "representation," which would be the most general of concepts and would constitute as simple (economical) a picture of the whole of experience as possible.

This systematization would entail a physiological description of physical phenomena, which would be built up into a concept of the totality of experience on the basis of an associationist psychology. The aim of the construction of this world-picture would be to simplify and systematize experience in such a way that we could more easily deal with it. Philosophy, then, becomes the activity of thinking about the world according to the "principle of least action." (So Avenarius entitled the prolegomena to his *Critique of Pure Experience.*)[30] Mach was in complete accord with this program, recognizing in it a significant presentation of the principle of the economy of thought, as well as an important contribution to the clarification of the relation between the physical and the psychical. These were the considerations foremost in Mach's mind when he came to analyze the nature of "representation" in physics.

Mach maintained that physical theories are descriptions of sense data which simplify experience by allowing the scientist to anticipate further events. Mathematical functions serve to simplify what the senses perceive through their organizing power. It is less correct to speak of theories as true or false than it is to speak of them as more or less useful, since it is their very nature to be descriptions of, rather than judgments on, sensations.

It is the object of science to replace, or *save* experiences, by the reproduction and anticipation of facts in thought. Memory is handier than experience, and often answers the same purpose. This economical office of science, which fills its whole life, is apparent at first glance; and with its full recognition all mysticism in science disappears.[31]

Metaphysical elements in science offend against its essential characteristic—that is, its economy. The notions of "absolute" space, time, and motion in Newton's physics are just superfluities. Mach's views on Newton's absolutes are well summarized in his statements regarding absolute time:

This absolute time can be measured by comparison with no motion; it has therefore neither a practical nor a scientific value; and no one is justified in saying that he knows aught about it. It is an idle metaphysical conception.[32]

For Mach, the way to understand—and so learn to peel away—these accretions is through a study of the principle of mechanics which is historical as well as critical. It is thus no accident that his major work should be entitled *The Science of Mechanics: A Critical and Historical Account of Its Development,* and that another should be *The History and Root of the Principle of Con-*

servation of Energy. In order to justify his claim that science is properly restricted to describing sense data in the most efficient manner, it was essential to explain how factors which were not descriptions of sense data had found their way into earlier physical theory. By analyzing the origin of certain scientific ideas, he was able to show how scientists had been led to form explanations which transcended the limits of the observable; the presence of metaphysical elements in mechanics, such as the notion of "force," is thus accounted for by pointing out that mechanics came of age during a period when men were immersed in theological problems.

Every unbiased mind must admit that the age in which the chief development of the science of mechanics took place was an age of predominantly theological cast. Theological questions were excited by everything and modified everything. No wonder, then, that mechanics is colored thereby. But the thoroughness with which theological thought thus permeated scientific inquiry, will best be seen by an examination of details.[33]

The historical element in Mach's critique of science serves to indicate the limits within which profitable scientific inquiry can take place; it also possesses a heuristic value, in that

the historical investigation of the development of a science is most needful, lest the principles treasured up in it become a system of half-understood precepts, or worse, a system of *prejudices.* Historical investigation not only promotes the understanding of that which now is but also brings new possibilities before us by showing that which exists to be in great measure *conventional* and *accidental.* From the higher point of view at which different paths of thought converge we may look down upon us with freer vision and discover routes before unknown.[34]

Thus, apart from endeavoring to explain that mechanics has no more than a historical claim to primacy among the different branches of physics, Mach is also concerned to open up new paths in mechanics through a reconsideration of its development.

Mach's stress upon the "conventional and accidental" character of the state of science in his own time also sprang from broader considerations. He believed that all knowing is directed toward the adaptation of the animal to its environment. All concepts, theories, maxims, and the like were for him functions of our instinct for biological survival.[35] Conceptual schemes are economical instruments for dealing with practical problems. As such, they are by nature colored by our motives—"In the reproduction of facts in thought, we never reproduce the facts in full, but only that side of them which is important to us, moved directly or indirectly by a practical interest."[36] For Mach, men are for the most part passive as knowers. Knowing consists primarily in describing the world of sensation to ourselves, as we must do in order to come to terms with our environment. In this context, intellectual history becomes the story of the "survival" of the "fittest" idea. Concepts too must compete with their rivals in order to gain adherents and consequently to survive. They must "adapt" themselves, both to facts and to one another.

One might expect that, when notions such as these were set forth by a scientist who claimed to be the foremost among the denouncers of metaphysics, someone would object that he had let the enemy in through the back door. One man who criticized Mach on these grounds was Max Planck. Planck maintained that Mach's biological theory of knowledge was every bit as metaphysical as those theories which he condemned; he also attacked Mach's concept of the nature of physical theory, denying that physical theories were based solely upon sense data.[37] In Planck's view, the physicist creates the system of the physical world by *imposing* form upon it. He held that the mind creates the mathematical structures which organize empirical facts into the unified system that is physical science. He accused Mach of anthropomorphism, the cardinal sin among physical scientists. To Planck, Mach's attempt to base physics on the description of sense data involved the assumption that "physical" states were somehow identical with "psychical" states.

On the other hand, Planck nowhere argued against basing science upon the principle of economy. On the contrary, he insisted that certain of the ideas which Mach most vehemently opposed were in fact in accord with the economy of nature. "It would not surprise me, if one day a member of Mach's school came up with the great discovery that the probability hypothesis, or the reality of atoms, is in fact a consequence of scientific economy."[38] Planck's words were prophetic, for Einstein's career was to reflect such a process of discovery. In fact, a strict adherence to Mach's principles led Einstein eventually to reject most of what Mach stood for.[39] In this debate with Mach, Planck's position was, curiously enough, a development of the work of a physicist whom Mach himself knew and respected. This physicist, who was, Helmholtz had asserted, "endowed with the rarest gifts of intellect and character''[40] and who died prematurely in the early 1890s, was Heinrich Hertz.

Mach expressed the fundamental antithesis between himself and Hertz when he remarked:

> It is not the business of a man of science to criticize or refute a philosopher like Kant, though it may be observed in passing that it would no longer be a particularly heroic achievement to show the inadequacy of Kant's philosophy as a guide to modern scientific research.[41]

Hertz, as a student of Helmholtz, could not overlook the significance of Kant's theory of knowledge for theoretical physics. For Mach, on the other hand, the surest guide in all epistemological matters was Hume's skeptical empiricism. It is certain that Mach read Hertz's *Principles of Mechanics* with great interest, but he does not appear to have grasped the significant difference between his own conception of the nature of physical theory and that propounded by Hertz in the introduction to his *Principles*. While praising Hertz's elimination of the ''physical'' side of mechanics, Mach failed to recognize that, in its basic conceptions, the Hertzian system was Kantian.

Mach's general misunderstanding of Hertz is typified by his comments on the word *Bild* (meaning, literally, ''picture'' or ''image''), which is the central concept in Hertz's physical theory. Mach claims that ''Hertz uses the term *Bild* in the sense of the old English philosophical term *idea,* and he applies it to systems of ideas or concepts relating to any province.''[42] A more careful reading of the introduction to the *Principles of Mechanics* does not bear out this claim. By ''images'' or ''pictures,'' Hertz means anything but the British empiricist notion of *ideas*. What he is trying to set forth is, in fact, a theory of mathematical models.[43] True, his choice of words may be unfortunate; though this is due in part to the vagueness of the term *Bild*. But it is significant that, in describing his *Bilder* as ''representations,'' Hertz consistently chose to employ the word *Darstellungen* rather than *Vorstellungen*.

If he had had the British philosophers' ''ideas,'' or sensations, in mind, *Vorstellungen* would have been the appropriate word. (That is the word ordinarily used by German philosophers to denote a mental picture of a sense datum.) Thus, in the title of his major work, Schopenhauer refers to *Die Welt als Wille und Vorstellung;* while Avenarius' philosophical goal is that of a

Centralvorstellung, which "represents" all that is essential to experience by means of a single completely general concept.[44] Hertz, on the other hand, employs the word *Darstellung* to refer to the function of his pictures or images. By this usage, he does not mean the kind of representation which is merely the reproduction of sense impressions, but rather (for example) the whole system of mechanics, in the sense in which even Mach's *Science of Mechanics in Its Development* is *historisch-kritisch "dargestellt."* In this mode of representation, men are not merely passive spectators to whom "representations," like Humean "impressions" or Machian "sensations," just *happen;* on the contrary, *Darstellungen* are consciously *constructed* schemes for knowing.

Hertz characterizes these "cognitive schemes," or "models," as follows:

Various models [*Bilder*] of the same objects are possible, and these models may differ in various respects. We should at once denote as inadmissible all models which implicitly contradict the laws of our thought. Hence we postulate that in the first place all our models shall be logically permissible—or briefly, that they shall be permissible. We shall denote as incorrect any permissible models, if their essential relations contradict the relations of external things, *i.e.,* if they do not satisfy our first fundamental requirement. Hence we postulate that in the second place our models shall be correct. But two permissible and correct models of the same external objects may yet differ in respect of appropriateness. Of two models of the same object that is the more appropriate which includes in it more of the essential relations of the object—the one we may call the more distinct. Of two models of equal distinctness the more appropriate is the one which contains, in addition to the essential characteristics, the smaller number of superfluous or empty relations;—the simpler of the two. Empty relations cannot be altogether avoided: they enter into the models because they are simply models,—models produced by our mind and necessarily affected by the characteristics of its mode of modelling them.[45]

The three tests to be satisfied by a representation of mechanical phenomena are logical consistency, correspondence with empirical data, and simplicity or elegance of presentation. We must accordingly distinguish the internal structure or articulation of our mathematical models of mechanical phenomena from their relation to the facts given in experience. The former, which includes the factors of mathematical deduction (consistency or permissibility) and systematic or formal presentation (simplicity or appropriateness), is the a priori element in Hertz's system and is explored in Book I of his *Principles*. In Book II, he goes on to consider how such an a priori deductive system is put into relation with experience. The two books taken together constitute Hertz's own representation of the science of mechanics. He compares this representation to a "systematic grammar"; and in order to give some indication of how his system relates to the traditional representations of mechanics, he compares those to the more elementary, simplified grammars constructed to help those who are beginning to learn a new language:

Our representation of mechanics bears towards the customary one somewhat the same relation that the systematic grammar of a language bears to a grammar devised for the purpose of enabling learners to become acquainted as quickly as possible with what they will require in daily life. The requirements of the two are very different, and they must differ widely in their arrangement if each is to be properly adapted to its purpose.[46]

To appreciate the novelty of Hertz's theory, we may return to the comparison between his ideas and those of Mach. For Mach, the critique of representations in physics is historical and polemical. He tries to explain, by recapitulating that development, why mechanics developed as it did, while all the time he himself is standing on the sidelines, to point out the spots where metaphysics entered in to confuse the physicist. Mach's program, then, is one that essentially involves the belief that the *limits,* both of mechanics in particular and of natural science in general, are determined by a process of "reduction," which relates statements about physical phenomena to their evidential basis in statements about sense data. He thus sets the limits of mechanics *externally*. The account of mathematical models introduced by Hertz possesses, by contrast, one great advantage. One can indicate the limits of these models *from within*.

Our fundamental law, although it may suffice for representing the motion of inanimate matter, appears (at any rate, that is one's first and natural impression) too simple and narrow to account for even the lowest processes of life. It seems to me that this is not a disadvantage, but rather an advantage of our law. For while it allows us to survey the whole domain of mechanics, it shows us what are the limits of this domain.[47]

So, in expounding his theory of models, Hertz simultaneously defines the limits of their applicability. As such, the model itself *shows us* the limits of all possible experience which can be called "mechanical."

Hertz's models, whose very structure prescribes their sphere of application, mark a great improvement over the basic conceptual apparatus which Mach had utilized—that is, symbols which are "copies" or "names" of actual sense experience—because their foundation is not psychological and descriptive, but logico-mathematical. Thus, on Mach's own principle of economy of thought, these structures fulfill the function of enabling the scientist to "anticipate experience" much more efficiently than Mach's descriptions had done. Indeed, it may be argued that a historical critique of the sort that Mach undertook is a "grammatical" propaedeutic to the systematic representation of the laws of mechanics, as conceived by Hertz. It establishes the historical fact that several systems of mechanics have explained the same phenomena and, further, that no particular system has any priority except that derived from the economy of its presentation. Nevertheless, the system which enables the scientist to anticipate experience remains the most efficient one by far, especially when it simultaneously bypasses as many philosophical pitfalls as does that of Hertz.

It is also significant that Hertz's theory developed not out of a general philosophical analysis, but as a way of solving a practical problem. Hertz had been trying to determine the precise nature of Maxwell's theory, by considering the several different sets of equations used by Maxwell to express his theory, and thus to discern what sorts of things Maxwell was asserting about the deeper nature of electromagnetic phenomena. It occurred to Hertz that, in actual fact, Maxwell was saying nothing at all about the physical nature of these phenomena. His equations were logical formulas which enabled him to deal with the phenomena and to understand how they operated. In short, Hertz realized that "Maxwell's theory is Maxwell's system of equation."[48] He thus became aware that mathematical formulas could provide a framework for dealing with all the problems of physics and, so, confer a logical structure on physical reality.

The elements of such a structure or model need not be *derived from* perception; they correspond, rather, to *possible sequences* of observed events. They thus simplified experience to a greater extent than psychological reproductions do. Mach had founded his theory of physical representation on the more general notion of a basic science of psychophysics, after studying the psycho-physiological theories of Herbart about the intuition of space and the organization of the senses; he thus began his analysis outside physics and never managed to expound physical theory from within. Indeed, he hardly appears to have considered this necessary. From the time of Carnot on, when it was discovered that the new science of thermodynamics did not require any sort of picture or model to explain the nature of heat, there had been a widespread hostile attitude among Continental physicists to any form of hypothetical model in science. By Planck's time, however, new developments in physics were requiring fresh patterns of explanation, and these warranted complex mechanical hypotheses, of which the atomic theory is the most familiar example. When he attacked both the theory of atoms and the hypothetical thinking which it typified, Mach was expressing the attitude of an earlier generation of scientists. For men like Planck and Boltzmann, on the other hand, atomic theory was very much a part of the economy of science.

The Kantian element in Hertz's interpretation of physical theory is evident also in the ideas of Ludwig Boltzmann, the man who founded the "statistical mechanics" which lies at the basis, not only of the twentieth-century approach to thermodynamics, but of the modern attitude toward theoretical physics generally. Boltzmann took Hertz's account of mechanics as defining a system of "possible sequences of observed events," and made it the starting point for a general method of theoretical analysis *in physics itself*. He did so, by treating each independent property of a physical system as defining a separate coordinate in a multi-dimensional system of geometrical coordinates. All the possible locations of each separate body in the physical system, for instance, were ordered along three spatial "axes of reference"; all values of, say, temperature along another axis; all values of, say, pressure along a fifth; and so on. The totality of theoretical "points" in the resulting multidimensional coordinate system gave one a representation of the "ensemble of possible states" of the physical system in question; and any actual state could be defined, by specifying the particular point in this "multidimensional space" whose coordinates corresponded to the actual values of all the variables. The general problem for statistical mechanics was then to discover mathematical relations governing the frequencies with which—on various assumptions and conditions—the *actual* states of a physical system would be distributed among its *possible* states; and, so, to compute the relative probabilities of finding the system, in actual fact, in one overall physical state rather than another.[49]

It would take us too far afield to explain here, even in brief, how Boltzmann's statistical method of analysis came to play so central a part in twentieth-century physics. Planck himself immediately picked on it as a stroke of genius. In this way, one could eliminate finally all subjective references, to "sensations of warmth" and the like, which lingered on in Machian accounts of heat theory, and replace them with rigorous mathematical descriptions.[50] With the new emphasis on statistical explanation characteristic of quantum mechanics, the importance of Boltzmann's method has only increased. In particular, his method of specifying the physical state of a system, by reference to a multidimensional space whose coordinates represent all the independent variables of the system, has been taken over entirely into the standard presentations of modern quantum theory. But—technicalities apart—it is worth pointing out that this notion of a "space of theoretical possibilities," which plays the key part in Boltzmann's method of analysis, can be summarized concisely in words from Wittgenstein's *Tractatus Logico-Philosophicus,* as follows:

The facts in logical space are the world; the world divides into facts; each item can be the case or not the case while everything else remains the same . . . We construct for ourselves representations [*Bilder*] of facts.

A *Bild* depicts reality by representing a possibility of existence and non-existence of states of affairs. A *Bild* represents a possible situation in logical space.

A proposition determines a place in logical space . . . In geometry and logic alike a place is a possibility: something can exist in it.[51]

As we shall be seeing later, it is a short step from Boltzmann's method of treating actual physical "states of affairs," as distributed statistically among the total ensemble of possible "states of affairs" defined within a particular multidimensional space, to Wittgenstein's "method of truth tables," in which the truth or falsity of the "molecular" propositions corresponding to different complex combinations of facts is treated as a function of the independent truth or falsity of the elementary propositions corresponding to all the independent "atomic" facts or states of affairs involved.

For the most part, twentieth-century science has come out in favor of Hertz's "models" rather than Mach's "descriptions." However, this did not come about without a struggle; and the influence of Mach's positivism is still clear in, for instance, the arguments of the quantum physicists (e.g., Bohr and Heisenberg) about the primacy of "observables."[52] For Planck, this disagreement meant a period of ostracism from the scientific community. Boltzmann, who identified himself as continuing the work of Hertz, was unable to cope with the harsh criticisms of Mach, Ostwald and their followers; this hostility was, indeed, a factor in the mental unbalance of his later years which finally led him to take his own life—just at the moment when the young Wittgenstein was preparing to study under him. By 1906, the struggle against metaphysics had become petrified into a dogmatic empiricism, which considered all hypothetical structures taboo. If this attitude has been largely displaced in science, this is thanks to the successors of Hertz, though in the philosophy of science this dogmatic attitude has survived far longer in the work of the Vienna Circle. Among historians, however, the pioneering importance of Hertz's work remains even today largely unrecognized, despite the high regard which a philosopher of such repute as Ernst Cassirer had for his work.[53] And the history of fifty years of interpretation of Ludwig Wittgenstein's *Tractatus Logico-Philosophicus* has been profoundly influenced by the philosophical successors of Mach—the Vienna Circle—who distorted the argument of a work on the philosophy of language which was, as we shall see, derived essentially from Hertz's and Boltzmann's theories, into an epistemological exercise in Machian empiricism.

One distinctive virtue of Hertz's analysis, we said, was that it showed how the scope of any theoretical representation can be *shown from within*. Unlike Mach's "reductionist" analysis, which related all physical theories back to a universal—and philosophically more fundamental—system of psychophysics, Hertz's method allowed one to define the totality of "theoretical possibilities" which the theory in question can meaningfully be used to represent in a way that makes no appeal to any more general principles, external to the particular representation. For anyone brought up to appreciate the full philosophical force of Kant's critical program, this was an important point in Hertz's favor. For one of Kant's central ambitions had, likewise, been to map the overall scope of boundaries of the "reason" by showing them from *within,* in a way that avoided all reliance on external metaphysical assumptions; and then not merely to *assert,* but to *show,* that metaphysics is—rationally speaking—concerned with the "unknowable," because its questions lie at or beyond the boundaries of the reason so mapped. In this sense, we can legitimately speak of Hertz's attitude toward physical theory as Kantian; as such, it falls squarely into place alongside the other attempts at which we have already looked, to define the scope, conditions of validity, and boundaries, of different media, symbolisms, modes of expression and/or languages, which were a dominant feature of Viennese intellectual and cultural debate from 1890 on.

In order to see most clearly the philosophical issues involved in proportion, we must place them in their historical perspective. This means seeing them in the light of the arguments put forward by the two men who did most to shape the questions under discussion in that debate—namely, Immanuel Kant himself and Arthur Schopenhauer. Kant never tired of reminding his readers that the human reason tends to run riot and "precipitate itself into darkness."[54] The whole of the "critical philosophy" is directed toward explaining the proper limits of reason and showing how these limits are overstepped because of reason's innate tendency to pass from sensible experience itself to an explanation of that experience, although such an explanation lies beyond it in the sphere of "things in themselves." There is a natural disposition on the part of reason to explain the world of perception in terms of an intelligible world beyond the possibility of perception; such explanation is characteristic of *metaphysics,* which claims to be not only a science, but the queen of the sciences. The critique of reason which Kant produced in 1781 was an attack upon these claims.

The point which made Kant suspicious of the assertion that metaphysics had the status of science was the multiplicity of diverse, and often contradictory, metaphysical systems. Physical science (or natural philosophy, as it was then called) exhibited no such multiplicity. The knowledge that it contained was cumulative. Each scientist could build on the work of his predecessors;

this was not true of the metaphysician. In natural science the work of many men stood together as a *body of knowledge.* The work of the metaphysicians was no such body of knowledge, but merely the work of several men contradicting each other. For this reason the claims of metaphysics to be a science were suspect. Metaphysics and natural science were both held by Kant to be works of reason; but, since they are in practice so different, it became necessary for him to reconsider the nature of the foundation of that knowledge which is denominated "scientific." The resulting *Critique of Pure Reason* was, in Kant's own words, the philosophical equivalent of the Copernican revolution in astronomy. It produced the most radical change of viewpoint in philosophy since Parmenides' discovery that logical coherence is essential to any explanation of the world, and it resulted in Kant's rejection of all claims of metaphysics to a scientific status.

It was, Kant concluded, in the very nature of reason itself to strive to pass beyond the scope of all experience, and even all possible experience. He referred to the "natural predisposition" (*Naturanlage*) of our reason to do so.[55] Since Kant insisted that he was not concerned with psychology or anthropology, this can only mean that it is an *essential* feature of reason that, in its desire to complete the world-picture it has created, it should strive to pass beyond the limits of possible experience. Metaphysics is thus the most "human" of man's activities.

For metaphysics, in its fundamental features, perhaps more than any other science, is placed in us by nature itself and cannot be considered the product of an arbitrary choice, or a casual enlargement in the progress of experience, from which it is quite disparate.[56]

Even though it is not possible for us to form a definite idea of what lies beyond experience, reason is never satisfied with what experience has to offer it. Consequently, it postulates without justification that its ideas correspond to something actually existing.

As for such ideas as those of the soul, of the world and of God, although these ideas do not extend our real knowledge, they are not without a function. For the scientist they function as "regulative ideas"—they furnish him, for example, with the idea of that unity which is proper to science, thereby aiding the scientist to "render experience within itself as nearly complete as possible."[57] Similarly, they provide the ethical theorist with notions which serve to protect him against the temptation to take materialism, naturalism or fatalism really seriously, to the point of actually accepting them. Thus, the ideas of reason are related to morality, not essentially, but as a scholium. The fact that reason transcends the limits of experience, then, does not entail that what it produces beyond those limits is wholly meaningless, but only that its products, the ideas, cannot extend our knowledge.

This theory of "the limits of reason" is of direct importance to us here, since it was the starting point of the whole debate about language and values, which came to a head in the Vienna of 1890–1914. In order to understand it more completely, one must look into Kant's distinction between limits and bounds (*Schranken* and *Grenzen*). "Bounds (in extended beings) always presuppose a space existing outside a certain definite place and enclosing it," says Kant; on the other hand, "limits do not require this, but are mere negations which affect a quantity so far as it is not absolutely complete."[58] Hence, "in mathematics and in natural philosophy, human reason admits of *limits* but not of *bounds:* namely, it admits that something indeed lies without it, at which it can never arrive, but not that it will at any point find completion in its internal progress."[59] Mathematics and physics will go on explaining appearances for all time. The number of phenomena that they may discover is *unbounded.* Nevertheless, their discoveries are limited to appearances. They are, by their nature, unequipped to discover the nature of things in themselves. These branches of knowledge are restricted to what can be known about objects of sense-experience. They can never explain anything in such a way as to transcend that experience. A science of metaphysics (if there could be such a thing) would lead, not to the limits of speculative reason, but to its bounds; in that case, one would reach the *bounds of the conceivable,* as opposed to the *limits of the actual.*

The implications of the Kantian critique were particularly far-reaching in the field of ethics. No longer could morality be based on any sort of "natural law" or "human nature." Kant was convinced that any such notion as that of human nature, regarded as a "thing in itself," was beyond the reach of human knowledge. For him, the absolute necessity which binds the will to perform moral acts—like the necessity of a particular class of propositions—springs from the reason itself, which is the source of all necessity. Reason can know, and therefore be responsible for, only that which it creates itself. Just as any systematic knowledge of forms, structures and necessary connections in nature is a result of the application of a priori forms of the understanding to what has been perceived through the a priori forms of sensibility, so too our moral actions must be based on the legislation of reason. In metaphysics, reason drives itself beyond the limits of understanding to the conception of an "unconditionally necessary" being, this being the only conception which entirely satisfies it. In the moral sphere, similarly, the only sort of motivation that can entirely satisfy the practical reason is an "unconditioned necessity," binding the will to act:

The speculative employment of reason *with respect to nature* leads to the absolute necessity of some supreme cause of the world: the practical employment of reason *with a view to freedom* leads also to absolute necessity, but only *of the laws of the actions* of a rational being as such.[60]

Here is the origin of the Categorical Imperative, the legislator and judge of all human actions. In its speculative function, reason legislates for sensible experience, thereby producing nature as a "system." In its practical function, reason legislates for itself as a cause of action. What to the speculative reason were illusions—the Transcendental Ideas of God, the world, and the soul—are now seen in a different light, as necessary fictions for organizing conduct according to reason. The practical application of reason to conduct necessitates that reason should think itself in a noumenal world; that is, an intelligible "kingdom of ends" in which the ideas of freedom, immortality and God have meaning. Only in such a context can the Categorical Imperative be meaningful. Thus, for Kant, ethics is concerned with the conduct of rational beings precisely insofar as they are rational; and he claims that such an ethic would be valid not only for men but for all rational beings whatever.

Having started from the idea that reason has an innate tendency to overstep its limits, Kant's critique of reason thus proceeds by positing—and distinguishing—two spheres of activity as the concern of reason: the sphere of facts, and that of values. In the first sphere, reason's drive to attain the source of all necessity (namely, the "unconditioned") creates intellectual monsters which fetter speculation. In the second sphere, the unconditioned becomes the very basis for the activity of reason and, so, the foundation of morality. Indeed, a primary concern of

Kant's critique of reason lies in the need to establish the true character of the sphere of values; one of the main reasons for undertaking it had been to prove that, regarded as systems of nature, such doctrines as materialism, naturalism, atheism, fatalism and the like are impossible. In fact, none of the systems of nature has anything at all to do with the nature of Man as a rational being; consequently they cannot provide a foundation for ethics. Reason alone is capable of this. Since he considered metaphysical systems to be a threat to human freedom and, so, to morality as well, Kant set out to show that they were at best fictions. Yet at the same time, in determining the limits of reason, he saw himself as performing a service to natural philosophy, for "we do not enlarge but disfigure the sciences if we allow them to trespass upon one another's territory."[61] (Logic provides him with a perfect example of a science that is limited in the way he describes; its great value in intellectual life is derived therefrom —"that logic should have been thus successful is an advantage which it owes to its limitations . . .")[62] In short, the critical philosophy determines the sphere of applicability of natural science at the same time that it defends the sphere of morality from a reason that has gone wild and overstepped its own proper limits.

In the last century no one defended Kant from German idealism more than Arthur Schopenhauer. He ceaselessly inveighed against those philosophers who had transformed the critical philosophy into the grandiose idealist systems of the early-nineteenth century. Hegel, in particular, was the continual object of his wrath. Thus he says,

People generally are beginning to be conscious that real and serious philosophy still stands where Kant left it. In any case, I cannot see that anything has been done in philosophy between him and me; I therefore take my departure direct from him.[63]

Curiously, time has proved that Schopenhauer had much more in common with the idealists than he ever cared to admit; he himself thought that he was taking up where Kant had left off. His main work, *The World as Will and Representation,* grew out of his marriage of Kant to Oriental thought, the importance of which for Western philosophy he was—leaving aside Leibniz' interest in the *I Ching*—the first to recognize.

The title of Schopenhauer's book reflects his basic notion that the world possesses two fundamental aspects—corresponding

roughly to Kant's practical and speculative reason, respectively
—which he refers to by the two words "will" and "representation." We are aware of ourselves both as knowers or thinkers
and as actors or agents. Like Kant, Schopenhauer was very much
concerned with limiting the sphere of abstract, intellectual
thought and, so with distinguishing and separating the sphere of
facts from that of values. In Schopenhauer's opinion, Kant's
two greatest achievements were the Transcendental Aesthetic,
in which he had proved that all that we perceive is "phenomenal"
(or mere appearance), and the associated distinction of the
"phenomenon" from the "thing in itself." For Schopenhauer,
these together give us ground for arguing that the two fundamental aspects of the world are separate, but related in a determined way—that is, the representation stands to the will as
"phenomenon" to "thing in itself." Schopenhauer considered
himself a Kantian on account of his development of these notions; and, when interpreted in his own fashion, they form the
cornerstone of his philosophy. In effect, while affirming Kant's
greatness and insight, Schopenhauer was simultaneously transforming the Kantian critique into something quite different.

An essential part of Schopenhauer's thought is the thorough
critical analysis of the Kantian philosophy, to be found primarily
in his dissertations *On the Fourfold Root of the Principle of
Sufficient Reason* and *On the Two Fundamental Problems of
Ethics* and, in a summary form, in the essay "Criticism of the
Kantian Philosophy," appended to his major work. Among the
gravest deficiencies Schopenhauer finds in the critical philosophy
is the fact that Kant fails to define his basic concepts. "Reason,"
"understanding," "concept," "category," and many other
terms are used and distinguished, without being properly explained.

Now as I have said above, if Kant had seriously investigated to what extent two such different faculties of knowledge, one of which is the distinctive characteristic of mankind, come to be known, and what reason
and understanding mean according to the use of language in all nations
and by all philosophers, then he would never have divided reason into
theoretical and practical without any further authority than the *intel-
lectus theoreticus* and *practicus* of the scholastics, who use the terms in an
entirely different sense, and he never would have made practical reason
the source of virtuous conduct. In the same way, Kant should really have
investigated what a *concept* is in general, before separating so carefully

concepts of the understanding (by which he understands partly his categories, partly all common concepts) and concepts of reason (his so-called
Ideas), and making them both the material of his philosophy, which for
the most part deals only with the validity, application and origin of all
these concepts.[64]

Here and throughout, the chief charge that Schopenhauer levels
at Kant is that a residual Scholasticism is allowed to distort the
brilliant insights from which it began. A prime example of such
scholastic vestiges is Kant's architectonic, which demands sym-
metry everywhere within his system. It is precisely this architectonic, Schopenhauer asserts, that ruins the *Critique of Pure
Reason.* Kant proceeds smoothly enough as far as the Transcendental Aesthetic, where he succeeds in formulating one of his
most brilliant notions; but after that the demands of the architectonic take control of him. Schopenhauer's dissertation *On the
Fourfold Root of the Principle of Sufficient Reason,* was an attempt to set this straight: simplifying the analytic, by removing
the unnecessary accretions which this externally-improved structure required. All that Kant was really concerned to establish in
the analytic was the principle of causality, as the basis of science;
but the architectonic compelled him to include, also, other superfluous judgments.

Schopenhauer set out to rectify this by demonstrating that the
a priori in human knowledge is based upon the principle of sufficient reason, which has four forms (the "fourfold root"),
depending on what it is required to ground. He begins by distinguishing science from a mere aggregation of facts—"For by
science we understand a *system* of notions, that is, a totality of
connected, as opposed to a mere aggregate of disconnected, notions."[65] It is the principle of sufficient reason that provides the
a priori basis for connecting our representations into a systematic body of knowledge, or science. For Schopenhauer, in
other words, science is a coherent representation of perceptions,
grounded a priori in the principle of sufficient reason. It is the
function of the understanding to represent and unify perceptions
into a science:

Now it is the Understanding which, by means of its own peculiar function, brings about the *union* [of space and time] and connects their
heterogeneous forms in such a manner, that empirical reality—albeit only
for that understanding—arises out of their mutual interpenetration, and
arises as a collective representation, forming a complex held together by

the forms of the principle of sufficient reason, but whose limits are problematical.[66]

Schopenhauer's attempt, then, is to prove that the a priori structure of the world, regarded as an object of knowledge—the *World as Representation*—is entirely based on the principle of sufficient reason, and in so doing to simplify and clarify the Kantian position with regard to the foundations of knowledge.

However, there was one fundamental point at which Schopenhauer claimed to advance beyond the Kantian position. This was his transformation of the sphere of pure speculative reason into "the World as Representation." In taking representation (*Vorstellung*) as his point of departure, Schopenhauer claimed to avoid the problems generated by the Kantian dichotomy between subject and object:

Now our method of procedure is *toto genere* different from these two opposite misconceptions (i.e. attempting to deduce the object from the subject or vice versa), since we start neither from the object nor from the subject but from the *representation*, as the first fact of consciousness.[67]

If we start from the object, we find ourselves in a pre-Kantian dogmatism. If we start from the subject, we are soon caught up in Fichtean idealism. Starting with the representation, or *Vorstellung*, the mental image of our perception, we do not face such difficulties. Representation, in this sense, must be distinguished from the abstract conceptions which are derived from it—that is, from the representation of species or the class concept, and from the Platonic Idea, the object of art. For Schopenhauer, the subject is not something in the world, but a precondition of its very existence:

Because in general no object without subject can be conceived without involving a contradiction, we must absolutely deny to the dogmatist the reality of the external world, when he declares this to be its independence of the subject. The whole world of objects is and remains representation, and is for this reason wholly and forever conditioned by the subject.[68]

Objects exist only insofar as they are known; subjects exist only insofar as they are knowers. Outside this context, nothing can be said of either. They are the reciprocal *limits* of the world as representation.

Yet this is not the only aspect of the world.

The objective world, the world as representation, is not the only side of the world but merely (so to speak) its external side. The world has an entirely different side which is its inmost being, its kernel, the thing-in-itself . . . i.e., Will.[69]

It is possible to know this noumenal aspect of the world, because men are capable of knowing themselves, insofar as they are acting, willing subjects, and therefore objects of knowledge. Kant's "practical reason" was a muddled way of discussing "the world as will." In Schopenhauer's thought, however, the meaning of the distinction between the world as representation and the world as will goes far beyond the distinction between the twin functions of reason in Kant; and, indeed, it goes in a direction contrary to some of Kant's basic notions. For Schopenhauer believed that he had opened the door to a new method of attaining the noumenal, or the "thing in itself." Thus he asserted:

Phenomenon means representation and nothing more. All representation, be it of whatever kind it may, all *object* is *phenomenon*. But only the *will* is *thing-in-itself;* as such it is not representation at all, but *toto genere* different therefrom. It is that of which all representation, all objects, are the phenomenon, the visibility, the *objectivity*. It is the inmost essence, the kernel, of every particular thing and also of the whole. It appears in every blinding acting force of nature, and also in the deliberate conduct of man, and the great difference between the two concerns only the degree of the manifestation, not the inner nature of what is manifested.[70]

Representations, thoughts, can be said to be objectifications of the will, inasmuch as they are the instruments of desire; they are tools which enable man to satisfy the needs of his physical structure. The function of thought is to fulfill the biological needs of nutrition and propagation; in this sense representations *serve* the will.

Schopenhauer was aware that his notion of the world as will constituted a divergence from the path that Kant had chosen to follow. His essay *On the Basis of Morality* helps to clarify the relation between Kant's practical reason and his own "world as will." It is an essay about the foundation of Kantian ethics—or, more precisely, about Kant's confusions over the nature of ethics. Like *The Fourfold Root of the Principle of Sufficient Reason,* it attempts to explain away the deficiencies of Kantian thought as residues of Scholasticism, but Schopenhauer's attack here is far more devastating than in *The Fourfold Root.*

For Schopenhauer, Kant's great contribution to ethics lay in liberating morality, at a single stroke, both from eudaemonism and from its dependence on theology. A great stride in this direction had been taken when Kant succeeded in distinguishing ethics proper from the exposition of its foundations. Consequently, Schopenhauer has a good deal of respect for the *Foundations of the Metaphysics of Morals* where Kant established that distinction, but he has only disdain for *The Critique of Practical Reason*. The former book was written, he maintains, by a genius at the height of his powers, the latter by a garrulous old man. In *The Critique of Practical Reason*, Kant let theology in through the back door, by basing morality on a categorical imperative, on the "ought" rather than the "is." For Schopenhauer, Kant's assumption that there exist purely moral laws is entirely gratuitous. He considers that this notion, like that of the Creator-God, had been part of Judaism's legacy to the intellectual enslavement of mankind. To base ethics on obligation is tantamount to the reintroduction of the divine judge and eudaemonism—"A commanding voice, whether it comes from within or from without, cannot possibly be imagined except as threatening or promising."[71]

Such an ethic rests, then, upon happiness and therefore upon egoism. Another muddled aspect of Kant's ethics is the notion of a morality proper to "all rational beings whatever." In this concept, says Schopenhauer, we have a genus the predicates of which apply to only one species, the only one we know or can know, that is, man. When Kant speaks of "rational beings apart from men," he might just as well be speaking of "heavy beings apart from bodies."

Contrary to Kant, Schopenhauer argues that the basis of morality must be, not a pure a priori conception, but something empirical. Only the empirical is real, and only the empirical can move the will. To say that something a priori and conceptual moves the will is tantamount to maintaining that the will is stimulated to action by *nothing actual*. In a devastating argument, he castigates Kant's idea that the reasonable and the human—and, consequently, the virtuous—are coterminous. Reasonable, for Schopenhauer, carries an ethically neutral meaning, neither virtuous nor vicious. It merely signifies the faculty which distinguishes man from the animals, and enables him to perform more varied types of activity—namely, the capacity of human beings to deal with their environment in terms of abstract conceptions. As a result of their ability to think abstractly, men are said to be "free," for in comparison with animals they are capable of far more varied modes of activity. Thus it is possible to be very reasonable without being virtuous, just as it is possible to be virtuous and quite unreasonable.

Schopenhauer found the true foundation of motivation in the Scholastic principle *operatio sequitur esse*. For him, this meant that the observable actions of different men were manifestations of each man's fixed nature. He saw this older principle as anticipating one of Kant's monumental discoveries, the coexistence of freedom and necessity in the willing subject. Schopenhauer considered the will to be identical with its acts, that is, its bodily manifestations. Both are thus capable of being known as "phenomena," strictly determined by the law of causality, and at the same time as "things in themselves," therefore free. His ethics begins, therefore, with an empirical search for truly moral acts—that is, for acts which are not motivated by egoism. Egoism is the manifestation of the will to live in man, which drives him to seek life under the optimum circumstances, and not to consider his means of attaining it. "The absence of all egoistic motives is thus the *criterion of an action of moral value.*"[72]

The only adequate basis for morality, in Schopenhauer's view, is one upon which men are able to act morally, justly and kindly, toward one another; it accordingly has little to do with what is taught in ethics courses at universities. Such a morality can only be one founded upon compassion, upon the actual giving of oneself to the other, in that kind of relationship which Buber was later to describe as proper to an "I" and a "Thou." Schopenhauer derived this notion from his studies of Hindu mysticism. For him, the Hindu ethics culminates in a kind of Solipsism, in which the good man

perceives that the distinction between himself and others, which to the wicked man is so great a gulf, belongs only to a fleeting, deceptive phenomenon. He recognizes immediately, and without reasons or arguments, that the in-itself of his own phenomenon is also that of others, namely that will-to-live which constitutes the inner nature of everything, and lives in all; in fact, he recognizes that this extends even to the animals and to the whole of nature; he will therefore not cause suffering even to an animal.[73]

No positive expression whatsoever of this feeling is possible; so Schopenhauer's ethics culminates in a mystical experience. The only other experience which closely resembles it is also one in the sphere of values—namely, the aesthetic experience which consists, to a large extent, in the fact that, when we enter the state of pure contemplation, we are raised for the moment above all willing, above all desires and cares; we are (so to speak) rid of ourselves.[74]

As such, this too is a moral experience, but only a temporary one, because as long as we are engaged in it we are not capable of doing harm to the other. By the act of giving ourselves over to contemplation, we have dissociated ourselves from willing.

Schopenhauer's attack on the Scholastic residue in Kantian thought thus terminated in a move which makes morality immediately dependent upon feelings and intentions. The sphere of facts and the sphere of values, which in Kant were distinct but by no means separate, come to be separated widely in the philosophy of Schopenhauer. In the thought of Søren Kierkegaard, this separation becomes an unbridgeable chasm.

Kierkegaard believed, as Schopenhauer did, that morality is not founded upon intelligence; and he attacked the abstractness of Hegelian morality, in the same way that Schopenhauer attacked Kant. For both men, ethics had to be rooted not in the conceptions of reason, but in the existing individual, and Kierkegaard was sufficiently impressed by Schopenhauer to concede that he was "unquestionably an important writer . . . who, in spite of complete disagreement, touches me at so many points."[75] Still, Kierkegaard was right to see that there was a "complete disagreement" between their respective conceptions of the moral life. For Schopenhauer, the moral man is essentially passive; his major moral effort consists in denying his instinctual urges. The "morality of compassion" is based upon the notion of the brotherhood of mankind, and is thoroughly social; a man is genuinely moral for Schopenhauer, only when he takes the sufferings of the other upon himself. Kierkegaard, on the contrary, maintained that true morality is asocial, because it consists in an absolutely immediate relationship between each man and God. The goal of Kierkegaardian man is the "leap into the absurd," the leap of faith by which the finite personality totally commits itself to the infinite. In this relationship, the friend or fellow man becomes the unnecessary other.

Kierkegaard spent his life attempting to make people aware of this truth. "The problem itself is a problem of reflection: to become a Christian . . . when one is a Christian of sorts."[76] This is Kierkegaard's point of departure: how do I become a Christian? The very question implies that, even though I may be one nominally, I am not a true Christian. Kierkegaard's problem is, then, taken from the way men live; he maintains that, between what men do and what they claim about themselves, there is a grave discrepancy. Hence, one essential element in Kierkegaardian thought was a thoroughgoing critique of conventional bourgeois mores; this is recurrent throughout his work, but it is perhaps best illustrated in his essay *The Present Age.* Comfort, reflection, temporary apathy and equally temporary enthusiasm, he asserts, characterize the present age. It is an age of abstract thought in which passion plays no role, an age of ideas in which true feelings play no role. In such an age of indolence, revolutions are inconceivable. It is thus an age without genuine values —"An age without passion has no values, and everything is transformed into representational ideas."[77]

In an age that cherishes abstractions, no morality is possible; all that such an epoch is capable of producing is a sham life. The age itself becomes an abstraction. As such, it is characterized throughout by a leveling process that leaves no room for individuality. In effect, the age becomes incarnated in "the public."

In order that everything should be reduced to the same level, it is at first necessary to procure a phantom, its spirit, a monstrous abstraction, an all-embracing something which is nothing, a mirage—and that phantom is *the public.*[78]

This abstraction has a way of crushing the individual, by means of the further abstractions that it produces—"public opinion," "good taste" and the like. In a deteriorating society, this "public" is the fiction of the press.

Only when the sense of association in society is no longer strong enough to give life to concrete realities is the Press able to create that abstraction "the public," consisting of unreal individuals who never are and never can be united in an actual situation or organization—and yet are held together as a whole.[79]

Thus, Kierkegaard in Copenhagen, like Kraus in Vienna some seventy-five years later, considered the press to be the special agent of demoralization, as a result of its impersonality and indifference to truth. To all of this, he opposes the individual, who is the sole bearer of responsibility and the sole subject of religious and moral experience. This individual has become lost in the stifling crowd, and Kierkegaard saw it as his responsibility to call people's attention to this situation in such a way as to remedy it.

In order to do this, Kierkegaard had to undertake a vast polemic against his society. This polemic formed an essential element in what he called *indirect communication*—"No illusion can ever be destroyed directly, and only by indirect means can it be radically removed."[80] The function of polemic was to destroy illusions, but at the same time its task was creative— ". . . everything creative is latently polemical, since it has to make room for the new which it is bringing into the world."[81] This is especially true of religious thought, for religion always enters the world as a stranger. Thus Kierkegaard's polemical critique of society is an indispensable element in his thought. Most significantly of all, in order to establish new *values,* the old must be swept away. To attempt merely to refute the values of another gets one nowhere. It merely strengthens and embitters him.

In all eternity it is impossible for me to compel a person to accept an opinion, a conviction, a belief. But one thing I can do: I can compel him to take notice. In one sense this is the first thing; for it is the condition antecedent to the next thing, i.e., the acceptance of an opinion, a conviction, a belief. In another sense it is the last—if, that is, he will not take the next step.[82]

The polemicist, then, puts a man in a position where he must make a choice, and this is—in the nature of the case—all that the teacher of ethics can do.

Kierkegaard's writings repeatedly emphasize that this "indirect communication" is, in fact, nothing more than the revival of the Socratic method in the service of Christianity. It is a "new militant science"[83] intended to replace the older apologetic method, which does not provide an adequate instrument for the Christianization of the modern world. Indirect communication, or (as Kierkegaard sometimes calls it) "communication by means of reflection," is intellectual and moral midwifery on the Socratic pattern. It endeavors to bring someone up to the threshold of knowledge, so as to permit him to cross over it by himself. In addition to polemic, the instruments of the moral teacher are, thus, irony, satire, comedy and allegory. By shocking or by poking fun at or attacking a position, these forms achieve what speculative argumentation cannot; they bring men to the point where they must choose. For Kierkegaard, the very notion of speculation itself is an object of derision, because it can never change a person's mode of *living*. In Kierkegaard's view, the greatest disaster that ever befell Christianity was the attempt to express its truths in speculative terms. As a result, Christianity contradicted itself. Speculative truth is a matter of universal and complete knowledge, *true for all time;* whereas Christianity has to do with the existing person, who is always in a state of becoming, always an individual. Speculation is concerned with "objective truth," Christianity is rooted in *subjective truth,* a notion which lies close to the heart of all Kierkegaard's thinking.

Kierkegaard defines "subjective truth" as "an objective uncertainty held fast in an appropriation process of the most passionate inwardness."[84] This is his existential truth. What Kierkegaard is speaking of here is, in fact, *faith*. Seen in this light, his attack upon the passionless society takes on a greater significance. In its passionlessness, his society refused to allow room for "inwardness" and, consequently, for faith. In this sense, the crowd is "untruth," for the crowd and its mentality are strictly opposed to inwardness and passion. Similarly, no amount of speculation can ever produce passion: a person cannot be reasoned into a confession of faith, and "indirect communication" alone can convey existential truth. This is also the source of Kierkegaard's doctrine of faith as a "leap into the absurd."

Christianity has declared itself to be the eternal essential truth which has come into being in time. It has proclaimed itself as the *Paradox*, and it has required of the individual the inwardness of faith in relation to that which stamps it as an offense to the Jews and a folly to the Greeks—and an absurdity to the understanding.[85]

The "absurd" is the passionate clinging to an objective uncertainty that by its nature offends the understanding. Faith, for Kierkegaard, is measured by the risk it involves. Thus the greatest possible faith becomes the greatest possible risk, placing a total commitment in what is most uncertain, the absurd. Speculative thought can never explain this—"To explain the paradox would then mean to understand more and more profoundly what a paradox is, and that the paradox is the paradox."[86] Speculation would have to transcend itself in so doing, and such notions can be conveyed only "indirectly."

In this way, Kierkegaard made the separation of the sphere of facts from that of values an absolute one. The process which Kant had set in motion by distinguishing the "speculative" and the "practical" functions of reason, and which Schopenhauer kept moving by separating the world as representation from the world as will, culminated in Kierkegaard's total separation of reason from anything that pertains to the meaning of life. Beyond this, for anyone who accepted this theory, yet nevertheless wanted to produce teachings, there would be only one recourse: to devote himself to the writing of parables expressing the points of view of those who had found the meaning of life in their own living.

The man who brought this conclusion to bear on the consciousness of the general reading public, at the end of the nineteenth century, was the novelist Leo Tolstoy. Between his work and that of Kierkegaard, there was no direct relationship. However, there are definite parallels both in their conceptions of art and in their attitudes to "indirect discourse" and the "meaning of life." Tolstoy conceived morality as essentially based upon feeling, and art as "the language of feeling"; speech, by contrast, was the medium of rational thought. Hence art was, for him, the medium through which moral teachings must be propagated. In his detailed views about the moral life, however, Tolstoy was more in agreement with Schopenhauer than with Kierkegaard; for Tolstoy, morality was nothing if it was not social. Art is thus a condition of human life, the transmission of feelings in which men are united. It produces a true "compassion," or "feeling-with," the situation of another person and thus may be said to be religious in nature. Yet it is religious, not in the sense that it is dogmatic, but in the sense that it makes men aware of the fundamental law of human life—that is, the principle that "I am my brother's keeper."

Inasmuch as this principle has the same meaning as the doctrines of the Sermon on the Mount, Tolstoy takes it to mean "Resist not evil." Thus, Tolstoy's version of Christianity is one which accepts a life dedicated to suffering and in this respect resembles Schopenhauer's conception of morality. At the same time, Tolstoy vehemently rejected all dogma—"I do not care to expound the doctrines of Christ; I should wish only one thing: to do away with all exposition."[87] Here, he is closer to Kierkegaard with the notion of subjectivity. Like Kierkegaard, Tolstoy had little use for speculative knowledge in his mission:

If we turn to the branches of knowledge which are not concerned with the problem of life but find an answer to their own particular scientific questions, we are lost in admiration of the human intellect, but we know beforehand that we should get no answer to our question about life itself, for these branches of knowledge directly ignore the question of life.[88]

We possess what is very probably an autobiographical account of the mental struggles by which Tolstoy himself came to his conclusion, in the novel *Anna Karenina.* The figure of Konstantin Levin represents, in many ways, Tolstoy's own self-portrait. Throughout the whole long story, Levin is striving to achieve an understanding of his own human situation—in relation to his family, the peasants who work on his estates, his fellow landowners, the Russian people, humanity at large, and finally God— which will permit him to see some meaning in his life and so feel confidence in the principles by which he guides his own conduct. Insofar as it is concerned with Levin's self-development, the whole novel chronicles his successive attempts to find the intellectual foundation for morality for which he is seeking—in public affairs, in marriage, in the rational organization of his own farming methods, and so on. Finally, at the very end of the story, he experiences a kind of conversion. The scales drop from his eyes. A casual conversation with one of his peasants produces in him "the effect of an electric spark, suddenly transforming and welding into one a whole group of disjointed impotent separate ideas," as a result of which he recognizes that his very attempt to base the principles of conduct on *intellectual* foundations had itself been misguided from the very start.[89]

I, and all other men, know only one thing firmly, clearly, and certainly, and this knowledge cannot be explained by reason: it is outside reason, has no cause, and can have no consequences.

If goodness has a cause, it is no longer goodness; if it has a consequence —a reward—it is also not goodness. Therefore goodness is beyond the chain of cause and effect. . . .

I have discovered nothing. I have only perceived what it is that I know. I have understood the Power that not only gave me life in the past but is giving me life now. I have freed myself from deception and learnt to know my master.

I used to say that in my body, in this grass, in this insect . . . there takes place, according to physical, chemical, and physiological laws, a change of matter. . . . And I was surprised that, in spite of the greatest effort of thought on that path, the meaning of life, the meaning of my impulses and my aspirations, was not revealed to me. . . .

I looked for an answer to my question. But reason could not give me an answer—reason is incommensurable with the question. Life itself has given me the answer, in my knowledge of what is good and what is bad. And that knowledge I did not acquire in any way; it was given to me, as to everybody, *given* because I could not take it from anywhere.

The meaning of life is thus a question of a different order from that with which the sciences deal. Tolstoy felt that in his version of Christianity he had found the answer to the problem of the meaning of life. It then became his vocation to teach this to men. The stories and tales of his later years—notably those short parables written between 1872 and 1903, and published together under the title, *Twenty-Three Tales*—are the fruits of his effort to teach morality through literature. These tales are extremely simple parables about simple people, and they exemplify men's major virtues and vices in a very direct, often very moving manner. As such, they are beautiful illustrations of what Kierkegaard had meant by "indirect communication." Their function is to teach Christianity as a way of life that everyone is capable of embracing, and they stress that often the observance of the Christian way of living may conflict with the formal beliefs of Christian doctrine.[90]

Finally, in his book *What Is Art?*, Tolstoy expounded his own theory of art, criticizing the aestheticism and esoteric character of the art of so many of his contemporaries. His attack on aestheticism was based on the idea that this art had become merely a palliative for the upper classes.[91] As these classes lost their faith in Christianity, beauty—that is, their satisfaction or pleasure in form alone—had come to be the sole criterion of "good" and "bad" art. In becoming secularized, art thus fell away from its proper function, the transmission of the artist's perception of the meaning of life. At the same time, the professionalism and academicism of art supported by the upper classes had the effect of estranging it from the common people. The result was an *immoral* art, an art that had forgotten its social obligations. When it became the servant of class interests, art became simply a matter of amusement. For the artist, this meant that sincerity was no longer required of him; with sincerity gone, the artist could produce esoteric works that no longer spoke to the common man; and all of Tolstoy's efforts, in his later years, went into counteracting this tendency. In short, *What Is Art?* represents his polemic against aestheticism on the level of theory, while his *Tales* represent his practical work to reinstate a religion-inspired popular art.

Although the historical continuity from Kant's critical philosophy to Tolstoy's stories is neither complete nor direct, there is a certain logical development, set in motion by Schopenhauer and completed by Kierkegaard, whose final outcome, as we can observe with the wisdom of hindsight (the Owl of Minerva takes wing only at dusk), is best exemplified in Tolstoy's *Tales*. What began as an attempt to chart the limits of reason in all its various spheres of activity ended in an outright denial of the validity of reason within the realm of values. So the attempt to set limits to the scope of the reason resulted ultimately in the assertion that values, morality and the meaning of life can be discussed only beyond the frontiers of rational thought, within the sphere of affectivity, by indirect means only. Despite all the differences between the resulting attitudes toward morality—Kierkegaard's being purely individualist, Tolstoy's collective—they were at any rate alike in strictly rejecting all attempts to give morality "intellectual foundations" in the world of facts—whether in the accepted codes of conventional morals or elsewhere.

In this respect, all the men involved in this development had a natural appeal to a generation of Viennese thinkers, artists and social critics who found themselves, as a class, alienated from the values of the society in which they lived. So, at this point we return to the cultural situation in Vienna at the turn of the century—in particular, to Karl Kraus and those who shared his attitudes in regard to social and artistic "critique" and the "creative separation" of facts and values. Given their own views, the Krausians were naturally receptive to the direction in which the post-Kantians had developed and, of all the post-Kantian philosophers, Arthur Schopenhauer—with the epigrammatic punch and elegant literary style which set him off from his academic and professional colleagues in philosophy—was the most widely read and influential in the Vienna of the 1890s. Before long, he was joined in popularity by Søren Kierkegaard. Meanwhile, as Paul Engelmann reports, there was an equally lively interest in the writings of the novelist-turned-moralist

Tolstoy—notably in his crucial essay *What Is Art?*, which effectively discredited the fashionable aestheticism of the time, and revived interest in art as the main channel of moral communication.

With this historical reconstruction as a background, we can now identify the general intellectual problem which faced men in all fields of thought and art in Vienna in the years just before the First World War—the problem which might well present itself to them as the central problem of philosophy itself. By 1900, we said, the time had already been ripe for a comprehensive critique of language, designed to draw together and generalize, in philosophical terms, all the more localized and particular critiques of established means of expression and communication already familiar in (for example) logic and music, poetry and architecture, painting and physics. Such a philosophical critique must presumably confirm and justify the separation between facts and values as a philosophical necessity, so going far beyond the boundaries of particular fields. Mauthner, with his *Critique,* had made a first attempt to provide such a general philosophical analysis, and up to a point the result was impressive enough. By exploring the ramifications of his nominalist principles, his final *Sprachkritik* certainly ended by supporting the core ethical position held in common by Schopenhauer, Kierkegaard and Tolstoy—namely, the view that the "meaning of life" is not a matter for rational debate, cannot be given "intellectual foundations," and is in essence a "mystical" matter. But it supported this proposition only at a steep price. For, according to Mauthner's arguments, it was not merely the "meaning of life" which ceased to be a possible object of knowledge. His principles had compelled him to deny, also, the possibility of any genuine knowledge going beyond a metaphorical description of the world, even in science and logic.

The road by which Mauthner had reached this conclusion was, however, open to criticism. Instead of mapping the scope and limits of language from within, in an essentially Kantian manner, he had followed the example of Mach: basing his analysis on general principles external to the subject in hand and so giving needless hostages to fortune. So was there any alternative road, by which one could reach the same end point in a more rigorous manner, without having to sacrifice logic and science in the process? An example of what might be done was already available in the work of Hertz and Boltzmann. These men had shown how the logical articulation and empirical application of systematic theories in physical science actually gives one a direct *bildliche Darstellung* of the world, in a sense of that phrase quite different from the *metaphorical description* of Mauthner—namely, a *mathematical model* which, when suitably applied, can yield true and certain knowledge of the world. And they had done so, furthermore, in a way that satisfied Kant's fundamental anti-metaphysical demands—namely, by mapping the limits of the language of physical theory entirely "from within."

For anyone approaching the ethical position of Kierkegaard and Tolstoy with a previous knowledge of Hertz and Boltzmann —for anyone who, with their help, had seen how the descriptive language of scientific theory acquires a "representational" use in the factual inquiries of physics—it was therefore only a single straightforward step to pose the further question:

Is there any method of doing for *language-in-general* what Hertz and Boltzmann have already done for the language of theoretical physics? Is there (that is) some way to map the scope and limits of the "sayable" exhaustively from within, so that *both* it can be seen how descriptive language in general is used to give a *bildliche Darstellung* in the Hertzian sense of a representation in the form of a mathematical model of all matters of fact, *and also* the "transcendent" character of all ethical issues—which make them amenable only to "indirect communication"—at the same time *shows itself* as the by-product of the analysis?[92]

In this question, the critical problems that had been the common concern of social, artistic, scientific and philosophical debate in Vienna, ever since the late 1880s, at last come to a single sharp focus. Philosophically, this question *epitomizes* the whole cultural debate in *fin-de-siècle* Vienna, as we have studied it here. And anyone who produced a completely general *Sprachkritik* which satisfied all these requirements—one which was more rigorous and less open to refutation than Mauthner's—could legitimately feel that, at one stroke, he had succeeded in resolving the central and most pressing intellectual problem of the epoch.

6

The Tractatus *Reconsidered:*
AN ETHICAL DEED

Alle Philosophie ist Sprachkritik.
Allerdings nicht im Sinne Mauthners.

—*Tractatus,* 4.0031

We are here at the nodal point of our argument. At the end of
the introductory chapter, we posed a question about Wittgenstein which, we claimed, would throw light on the real significance of his *Tractatus Logico-Philosophicus,* a question which
explained why, even at the time, this book appeared to be an
epitome or final culmination of the contemporary intellectual debate. This was the following:

What was the philosophical problem by which Wittgenstein was *already*
preoccupied—the problem whose solution he saw as a key to all the outstanding difficulties in philosophy—*before* he even got in touch with
Frege and Russell in the first place?

In the four intervening chapters, we have been reconstructing
a picture of the social and cultural situation in late Habsburg Vienna, indicating the importance of the continuing post-
Kantian critique for the men of that milieu—not just for professional philosophers, but for all educated, thinking men. As
the outcome of this investigation we have recognized (1) that the
need for a general philosophical "critique of language"
(*Sprachkritik*) was already acknowledged in Vienna some fifteen
years before Wittgenstein wrote the *Tractatus;* and (2) that the

shortcomings of Mauthner's first attempt at such a comprehensive *Sprachkritik* had left unresolved one quite specific difficulty, which might nevertheless be overcome, if some method could be found of reconciling the physics of Hertz and Boltzmann with the ethics of Kierkegaard and Tolstoy, within a single consistent exposition. The hypothesis to which our analysis has led is, quite simply, that *this was the problem with which Wittgenstein was originally preoccupied, and which determined the goal at which the writing of his* Tractatus *was directed.*

So far, our inquiries have been progressively narrowing down from a broad study of Habsburg society and its structural problems, by way of certain general preoccupations of *fin-de-siècle* Viennese culture, to the specific difficulties of early-twentieth-century philosophy proper. From this point on, we shall be moving in the reverse direction: seeking first to establish that the *Tractatus* did indeed have the aims and implications we have here proposed, and subsequently exploring the wider ramifications of this hypothesis and the light which the later development of Wittgenstein's own philosophical ideas can throw on more recent cultural and social developments. But, to begin with, we must set about justifying our central hypothesis.

This cannot be done by appealing only to internal evidence, taken from within the text of the *Tractatus*. Wittgenstein's formal arguments—and the reasons why he saw the book as solving, in all essential respects, the outstanding problems of philosophy —are anything but self-explanatory; and, once we have recognized his evident determination to present his analysis by the strictly Kantian method of "mapping from within," that is only to be expected. Anything that he had chosen to say within the book to explain "what his argument was *for*" would have involved a deviation from this Kantian method, so laying him open to avoidable criticism. Yet, if we are ready to look in the right direction, the text itself is by no means devoid of evidence—especially if we are to take the final ten pages of the book as seriously as the previous sixty or sixty-five. Let us merely suppose that, in actual fact, these final ten pages were not intended as a string of *obiter dicta* thrown in as an afterthought or makeweight, but that they are—as their position suggests—meant to be the climax of the book. In that case, a further question immediately arises:

Why, then, did Wittgenstein devote so much of section 6.3 to the relative positions of logic and of theoretical mechanics *à la* Hertz, of section 6.4 to the "transcendental" character of ethics, and of section 6.5 to the problem of the "meaning of life"?

Inevitably, however, much of the argument to confirm our present account of Wittgenstein's pre-Fregean preoccupation depends upon circumstantial evidence. Given the social, cultural and philosophical situation we have depicted here, and given also Ludwig Wittgenstein's own family background and education, he was—we shall see—uniquely placed (1) to feel the full force of that problem, (2) to recognize the possibility of attacking it by the methods of the new propositional logic, and (3) to produce a completely general and formal solution of just the kind he did. True, without the example of Russell and Frege before him, Wittgenstein could never have written the *Tractatus* as we have it. But what Frege and Russell did for him was to provide new techniques, using which he was able to solve his own preconceived problems. If this diagnosis is once accepted, no difficulty remains in reconciling the "logical" and the "ethical" aspects of Wittgenstein's ideas. The *point* of his book—as he himself was in due course to insist—is an *ethical* one; its *formal techniques* alone are drawn from propositional logic. And, once this is recognized, it becomes clear also just why, in addition to being a characteristically Viennese document, the *Tractatus* was a key book for Wittgenstein's contemporaries.

Certainly, Wittgenstein's family situation placed him at the focus of the Austrian quandaries and paradoxes.[1] Ludwig was the youngest child of Karl Wittgenstein, a millionaire industrialist, the peer of Skoda and Krupp in Central Europe, whose home was one of the most important musical salons in the Vienna (and a fortiori the Europe) of his day. In public life, Karl Wittgenstein combined a thoroughgoing knowledge of the latest technological advances with a keen business sense, and he thereby became a giant in Habsburg industry and finance. In private life, he was a great patron of the musical arts, to whose home such musicians as Brahms and Joachim, Mahler, Walter, and the youthful Pablo Casals were no strangers. The elder Wittgenstein was convinced that the only genuine educational foundation for life was a rigorously disciplined course of private tutoring, so his youngest son was educated at home until the age of four-teen. Furthermore, the Wittgensteins seldom went outside their own household to satisfy their cultural wants—a prerogative of the wealthy few. As a result, it is particularly relevant at this point to consider the idiosyncratic atmosphere of the Wittgen-stein family and household itself. (This individual quality helps to explain why the philosopher was so seldom "at home" any-where else.) But, if we are to understand the special character and atmosphere of this household, something more must first be said here about the life and times of Karl Wittgenstein himself.

Karl Wittgenstein was the youngest of the three sons of Her-mann Wittgenstein, a man of solid middle-class background who also had eight daughters and earned his living partly by dealing in wool, partly by purchasing inefficient farms and making them profit-making before selling them. The love of music so char-acteristic of his descendants was by no means lacking in the family of Hermann Wittgenstein. His eldest daughter, Anna, studied piano with Clara Schumann's father, Wieck, and with Brahms; Fine was a *Lieder* singer who studied with prominent practitioners of that art; Clara was a pupil of Goldmark, while Karl himself played the violin and always took his instrument with him on trips away from home, even at the height of his busi-ness career, so that he could play some sonatas before retiring to bed. So it is no surprise that Hermann was well aware of the considerable musical talents of Joseph Joachim, who was his wife's cousin, and whom he raised with his own eleven children; his concern for the thirteen-year-old Joachim, in fact, led Her-mann to send him to Mendelssohn to study. Among his charities, Hermann acted as a patron to other musicians too.

For all his artistic tastes, Hermann was a stern father, who would not permit his absolute authority to be questioned. For example, he rejected a suitor to one of his daughters without consulting her at all. This sternness and inflexibility in due course brought him into conflict with his youngest son. Karl very much desired to attend the Technical Institute in Vienna, but his father considered such an education unsuitable for a gentleman and refused to consider the suggestion at all. How-ever, Karl was his father's son and could be equally intransigent. Since the conflict of wills was apparently irresoluble, there was nothing to do but to escape from his father's influence, and escape he did. In January of 1865, he left Vienna, arriving in

New York in April of that year with nothing but his violin. His stay in the United States lasted for less than two years, and during this time he took various employments. He was a waiter and violinist in a restaurant, a steersman on a canal boat, a bartender, a night watchman, a teacher at an orphanage for destitute children and also at a Christian Brothers school in New York, where he taught Latin, Greek, mathematics, violin and tenor horn!

Karl Wittgenstein's American experience deeply impressed him. Later on, in a series of essays which he wrote as a successful businessman for the *Neue Freie Presse,* filling three volumes, he expressed his admiration for the standard of living attained by the American worker in comparison with his Austrian counterpart.[2] Not without difficulty, a *rapprochement* was arranged between Karl and his father: this led to the return of the twenty-year-old son to Vienna in 1867, on the understanding that he should be allowed to attend the Technical Institute. Over the next twenty years, the financial world of Vienna witnessed the meteoric rise of Karl Wittgenstein to the heights of business success. He had an extraordinary capacity for utilizing his technological knowledge to transform failing factories into booming and productive enterprises. No small part of his success sprang from his fantastic capacity for work—day and night, and days upon end, without rest. By 1895, he was an undisputed master of the technique which came to be known as the "rationalization of industry," eventually dominating the steel industry of the Habsburg Empire, which was located mainly in Bohemia. Taking this devotion to work together with his strict Protestant morality, we can see in Karl Wittgenstein an all-but-perfect representative of Weber's "Protestant Ethic."

In 1872, he met Leopoldine Kalmus, whom he married. The couple had nine children, of whom eight grew to adulthood. Aside from Ludwig, the best-known of these was Paul, who, despite losing his right arm, went on to become a successful concert pianist, commissioning a piano work for one hand by Richard Strauss as well as Maurice Ravel's famous *Concerto for the Left Hand,* to constitute his repertoire. (The determination and discipline so required of him, as well as his steadfast and single-minded devotion to perfection of technique, were integral elements in the heritage of stern Protestant morality characteristic of the world-view which Karl Wittgenstein transmitted to his entire family.) The very fact that Paul and Ludwig, who were the two youngest children, were not considered exceptional by the rest of the family, is itself evidence of the exceptional standards which they all set for themselves.

Karl and Leopoldine's other children were equally talented. The eldest, Hermine, was a painter of no mean ability, whose works reveal a mastery of technique and aesthetic sensibility. Hermine's deep admiration and enthusiasm for Klimt, indeed, prompted Karl Wittgenstein to supply the funds needed for the Secession Building, which bore an inscription recording the fact until Hitler's barbarians effaced it. The second son, Rudi, was similarly inclined to the theater. Margarete, the youngest of the three daughters, was the rebel of the family and its brightest intellectual light. At a time when her parents could recognize only the merits of the established classics—Latin and German— she was immersed in the shocking "modernism" of Ibsen; nor did she shy away from abstruse theories in philosophy, social sciences and the humanities. She became a close friend of Sigmund Freud, and she helped Marie Bonaparte to arrange his escape from Austria after Hitler's *Anschluss*. It was very likely Margarete who put the writings of her favorite philosopher, Schopenhauer, as well as those of Weininger and Kierkegaard, into the hands of her youngest brother, for she kept her finger always on the pulse of intellectual and cultural life.

For the Wittgensteins as a family, however, culture was preeminently musical culture. Leopoldine Wittgenstein—"Poldy," as she was affectionately called—was herself an accomplished pianist. It was she who brought the blind organist and composer, Josef Labor, to their home; and, to the end of his days, her youngest son, Ludwig, was to admire Labor's music, which is sadly too little known today. Kurt Wittgenstein, the third son, was a cellist; but the most talented of the children, musically, was Hans, the eldest son, who played several instruments like a virtuoso. It was with Hans that the drama played out in the previous generation between the father and grandfather was to be re-enacted, this time with tragic consequences.

The attitude of the Wittgensteins toward their Jewish heritage further complicated matters. Although Karl Wittgenstein's children adopted his Protestant outlook on life, they thought of themselves as entirely *Jewish* by extraction. A story is told that one of Karl Wittgenstein's sisters once approached her brother

Louis, the prominent Protestant presbyter, in a state of perplexity, asking him if the rumors about the family's Jewish blood were true. Louis is said to have replied, *"Pur sang,* Milli, *pur sang!"* They identified with what they took to be a tradition of aesthetic idealism in Judaism, although still remaining very much apart from its religious teachings and observances. The identification penetrated their character so deeply that Margarete Stonborough (Wittgenstein's youngest sister) insisted upon being jailed with other Viennese Jews after the *Anschluss, over the expressed objections of the Nazis,* who were content to consider her and her family non-Jews. These conflicts of religious loyalty were, however, by no means the main source of family stress. The fact was that Karl Wittgenstein was prepared to allow his sons even less choice than his father had granted him in deciding on their life's work. He insisted that Hans's extraordinary musical talents must be sacrificed to a career in finance and industry, following in his footsteps. Here the *fin-de-siècle* generation gap—with the more practical father pitted against the artist son—was evident once again and was made tragic by the fact that Hans had inherited his father's determination. Even as a youth, when his father forbade him to play upon the family instruments, he would slip away to church to play the organ. Since father and son were simply unable to communicate, Hans could eventually no longer bear to go on living in his father's house. Like Karl before him, he had to escape, and escape he did, also to North America, where he met a tragic end, probably committing suicide.

Incredible as this may seem, this episode does not appear to have affected Karl—at least, his attitude did not change in any observable manner. When his second son, Rudi, committed suicide in similar circumstances, the impact on him was more pronounced. Whether or not this event would have produced a lasting change in his attitudes is impossible to tell, for he himself died of cancer in 1913, and so did not live to hear of the suicide in 1918 of his third son, Kurt, who killed himself after his defeated troops deserted on the Italian front. Thus, Ludwig Wittgenstein's elusive remarks about suicide, in his *Notebooks of 1914–1916,* and the references to his own thoughts of suicide in his correspondence with Engelmann, are in no sense idle speculation on a tragic subject.[8] Similarly, with his reflections on his "lack of decency" in the Engelmann correspondence; these must be considered in the light of the morality of absolute duty, with its total opposition to all sham and compromise, which permeated the cast of mind characteristic of the whole Wittgenstein patrimony.

Evidently, then, we scarcely need to *prove* that Wittgenstein was personally exposed to the crises in art, morality, and even family life, that were the central sources of cultural and ethical debate in prewar Vienna. Rather, the burden of proof is the other way. Given that the very house in which he grew up was itself such a cultural center and comprised within itself many of the crucial tensions out of which this debate issued, he would have had to insulate himself quite consciously, in order to avoid being immediately aware of the discussions which were being so vigorously carried on around him.

In one final respect, also, Ludwig Wittgenstein's background and upbringing were, from our present point of view, remarkable. We have referred already to Karl Wittgenstein's peculiar opinions about the only genuine bases for a first-rate education. Instead of sending his children away to school, he had had them educated at home by tutors, which made it possible for Ludwig to develop his intellectual powers at his own pace. This was also a determining factor in his later education. Without Greek, the humanistic *Gymnasium* was closed to him; as a result, he ended up attending the Linz *Realschule* beginning in 1904—just about the same time, incidentally, that the young Adolf Hitler left that same institution! In view of the extraordinary talent he had already displayed for constructing things—at the age of ten, he made a model sewing machine out of matchsticks that actually worked, the only special talent he displayed as a child—he naturally chose to study engineering at Linz. At this point, it is important not to be misled by irrelevant associations. In Britain and America, the training of engineers has always had a much more practical emphasis than it has in Continental Europe, and especially in the German-speaking countries. In Zurich, in Berlin and Vienna, the prime intellectual foundation demanded of a first-rate engineer around 1900 was a thorough intellectual grasp of theoretical physics, especially Newtonian mechanics. So the first goal that a young man in Ludwig Wittgenstein's position had to set himself was a proper understanding of mathematics, especially in its application to physics. (In this respect, Ludwig Wittgenstein had the same *formation pro-*

fessionelle as a Swiss "engineer" only a few years older than he, Albert Einstein.)[4]

Accordingly, Heinrich Hertz's book *The Principles of Mechanics* will have come into Wittgenstein's hands in the ordinary course of his education. And it will have done so, not just as one more textbook among others, but as the authoritative and magisterial analysis of fundamental ideas about the physical world. The admiration that Wittgenstein conceived for Hertz in his youth was something he never lost. Later in life, we find him entering reservations about almost everyone else—even about Frege[5]—but, right up to the end of his years, he continued to quote Hertz with approval and agreement. As for Ludwig Boltzmann, we have already remarked on the echoes of Boltzmann apparent in Wittgenstein's remarks about "logical space"; and the moment he returned to active philosophy, from 1927 on, he took up this particular topic again.[6] If the late lamented Heinrich Hertz gave Wittgenstein his first magisterial example in physics, Boltzmann was the man he hoped to learn from directly, when the time came to leave Linz in 1906—only to be frustrated by Boltzmann's suicide at Duino in September of that year.[7]

By now, we also have a good deal of evidence about Wittgenstein's broader interests. Music was the chief of these. Schopenhauer used to argue that the musician somehow possessed a power, which the metaphysician inevitably lacked, to transcend the limits of representations and to convey deeper feelings, attitudes and convictions, which the verbal language of formal philosophy strives in vain to express. In his more relaxed moments, Wittgenstein used in later life to discuss the expressive power of music—a topic which continued to fill him with philosophical perplexity—in terms which allotted to it little less significance than Schopenhauer had given it.[8] Philip Radcliffe, lecturer in music at King's College, Cambridge, describes how during Wittgenstein's time as professor of philosophy at Cambridge he used to bring him bulky scores to play over on the piano—notably, some forgotten works by his mother's old friend Josef Labor. Wittgenstein placed importance on the precise manner in which the scores were played, and seemingly found in them something of that preterlinguistic significance that Schopenhauer had claimed. Nor was his range of musical tastes and interests limited or conventional. Hearing that G. E. Moore's younger son, Timothy, had organized a successful jazz "combo,"

Wittgenstein persuaded him to sit at the piano and explain at great length the structure and development—what Schönberg would have called the "logic"—of jazz.[9]

Within philosophy itself, by contrast, Wittgenstein seems to have read comparatively little. Like Schönberg in music and Kokoschka in painting, he set no store by professionalism and saw himself as none the worse for being a self-taught philosopher. One of the few philosophical writers who impressed him from early on was Georg Christoph Lichtenberg. Lichtenberg, an eighteenth-century professor of natural philosophy at Göttingen, had been admired by Kraus and was a major influence on Mach too. Lichtenberg's writings became very popular among Viennese intellectuals at the turn of the century.[10] Even more than Schopenhauer, he set the aphoristic style of philosophizing that became fashionable at this period, of which the aphorisms of the *Tractatus* are only one illustration. He wrote about both theoretical physics and the philosophy of language, indeed, in a spirit which (as Wright has said) shows "a striking resemblance to Wittgenstein."[11]

(To anticipate a point about Wittgenstein's later ideas: Lichtenberg's writings were also the source of the term "paradigm," which played so large a part in Wittgenstein's later discussions. Lichtenberg used the notion of *paradeigmata* to link the formal patterns of grammatical analysis in linguistics with those of theoretical analysis in physics. Just as in grammar we relate the declension of nouns and the conjugation of verbs to certain general, standardized forms, or *paradigms,* so too we "explain" natural phenomena in physics by relating puzzling events and processes to certain standard and self-explanatory forms or patterns. This notion of *paradigms*—by which our thought can be either directed fruitfully, or alternatively misled—has a central place in Wittgenstein's later accounts of "logical grammar" and its role in philosophy.)[12]

Finally, as for Wittgenstein's own contemporaries in Vienna, we know directly of his admiration for Weininger, Kraus and Loos. In particular, he was personally acquainted with the architect Adolf Loos, whose ideas about ornament and decoration were so congenial with his own and whose conceptions of "function" throw light on Wittgenstein's own later excursions into the architectural field.

Like so many of his contemporaries, Ludwig Wittgenstein was

swept up in the Kierkegaard revival, which was associated with
the Brenner Circle in general, and with Theodor Haecker in particular, though it was Tolstoy who seems to have exerted the
deepest and most direct moral influence upon him. From the very
beginning, he was undoubtedly a man of great moral earnestness.
(As his father's son, how could he have been anything else?)
Thus, in writing about Moore, Russell and their associates, who
were later to be the core of the Bloomsbury group, John Maynard Keynes bracketed "Ludwig" with D. H. Lawrence as having objected to the brittleness, superficiality, and above all the
irreverence, of these young Cambridge intellectuals.[18] Wittgenstein's natural gravity was greatly enhanced by his experience
during the war. Just as his family had seen in him a happy sunny
child, so his English acquaintances from before 1914 knew him
as capable of great gaiety and sparkling intelligence; at that
time, any shadows there may have been were normally below the
surface. From 1919 on, he became a lonely and introverted figure.
He admitted to having been impressed by Oswald Spengler's
Decline of the West, and he retreated more and more into ethical
attitudes of extreme individualism and austerity. For Wittgenstein as for Tolstoy, the demands of personal integrity were
associated with a theoretical commitment to an absolute egalitarianism and an overriding concern with his brother men. Yet
this commitment remained largely theoretical. His normal habit
of life was that of a recluse, and it was only during the Second
World War that his convictions had a chance to express themselves practically, in his decision to take up war work in the
most menial of occupations, as a hospital porter and orderly.

To begin our reinterpretation of the *Tractatus,* we can best
indicate how its preoccupations grew out of Wittgenstein's upbringing and cultural background by considering his connections
with Ludwig Ficker and the group of young avant-garde
intellectuals which was centered around Ficker's periodical *Der
Brenner,* published in Innsbruck, and more particularly, with the
work of Theodor Haecker, with which Wittgenstein explicitly
identified his own tasks in the *Tractatus.*

Haecker's career as a writer was largely devoted to making
the name of Kierkegaard the household word that it has since
become. When he published his first monograph, *Søren Kierkegaard and the Philosophy of Subjectivity,* Kierkegaard was still

all but unknown, and Haecker's activities as an expositor have been in no small measure responsible for the new twentieth-century enthusiasm for Kierkegaard. In this first monograph, Haecker—among other things—draws a direct and open contrast between Kierkegaard and Mauthner, as between the true "critique of language" and its counterfeit.[14] A little unfairly, he dismisses Mauthner as an armchair skeptic, whose life was unaffected by his philosophy. As Haecker saw it, Mauthner merely embraced skepticism as an intellectual thesis, rather than as an existential posture, and therefore had more in common with Descartes than with Pascal. By contrast, Kierkegaard's skepticism was existential and filled with *Angst*. In spelling out just how Kierkegaard was the genuine skeptic and the genuine critic of language, Haecker may thus have drawn Wittgenstein's attention once again to the problems which Mauthner's critique of language either had left unsolved or, more significantly, had failed to raise at all.

As Kierkegaard came in due course to discover, however, these very questions are in principle unanswerable. The problem of life, the meaning of human existence, is the sole object of his contemplation; yet it is impossible for reason, his own tool, to find any solution to the resulting paradoxes of life. Reason can only lead Kierkegaard to paradox; faith is needed to overcome it. This is the task of the "subjective" thinker—to attain the higher sort of truth which is beyond reason and once again integrates life and thought. Within the terms of factual description, subjective truth—the truth that is life, moral truth—is incommunicable. The subjective thinker, who would possess and teach values, must assume the intellectual posture of Socrates; irony, satire, comedy and polemic are the instruments of "indirect communication" and so the means to this end. The true critique of language, says Haecker, consists not in studying words in Mauthner's manner, but in transforming language from an instrument of practical utility into an instrument of the spirit which will change people's lives. In this sense, Haecker presented Kierkegaard as a "language philosopher" who, like Tolstoy, viewed art as man's means of access to the realm of the spirit.

Among his contemporaries Haecker acknowledged one such subjective thinker:

Probably one person is capable of leading a life of the spirit unnoticed, and he comes infinitely closer to this than most people writing today, who have at bottom only two possibilities of proving their honor in his presence: silence and self-deprecation. Indeed, without having to think twice, a name occurs to me instantly: Karl Kraus.[15]

Kraus was the true disciple of Kierkegaard without even knowing his name, in Haecker's opinion, for Kraus continued Kierkegaard's work in his satires and polemics. Kraus, like Kierkegaard, knew all too well that ethics is not a science of morality, nor a branch of knowledge like geometry or chemistry. Ethics has nothing to do with facts. Its basis is the subjectivity of conviction, and its sphere is not that of science but that of the paradoxical. Kraus further agreed with Kierkegaard that the unity of form and content in a work of art was absolutely essential. Aesthetic form and ethical content are two faces of the same coin. Only the good man knows what values are, and only he can communicate them. No amount of scientific knowledge can ever make a man good. On Kierkegaard's and Kraus's view of ethics, Haecker insists, the notion of "moral sciences" (*Geisteswissenschaften*) presents a contradiction in terms. Ethics is rooted in the paradoxical, and there can be no science of the paradoxical. Only the aphorism was equal to expressing the immediacy of the ethical. Thus Haecker's ideal for a critique of language was to be found in the aphorisms and polemics of Kraus, who was Kierkegaard *redivivus.*

However, even though in Haecker's eyes Karl Kraus might represent the best practical exponent of a Kierkegaardian "critique of language," that did nothing to resolve the problem left over by Mauthner's analysis—the problem of reconciling, so to say, Hertz and Boltzmann on the one hand with Kierkegaard and Tolstoy on the other. As an engineer trained in the physics of Hertz and Boltzmann, Wittgenstein was well aware that, despite the philosophical skepticism of a man like Mauthner, a "representational" language was not impossible; in physics, at least, it was possible to represent natural phenomena meaningfully in a *bildliche Darstellung,* if that phrase could be radically reinterpreted in the sense of Hertz. The proof of this lay in the very fact that those same principles which physicists speak of theoretically are also applied practically in the construction of machines. As an enthusiastic Hertzian, then, Wittgenstein knew that *Darstellungen*—in the form of *Bilder* or "models"—were possible in mechanics. In fact, the certitude by which mechanics could be distinguished from the rest of human knowledge and regarded as the most fundamental branch of physics was a consequence of the mathematical structure which the physicist imposes on mechanical phenomena in the process of constructing his "models" of those phenomena.

Furthermore, these representations have the advantage of being self-limiting, in that the range of their applicability is largely determined by their mathematical form. So there existed one area of language, at least—namely, the language of mechanics— which was sufficiently univocal and well-structured to convey "facts" about the world, that is, to provide a "representation" of the world, in the form of a mathematical *Bild*. The univocity of this language, and its consequent capacity to remain free of ambiguity, were direct results of its mathematical structure, its form. This form did not arise out of experience; yet neither was it the product of arbitrary conventions and definitions. Rather, it was imposed upon experience in such a way as to order it economically—the feature which had been the source of Mach's praise for Hertz's *Principles*. Thus, as Wittgenstein was in a first-hand position to know, Mauthner's conception of knowledge was directly challenged by the Hertzian representation of the language of mechanics, in the form of a mathematical model. And, if one could only establish a corresponding—but all-embracing—"mathematics of language," it might then be possible to carry through a "critique of language" which would explain "from within" the nature and limits of language in general in the same way that Hertz had been able to transform the critique of mechanics, placing it on a philosophically secure basis by considering its *mathematical structure,* rather than studying the *psychological and historical development* of its concepts, as Mach and Mauthner had done.

The central task of Hertz's own treatise on *The Principles of Mechanics* thus had curious parallels with the one that was now engaging Wittgenstein. Hertz had been concerned to explain how, at one and the same time, the classical theory of Newtonian dynamics can both form a mathematical system of axioms and deductions, and describe the *actual* world of nature, as contrasted with all *logically conceivable* worlds; and this is a topic to which Wittgenstein was subsequently to devote an unusually sustained passage in the *Tractatus,* in Propositions 6.34 to 6.3611. If only, Hertz had argued, one distinguishes with sufficient care between the formal steps by which such a mathematical calculus is articulated and the empirical or pragmatic steps by which the resulting axiom system is applied in actual experience, that question will answer itself.[16] Furthermore, it will do so in a way that circumvents many fruitless and confused metaphysical debates—for example, those disputes about "the essential nature of force" which had disfigured and obstructed the development of nineteenth-century physical science.

If Wittgenstein was to establish a comprehensive "model" theory of language, we have said, he needed a similar "mathematics of language," which could account for its formal structure in completely general terms. It was at this point that he might naturally turn to the work of Frege and Russell. For the philosophical program in Russell's early writings could immediately be read as providing the means of solving the generalized form of Hertz's problem. Suppose one reconstructed language as Russell proposed, on an explicitly defined formal model, and arrived in this way at a "propositional calculus" capable of expressing the real forms of propositions; the resulting formalism would enable one to *show* how the internal structures of language represent the corresponding structures by which "objects" in the real world are linked together into "facts." So Russell's claim that the real logical form of propositions is often disguised by the misleading grammatical garb of natural languages—and that this real form is best captured by expressing it in the logical symbolism of *Principia Mathematica*—gave Wittgenstein his essential clue. By using the "propositional calculus" as a formal model of language, it would be possible to construct a critique of language of a new kind, which would escape the criticisms incurred by Mauthner's earlier effort. This is why Wittgenstein contrasts his own work with Mauthner's, in terms that appeal to Russell's new distinction between "apparent" and "real" logical form.

All philosophy is a "critique of language" (though not in Mauthner's sense). It was Russell who performed the service of showing that the apparent logical form of the proposition need not be its real one.[17]

The logical symbolism of Russell and Frege was thus the *means* by which Wittgenstein could now provide a generalized critique of language capable of doing justice both to Hertz and to Kierkegaard. In particular, Russell's "propositional calculus," of which Mauthner had been ignorant, gave him precisely the "logic of language" he needed. In their revision of logic on the basis of mathematics, Russell and Frege had summoned up powerful arguments against the kind of "psychological reductionism" characteristic of Mauthner's rejection of logic. Frege in particular devoted much of his efforts to this antipsychologistic task, and his monograph on *Concept Writing* (*Begriffsschrift*) was the first attempt to systematize mathematical logic; Whitehead and Russell's *Principia Mathematica* provided a well-ordered compendium of such a system. Here, then, was a basis for the new "calculus of language" that Wittgenstein sought.

Mauthner's arguments, being basically nominalistic, had attempted to demonstrate the limits of language by means of a theory *about* language; they thus contained an element of circularity. In this respect, they resembled Mach's critique of mechanics, which was based on a psychological theory *about* mechanical concepts. Hertz's critique of mechanics was far more penetrating than Mach's, because he was able to focus clearly upon the structure of these concepts as they are *used*. His position entailed an understanding of the nature and limits of mechanics from within the discipline. He did not have to take refuge in theories *about* mechanics; the limits of mechanical explanation were evident, once the structure of its concepts was elucidated, and did not require further demonstration. The model (*Bild*) simply displayed the limitations on its own application. With a propositional calculus at his disposal, Wittgenstein could eliminate the corresponding circularity, which—as Mauthner had admitted—characterized the earlier critique. In this way, one could expound the nature and limits of language in terms of its structure; the limits of language could be made evident and did not have to be stated explicitly. These are precisely the merits Wittgenstein claims on behalf of his so-called "picture theory of language."

British and American interpretations of the *Tractatus* have suffered as a result of difficulties over the German word *Bild* and its associated word forms, *abbilden* et cetera. When writing in English, philosophers have tended to discuss Wittgenstein's "picture" theory as though it invited us to think of "propositions'' as providing, so to say, *snapshots*—or even *mental images* —of ''facts.'' Such an interpretation misses two central points about Wittgenstein's discussion of *Bilder*. In the first place, all his discussions of the relation between propositions and facts are given in active, constructive terms. In the revised translation of the *Tractatus*, for instance, the crucial Proposition 2.1 is rendered into English as ''we picture facts to ourselves.''[18] whereas the original German says, ''Wir machen uns Bilder der Tatsachen.'' A *Bild*, or ''picture,'' is for Wittgenstein something which we make, or produce, as an artifact; just as the painter produces an ''artistic representation'' of a scene or person, so too we ourselves construct, in language, ''propositions'' having the same forms as the facts they picture. And, again and again, we understand Wittgenstein's aphorisms better if we think of linguistic *Bilder* as ''deliberately constructed verbal representations,'' instead of misleading ourselves by the use of the much looser English term ''pictures.''

In the second place, too, the current translations of the *Tractatus* conceal the essential continuity between Hertz's uses of the term *Bild* in physics and Wittgenstein's in philosophy. Just as we understand Hertz's account of theoretical mechanics best if we translate his word *Bild* as ''model,'' so also with the *Tractatus;* for example, Wittgenstein's notion that a gramophone record, the musical idea, the written notes, and the sound waves, are related to one another by virtue of a common *abbildenden internen Beziehung* (4.014) is best understood in terms of a common ''model,'' rather than of a ''picture.'' The spatial order presented in a picture is of a very different type from the logical order characteristic of a theoretical or mathematical model in natural science. Like their Hertzian counterparts, again, Wittgenstein's models are referred to as ''representations,'' in the sense of *Darstellungen;* this too helps to underline the fact that they are logical constructs and, so, totally different from reproductions of sensory experience, or *Vorstellungen*. Indeed, although the verb form *stellen vor* appears in the *Tractatus* twice, alongside the more frequent *stellen dar*, *Vorstellungen* as such are never mentioned.

The term *Darstellungen* covers ''models'' in the widest sense. It embraces architects' blueprints, children's model toys, painted portraits (though not photographs), and all sorts of patterns; mathematical models (*Bilder*) thus constitute only one species of representations or *Darstellungen.* Wittgenstein emphasizes the logical structure of his models when he says, "Every model is *at the same time* a logical one. (On the other hand not every model is, for example, a spatial one.)"[19] He emphasizes the fact that his models are constructed when he says, "We *make* models of facts for ourselves,"[20] and that a model is "laid against reality like a measure."[21] Indeed, in his *Notebooks* he claims that

the world could be completely described by completely general propositions, and hence without using any sort of names or other denoting sign. And in order to arrive at ordinary language one would only need to introduce names, etc., by saying after an "$(\exists x)$," "and this x is A" and so on.[22]

Here he implies that it should be possible to create a "logical scaffolding," or *logisches Gerüst*—that is, an a priori system capable of modeling the whole world and, so, of furnishing the logical structure of all description. If this were done, it would do for language in general what the first part of Hertz's *Principles* had done for the language of mechanics. By introducing names into this general system, we could then apply it to reality. The result would be "ordinary language"; and this, Wittgenstein claimed, is what we in fact do. So he saw himself as having universalized Hertz's approach to the language of mechanics in such a way that it became applicable to all discourse; and he had thus been able to execute the very *bildliche Darstellung der Welt* that, in virtue of its isomorphic character, went far beyond a mere metaphorical description.

In order to understand just how Wittgenstein's models "represent" experience, it is necessary to look at their mode of modeling—that is, at the way in which these models are constructed. Propositions are representations that we make of situations or arrangements of objects, more commonly called "facts." They are not exact reproductions of these facts, but only of what is *essential* in them—objects designated by names, and the logical relationships between them represented by connectives. Thus, Wittgenstein says:

The fact that the elements of a model are related to one another in a determinate way represents that things are related to one another in the same way. Let us call this connection of its elements the *structure* of the models, and let us call the possibility of this structure its *form of modeling.*[23]

He adds: "Only the end points of the graduating lines actually *touch* the object that is to be measured."[24] In this respect, Wittgenstein's models resemble Hertz's ones, which also model only what is essential to the structure of the corresponding phenomena. Beyond naming objects and describing their configuration, Wittgenstein's models cannot, in principle, assert anything about them. The determinate relationship between names or symbols is the *sense* of a proposition. "What a model represents is its sense";[25] this is what it *shows* about the symbols. If the objects to which the name or symbols refer (*bedeuten*) actually have this configuration, the proposition is true, and the model is correct; if not, it is false, and the model is incorrect. In either case, "in order to tell whether a model is true or false, we must compare it with reality."[26]

Two things, accordingly, are essential to Wittgenstein's model theory of language: a correspondence theory of truth, and the assumption that there exists a sufficient "isomorphism" (*Verbindung*) between language and reality to permit—and validate —all our descriptive use of language. The logical structure of language makes it possible for us to ascertain a priori that certain configurations of objects are, or are not, "possible." This is the function of "truth tables" in Wittgenstein's system; they establish the a priori truth possibilities of any model. Given all the possible "truth values" for the symbols a proposition contains, it can be determined which of these are truth possibilities, given the sense of the proposition—that is, what relation it asserts or denies to hold between the symbols. This is how "a model presents a situation in logical space."[27] It determines a certain configuration of objects by asserting or denying a logical connection between symbols; and by assigning all possible truth values to these symbols, the conditions under which the proposition *can* be true or false are established. Thus "a proposition can determine only one place in logical space; nevertheless, the whole of logical space must already be given."[28]

As we remarked earlier, Wittgenstein's "logical space" is similar to a coordinate system in theoretical physics. Any one set of coordinates presupposes the whole system. Indeed, the spatial metaphor is similar to that of "phase space" in statistical mechanics.[29] The latter is an artificial space of $6n$ dimensions, where n is the number of molecules in a given volume of a given gas. The $6n$ dimensions represent the microscopic state of the gas, as defined by the position and momentum of each molecule at a given instant. (Thus the $6n$—three coordinates for the position of any molecule, and three for its momentum.) This notion of phase space is a device for representing all possible states of the individual molecules, and it furnishes the a priori probabilities from which the most probable macroscopic state can be computed by means of the probability calculus. In the light of Wittgenstein's scientific background and his expressed interest in the work of Ludwig Boltzmann, this similarity of metaphor is certainly more than a coincidence.[30]

The model theory of propositions and the theory of truth associated with it had one further advantage. It was also capable of dealing with a problem which initially had been raised by Meinong but had not been solved to the satisfaction of logicians. Briefly: suppose that we are given a proposition such as, "The pot of gold at the end of the rainbow is full," and asked whether it is true or it is false. Either answer is unsatisfactory, for either of them seems to imply that there indeed exists a pot of gold at the end of the rainbow. Meinong held that affirmative propositions with "sense" must have "reference"; his reason for maintaining this was a belief that *names* continued to refer to things, whether or not they were functioning as symbols in a *proposition*. For do not names convey a meaning—that is, have a sense of their own? Meinong inferred, there must exist somewhere a realm comprising such possible objects of reference as golden mountains, reigning kings of France, and pots of gold at the end of the rainbow; and Russell's celebrated "theory of descriptions" was an attempt to extricate logicians from this morass.

Wittgenstein proceeded from Hertz's view of models and followed Russell's theory of meaning which made the meaning of *propositions* prior to that of *names*. For him, propositions "model" situations relating objects in configurations; the sense of the proposition is the logical relation it expresses between the symbols. If the objects for which the constituent symbols or names stand form the configuration which the logical relation "models," then the proposition is true; if this is not the case, it is false. "Only propositions have sense; only in the nexus of a proposition does a name have reference."[31] Names on their own are without sense; it is only in the context of the logical relations between them that they are intelligible. Thus, thanks to the model theory of propositions, Wittgenstein was able to incorporate into his new critique of language a yet more elegant solution to a critical problem in logical theory also.

With this logical problem in mind, it is worthwhile asking, "Just how did Ludwig Wittgenstein stand *as a logician* in relation to Gottlob Frege and Bertrand Russell?" Russell himself took it for granted that Wittgenstein was, first and foremost, his own pupil and disciple; and he became disillusioned with Wittgenstein later on, when his own natural philosophical development took him off in uncongenial directions. Other commentators, such as Elizabeth Anscombe, have seen Wittgenstein as a follower of Frege. Certainly, they allow, Wittgenstein introduced a number of important logical novelties, but Frege was his essential starting point and must be kept in the center of attention if Wittgenstein's logical techniques are to be properly understood.

Our own analysis, however, suggests yet a third possibility: this is, that Wittgenstein was, all along, an independent and original contributor to philosophical logic. He was, of course, deeply indebted to Frege and Russell for inaugurating the whole program of symbolic logic and the propositional calculus; but he had come to logic and the philosophy of language from his own, independent starting point, and he had developed his own original standpoint for dealing with the problems that were in the center of his mind. Even in logic itself, he was in fact indebted to Frege and Russell more for their methods and for his initial stimulus than for the detailed doctrines which he subsequently developed. And, when the occasion arose, he could himself be quite critical of his colleagues in logic. In a retrospective conversation with Waismann in 1929, for instance, he made a remark which was —philosophically—highly damaging to both men:

In constructing symbolic logic, Frege, Peano and Russell always had their eye on its application to mathematics alone, and they never gave any thought to the representation [*Darstellung*] of real states of affairs [*Sachverhalte*].[32]

For his own part, the use of language within pure mathematics was always of secondary interest. From the beginning, it was his goal to establish a formal "theory of language" capable of showing how propositions succeed in representing real states of affairs and serving the purposes of real life.

Wittgenstein's critique of language is based, then, upon the logic inherent in ordinary language; just as Schönberg had sought the essence of music in the logic of composition. The propositional calculus becomes for him the a priori "scaffolding" of language and, so, the basis for any scientific description of the real world. Logic makes the very existence of a describable world possible, simply by making description itself possible. Just as, in Kant, the understanding creates the order in nature, logic makes Wittgenstein's "world" possible, by providing it with a form—"It is obvious that an imagined world, however different it may be from the real one, must have *something*—a form—in common with it."[33] To put the same point negatively: "We could not *say* what an 'illogical' world would look like."[34] Here the link between the logical form of propositions and Wittgenstein's critique of language comes sharply into focus. "What a model must have in common with reality, in order to be able to model it—correctly or incorrectly—in the way that it does, is the *form* of modeling";[35] and again, "A model cannot, however, model the form of modeling; it displays it."[36] And finally, "What *can* be shown *cannot* be said."[37]

At this point in Wittgenstein's analysis, however, a fundamental difficulty presents itself. Russell had been prepared to take for granted the possibility of expressing the "real" logical forms of propositions capable of describing the real world in the symbolism of the propositional calculus, and he was accordingly content to reconstruct language on an explicitly defined mathematical model, without paying close attention to its actual application. Yet, what guarantee was there that the resulting formalism had any application to our actual descriptive language, and through it to the real world? Calling Russell's formal system by the name of "the propositional calculus" was all very well; but this begged the fundamental question, instead of answering it. (Treating the formal expressions of the system as propositions, without further ado, was merely arbitrary.) What had to be shown, further, was on what conditions such a formally defined calculus could serve a *propositional* function at all. As Hilbert and Hertz had demonstrated, no axiomatic system can by itself *say* anything about the world. If such a system is to perform a propositional—that is, a linguistic—function, something more is required: it is necessary to demonstrate, in addition, that the relations actually holding between language and the world make such a formalization possible.

As Wittgenstein very soon saw, his own fundamental principles were such that this could not be demonstrated. The possibility of relating propositions to facts was something which might *show itself,* and which might therefore be *seen;* yet there could be no question of asserting or of "proving" it. In this one respect, Wittgenstein's general critique of language was in a different position from Hertz's more specialized critique of theoretical physics. In the case of physics, it was legitimate enough to analyze explicitly the relations between the language of physical theory and the natural phenomena it is used to explain; this could be done in a language other than that of the theory under discussion, without presupposing the very thing that it was meant to justify. In the case of language-as-a-whole, by contrast, no "extralinguistic language" was—in the nature of the case—available in which to conduct the critical analysis required. Russell's program required one to assume, at one and the same time, *both* that the "true structure" of language is "propositional" in the required, formalizable sense, *and* that the real world is describable by means of such a language. These assumptions, as Wittgenstein saw, were substantial ones; yet what more could legitimately be said to clarify the situation? Once the validity of using language to describe the world at all was called into question, we did not improve matters by using this same language in the attempt to describe and validate the relations *between* language and the world. That whole enterprise, he hinted, would be a kind of Indian rope trick—like trying to climb up an unsupported ladder and hold it up at the same time.

This dilemma is fundamental to our understanding of the *Tractatus.* At this early stage, Wittgenstein evidently accepted Russell's program as being legitimate and worthwhile not only for mathematics, but also for philosophy. Initially, his questions about the applicability of the propositional calculus reflected no active doubts; on the contrary. Yet his quandary was genuine. He might urge his readers to think of the world as being "composed of the totality of facts, not of things";[38] of the unit elements in a fact as "fit[ting] into one another like the links in a chain,"[39] and so on, and so on. Yet, if he were challenged to explain *why* we must suppose that language is related to the world in that particular way, he was—on his own confession—in no position to give any literal reply. If the propositional calculus is to provide the sole instrument for making literal, meaningful statements, one can then speak *about* its linguistic role only figuratively. In a manner of speaking, therefore, the whole *Tractatus* had been (as he acknowledged later) a kind of Platonic myth. Rather than provide a straightforward theoretical account of the relation between language and the world, for which any literal defense could be given, it had given at best a helpful image, capable of providing insight into the nature of the language–world relationship—but one which, in the long run, had to be transcended. The propositional calculus had attracted Wittgenstein, in the first place, as the intellectual instrument required for a fully rigorous "critique" of language in general. By the time he had finished, it turned out to have given him only the scaffolding for an elaborate metaphor.[40] Unless one *saw* the possibility of modeling "facts" by "propositions" having the same "real logical form," no independent demonstration was possible to prove that the propositional calculus can be used to describe real "states of affairs."

In the last resort, then, the relationship between language and the world itself became, for Wittgenstein, as *ineffable* as all other nonfactual considerations. Propositions were capable of modeling and, so, describing reality; but they could not simultaneously describe *how* they describe it, without becoming self-referential and consequently meaningless. Wittgenstein's models *showed* the limits of what they were capable of *saying:* they modeled the way things were in the world, and accordingly made scientific knowledge of phenomena possible, but they could do nothing more. This was clear from the nature of the models themselves; they were not even *capable* of representing anything that was not factual. Thus Wittgenstein says, "And so it is impossible for there to be propositions of ethics"; and he at once goes on to add—rather startlingly—"Propositions can express nothing that is *higher*."[41] This very last word indicates that, in one crucial respect, the content of the *Tractatus* had been radically incomplete. The word "higher" intimates that there is more to the doctrine of "showing" than the model theory, for Wittgenstein goes on to pronounce in the next proposition that—

like logic—''Ethics is transcendental.''[42] At this point, the circle of Wittgenstein's argument closes itself, and we are brought face to face once again with what is, *for him,* the fundamental point and purpose of the entire ''critique.''

The problem on which Wittgenstein embarked—according to our hypotheses—was that of constructing a general critique of language capable of showing, at one and the same time, *both* that logic and science had a proper part to play within ordinary descriptive language, by which we produce a representation of the world analogous to a mathematical model of physical phenomena, *and* that questions about ''ethics, value and the meaning of life,'' by falling outside the limits of this descriptive language, become—at best—the objects of a kind of mystical insight, which can be conveyed by ''indirect'' or poetical communication. The first part of his task had been accomplished by extending Hertz's analysis of *Bilder* and *Darstellung* in the language of physical science, using Frege and Russell's propositional calculus as the framework for this extension. The second part of his task could scarcely be accomplished in words at all, except in a negative way. As Paul Engelmann has put it:

Positivism holds—and this is its essence—that what we can speak about is all that matters in life. *Whereas Wittgenstein passionately believes that all that really matters in human life is precisely what, in his view, we must be silent about.* When he nevertheless takes immense pains to delimit the unimportant [i.e., the scope and limits of ordinary language], it is not the coastline of that island which he is bent on surveying with such meticulous accuracy, but the boundary of the ocean.[43]

The evidence that Wittgenstein's aim in the *Tractatus* was as much ethical as logical cannot, accordingly, be looked for within the text of the book itself. What we must here point to, accordingly, is the circumstantial evidence which allows us to support that claim.

Let us here recall Wittgenstein's relations with Ludwig Ficker and the Brenner Circle. Ficker was the only editor in Austria who would even mention the work of Karl Kraus, let alone concede its importance; Kraus reciprocated, by referring to *Der Brenner* as the only honest periodical in Austria.[44] When, in due course, Wittgenstein used part of his patrimony for the benefit of writers and artists, he entrusted to Ludwig Ficker the sum of one hundred thousand crowns, asking him to distribute it among worthy artists. (Rainer Maria Rilke was one of the first beneficiaries.) From the outbreak of war, right up to 1919, Wittgenstein was in continual contact with Ficker by mail.[45] Having made three unsuccessful attempts to publish the *Tractatus*—first through Kraus's printers, Jahoda and Siegel, then through Braumueller, who had published Weininger, and finally through "a German professor of philosophy" who Wright conjectures was probably Frege and who had a connection with the periodical *Beiträge zur Philosophie des Deutschen Idealismus*—he turned to Ficker for advice, and the resulting correspondence casts significant light on what the *Tractatus* was intended to do.

In one letter, Wittgenstein writes about his book, "It is concerned with the representation of a system. And besides the representation is completely worked out."[46] In another he says, "The work is strictly philosophical and literary at the same time . . ."[47] while, in a third, he remarks:

I believe that in such cases things are related as follows: even if a book is entirely respectably written it is always from one standpoint worthless. For really, no-one has to write a book, because there are many completely different things to do on the face of this earth. On the other hand, I believe that I can say: if you publish Da[l]lego and H[a]ecker, etc., you can also publish *my* book.[48]

So he identifies what he is doing with Ficker's own literary and philosophical interests, and with what Haecker had been doing. In yet another of these letters, he gives what is the most explicit idea of what he conceived he had accomplished in the *Tractatus:*

The book's point is an ethical one. I once meant to include in the preface a sentence which is not in fact there now, but which I will write out for you here, because it will perhaps be a key to the work for you. What I meant to write, then, was this: My work consists of two parts: the one presented here plus all that I have *not* written. And *it is precisely this second part that is the important one.* My book draws limits to the sphere of the ethical from the inside as it were, and I am convinced that this is the ONLY rigorous way of drawing those limits.

In short, I believe that where *many* others today are just *gassing,* I have managed in my book to put everything firmly into place by being silent about it. And for that reason, unless I am very much mistaken, the book will say a great deal that you yourself want to say. Only perhaps you won't see that it is said in the book. For now I would recommend you to read the *preface* and the *conclusion* because they contain the most direct expression of the point of the book.[49]

Here, at last, Wittgenstein's remark that there can be no ethical propositions, because they are "higher," finally becomes intelligible.

Wittgenstein is trying to set the ethical off from the sphere of rational discourse, because he believes that it is more properly located in the sphere of the poetic: "Ethics and aesthetics are one and the same."[50] Just as the logical scaffolding of the world is a priori, so too ethics is a condition of the world: "Ethics is transcendental."[51] However, like logic, the ethical is not dependent upon the facts: "*How* things are in the world is a matter of complete indifference for what is higher."[52] Much of the difficulty that people have experienced in interpreting the *Tractatus* revolves around the fact that both ethics and logic relate to what can be "shown" but not "said"; consequently, "the mystical" is ambiguous. In the first place, it refers to what the world has in common with its representation, its mirror, that is, language. Secondly, it refers to the poetic power of language to convey the "meaning of life." Language can present experience, but it can also infuse experience with meaning. The former is possible because the propositions that represent facts are models with a logical structure. The latter is poetry. The sound which the musical notation, the record and the musical idea alike represent, through their common form, also conveys a particular feeling.[53] Language can thus represent facts by means of propositions, or alternatively convey emotions in poems. The aim of the *Tractatus* is to distinguish the two, and thereby protect them from confusion.

In the world of facts, there is nothing of value—"The sense of the world must lie outside the world"[54]—and there are no riddles —"the *riddle* does not exist."[55] The meaning of the world lies outside the factual. In this sphere of value and meaning, there are no propositions, no facts—only paradox and poetry. "Only he is an artist," as Kraus puts it, "who can make a riddle out of the solution."[56] The question of how logic can represent the world, and the question of the sense of the world, together constitute "the mystical." Both are spheres in which propositions cannot possibly be meaningful. Thus the notion of "showing" is rooted in two relations; that between the world and logic, and that between the facts that constitute the world and the sense, or meaning, of the world. The virtue of having shown this *from within* the logical structure of propositions is that the sphere of facts will thereby, once and for all, have been distinguished scientifically from that of values. This last letter to Ficker, in short, unifies Wittgenstein the formal logician with Wittgenstein the ethical mystic, and explicitly places him in the mainstream of Austrian culture.

Wittgenstein's abiding convictions that one must renounce all attempts to put ethics on "intellectual foundations" is evident again in his later conversations with Waismann and Schlick. In December, 1930, for instance, we find him criticizing Schlick's approach to philosophical ethics, in the following remark to Waismann:

Schlick says that in theological ethics there are two interpretations of the Essence of Good. On the shallower interpretation, the Good is good, in virtue of the fact that God wills it: on the deeper interpretation, God wills the Good, because it *is* good. On my view, the first interpretation is the deeper: that is good, which God commands. For this blocks off the road to any kind of explanation, "why" it is good; while the second interpretation is the shallow, rationalistic one, in that it behaves "as though" that which is good could be given yet some further foundation.[57]

And, a little later on, he cites a remark from Schopenhauer: "To preach morality is hard; to give it an intellectual justification is impossible."[58]

Almost exactly a year before (in December 1929), Wittgenstein had made the affiliation between his own views and those of Kant and Kierkegaard quite explicit, in a conversation during which he also denounced as "babble" the philosophical ethics of professional philosophers like G. E. Moore. This passage, some of which was later included in a posthumously printed *Lecture on Ethics,* is worth quoting at length:

I can well understand, what Heidegger means by Being and *Angst.* Man has an impulse, to run up against [*anzurennen*] the limits of language. Think, for example, of the wonder that anything whatever exists. This wonder cannot be expressed in the form of a question, nor is there any answer to it. All that we can say about it can a priori be only nonsense. Nevertheless, we run up against the limits of language. This running-up-against [*anzurennen*] Kierkegaard also saw, and indicated in a completely similar way—as running up against the Paradox. This running up against the limits of language is *Ethics.* I regard it as of great importance, that one should put an end to all the twaddle about ethics—whether it is a science, whether values exist, whether the Good can be defined, etc. In ethics people are forever trying to find a way of saying something which, in the nature of things, is not and can never be expressed. We know a priori: anything which one might give by way of a definition of the Good—it can never be anything but a misunderstanding . . .[59]

Once again, however, this is not to say that the *attempt* to express the "unsayable" in ethics must be totally renounced. It is only that we must, at all costs, avoid overintellectualizing and so misrepresenting the true character of the issues involved.

Perhaps the most important prerequisite for understanding the *Tractatus* is a grasp of the distinction between the *philosophy* it contains—the model theory, the critique of Frege and Russell, and so on—and the *world-view* which Wittgenstein is expounding in it. His philosophy aims at solving the problem of the nature and limits of description. His world-view expresses the belief that the sphere of what can only be *shown* must be protected from those who try to *say* it. The philosophy of the *Tractatus* is an attempt to show, from the very nature of propositions, that poetry does not consist of propositions. In this world-view, poetry is the sphere in which the *sense* of life is expressed, a sphere which therefore cannot be described in *factual* terms.

It is the will, rather than the reason, that introduces value into the world: "I call 'will' first and foremost the bearer of good and evil."[60] The world—the totality of facts—relates to the will, in Wittgenstein's view, in very much the same manner as Schopenhauer's world as representation relates to the world as will, as husk to kernel, as *phenomenon to noumenon.*

If the good or bad exercise of the will does alter the world, it can alter only the limits of the world, not the facts—not what can be expressed by means of language.

In short, the effect must be that it becomes an altogether different world. It must, so to speak, wax and wane as a whole.[61]

In science, we want to know the facts; in the problems of life, facts are unimportant. In life, the important thing is the capacity to respond to the suffering of another. It is a matter of right feeling. The *philosophy* of the *Tractatus* is directed toward showing how "knowledge" is possible. But, in its world-view, this knowledge is relegated to a secondary role. The vehicle for conveying feeling, which has the primary role in life, is the poem or the fable. Tolstoy's *Tales* especially impressed Wittgenstein in this respect, as Paul Englemann tells us;[62] and so also did the early American Western films, which he viewed as fables or moralities.[63] These fables reach out to a man in his *Innerlichkeit,* and so are the means of touching the fantasy, which is the fountainhead of value.

To sum up: our present interpretation of the *Tractatus* reads it as taking over from Frege and Russell certain logical instruments, and applying these to the problem on which Mauthner himself had embarked earlier—that of producing a critique of language in complete general and philosophical terms. Where Mauthner had ended in philosophical skepticism, however, the use of this logical framework permitted Wittgenstein to show how far ordinary factual or descriptive language can legitimately be thought of (even if only metaphorically) as getting its literal, straightforward meaning in the same kind of way as the "mathematical models" around which Hertz had built his account of scientific knowledge. Yet, in the last resort, the fundamental point of this whole critique was to underline the ethical point that all questions about value lie *outside* the scope of such ordinary factual or descriptive language. And, by starting from this *ethical* emphasis we can begin to work our way back to the larger Viennese cultural situation within which Wittgenstein grew up, and which—if we are right—played a substantial part in shaping his own problems and preoccupations.

Engelmann has argued that the *Tractatus* is very much a product of Viennese culture; that Wittgenstein was to philosophy what Kraus was to letters and what Loos was to art and architecture. By now, we can see how far that is an accurate characterization. Wittgenstein's critique of language, as expressed in the *Tractatus,* is in fact—as he himself claimed—only *half* a critique. The half that he did not write ("this second part, that is the important one") comprises the corpus of Karl Kraus's writings. Rationalistic ethics and metaphysics are to Wittgenstein what the feuilleton is to Kraus: conceptual monsters, which only succeed in mixing up essentially different things. Just as in the feuilleton fact and fantasy produce an artistic bastard, so in metaphysics science and poetry mate to produce a conceptual mongrel. In art, ornament and use mate to produce objects, such as filled prewar houses, that are both ugly and useless. In music, the quest for theatrical effects has displaced the inherent logic of the musical idea itself. The principles of composition had been applied to produce effects mimicking other kinds of sound, and the true art of composition had been lost in the shuffle.

All of these distortions were the result of telescoping elements which were essentially unrelated and which in combination were destructive of one another. Since society not only condoned but demanded the production of such aberrations, a critique of any of the arts was implicitly a critique of culture and society as a whole. Wittgenstein's *Tractatus* furnished the most abstract of these and therefore the least readily comprehensible. Nonetheless, it was—as Engelmann claimed—one central and essential element in the twentieth-century Viennese critique of language, communication and society.

Seen in this Viennese context, then, the *Tractatus* attempts to provide a theoretical groundwork for the distinction between the spheres of reason and fantasy, upon which the Viennese critique of society in the early decades of this century was based. So understood, Wittgenstein's radical separation of facts from values can be regarded as the terminus of a series of efforts to distinguish the sphere of natural science from the sphere of morality, which had begun with Kant, had been sharpened up by Schopenhauer, and had been made absolute by Kierkegaard. Like Kant, Wittgenstein was concerned at the same time to defend the adequacy of language as a scientific instrument from Mauthner's skepticism; the model theory of the proposition became the basis upon which Wittgenstein could give scientific language a sure basis, while drawing an absolute distinction between what language *says* and what it *shows*—that is, what is "higher."

On this interpretation, the *Tractatus* becomes an expression of a certain type of language mysticism that assigns a central importance in human life to art, on the ground that art alone can express the meaning of life. Only art can express moral truth, and only the artist can teach the things that matter most in life. Art is a mission. To be concerned merely with form, like the aesthetes of the 1890s, is to pervert art. So in its own way, the *Tractatus* is every bit as much a condemnation of *l'art pour l'art* as Tolstoy's *What Is Art?* For Wittgenstein, indeed, the implications of the *Tractatus* were even more far-reaching than those of Tolstoy's essay, since they were based upon a completely general understanding of the nature of language and other means of expression.

In short, the primary concern of the author of the *Tractatus* is to protect the sphere of the conduct of life against encroachments from the sphere of speculation. He sought to protect the fantasy from the incursions of reason, and to prevent spontaneous feeling from being stifled by rationalization. He was aware, as Kraus was, that reason is only an instrument for good when it is the reason of a good man. The good man's being good is a function not of his rationality, but of his participation in the life of the fantasy. For the good man, ethics is a way of life, not a system of propositions—"There are no ethical propositions, only ethical actions," as Engelmann puts it.[64] Thus the *Tractatus* was, first and foremost, an attack on all forms of rational systems of ethics—that is, theories of ethics that would base human conduct upon reason. It did not, of course, claim that morality is *contrary to* reason; merely that its foundations lay elsewhere. So, in contradistinction to Kant, both Schopenhauer and Wittgenstein find the basis of morality in "right feelings" rather than in "valid reasons."

In separating reason from fantasy, the mathematical representation of the physicist from the metaphor of the poet, straightforward descriptive language from "indirect communication," Wittgenstein was convinced that he had solved "the problem of philosophy." The model theory explained how knowledge of the world was possible. The mathematical (logical) basis of that theory explained how the very structure of propositions *showed* their limitations—that is, how the structure of propositions determined the limits of scientific (rational) inquiry. The implication of the model theory was that the "meaning of life" lay outside the sphere of what could be said; the "meaning of life" should properly be referred to as a riddle, rather than as a problem, since there is no question of solving it, or answering it. So the model theory corroborates Kierkegaard's notion that the meaning of life is not a topic which can be discussed by means of the categories of reason.

Subjective truth is communicable only indirectly, through fable, polemics, irony, and satire. This is the only way that one can come to "see the world aright." Ethics is taught not by arguments, but by providing examples of moral behavior; this is the task of art. It is fulfilled in Tolstoy's later *Tales*, which explain what religion is, by *showing* how the truly religious man lives his life. The meaning of life was no more an academic question for Wittgenstein than it had been for Tolstoy. It was not, and could not, be answered by the reason, since it is resolved only by the way in which one lives. For Wittgenstein all this was implied in the model theory, which—by refuting Mauthner's skepticism—at last enabled one to restore objectivity to science, while establishing the subjectivity of ethics.

If the world-view of the *Tractatus* is *au fond* the world-view of Kraus, Wittgenstein's conception of philosophy is also Krausian. If Kraus's journalism is polemical, so is Wittgenstein's philosophy.

The correct method in philosophy would really be the following: to say nothing except what can be said, i.e., propositions of natural science— i.e., something that has nothing to do with philosophy—and then whenever someone else wanted to say something metaphysical, to demonstrate to him that he had failed to give a meaning to certain signs in his propositions. Although it would not be satisfying to the other person—he would not have the feeling that we were teaching him philosophy—*this* method would be the only strictly correct one.[65]

The task of philosophy is not to seek to build up a body of doctrine, but to be on guard continually against just that. There simply cannot be any meaningful propositions except those of natural science; there are no metalanguages; logic is meaningless (*sinnlos*) and philosophy is nonsense (*Unsinn*). Yet even here there is a certain Krausian irony, for Wittgenstein considers that this "nonsense" is anything but *unimportant*.

A common objection to the *Tractatus* is that it ends in contradiction, since, in its attempt to transcend the sayable, it too must fail. Certainly, it is difficult for academic philosophers to arrive at any other conclusion, in the face of such statements as the penultimate aphorism of the whole book, 6.54.

My propositions serve as elucidations in the following way: anyone who understands me eventually recognizes them as nonsensical, when he has used them—as steps—to climb up beyond them. (He must, so to speak, throw away the ladder after he has climbed up it.) He must transcend these propositions and then he will see the world aright.[66]

To those who saw Wittgenstein as a follower of Russell, these statements were inevitably paradoxical and self-defeating. Taken, instead, as one aphorism from a book of aphorisms written by a thinker under the spell of the Krausian vision, such a statement is less astonishing. Had not Kraus asserted that "the aphorism never covers itself with truth, it is either half true, or one-and-a-half-times true''?[67] Wittgenstein's propositions are thus neither statements of a scientific nature, nor are they meta-linguistic. Rather, they are *aphorisms* which, by giving a generalized critique, at the same time convey a world-view: they are a Krausian medium for a Krausian message.

Once the meaning of these aphorisms has been grasped they are no longer necessary. Once one has seen that values are something not to be debated, but to be acted upon, one no longer needs the *Tractatus*. For the *Tractatus* is itself, by intention, a polemic against the kind of rationalism that maims and shackles the human spirit. This rationalism had been the result of a failure to distinguish the legitimate sphere of rational speculation from that of fantasy; and the only way of demonstrating its limitations was by a book of aphorisms, which showed how the two spheres of facts and value were to be distinguished.

The result was those cryptic seventy-five pages which Wittgenstein himself feared would be very difficult to comprehend, save for the man who "has himself already had the thoughts which are expressed in it."[68] (Just how soon, and how completely his fears were to be realized, we shall see in the next chapter.) This statement also provides us with something of an explanation of the reasons why Wittgenstein had so little to say about his book after it was published, even though he insisted that no one had grasped his point, least of all Bertrand Russell. In order to have had the same thoughts as the author of the *Tractatus Logico-Philosophicus,* one would have to have lived in the milieu of *fin-de-siècle* Vienna; but, more than that, one would have to have undergone the experiences that Ludwig Wittgenstein himself had undergone during the First World War. For it was during that war that these thoughts—drawn from Kraus and Loos, Hertz and Frege, Schopenhauer, Kierkegaard and Tolstoy—coalesced into the unity which was the *man* Ludwig Wittgenstein.

Just what those experiences were remains to be fully discovered. Perhaps they began with his visit to Trakl, whom he had been supporting through the agency of Ludwig Ficker. What can Wittgenstein have felt, on arriving at the military hospital in Kraków, where he had sought him out, when he discovered that this brilliant young poet had taken his life but three days before? Certainly, Tolstoy was as much in his thoughts as Frege during this crucial period; his fellow soldiers nicknamed him "the man with the Gospels," because he never was seen without his copy of Tolstoy's *The Gospel in Brief,* which he mentions acquiring in a letter to Russell, and which he also referred to as the book which "saved my life." Taken as a whole, in short, the *Tractatus* expressed an intensely personal view of the world, a view that had been forged out of many sources and was all the more individual and creative for bringing together such disparate elements. Clearly, a set of aphorisms which emerged from such a complex situation was not to be grasped with ease. Indeed, a man of Russell's background and mentality was bound to find much that was of the greatest significance to Wittgenstein entirely incomprehensible.

Herein lies the source of the myth that still surrounds the image of Ludwig Wittgenstein, the "odd-ball genius"—the myth which has bred such curiosities as the Eugene Goossens oboe concerto supposedly inspired by the *Tractatus,* and the "Wittgenstein Motet" *Excerpta Tractati Logici-Philosophici* by Elizabeth Lutyens, as well as the sculpture and poetry which claim to be based on Wittgenstein's work. All of these reflect the esoteric qualities found in the book by nonphilosophical readers in the nineteen-twenties and the thirties—and in the sixties and seventies—qualities of a kind that were entirely foreign to Russell and the logical positivists. Yet, by this stage, it should be evident that Wittgenstein would have had even less to do with these compositions than with Russell's preface; just as Schönberg steadfastly turned away those students who came to him to learn "the new music" before they had mastered the old.

The question remains: Why, in the face of all of this misrepresentation, did Wittgenstein himself remain silent? To explain this reaction fully might well require an exercise in psychobiography that would involve laying bare the whole development of his personality. Such an interpretation would suit the existentialist attitudes of the author of the *Tractatus,* who could no more have explained his book to anyone else than the author of *Either/ Or* could have written a scholarly commentary on his own work. Indeed, the closest we may be able to come to understanding Wittgenstein's mind, at this point, is to call to mind the aphorism of Karl Kraus:

Why does many a man write? Because he does not possess enough character not to write.[69]

7

Wittgenstein the Man, and His Second Thoughts

*Anrennen gegen die Grenze der
Sprache? Die Sprache ist ja
kein Käfig.*

—LUDWIG WITTGENSTEIN,
December 17, 1930

As the book, so the man; if the message of the *Tractatus* was a Krausian message, so was Wittgenstein's life a Krausian life. In the Cambridge of the 1940s, we saw Wittgenstein's extraordinary character and unconventional behavior as irrelevant to his philosophy—even as distracting attention from the pure-spring-water clarity and transparency of the truths he had to teach us. In retrospect, this was a mistake: there was no such division between the philosopher and the man. From the beginning, Wittgenstein's philosophical reflections were just one expression, among others, of an integral personality; and, if we found it difficult to penetrate to the heart of his *arguments,* this is—not least—because we did not fully understand *him.*

There was probably no reason why we should have understood him. Between Vienna in the years before 1919 and the Cambridge of 1946–47, there were too many barriers of time, of history and of culture. Intellectuals and artists in Britain may at times have felt neglected, ignored or even derided; but they have never been completely ''shut out'' from the world of affairs or compelled to serve a culture and society whose values they totally rejected. In this respect, they have been spared the absolute alienation out of which the intransigent and uncompromising integrity of a Kraus or a Wittgenstein is born. As a result, they have usually been able to play things much more lightly, so exposing themselves to the charge of superficiality and irreverence from the Wittgensteins and D. H. Lawrences of the world.[1] In return, the English have always viewed such quintessentially Krausian remarks as "If I must choose the lesser of two evils, I will choose neither" as manifesting a certain distasteful pomposity and self-importance.

Yet those very things about Wittgenstein that his English students and associates most misunderstood were very largely matters of *style*. Every generation of alienated intellectuals finds its own characteristic way of expressing its rejection of conventional worldly values. At one time, young men grow beards and shoulder-length hair; reject all external discipline as authoritarian, in favor of a "life style" of unregulated freedom; regard all questions of ethics and morality as matters of aesthetic taste; and take a perverse pride in "letting it all hang out." At another time, by contrast, long hair and beards will themselves appear completely "square." The eminent doctors, businessmen and academicians of the late nineteenth century, with their great furry heads and shovel beards, turned on their pupils and children an eye of misleadingly self-confident complacency; while, throughout Austria itself, the grizzled sideburns of the Emperor Francis Joseph gazed down from the walls of every public office. The results (as we can now see) were predictable. In a culture overloaded with tawdry rubbish and meaningless etiquette, the rebellious young men who were seeking to achieve consistency and integrity rejected facial hair along with all other bourgeois superfluities. To them, mustaches and sideburns were mere ostentation, like velvet smoking jackets and fancy neckties. A serious, uncluttered mind called for a clean-shaven chin and an open-necked shirt; artistic matters became, for them, matters for moral reflection and judgment, rather than morality a matter of aesthetic taste; the proper alternative to the arbitrary authoritarianism of society was not anarchism but self-discipline. A man must take his own life in hand, on his own responsibility before God—or, at least, before his own "understanding of goodness,'' that "knowledge unattainable by reasoning" which (as Tolstoy put it) is "indubitably revealed" to each man's heart.[2]

In their fundamental aspirations and ideals, therefore, the generation of the *Wandervögel* in the 1920s were, after all, not as different from the generation of the Hippies as their external appearance might suggest. If the young Germans and Austrians of the early twentieth century questioned the moral integrity of their fathers' culture and society even before 1914—seeing in the apparently endless reign of Francis Joseph the perpetuation of a despotic regime from which all life and virtue had departed— the agony and bloodletting of 1914–1918 merely reinforced their feelings of doom. These were indeed *The Last Days of Mankind.* The worldly, bourgeois society of the late nineteenth century had cut its own throat, and the survivors were free of all moral obligations to their past. It was time to make a fresh start. Redemption would come only through a new austerity, of dress, of manners, of taste, of style. (In the 1920s, it was easier to get yourself expelled from school as a troublesome radical for having a crew cut, than for wearing your hair too long.) With bared chests, sandals on their feet, and rucksacks on their backs, the young men of Germany and Austria marched out of the corrupt cities and back into the pine forests, where, in a spirit of *Brüderschaft,* they hoped to recapture the purer and simpler values to which the generation of their fathers had been blind.[3]

Ludwig Wittgenstein himself was born too early to belong to the *Wandervögel* generation. Yet it is clear that he shared many of their values; indeed, those values were themselves molded on the example of men like Kraus, Loos and Wittgenstein. For Wittgenstein personally, the years of war service, first on the Russian and later on the Italian front, had been a time of spiritual self-questioning, but also a time of fulfillment. As though his army life—much of it on active service—had not been enough to keep him busy, he was also in the last stages of composing the *Tractatus,* which was apparently finished during the summer of 1918; while army life brought him closer to his fellow-soldiers, and fellow-citizens, than he had ever been as a rich man's youngest son in Vienna or ever subsequently became. Here as elsewhere, one is reminded of Tolstoy's Konstantin Levin, who recognizes that the "meaning of life" shows itself only in the living, to the man who gives himself over, honestly and wholeheartedly, to the practical, everyday tasks of tilling the soil, of family life and of human kindness.[4]

In music, art and literature, meaningless decoration and superfluity might fill men like Kraus and Loos with a morally tinged distaste. When enshrined in the conventions of society and personal relations, Wittgenstein found them a matter for authentic disgust. When first elected a Fellow of Trinity College, Cambridge, he could not bring himself to dine at High Table. His reasons had nothing particularly to do with the fact that the Fellows were given more or better food; nor did it spring from any populist desire to mingle with the undergraduates. He objected, rather, to the symbolic fact that the High Table itself was placed on a platform, six inches higher than the main floor of the dining hall; and, for a while, the college agreed to serve him separately, at a small card table placed on the lower level.[5] (Later on, he scarcely dined in Hall at all.) Nor was it the artificialities of social convention alone that horrified him; those of the intellectual life were, if anything, worse.

He acquired from Tolstoy a feeling that "humanly useful" work—particularly manual labor—alone had dignity and value. He briefly visited Russia,[6] though there is no suggestion that he found Soviet society any more to his taste than the society of Western Europe; and he gave the impression of being a man who would, above other men, have found integrity and fulfillment within the framework of a *kibbutz*. Nor was this impression an accidental one. When the first Jewish collective farms were set up in Palestine, during the 1880s and 1890s, the ethos and social ideology of the *kibbutz* movement were worked out and expounded by a new Russian immigrant called Gordon, who was himself an immediate disciple and follower of Tolstoy.[7]

Wittgenstein's respect for "humanly useful" work could be evoked in surprising ways. One day in 1946 or early 1947, Dorothy Moore—the wife of G. E. Moore, his predecessor in the chair of philosophy at Cambridge—was pushing her bicycle up Castle Hill, on her way out to do part-time work in the Chivers jam factory at Histon, when she met Wittgenstein out for a walk. He inquired where she was going, and—she later reported—was more delighted than she had ever known him to be, to see the wife of Britain's most abstractly intellectual philosopher going off to do "real" work at the factory bench.[8] His belief that intellectual, and especially academic activities did not represent "real" or humanly useful work extended, of course, to his own philosophizing. Those students who were sufficiently close for him to be able to influence their personal decisions, he strongly discouraged from taking up academic philosophy as a career: that would, in itself, show that they had misunderstood the point of his teaching. Instead, he urged them to take up medicine, like Drury, or at least—if they had to be academics— to go into some serious field such as physics, like W. H. Watson. If he himself went on doing philosophy, that, he would have said, was because he was "not fit for anything else"—in any event, he was "not harming anyone besides himself." Somebody had to scrub out the Augean stables of the intellectual world, and it just happened to be him who had been fated to perform this task of intellectual sanitation.[9]

Some people have seen, in Wittgenstein's attitude toward his own philosophy, an inconsistency amounting almost to nihilism. Yet, once again, this objection misses the heart of the matter.[10] Coming from an authentic positivist, this point of view might have been criticized as self-refuting; in the same way that, for instance, the so-called "principle of verification" was repeatedly challenged in the later 1920s and 1930s, as being itself "unverifiable." But what Wittgenstein rejected as discreditable and rationalistic was only a certain *kind* of philosophizing—though admittedly a kind to which academic philosophers were particularly prone. (In this respect, one is reminded afresh of Schopenhauer and Kierkegaard.) That is the kind of philosophical discussion which "obliterates the distinction between [i.e., confuses] factual and conceptual investigations."[11] This sort of intellectualistic discussion was "meaningless" in a way that did not warrant rescuing. Yet, alongside it, there existed also another type of philosophical discussion, the sort one finds in a man like Kierkegaard or Tolstoy, and which struggles to convey—though in an "indirect" manner—profound human truths, of a kind that cannot be stated in straightforward, everyday language. Man's tendency *an die Grenze der Sprache anzurennen* can thus lead one either (as in Moore) into a philosophical *Geschwätz*,[12] which confuses conceptual issues and empirical ones, or alternatively (as with Kierkegaard) into a religious attempt to articulate the essentially unverbalizable. These two kinds of philosophy may be hard to tell apart at first sight. As he said at one of his at-homes during his last year at Cambridge:

Sometimes, we go into a man's study and find his books and papers all over the place, and can say without hesitation: "What a mess! We really must clear this room up." Yet, at other times, we may go into a room which looks very like the first; but after looking round we decide that we must leave it just as it is, recognizing that, in this case, *even the dust has its place.*[13]

In any event, the activity of "doing philosophy" was not the *only*—perhaps, not even the *central*—thing in Wittgenstein's life. His colleagues at Cambridge, we remarked at the outset, regarded him as "a philosopher of genius," who just happened to have come from Vienna. The comparison with Kraus and Schönberg helps us to see that he was, rather, one of Kraus's "integral men," whose genius just happened to find expression through philosophy, among other things. Once he had completed the *Tractatus* in 1918–19, he felt he had done all there was in him to do for the subject. So he dropped it. With that out of the way, his creative fantasy needed to turn to other channels. He spent the academic year 1919–20 at the Vienna Teachers' Training College, in the Kundmanngasse—a street to which he was to return in a quite different capacity, six years later—and then took up a series of appointments as an elementary-school teacher. Though he did not find the school authorities or his pupils' parents easy to deal with, he threw himself into the actual work, and seems to have been quite remarkably effective, especially in the teaching of mathematics.[14]

Later on, when his mood was very dark and he could not continue teaching, he worked for a while as a gardener, until his sister Margarete Stonborough invited him to participate in the construction of her new city house. Wittgenstein had a strictly antiprofessional attitude, and he approached this task as just one more legitimate challenge to his own individual clear-headedness and sense of function. (As Loos had repeatedly said, architectural design is strictly in the service of function: "the meaning is the *use*.")[15] To begin with, he collaborated with his younger friend Paul Engelmann, who himself had an architectural training; but very soon he was able to take sole responsibility, and the greater part of their resulting design—especially, the interior details of the house—was strictly his own conception. A recent architectural commentator has written about the Kundmanngasse house:

Academies and architectural offices can find no formal dogmas or recipes in this building. They will look in vain for details to copy, as columnless glazed corners or ribbon windows. Instead of formulas or clichés, a philosophy . . .

The building is important because it is an example of going beyond limits, because it demonstrates how enriching "unprofessional encroachment" can be, and because it questions the limits of a profession that are mainly set by the very members of that profession. Wittgenstein, the philosopher, was an architect.[16]

The message is again a Krausian one. The institutional barriers between the professions can serve as arbitrary restrictions on the creative fantasy, just as much as any intellectual barriers in philosophy itself. Whether he was concerned with architecture or with music, with schoolteaching or with writing, it was the same individual Ludwig Wittgenstein whose personality and fantasy found expression through all these different media and techniques—whether as artist, or as moralist, or as both at the same time.

Almost from the moment of its publication, the nature and purpose of Wittgenstein's *Tractatus* gave rise to misunderstandings among his Viennese contemporaries, and his own disappearance from the philosophical scene did nothing to help the situation. If one only sets aside those last five pages (Proposition 6.3 on), the intellectual techniques developed in the rest of the book lend themselves to quite different uses, both in mathematics and in philosophy, and can be quoted in support of intellectual attitudes quite antagonistic to Wittgenstein's own. As a result, both in England and in Vienna itself, the *Tractatus* became the foundation stone of a new positivism or empiricism; and this developed into a thoroughgoing antimetaphysical movement, which held out scientific knowledge as the model of what rational men should believe—aiming to put the more loosely expressed positivism of Comte and his nineteenth-century followers on a new and more rigorous basis, by the proper application of Russell and Frege's propositional logic. At this point, therefore, we must look briefly at the origins of these other philosophical movements—Cambridge "analytical philosophy" and Viennese "logical positivism"—and see how a document written as the final and definitive stage in post-Kantian "transcendental philosophy," in order to liberate ethics from any kind of science-based empiricism, could at once be stood on its head and used to justify reimposing just such an empiricist system.[17]

Let us start in Cambridge at the turn of the century. The alliance between formal logic and philosophical analysis personified by the early Bertrand Russell had, to begin with, nothing specifically positivistic about it. In intention, at any rate, it had been philosophically neutral. True, both Russell and his closest ally, G. E. Moore, were in revolt against the British post-Hegelian idealists, notably Bradley. Yet their quarrel with Bradley was not so much with what he *said;* it was with his failure, as they saw it, to say anything significant at all. Absolute idealism was not so much a philosophical doctrine as an intellectual debauch. One could laugh at it, like F. C. S. Schiller in his spoof issue of *Mind;*[18] one could clear it out of the way and start again from scratch; but one could not contradict it, because its arguments were confused beyond the point of rational discussion.[19] So Moore and Russell scorned to debate with their predecessors, and embarked rather on a "new instauration"—a cleansing of the Victorian philosophical stables, to be followed by the reconstruction of philosophy in new and unambiguous terms.

Looking back at the intellectual situation at Cambridge in the years around 1900, of course, we must now distinguish more carefully than was possible at the time between the explicit content of this "philosophical reformation" on the one hand, and its revolutionary manner and motives on the other. If we look carefully enough at the writings of Moore and Russell's immediate predecessors, indeed, it begins to be somewhat mysterious how these younger men could present their own philosophical positions as such great *intellectual* novelties. Russell's much-heralded distinction between "knowledge by acquaintance" and "knowledge by description," for instance, is spelled out already in Bradley's *Logic;*[20] while Moore's account of value predicates, as "indefinable" terms referring to "non-natural" properties, now appears only a small step on from McTaggart's position in philosophical ethics.[21] And perhaps we shall do better to pay attention less to this content than to the words of Roy Harrod who, in his biography of John Maynard Keynes, wrote of the profound influence exercised on Keynes and his Cambridge contemporaries by the "flaming advocacy" of G. E. Moore's *Principia Ethica.*[22]

If the arguments of Moore and Russell were self-consciously

revolutionary, this was as much a matter of personal style as of intellectual content. Many of Moore's close friends and successors—for example, Keynes himself in his revealing essay, *My Early Beliefs*—have testified to his personal dominance.[23] So, for the self-selected élite of Cambridge between 1903 and 1914, *Principia Ethica* became a kind of secular Bible, or theoretical manual of right conduct—"the Ideal is Indefinable, and G. E. Moore is its prophet." As such, Moore and his book need to be reconsidered in the context of their time. Certainly, it is hard now to recapture at first hand the passions which they initially aroused and which helped to channel the intellectual and emotional energies of a whole generation of writers and thinkers in Cambridge and London, ranging from Keynes and Russell, by way of E. M. Forster and Leonard Woolf, to Roger Fry and Lytton Strachey.[24] (The last phrase a philosophy student would apply to *Principia Ethica* in the 1970s is "flaming advocacy.")

So at this point it is necessary to recall, quite deliberately, the social position of the entire Cambridge and Bloomsbury group, and the part they played in demolishing the Victorian way of life. Secure in their private incomes, they could safely mock at the Established Church. (How could the Indefinable Good be thought of as incarnated in Church Hall, Westminster, or still more in Buckingham Palace? As for Benthamite utilitarianism, that was not merely narrow-minded but vulgar.) In this case as in others, the *revolutionary* character of the new philosophical movement is more intelligible, in retrospect, as a matter of social psychology than as a phenomenon in the history of ideas.

Like so many of the leading figures in the history of early-twentieth-century philosophy, Moore and Russell, we may say, were personal revolutionaries operating in a strictly intellectual field. Where the moral critique of contemporary Catholicism, as undertaken on an emotional level by Péguy, became intellectualized in the philosophical teachings of Maritain, the "ideal utilitarianism" of G. E. Moore represented an abstract refinement and justification, on an intellectual level, of the moral aestheticism associated earlier with the name and the writings of Oscar Wilde. There was, thus, a closer connection than books on the history of philosophy sometimes suggest between the intellectual views of Moore and Russell, the life style which their younger associates built on the basis of those views, and the radical transformations in practical ethics and aesthetics with which those followers were associated—as represented, for example, by Roger Fry's Post-Impressionist Exhibition, the immense success of Diaghilev's Russian Ballet, and the novels of Leonard Woolf's wife, Virginia. The philosophical reformation inaugurated in the writings of Moore and Russell accordingly had ulterior motives, also, which severely limited the respects in which it was possible for either them or their immediate successors in British analytical philosophy to grasp the real point of Wittgenstein's philosophical concerns.

The analytic methods employed in Russell and Moore's reconstruction of philosophy were of two alternative kinds: those of a refined lexicography, as in *Principia Ethica,* and those of a purified mathematics, as in *Principia Mathematica.* But in each case the key word was *Principia.* Theirs was a new and initially uncommitted beginning. Indeed, if we go back to the earliest papers of both Moore and Russell, written in the late 1890s, we shall find that even so characteristic a notion as that of sense data is not yet in evidence. Those ideas came later. For the moment, the task was to assemble a disinfected language for philosophy—to insist on clear definitions of those terms that could be defined, to rebut all misleading attempts at defining terms that were essentially indefinable, and to reveal the "true" logical forms and articulations underlying the sometimes deceptive clothing of grammar and syntax in which everyday language dresses up our thoughts. Were these humdrum ambitions, or "underlaborer's tasks," as John Locke called them?[25] They may appear that way to us; but a missionary, reforming zeal will carry one through even the most tedious-sounding enterprises.

To begin with, the aims of Schlick and the other Vienna Circle positivists had been scarcely more doctrinal than Moore's and Russell's early programs. During the years before 1914, scientific-minded intellectuals in Germany and Austria were disgusted with the entire state of official European philosophy. If they had any patience with professional philosophers at all, they reserved it for Schopenhauer; but this could be attributed as much to his polemical attacks on Hegel as to his personal doctrines. Their own preoccupations arose, rather, out of the exact sciences. They followed with sympathy and interest the mathematical innovations of Frege and Hilbert, the theoretical physics of Poincaré, Lorentz, and the meteoric young Albert Einstein, the chemical skepticism of Ostwald, Mach, and other critics of literal-minded atomism. All these arguments relied on a new kind of critical analysis, and it was this critical movement within the exact sciences that now provided the inspiration for the new positivism.

The philosophical aims of the young Viennese positivists were thus similar to those of Moore and Russell; but their methods were different. Whereas the young Cambridge radicals had set out to reform philosophy by analysis, the Viennese positivists were determined to reform it by generalizing methods that were already proving their worth in scientific theory. Philosophy must be set on "the sure path of a science"—indeed, integrated with physics and biology into a single "unified science."[26] In practice, this involved reconstructing both philosophy and science in the form of axiomatic, mathematical disciplines, as the example of Frege suggested; as empirical, inductive disciplines, in which all generalizations and abstract concepts could be legitimated directly by appeal to observation; or *ideally* (and here they ran into the same problems that Hertz and Wittgenstein encountered) as empirical, inductive sciences whose inner articulations were, at the same time, formalized on the axiomatic pattern of systems in pure mathematics.

If there *was* a streak of positivism present at this stage, it came in through such men as Mach, Avenarius and Vaihinger. Above all, Ernst Mach was to be the godfather of logical positivism, if not its chief progenitor; and the insistence on the primacy of experience and observation, characteristic of his work in both physics and the history of science, was associated (as we saw earlier) with a philosophical commitment to "phenomenalism." All claims to knowledge of the world around us, Mach argued, derived their justification from the evidence of our senses, and this "evidence" must ultimately be interpreted in terms of the direct content of our individual sense fields. Accordingly, the theory of knowledge, if not the whole of science, was reducible to *Die Analyse der Empfindungen*—the analysis of sensations. Mach's epistemological position, like Hume's, was a "sensationalist" one.

This last idea was of great significance for the Vienna Circle philosophers of the 1920s. When they set about finding an epistemological starting point for their theories, they turned in vain to Wittgenstein's *Tractatus*. Although the *Tractatus* provided the basic logical structure for the new positivism, the Vienna Circle philosophy was completed only when the logic of the *Trac-*

tatus was dovetailed with Mach's sensationalist theory of knowledge. The argument of the *Tractatus* had employed the notion of "atomic facts," to correspond with the "unit propositions" of an idealized formal language; and it had gone on to show how the significance of more complex propositions might—in theory, at any rate—be analyzed by "truth-functional" methods.[27] But Wittgenstein had said nothing to indicate how one was to recognize "atomic facts" or "unit propositions" in practice; this had not been his purpose. The logical positivists now remedied his omission. Taking a hint from Mach and from Russell's doctrine of "knowledge-by-acquaintance," they equated Wittgenstein's "atomic facts" with the indubitable, directly known "hard data" of Mach's and Russell's epistemologies. The "unit propositions," which were the ultimate carriers of meaning, thus became *Protokollsätze,* and thereby the ultimate carriers of knowledge, each of them recording one single item of sensory evidence, vouchsafed by one single sensation, or "sense datum."

For the most part, therefore, the Viennese positivists were content, like Mach, to operate with an epistemological unit taken over with little change from David Hume's notion of "impressions." Like Hume again, they identified the realm of the "necessary" and the a priori with that of the "analytic" or "tautologous"; and this at first appeared to be in line with the *Tractatus* account of logical truth or falsity. Propositions were to be considered meaningful only if they were *either* confessedly logical, and thereby tautologous or inconsistent, or *else* genuinely empirical, in which case their semantic value would be determined by cashing them in for actual or possible observation reports or *Protokollsätze.* The formal truth calculus of the *Tractatus* thus became a method for the logical construction of human knowledge, by which higher-level abstractions and propositions of scientific theory were to be built from, or anchored onto, the concept-free "hard data" of the *Protokollsätze.* The fundamental dichotomy between empirical propositions and logical ones was accepted as absolute and exhaustive; and whatever could not be expressed in either form was not truly a meaningful proposition. This ax, it was true, threatened to sever ethical utterances (and much else) from the realm of the meaningful; but a place was soon found for many of the disputed utterances, even though as second-class speech, under the heading of "emotive" rather than "cognitive" expressions.[28]

The resulting philosophy was a clean, functional one, worthy of Gropius—geometrical in its lines, with none of that unpositivistic muddle-headedness so common among working scientists. (The logical positivists would cite with admiration Mach's slashing attack on the Newtonian concepts of absolute space and time.)[29] Thus, the transformation was under way and proceeded, step by step, from the *Tractatus,* through Russell's *Philosophy of Logical Atomism,* to Carnap's *Logische Aufbau der Welt,* and so on to Ayer's *Language, Truth and Logic.* And, despite a dozen subsequent qualifications and changes of name, the same basic dichotomies (e.g., between the factual and the logical, the cognitive and the emotive) still preserve a central place in the "logical empiricism" of the present day.

The seeds of Wittgenstein's misunderstanding with Bertrand Russell had accordingly been sown very early on; and Wittgenstein's failure to explain publicly, at the time, the reasons why he rejected Russell's interpretation of his book helped only to encourage the development of the rival, positivist interpretation. Russell himself was quite content to see his own "propositional logic" expanded, to provide the core of a new epistemology. After all, he himself had interpreted the idea of "atomic facts" in this epistemological way in his own 1914 Harvard lectures, *Our Knowledge of the External World.*[30] So, for some five years from 1922 on, professional mathematicians, philosophers and physical scientists at the University of Vienna, many of them strongly influenced by Mach and Russell, were holding intense discussions of the *Tractatus* and its wider implications, without Wittgenstein's participation. Wittgenstein, meanwhile, acquired the reputation of being a kind of mystery man, lurking in the background. As early as 1924, Moritz Schlick was already writing to him, trying to arrange a meeting, but nothing came of this. It was not until the spring of 1927, in fact, that the two men met and inaugurated the series of discussions—mainly between Wittgenstein and Waismann, but with Schlick also taking part on occasion—which continued right through to 1932.[31]

By 1927, however, the damage was done. There was a touch of irony about these encounters from the beginning. Schlick's wife reported afterward that he approached the luncheon meeting with Wittgenstein, arranged by Margarete Stonborough, with "the reverential attitude of the pilgrim." Afterward, "he returned in an ecstatic state, saying little, and I felt I should not ask questions.'' For his part, Wittgenstein reported to Paul Engelmann, after the initial meeting, ''Each of us must have thought that the other was crazy.'' At Schlick's request, Wittgenstein agreed to meet Carnap and some of the other members of the Vienna Circle, but it immediately became apparent that their intellectual positions were far apart—perhaps, unbridgeably so. To begin with, Wittgenstein was unwilling to discuss technical points in philosophy with the members of the Vienna Circle, and he insisted rather on reading poetry to them, especially the poems of Rabindranath Tagore. (Given his Tolstoyan position, this insistence may not have been as willfully irrelevant as it must have appeared to his audience.) Only gradually did he gain enough confidence to engage in philosophical discussion on frank and equal terms; and even so, he found this much easier with Schlick and Waismann than with Carnap and the more fervently positivistic members of the Circle.

The differences separating them were, after all, real enough. Within philosophy of mathematics, their conversations could proceed in a reasonably constructive spirit; and most of the discussions that Waismann has preserved for us were in this general area. As soon as they went further afield, however, radical disagreements arose. At one point, for instance, the conversations strayed into the field of perception. Here, we find Schlick pressing an empiricist point of view in the tradition of Locke, Hume and Mach:

You say that the colors form a system. By that, do you mean something logical, or something empirical? Suppose, for instance, someone spent his whole life shut up in a red room, and could see only red . . . could he then say, ''I see only red, but there must be other colors also?''

Wittgenstein's reply to this question echoes Kant's earlier reply to Hume—namely, that all perception involves the formation of a judgment:

I do not see red, rather I see *that the azalea is red.* In this sense, I also see that it is not blue. . . . Either there is a state of affairs, which can be described, in which case the color red presupposes a system of colors, or alternatively ''red'' means something quite else, in which case there is no sense in calling it a color.[32]

During the crucial years in the middle 1920s, when the logical positivism of the Vienna Circle was taking shape, the philosophers and scientists involved deeply respected the authority of

Wittgenstein and his *Tractatus.* Yet he himself remained an on-looker, and an increasingly skeptical one, so that by the early 1930s he had dissociated himself entirely from ideas and doctrines that others continued to regard as *his* brain children. For his own part he hoped that he had "climbed through, on, over" the metaphors of the *Tractatus,* that he had finally "surmounted" them;[33] and, having kicked away the temporary scaling ladder he had used to get there, he was distressed to see others picking it up and embedding it permanently in intellectual concrete. That had never been his intention. The logical positivists were overlooking the very difficulties about language which the *Tractatus* had been meant to reveal; and they were turning an argument designed to circumvent *all* philosophical doctrines into a source of *new* doctrines, meanwhile leaving the original difficulties unresolved.

It would be easy to write this reaction off as a display of temperament by a man who had the nature of a prima donna. But that would be a mistake. We are at liberty to speculate about ulterior motives if we please, but Wittgenstein also had powerful *reasons* for dissociating himself from the logical positivists; and if we take the trouble to analyze those reasons, it will help us to define more exactly the scope, strengths and limits of the Vienna Circle approach itself. The fundamental point at issue can be clarified by comparing two approaches to the philosophy of science. In the course of the *Tractatus,* as we said, Wittgenstein had cited Newtonian dynamics as providing an extended illustration of his views about the nature of language, and this discussion can usefully be contrasted with the "logic" of scientific theories subsequently elaborated by such men as Carnap, Hempel and Nagel.[34] For logical empiricists, one of the main functions of a "logic of science" has been to provide epistemological guarantees for science; but, for Wittgenstein, the *Tractatus* was in no sense an exercise in the theory of knowledge. On the contrary, as he saw it, epistemological preoccupations were distracting his Vienna Circle colleagues from his real topic—namely, the relations of language to the world—and were leading them to take for granted an impossible theory of language.

This difference is worth spelling out. According to the *Tractatus,* the function of a formalized theory in science was to provide a possible "method of representing" the relevant kinds of fact about the natural world. As Wittgenstein had learned from

Hertz, the applicability of any axiomatic formalism—whether Euclid's, Newton's or Russell's—is necessarily problematic. It is one thing to lay out such a system in the form of explicit definitions and deductions; it is another thing entirely to show how the resulting categories and logical articulations can be applied to the world as we know it. Up to that point there was no disagreement between Wittgenstein and the positivists. But now the old epistemological question arose: Have we any guarantee that a given theory—for example, Newtonian dynamics—does in fact apply? And here we reach the parting of the ways. For Mach and the early logical positivists believed that, in principle at any rate, all the abstract terms of a meaningful theory have their "physical meaning" conferred on them through their association with appropriate collections of sensations or "observations"; and, interpreted in this way, the statements in the abstract formalism become empirical descriptions of the natural world as we perceive it. Accordingly, in a completely candid science, every general abstract term or proposition will be anchored down, both logically and epistemologically, to a corresponding set of *Protokollsätze*, while the terms used in the *Protokollsätze* themselves are defined "ostensively," by associating them with the contents of our observations—ideally, of our sensory fields.[85]

This was once again a return to Hume, with "sensations," "sense data," and/or *Protokollsätze* standing in for "impressions" and statements recording "impressions." Wittgenstein had no use for any such doctrine. An axiomatic theory, he had argued, defines only a formal *ensemble* of possibilities in "logical space." This formal ensemble of possibilities—this "symbolism," "mode of representation," or "language"—could never be anchored *logically* to the world we use it to describe, because logical relations hold only *within* a symbolism. No set of authentic definitions can be contrived which will by itself transform the Newtonian formalism, or any other set of symbolic articulations, into a plain description of the world; if we *do* use the possibilities defined by such a theory as the stock in trade of our scientific descriptions and explanations, that fact inevitably remains a fact as much about *us* as about the world. "That Newtonian mechanics *can* be used to describe the world," Wittgenstein had declared, "tells us nothing about the world. But this *does* tell us something—that it can be used to describe the world *in the way in which we do in fact use it.''*[36] If Mach had played Hume, then Wittgenstein was here playing Kant—repeating Kant's countermove against Hume, but in a linguistic rather than an epistemological mode. The crucial idea of ''ostensive definitions,'' by which the logical positivists had hoped to account for the connection between language and the world, was a delusion. In the last resort, the connections between the linguistic realm and the world—the meanings, uses, or *modes d'emploi* it involves—cannot be made a matter for formal definitions; they are something which we must simply ''catch on to.''

Using this last phrase, of course, involves running ahead. The idea of ''language uses'' as something we have to ''catch on to'' becomes open and explicit only in Wittgenstein's later phase, after his break with the logical positivists was complete and open. Yet the arguments that led him to this idea were implicit in his earlier views. Working on the *Tractatus* had taught him that the relationship between language and reality was not, and could not be, a ''logical'' one. The relationship between a ''simple sign'' and that to which it corresponds in the real world was something that could be demonstrated or shown; but that demonstration (*Erklärung*) was in no sense a ''definition.'' This relationship could be shown but not stated (*gezeigt* but not *gesagt*). Definitions have a logical force only as between one set of words and another; thus the ambition to establish formal relationships between words and the world, whether by ''ostensive definition'' or otherwise, was unacceptable. Yet, for Mach, that ambition had been fundamental, if epistemology was to give the guarantees for natural science that he required.

This was the breaking point between Wittgenstein and the logical positivists. They would have to choose between him and Mach; and by and large they chose Mach. (Waismann was the one exception.) Yet they did so without at first consciously renouncing Wittgenstein; for, as they saw it, there was nothing incompatible between the insights of the two *maestri*. In the *Tractatus*, the basic symbolism of *Principia Mathematica,* as generalized by the truth-table method, had apparently provided positivism with the logical skeleton it had lacked in the writings of Auguste Comte. The idea of ''atomic facts'' could at once be given an epistemological use by identifying these facts with the evidence of Mach's ''sensations''; and a dozen other gnomic remarks thrown out in passing in the *Tractatus* could be reinterpreted in the same sense. For example, Wittgenstein's insistence that the relationship between language and the world was fundamentally "ineffable," that the mode of projection of a map cannot itself be "mapped," any more than we can *see* the light rays we are *seeing with*—this insistence, which he had expressed in the closing proposition, *Wovon man nicht sprechen kann, darüber muss man schweigen,* was interpreted by his Viennese associates as the positivist slogan "Metaphysicians, shut your traps!" Thus was born the hybrid system of logical positivism, which professed to put an end to all metaphysics but succeeded, rather, in rewriting the metaphysics of Hume and Mach in the symbolism of Russell and Whitehead.

To young Central European intellectuals growing up in the political and cultural wreckage of the Habsburg Empire, this philosophical reformation came like a breath of fresh air. And, indeed, some four fifths of the *Tractatus* could, without obvious misrepresentation, be used as a source of forthright, no-nonsense positivist slogans. As these younger men read it, the book was a grand, highly professional, and seemingly final denunciation of superstition (*Aberglaube*), and its closing motto was inscribed on the banners of all high-minded young freethinkers.[37] Once Wittgenstein had thus been labeled as a positivist, men found it hard to see him in any other light. So when, from 1929 on, he returned to philosophy and moved gradually into his second, contrasted phase of philosophizing, his new style was not regarded as a *rejection* of positivism. Rather, it was seen as a reconstruction of his earlier positivistic position on new and deeper foundations. In the late 1940s, for instance, an influential pair of articles in *Mind,* written by Brian Farrell, characterized Wittgenstein's newer position as "therapeutic positivism."[38] On this interpretation, men still had to be talked out of superstitious, unverifiable and/or meaningless beliefs; but the arguments designed to produce this result were to have a new starting point and a new method. The idea that the realm of the significant could be demonstrated by an analysis of language in the symbolism of mathematical logic was now abandoned. Instead, philosophical theories were to be diagnosed as symptoms of misconceptions about our *everyday language*—"cerebroses" (so to say) comparable to the "neuroses," which spring from misconceptions about our affective relationships.[39]

Far from being a positivist, however, Wittgenstein had meant the *Tractatus* to be interpreted in exactly the opposite sense. Where the Vienna positivists had equated the "important" with the "verifiable" and dismissed all unverifiable propositions as "unimportant *because* unsayable," the concluding section of the *Tractatus* had insisted—though to deaf ears—that *the unsayable alone has genuine value.* We can, it tells us, recognize "the higher" only in that which the propositions of our language are *unfitted* to capture; since no "fact," such as can be "pictured" by a "proposition," has any intrinsic claim either on our moral submission, or on our aesthetic approval. Wittgenstein's silence in the face of the "unutterable" was not a mocking silence like that of the positivists, but rather a respectful one. Having decided that "value-neutral" facts alone can be expressed in regular propositional form, he exhorted his readers to turn their eyes away from factual propositions to the things of true value— which cannot be *gesagt* but only *gezeigt.* No wonder Wittgenstein saw the completion of his *Tractatus* as a moment to give up doing philosophy and set out to devote himself to humanly important activities!

Paul Engelmann puts the point:

A whole generation of disciples was able to take Wittgenstein as a positivist, because he has something of enormous importance in common with the positivists: he draws the line between what we can speak about and what we must be silent about just as they do. The difference is only that they have nothing to be silent about. Positivism holds—and this is its essence—that what we can speak about is all that matters in life. *Whereas Wittgenstein passionately believes that all that really matters in human life is precisely what, in his view, we must be silent about.*[40]

Nor did Wittgenstein's interests in "atomic facts" and the rest have any epistemological implications for him. Both in Cambridge and in Vienna, the *Tractatus* was initially read as elaborating the very same theory of "logical atomism," applied to the analysis of our knowledge of the external world, that had previously been developed less formally by Mach and Russell. Wittgenstein had apparently completed the work, on which Mach and Russell had begun, of explaining how propositions about "material objects" could be "logically constructed" out of propositions about immediate sense experience. And one can fairly comment that Wittgenstein was acting imprudently, when he took over Russell's phrase "atomic facts" and analyzed the logical relationships between these facts and the propositions that "mirror" them, without distinguishing his own use of this phrase from that which it had had in Russell's epistemology—where it referred to the "hard data of sense." Once this confusion had been made, it was not hard to read Wittgenstein's later *Philosophical Investigations* too in an epistemological sense. Whereas philosophers like Russell had treated Wittgenstein's "unit propositions" as units of *knowledge,* as well as units of *language,* one could now read Wittgenstein's later polemic against the idea of a "private language" (whose terms would draw their meaning directly from "sensations") as an *epistemological* critique of the theory that sense data are the foundation of all our knowledge.

Nevertheless, Wittgenstein's preoccupation remained throughout what it was in the beginning: a preoccupation, less with the foundations of knowledge, than with the nature and limits of language. He was above all a "transcendental" philosopher, whose central philosophical question—as contrasted with his ethical questions—could be posed in the Kantian form, How is a meaningful language *possible at all?* And in this sense, it is a mistake to see him even as a "linguistic philosopher" in the sense in which G. E. Moore and the recent Oxford analysts have undoubtedly been. Wittgenstein was undeniably concerned with language and with the manner in which language operates within our lives; yet he never saw this as the self-sufficient subject matter of philosophy. Lexicography and linguistics were both perfectly reputable disciplines, but neither of them was specially *philosophical.* The philosopher's task, is not, in Wittgenstein's view, to instruct the ordinary man by analyzing the meanings of words; he himself rejected this notion, commenting,

There is no common-sense answer to a philosophical problem. One can defend common sense against the attacks of philosophers only by solving their puzzles, i.e., by curing them of the temptation to attack common sense, not by restating the views of common sense. A philosopher is not a man out of his senses, a man who doesn't see what everybody sees; nor on the other hand is his disagreement with common sense that of the scientist disagreeing with the coarse views of the man in the street.[41]

To Wittgenstein, language was interesting only as an element in a larger inquiry; and linguistic investigations had implications for philosophy only when they were placed in a broader intellectual context. In this sense, he was no more of a "linguistic philosopher" than, say, Plato or Kant or Schopenhauer.

Though all these men were interested in discovering how "thoughts" are related to "things," "language" to "facts," "judgments" to "things in themselves," or "representations" to "that which is represented," none of them posed that question—any more than Wittgenstein did himself—merely as a problem in linguistics.

From 1929 on, Wittgenstein was once again working at philosophy, and was in more or less continuous touch with his philosophical colleagues. By the time of his death, he had reached a position—best represented by his posthumous *Philosophical Investigations* (1953)—which appears, at first sight, to have little in common with that of the *Tractatus*. On the surface, the *Tractatus* had been a contribution to symbolic logic, in the tradition of Frege and Russell. By contrast, the *Investigations* presents an empirical-looking argument designed to demonstrate the "prodigious diversity" of ways in which language is put to use in human life; and it continually seems to be verging, not into mathematical logic, but rather into anthropology and psychology. This surface contrast is, however, misleading. Waismann has recorded a conversation (December 9, 1931) in which Wittgenstein talked about his progressive disillusionment with logical symbolism as an instrument for explaining the significance and scope of actual linguistic behavior.[42] Seven months later (July 1, 1932) he was telling Waismann,

In the *Tractatus*, I was unclear about "logical analysis" and ostensive demonstration [*Erklärung*]. I used to think that there was a direct link [*Verbindung*] between Language and Reality.[43]

Having taken it for granted, in the *Tractatus*, that the relationship between "simple signs" and that to which they corresponded could be immediately seen (even if it could not be *stated*) he had been too readily satisfied with a formal analysis of language as representation; and he had, as a result, paid too little attention to the steps by which formalized representations are *put to use* in real-life linguistic behavior. Even in physics—as Hertz had taught him—a mathematical system can be applied to scientific problems in the real world, only if we also have well-defined procedures for relating mathematical symbols with empirical magnitudes or measurements. So it had been an error, in his earlier book, to take for granted the existence of some self-explanatory and immediately recognizable *Verbindung der Sprache und der Wirklichkeit*. On the contrary, the crucial question now became, ''By what procedures do men *establish* the rule-governed links they do between language, on the one hand, and the real world, on the other?''

To arrive at a language suitable for the expression of ''propositions,'' accordingly, it is not enough for us to ''make for ourselves pictures of facts.'' The expressions in our language acquire their specific *meanings* from the procedures by which we give them definite *uses* in our practical dealings with one another and with the world, not from their inner articulation alone, nor from any essentially ''pictorial'' character in the utterances themselves. So the writing of the *Tractatus* had not, after all, completed Wittgenstein's philosophical task. His earlier solution of the ''transcendental'' problem—that is, his earlier account of the scope and limits of language—had been given in terms of a ''picturing'' relation which (as he saw now all too clearly) had been at best a helpful metaphor. Now he was faced with the complementary task, of showing how *any* linguistic expression—whether ''pictorial'' or not—acquires a linguistic significance, by being *given a use* in human life.

This was the starting point for the characteristic investigations of Wittgenstein's later period. His concern was no longer with the ''formal structure'' of language or with any supposed similarity of structure between ''propositions'' and ''facts.'' Men might have special reasons within physics, say, for giving a direct, ''pictorial'' representation of phenomena; but elsewhere there was less reason to regard the propositions of our language as ''pictures of facts.'' So, from now on, Wittgenstein focused his attention instead on *language as behavior:* concentrating his analysis on the pragmatic *rules* that govern the uses of different expressions, on the *language games* within which those rules are operative, and on the broader *forms of life* which ultimately give those language games their significance. The heart of the ''transcendental'' problem thus ceased (for Wittgenstein) to lie in the formal character of linguistic representations; instead, it became an element in ''the natural history of man.''[44] Unlike Kant, who had forever resisted any move that threatened to debase the discussion of philosophy from the analysis of rational thought as such into ''mere anthropology,'' Wittgenstein came to see the philosophical task as one of human self-understanding. (As he came to say, "Language is *our* language.") Yet, for all this shift of focus, the deeper preoccupation of his later years remained the same as that of his youth: to complete the logical and ethical tasks begun by Kant and Schopenhauer.

So that same humane and cultivated Viennese who had begun, in his youth, by mastering the mechanics of Hertz and the thermodynamics of Boltzmann; who had gone on, in his twenties, to play a leading part in the development of symbolic logic; who had abandoned philosophy, at the age of thirty, in favor of other, humanly more valuable occupations—that same philosopher found himself, at fifty, urging his hearers to reflect more carefully on the ways in which children do in fact learn (or might alternatively learn) the standard patterns of behavior within which our language has a practical function, and on the metaphysical confusions that can flow from any failure to keep these practical functions clearly in mind. Yet, for all its seeming changes, his intellectual Odyssey had been directed along a single, constant compass bearing. A man could obey the Socratic injunction, *Know thyself,* only if he came to understand the scope and limits of his own understanding; and this meant, first and foremost, recognizing the precise scope and limits of language, which is the prime instrument of human understanding.

Wittgenstein had entered philosophy with both intellectual and ethicoreligious preoccupations, the former derived from the transcendental inquiries of Kant and Schopenhauer, the latter inherited from Tolstoy and kept alive by Kierkegaard. The two groups of preoccupations together focused his attention on the scope and limits of linguistic expression; and his concern with this problem took several different forms in succession. First, as a young student of applied mathematics, he hoped to solve this "transcendental" problem by generalizing the ideas of Hertz and Boltzmann. Next, he found in the new logic of Frege and Russell an instrument—and a symbolism—with the help of which, he believed, one could demonstrate the scope and limits of language in general; the outcome was his *Tractatus Logico-Philosophicus.* Returning to philosophy after a break of some years, he now saw that deeper problems require one, even in mathematics, to consider not the inner articulations of mathematical calculi, but rather the rule-conforming behavior by which such calculi acquire some external relevance. (This is the burden of his conversations with Waismann and Schlick.) And finally, back at Cambridge, in a philosophical situation dominated by the example of G. E. Moore, he generalized his analysis yet again, with the aim of demonstrating how the meaning, scope and limits of *any* symbolic representation—linguistic as much as mathematical—depend on the relations by which men link it to a wider behavioral context.

For the later Wittgenstein, therefore, the "meaning" of any utterance is determined by the rule-conforming, symbol-using activities ("language games") within which the expressions in question are conventionally put to use; and these symbol-using activities in turn draw their significance from the broader patterns of activities (or "forms of life") in which they are embedded and of which they are a constituent element. The final solution of Wittgenstein's initial "transcendental" problem then consists in coming to recognize all the multifarious ways in which "forms of life" create legitimate contexts for "language games," and how these in turn delimit the scope and boundaries of the sayable.[45]

The continuity in Wittgenstein's thought is reflected in the loyalty and admiration he retained throughout his whole career for Heinrich Hertz. It was from Hertz's example that he first learned how progress might be made in solving the "transcendental" problem. It was to Hertz he would return, in the late 1940s, for the classic description of philosophical perplexity—namely, to the passage in the Introduction to Hertz's *Principles of Mechanics,* where he diagnoses the confusions underlying the nineteenth-century debates about the nature of *force* or *electricity:*

Why is it that people never in this way ask what is the nature of gold, or what is the nature of velocity? Is the nature of gold better known to us than that of force? Can we by our conceptions, by our words, completely represent the nature of any thing? Certainly not. I fancy the difference must lie in this. With the terms "velocity" and "gold" we connect a large number of relations to other terms; and between all these relations we find no contradictions which offend us. We are therefore satisfied and ask no further questions. But we have accumulated around the terms "force" and "electricity" more relations than can be completely reconciled amongst themselves. We have an obscure feeling of this and want to have things cleared up. Our confused wish finds expression in the confused questions as to the nature of force and electricity. But the answer which we want is not really an answer to this question. It is not by finding out more and fresh relations and connections that it can be answered; but by removing the contradictions existing between those already known, and thus perhaps by reducing their number. *When these painful contradictions are removed, the question as to the nature of force will not have been answered; but our minds, no longer vexed, will cease to ask illegitimate questions.*[46]

Throughout this later phase, Wittgenstein's philosophical development was diverging further and further from that of the Viennese positivists. They had, of course, been able to treat the *Tractatus* as a foundation for their own philosophical system, only by reading his remarks about "ostensive demonstration" (*hinweisende Erklärung*)—by which a man is brought to "see" the *Verbindung* between any simple sign and the corresponding reality—as a kind of "definition." Even in the *Tractatus* itself, Wittgenstein had denied that this *Erklärung* could properly be thought of in these terms. And the more that he now thought about the things that Moore and the sense datum theorists, Mach and the logical positivists, had alike been taking for granted in their theories of language, the more puzzling he found them. For how could "private sensations" be used, definitionally, as an anchor for language? And if, as he believed, they could not perform this definitional function—if the notion of "ostensive definitions" was in fact quite nonsensical—how then could one break the hold of the intellectual model that Moore, Mach, and their followers had found so seductive? Wittgenstein soon saw that he must find some alternative way of indicating how language *does* operate. It was all very well to insist that—literally speaking—the uses of language could not be "stated" but only "shown"; but that could no longer be accepted as an argument for silence (*darüber muss man schweigen*). After all, he had managed incidentally in the *Tractatus* to "show" a good deal about the relation between formalized scientific theories and the world, using as his expository device the model of a picturing relationship (*Abbildung*). The problem was now to find comparable ways of showing how language operates in other spheres of thought, reasoning and meaning, to which the "picture" model of language has no relevance—not even mythical or analogical.[47]

At the corresponding point in his own antisensationalist argument, Kant had launched into his "transcendental deduction," arguing that our existing system of concepts, categories, and forms of intuition alone is capable of yielding a *coherent* understanding of experience. Kant was prepared to settle for nothing less than a "deduction" because, in his eyes, it was essential to insulate the fundamental structure of our rational concepts from what he called "mere anthropology"; it would never do, for instance, to make the *necessary* truth of Pythagoras' theorem contingent upon the *empirical* fact that carpenters, surveyors and other human geometry users habitually employ in their actual practice procedures the effect of which is to guarantee the Euclidean system's relevance and applicability. Wittgenstein's ambitions were more modest. Certainly the positivistic equation of the "necessary" with the "tautologous" had been too shallow. Tautologies are two-a-penny, and we can construct as many more as we require, Humpty-Dumpty-wise, whenever we please—"It's a question of who's to be master, you or the words." But this left one central fact unexplained: the fact that some such tautologies are manifestly more indispensable than others, that we "feel" the necessity of some of them (in Keats's phrase) "on our pulses," while we could throw others overboard with equanimity.

This point was not met by turning it, as G. E. Moore had done, into a conundrum—"Is the proposition that *p* is a necessary proposition *itself* a necessary proposition?"[48] To do this only concealed the fact that we are concerned here with two kinds of "necessity," one of which can plausibly be equated with "tautology," the other of which cannot. (We should do better to rephrase Moore's question in the form, "Could we get along without the tautology *p?* Or is this tautology indispensable?") Nor was it met by replying, with Quine, that the original distinction between the "necessary" and the "contingent" was never applicable in the first place, except perhaps contingently.[49] For the very question at issue is: On what actual conditions does this distinction remain applicable? In what contingencies should we be obliged to admit that the applicability of some fundamental concept (or the relevance of some "necessary" relationship) was once again in doubt? Rather, some way must be found of bringing into the open the *human contingencies*—the "anthropological" facts, as Kant would have called them—presupposed in the adoption of our existing categories and concepts. In this way, the central philosophical problem with which Wittgenstein had been concerned throughout drove him away from all questions about syntax and formal semantics, and into that area of "pragmatics" and "psychologism" which logical positivists and logical empiricists have always dismissed as a formless intellectual slag heap.

In this second phase, Wittgenstein's style of exposition was as idiosyncratic as before; and those who never attended his lectures can hardly be blamed for missing the point. Whereas in his *Tractatus* he had resorted to myth, he now used parables or fables. To reconstruct two typical samples from memory:

Suppose a young child who has been playing outdoors runs into the house and grasps the kitchen tap, calling out as he does, "Water, water" —this being a word he heard used for the first time only yesterday. And suppose someone now raises the question, "Is the child telling us something, or showing that he has learned the meaning of this word, or asking for a drink?" What are we then to do? Need there be any way of answering that question?

or again:

Suppose an anthropologist finds the members of a tribe, whose language he does not yet understand, cutting up bolts of longitudinally striped cloth and exchanging them for small cubes of wood, uttering as they hand over the cubes the sounds "eena," "meena," "mina," "mo," and so on, always in the same regular sequence. And suppose he discovers that this exchange proceeds always up to the same point, regardless of whether the cloth is (as we should say) single-width or folded double. What should the anthropologist then conclude? Is he to infer that the tribe values cloth only by its length as measured along the stripes; or that the merchants who sell the cloth single-width are rogues; or that the tribe's arithmetic has a different structure from ours; or that "eena," "meena," "mina," "mo" are not their words for "1," "2," "3," and "4" after all; or that this is not really a commercial exchange, but some kind of a ritual . . . ? Or might we have no effective way of deciding among these alternatives?[50]

These little stories, with the sting in the final question, all had the same general effect. They forced the hearer into a corner from which he could escape in only one way: by conceding that the applicability or inapplicability of some actual category or concept depends, in practice, always on previous human decisions, and that these decisions have become "second nature" to us, for one or both of two distinct reasons. Either, the choices in question were made long ago in the development of our culture, and—no occasion having arisen for challenging them—their outcomes have been preserved within our conceptual traditions ever since; or, alternatively, the practice of using an expression in our conventional way, rather than in some conceivable alternative way, is drilled into us so early in life that, until some unforeseen contingency compels us to reconsider it, we cease to think twice about it; or, most commonly, the conceptual feature under discussion reflects choices taken at forgotten branch points in conceptual development, which are both ancient in terms of cultural history and early in the development of the individual's habits of speech and thought.

By explicitly reconstructing for ourselves the issues arising at these branch points, we shall normally (though not necessarily) come to see that, given all the circumstances, our actual conceptual practices are understandable and natural—even the most eminently practical—ones to have adopted, and so not readily "dispensable." To that extent, we shall have done what can be done to satisfy Kant's demand for a "transcendental" proof of the "synthetic a priori." The concepts and categories we actually employ may not provide the only conceivable or consistent basis for a coherent, describable experience of the world; but they do represent a legitimate equilibrium, resulting from a sequence of interlocking choices none of which, in the actual context of decision, could have been taken differently except at a certain price. And we can demand more than that, only if we misunderstand what is involved in the building of our language.

In expounding these fables or parables, Wittgenstein had not actually moved as far from his earlier *Tractatus* position as many people thought. For such "imaginary tales" amounted, as he said himself, to no more than "assembling reminders of the obvious"; in this way, he was simply bringing his hearers to the point of *recognizing for themselves* something implicit in their own linguistic practices which he could not explicitly *assert* without abandoning his own principles. There might not be a directly visible *Verbindung* between language and the world, yet this relationship was still something which had to be shown rather than stated; and it could be made a matter for teaching, only through indirect communication. What Tolstoy's *Tales* had done for the unsayable in ethics, these fables of Wittgenstein's did for the unsayable in the philosophy of language. So, in philosophy as in ethics, Wittgenstein believed, teaching could bring a man only to a point at which he recognized what you were getting at, for himself; and it was no good attempting to draw an explicit conclusion for him.

Nor, for that matter, did Wittgenstein's transition from the formal theory of "truth tables" to the informal analysis of "language games" do anything to break the links with his own Krausian inheritance. The arguments in the *Philosophical Investigations* need to be seen against his earlier Viennese background, quite as much as those of the *Tractatus*. We can, for instance, compare the considerations underlying his abandonment of a "representational" view of language in favor of an analysis in "functional" terms with the considerations that had earlier led Hugo von Hofmannsthal to abandon lyric poetry (based on the poetic image as *Bild)* in favor of morality plays that were *Gesamtkunstwerke*. Similarly, the notion of "forms of life" as the contexts for the language games within which linguistic expressions acquire their meaning, is itself a strikingly Loosian notion. Loos himself had insisted that the design of any meaningful artifact must be determined by the "forms of culture" within which it is used—the form of a chair by the way in which we sit, et cetera—so that changes in design have to be justified by changes in our manner of life, rather than vice versa. Even the very term *Lebensformen* (or "forms of life") itself, which Wittgenstein used at this point in his argument, had a recognizable Viennese origin. It was in fact part of the title of *Fackel* author Otto Stössl's study, *Lebensformen und Dichtungsformen,* published in Vienna on the eve of World War I, while Eduard Spranger's characterological study, *Lebensformen,* which appeared shortly thereafter, had sold 28,000 copies by the end of the decade. Given Wittgenstein's Viennese background, therefore, he was no more in a position to *invent* the term "forms of life" than one could today invent the phrase "territorial imperative"; in the Vienna of the 1920s, this was just one of those cultural commonplaces that did not need explaining.

Once again, however, the use that Wittgenstein made of this notion was highly original. Kant had argued that all our thoughts, perceptions and experiences are subject to a single, uniquely coherent system of concepts, categories and forms of organization; that these "rational forms" are, so to say, *compulsory* for all truly rational thinkers and agents. The neo-Kantian characterologists made one significant amendment to this view. They denied that the pure and practical reason had any single, unique and universal structure that was compulsory for thinkers of all interests and all cultures and was expressed in a common system of "synthetic a priori principles." Rather, different thinkers and agents structure their experience in a variety of ways, characterized by different systems of regulative principles. Any particular structure of interpretation is then compulsory—and the "synthetic a priori truths" which express that structure are relevant and applicable—only within the scope of a particular *Lebensform.*

By the 1920s men like Stössl and Spranger were teaching that forms of life are the ultimate data in philosophy, and that our basic categories and forms of thought gain a significance and application from this relationship to these forms of life and culture. Yet how this relationship was itself to be understood they never made clear. Spranger himself declared that alternative rational systems were characteristic of rival types of mind. The "military mind," for instance, conforms to one set of regulative principles, the "contemplative mind" to another, the "artistic-creative mind" to a third. Alternative systems of regulative principles thus define different *styles of thought,* and these styles in turn reflect parallel modes—or forms—of life style. Yet, in the last resort, Spranger's analysis remained curiously shallow and circular. For what, we may ask, is the essential difference between, say, the "military" and the "contemplative" styles of life? Can we characterize this difference independently, without using conformity to the respective regulative principles as a defining criterion, or differentia?

Reading the characterologists, we are never far from this central tautology; and we miss the feeling for a genuinely "anthropological" dimension that Wittgenstein brought to his own account of *Lebensformen.* In the *Philosophical Investigation,* by contrast, the alternative *Lebensformen*—all the possible human styles of thought, character and language—are no longer bare, abstract schemata. Wittgenstein says to us, rather: "Look and see how our life is *in fact* structured; thus it is, and thus it has to be, if our crucial concepts (e.g., 'proof,' 'time,' or 'sensation') are to have the meanings they demonstrably do have for the men who use them." So, in the *Investigations,* we can at last begin to see how one might go beyond the abstract discussion of schematic life styles, and identify the *actual* features of human life on which the validity of our fundamental concepts, categories and forms of thought depends. And over this point, as over the *Tractatus,* the true direction of Wittgenstein's line of attack becomes clear, only when we set aside for the moment the empiricism of Mach and Russell and place his problems in a transcendental tradition that leads back to Kant.

In just one respect, Wittgenstein's abandonment of the idea that language has a self-evident *Verbindung* to reality did have ironical consequences for him. In the *Tractatus,* he had committed himself to Russell's distinction between the "apparent logical form" of a proposition and its "real form"; and it was by appealing to precisely this distinction that he justified his remark (4.0031) that all philosophy is a "critique of language"—though *not in Mauthner's sense.* When he finally gave up the idea of a direct *Verbindung,* sometime around 1928–29, he gave up also Russell's associated distinction between "apparent" and "real" logical form; and he was left, as a result, in a position very much closer to Mauthner's than before. True, he did not explicitly share Mauthner's cultural relativism, nor any of the other consequences in which Mauthner was involved as a by-product of accepting a Machian nominalism. All the same, regarded as a general philosophical critique of language, Wittgenstein's later writings revived many positions and arguments already put forward by Mauthner in 1901—for example, the view that the rules of language are like the rules of a game, and that the very word "language" is itself a general abstract term, which we need to unpack by looking to see how, in actual practice, men put the expressions of their languages to use, within the contexts of all their varied cultures. The "logical structures" of the *Tractatus* had, after all, been only a metaphor that Wittgenstein had adopted temporarily, with an eye to certain larger philosophical purposes. And, as a long-standing admirer of Kraus and Loos, he was—in the light of his own subsequent self-criticism—entirely happy to accept an alternative point of view, within which "logical form" was by-passed and "meaning" was related directly to "functions" and "forms of life."

We shall shortly be ready to broaden our view, and to consider how far the changes that have taken place in philosophy since 1920 themselves reflect—and are reflected in—wider features of culture and society. However, the contrast between Wittgenstein's two main philosophical positions gives rise to one last question, a question which, in retrospect, calls into doubt his original claim that the solutions to "the problems of philosophy" given in the *Tractatus* were "unassailable and definitive." For the formal techniques of analysis that he had taken over from Frege and Russell apparently gave him the means of demonstrating the "unsayability," not just of the *Verbindung* between language and reality, but also of all questions of value. And we must here reconsider the question how far, in demolishing the basis of his earlier *linguistic* conclusions, Wittgenstein may not inadvertently have destroyed the basis for his *ethical* conclusions also.

At the outset, we argued, Wittgenstein's two main preoccupations—with "representation" and the problem of "the ethical" —were related, yet distinguishable. The conclusions of the *Tractatus* had the apparent merit of satisfying both preoccupations at the same time; for his formal mapping of *die Grenze der Sprache* effectively thrust the whole of ethics, values, and "the higher" too, outside the boundaries of the "sayable" and, so, underpinned his original Kierkegaardian attitudes. From 1930 on, we find him still adhering to the same ethical standpoint, yet in a new philosophical context; and it is not clear that his new account of *language* continued to provide any longer the kind of support for his *ethical* point of view that the *Tractatus* position had given. Even in Wittgenstein's later days, we saw, he firmly rejected the philosophical ethics of men like Schlick and Moore, as being overintellectualistic; and he held himself to the view that "the nature of the Good has nothing to do with the facts, and so cannot be explained by any proposition."[51] Yet the argument by which he had underpinned this absolute separation between "facts" and "values"—between what can be directly stated and what can be only "indirectly communicated"—had relied crucially, hitherto, on the ability to draw a correspondingly hard and fast distinction between the "representational" and the "poetic" uses of language. And, as we read the conversations with Waismann during the period 1929–31, we see Wittgenstein edging toward his own later position, in a way that immediately creates new difficulties for him about ethics.

At one point, for instance, Wittgenstein asks, "Does speech play an essential part in religion?"[52] And in answering this question he seems at first glance to be anticipating his later general account of language *as behavior*.

I can well imagine a religion in which there are no doctrines, so that nothing is spoken. Clearly, then, the essence of religion can have nothing to do with what is said—or rather: if anything is said, then that itself is an element [*Bestandteil*] in religious behavior [*Handlung*], and not a theory.

From this, we are tempted to conclude that the language games of religion derive their meaning from the religious forms of life in which they are elements. Yet he immediately goes on to say:

Further, no question accordingly arises, whether the words used are true or false or meaningless. Religious utterances are no sort of *likeness* [*Gleichnis*] : otherwise one would have to express them also in prose.

Here, the use of the word *Gleichnis* looks backward to a representational view of language, rather than onward to the behavioral semantics of the *Philosophical Investigations*. At this point, therefore, Wittgenstein is still contrasting religious and poetic languages (which are *not* representational) with ordinary descriptive language (which presumably *is*). Later on, however, Wittgenstein was to generalize the behavioral account of "meaning," and warn us against assuming that anything in language derives its truth, falsity or meaningfulness merely from being a *Bild;* so his later arguments present *all* linguistic expressions as being meaningful because of their roles as *Bestandteilen der Handlung*. By the time this final transition was completed, he had apparently abandoned any absolute or hard and fast contrast between literal, descriptive utterances (language as *Bild)* and ritual or performative speech (language as *Handlung);* and, by taking this final step, he had dismantled also the very criterion by appeal to which he had drawn his original absolute distinction between "sayable" facts, which language can encompass, and "transcendental" values, which must in the nature of things remain forever inexpressible.

In this final phase, Wittgenstein has no obvious defense against the argument that ethics and religion involve forms of life of their own or that, within these *Lebensformen,* ethical and religious language games become, in their own ways, as verbalizable and as meaningful (even as true or false) as any others. At the very least, he is no longer in a position to underpin his own individualistic view of ethics by appeal to a sharp dichotomy between the expressible and the transcendental. From his later conversations about religious beliefs, it is clear that he remained to the end as puzzled as he had ever been about the character of religious discourse.[53] But the formal writings of his later years touch on the subject only in isolated aphorisms—odd, parenthetical phrases such as "(theology as grammar)."[54] They give no explicit answer to the central question whether ethical or religious discourse does not comprise a legitimate system of meaningful language games. And, meanwhile, plenty of modernist theologians are ready enough to analyze religious discourse as *ein Bestandteil der religiösen Handlung,* and so to use Wittgenstein's later methods as the basis for a theological counterattack against the positivists.[55]

Clearly enough, too, Wittgenstein's change of philosophical method was for him only a continuation of his earlier intellectual policies by other means; it did not lead him *in fact* to abandon his long-standing ethical individualism. So we can only speculate about the response he would have made, if anyone had pressed the legitimacy of "ethical" forms of life and language games against him with determination. For might one not have urged that, on his own later principles, the very *intelligibility* of words like *good* and *right* is as dependent as that of all other linguistic expressions on the acceptance of those shared language games and forms of life within which they are given their standard uses, and by reference to which alone we can understand one another's choices, decisions and scruples? Surely, his own later position implies that the concept of "values" itself relies for its meaning on the existence of certain standard and recognizable modes of "evaluative" behavior? To this extent, Wittgenstein's later philosophy of language could neither justify nor refute, *in principle,* any complete dissociation of the realm of values from the realm of facts. Perhaps, he might at this point have replied by distinguishing the "sense" of ethical judgments from their "content" and appealing to their essentially private *content* as exempting the discussion of their "truth" or "validity" from the public criteria which necessarily govern their *sense;* so perhaps, in this way, even the "private-language" arguments that played a large part in Wittgenstein's later writings may, for him personally, have had an implicit ethical significance. As to this, we can only speculate. All that is certain is that, whatever the strict implications of his later position, the absolute dichotomy of facts and values was of great importance to him—of greater importance, indeed, than any particular philosophical argument that might have been put forward to underpin or justify it.

What, then, lay behind this dichotomy for him? Can we penetrate behind it to some yet deeper layer of Wittgenstein's thought? In point of philosophical theory, that separation of values from all matters of fact was evidently the end of the road. But there are hints—especially in the letters to Engelmann—that, for Wittgenstein personally, something else may have underlain that irreducible contrast. These hints might be followed up in either of two directions: psychological or sociological. In attempting to go further, that is, we might look more closely, either at Wittgenstein's own personal makeup or at the historical setting within which his mind was formed. Psychologically speaking, to begin with, one can say this much: that, whether or no Wittgenstein could have continued to offer any further justification *in principle* for dissociating the realm of facts from the realm of values, he did not succeed *in his own life* in creating any effective correspondence between them. In his letters to Engelmann, for instance, he several times reports thought of suicide. He writes repeatedly in tones of self-disgust about his own "lack of decency" (*Unanständigkeit*); and he hints at emotional pressures which it was equally difficult for him to suppress or to sublimate. On October 11, 1920, he writes:

At last I have become a primary-school teacher, and I am working in a beautiful and tiny place called Trattenbach. . . . I am happy in my work at school, and I do need it badly, or else all the devils in Hell break loose inside me. How much I should like to see you and talk to you!!!!! A great deal has happened. I have carried out several operations which were *very* painful but went off well. I.e. I may miss a limb from time to time—but better have a few limbs less and the remaining ones sound.[56]

Whatever the cause, he was still struggling in 1922. He wrote again in 1925, "Anyway, I am not happy, and not because my rottenness troubles me, but within my rottenness."[57] And, even in 1937, he is writing from Trinity College, Cambridge, "God knows what will become of me."[58]

Still, to grope after the ultimate source of Wittgenstein's deepest intellectual attitudes in his personal temperament and makeup would, very likely, betray us into unprofitable and irrelevant speculations. (As he says to Engelmann in a letter written from England, in the summer of 1925: "How could I expect you to understand me, when I barely understand myself!")[59] Instead, we shall do better to recall the social and cultural parallels that we came across in earlier chapters—that is, at those respects in which Wittgenstein's life and background make him so representative a figure of the last days of Austria-Hungary. The extreme individualism of Wittgenstein's position thus needs to be viewed against the backcloth of late-nineteenth-century Viennese bourgeois society and culture, just as that of Kierkegaard needs to be viewed as a reaction against the social artificialities of early-nineteenth-century Danish Lutheran society.

Where the character of society provides scope for the open recognition and discussion of collective moral problems, and the social structure is flexible and adaptable enough to respond to these deliberations, the uncompromising sort of stand Wittgenstein took over the separation of facts and values will appear paradoxical. Where no such scope exists, the claims of extreme individualism become more understandable. If the culture and society into which Wittgenstein grew up offered no more prospect for the rational discussion of morality or values than it had offered, say, to Karl Kraus, the ultimate reasons for Wittgenstein's divorce of values and facts accordingly lay, not in any individual quirk of his personal temperament, but rather in those features of the broader social context which had led, in the first place, to the absolute alienation of so many serious-minded bourgeois intellectuals. If the realm of values was completely dissociated, for Kraus and Wittgenstein alike, from the realm of facts, this is a comment on the fossilization which had overtaken the *Lebensformen* of upper-middle-class Kakanian existence. Given life as it was lived in the Vienna of the early 1900s, no recognized public forum of opportunities existed for the sincere and serious-minded discussion of ethics or aesthetics. The man who truly understood the deeper character of value judgments could, thus, find room for them only in the private world of his own personal life.

After the collapse of the Habsburg Empire and the abandonment of the dynastic *Hausmacht* around which it had been built, how far did that remain the case? Certainly, the men of 1920, who set about constructing a new democratic Austria free of the imperial encumbrances of the older regime, embarked on their task with idealistic hopes. And certainly, also, the artists and musicians, architects and poets of the interwar years believed that their revolutionary new techniques were capable of liberating them from the conventional artificialities of pre-1914 Vienna.

So we must now turn and ask how far, in the event, the reconstruction of culture and society which followed the collapse of the dynastic systems of Central Europe in 1918 succeeded in liberating the "creative fantasy" of artists, writers and philosophers in the kind of way the Krausians had demanded.

8

Professionalism and Culture:
THE SUICIDE OF THE MODERN MOVEMENT

*Do not let us introduce an Act
of Uniformity against poets.*
—COLERIDGE

For the Austrians, even more than for most other Europeans, the 1914–18 war was a trauma and a turning point. In Germany and Italy, national unity itself was still so recent a fact that the turmoil resulting from the First World War—whether from victory or from defeat—came as only one more episode in a long and confused history: the Germans, in particular, could say goodbye to the Hohenzollern dynasty without nostalgia. For the French, the immediate effects of the war were surgical, but it could be seen as merely the latest in a long sequence of similar wars of national defense along the line of the Rhine. For the British, it is true, the war represented a bloody and unwanted reinvolvement in the affairs of continental Europe, from which England had largely succeeded in disengaging itself ever since the year 1815; and it set in train a social transformation and a redistribution of political power which have been going on ever since. But only in Russia and Austria did the years from 1914 to 1920 bring a complete break with the past. In each country, the ruling dynasty had held power for so long that it seemed to incarnate the national identity; but by 1914 its rule had hardened into a petrified autocracy that had lost any capacity it might once have had for dealing on realistic terms with rival loyalties—

whether religious, ethnic or social—among its own subjects. So the dismemberment of the Habsburg inheritance, like the more forcible dispossession of the Romanovs, destroyed at a single blow a regime and a power structure whose very survival in the face of irresoluble paradoxes had seemed hitherto the best guarantee of its own unlimited durability.

This situation bore most heavily on the Viennese, especially on the generation born in the late 1880s and the 1890s, who now saw the framework of their social and national existence dismantled, just as they were approaching maturity as individuals. Whether or no late Habsburg Vienna was (in Kraus's phrase) a "proving ground for world destruction," it was certainly a severe testing ground for intelligent young men of Wittgenstein's own generation. The entire familiar scaffolding of political authority and social administration—the Dual Monarchy; the Habsburg *Hausmacht;* that great, continuous territory, stretching from the Po Valley to the Carpathians, which had been created three hundred years before to protect Europe from the infidel Turks and had been quietly fossilizing ever since, alongside its Ottoman rival; above all, the centralized autocracy first created by the Emperor Francis before 1800, and perpetuated by Metternich and Francis Joseph—all this was suddenly stripped away, leaving the Viennese to devise what future they could, in the Europe of the 1920s, for their own truncated Republic. This was amputation on a scale even the Russians escaped. Despite the abruptness and violence of the two 1917 revolutions and the subsequent years of confusion and civil strife between the Whites and the Reds, the eventual territory of Soviet Russia retained the traditional heartland of Tsarist power, together with most of its conquests; while the administrative machinery of the traditional autocracy was quickly and easily adapted to the Dictatorship of the Proletariat—or, rather, the proletariat's self-appointed representatives. So, in our preoccupation with Soviet Communism, we should not overlook the even more striking discontinuities facing the intelligent and potentially creative young men from influential Austrian families, when they returned to Vienna from prisoner-of-war camps or military surrender.

It was a situation which quickly sorted out the absolutists from the pragmatists. A very few of the traditional aristocracy dismissed the whole situation as "impossible" and retired from the scene in disgust, nursing the same unrealistic and unrealizable hopes as the White Russian princes and grand dukes of interwar Paris café society. (The clearest testimony of Francis Joseph's ultimate failure was the total absence from postwar Austria of any convincing movement for a restoration of the monarchy.) As contrasted with these residual aristocrats, there was another minority of equally "absolute-minded" men, who had lost all faith in the value and virtue of political power itself and who set aside all collective discussion of communal problems for the pursuit of their own individual, anxiety-laden lives. These men were a ready-made audience alike for the extreme individualism of a Kierkegaard, for the poetic introspection and artistic expressionism of the postwar years, and for the antiauthoritarian nightmares of the novelist Franz Kafka. During the last decades of Habsburg power, the situation had been described as "always desperate, but never serious." Now, the tables had apparently been turned; and the existentially minded diagnosed a situation of real gravity, just when there existed —at long last—constructive possibilities for social and political action.

For the pragmatic majority, the first and most important thing was to take advantage of these possibilities. Those men who set out to build the institutions and social practices of the new Austrian Republic no longer saw the same cause as before for alienation—particularly, for alienation of an extreme, Kierkegaardian variety. In the new Austria, there was plenty of positive work for intellectuals to do. A Kelsen, a Bühler or a Lazarsfeld need have little doubt that values could be practical. There was a constitution to be framed, a parliament to be established, an effective system of social democracy to be put into working order.[1] All the long-neglected consequences of industrialization to which Francis Joseph had turned a blind eye—above all, the housing shortage in Vienna—were waiting to be tackled; and the universal obstacle of Habsburg ultraconservatism had at last been spirited away. It was, the pragmatists thought, a time for looking forward, and for construction; and to these men the historicocritical and constructive positivism of Mach, for all its metaphysical defects, had an obvious appeal. Mach himself had died in 1916, disillusioned and disappointed with the contemporary reception of his ideas.[2] He need not have worried; within a few years the very substantial academic influence he exerted during his own lifetime was, if anything, eclipsed by the practical influence of his teachings in law, politics and social thought.

Given this changed historical situation, there is less cause for surprise at the fact that the *point* of Wittgenstein's *Tractatus* was so widely misunderstood. We have described the book as an epitome of the "contemporary" Austrian critique of communication and expression; but—we must be clear—contemporary with *what?* As we can now see, the *Tractatus* epitomized the philosophical and intellectual problems of Viennese art and culture, as they existed *before 1918.* So, from 1920 on, Wittgenstein was speaking, if for anyone, for the second of the three groups we have distinguished—that is, for the Viennese intellectuals who were traumatized by the Kakanian experience to the point of abandoning all belief in collective values, and who fell back instead on an individualism as absolute and antihistorical, in its own way, as the situation against which they were reacting. (This situation embraced, of course, both the uninformed "good taste" and "manners" of the Viennese bourgeois, and also the unprincipled autocracy of the Habsburgs themselves. When one of the Emperor Francis' public servants was described as a "patriot," the Emperor's own response was to ask, "Ah, but is he a patriot *for me?*")

If one were writing a psychobiography of Wittgenstein, indeed, one might well argue that, in his own person, he never overcame the crisis provoked by the collapse, in 1918, of the seemingly eternal framework of worldly falsehood into which he had grown up. The nineteenth-century Habsburg system had been established on an attempt to abolish the effects of history; and its constitutional structure claimed divine right, simply as a means of removing its operations from the sphere of moral judgment. The counterweakness of the existentialists lay in taking these very claims for existing society and political authority too seriously.

The moral defects of early-nineteenth-century Danish small-town Protestant society had, in Kierkegaard's eyes, nothing to do with the fact that this society was early-nineteenth-century, or Danish, or small-town, or Protestant. No; these moral defects must be seen—more cosmically—as springing from the central sinfulness of man and from his unchanging relationships with his fellow men and with God. There was no hope of drawing valid ethical distinctions *within* the sphere of social action, or *between* rival collective "moral codes," any more than one could hope to redeem institutional "Christendom" from its essentially non-Christian, or even anti-Christian, condition. Rather, one must first bring men to a recognition of the crucial *ahistorical* truth—namely, that salvation comes entirely from the individual's relations with his God and, aside from that, has nothing whatever to do with good works.

Wittgenstein's approach to problems of ethics and valuation, in the *Tractatus*, was equally *ahistorical*. His own opposition between the sphere of facts (which lent itself to representational description) and the sphere of values (about which one could speak at best poetically) was no more qualified, conditional or open to historical reconsideration than Kierkegaard's denunciation of Christendom, or the morality of moral codes. On the contrary, it was as important for Wittgenstein as for Kierkegaard to put the "transcendental" character of ethics on a *timeless* basis; after that, there could be no doubt about it, no subsequent going back. This meant, of course, that Wittgenstein's approach to ethics was also entirely *apolitical*. However much we may see a connection in retrospect between the collapse of the Habsburg Empire and Wittgenstein's own personal crisis of the early 1920s, he himself would probably have seen no connection between these two things.

It was, by contrast, the historical element that Ernst Mach shared with his empiricist predecessor, David Hume, that made his position so formidable an opponent for Lenin and the Marxists. For a Marxist and a Machian equally, there was no reason to doubt that one could do real good or ill in this world, by collective social action. History was thus a legitimate object for moral appraisal, and also an arena for moral choice. Hitherto, the power of the obsolete dynastic regimes might have stood in the way of any practical realization of these ambitions; but there was nothing essentially amoral—still less antimoral—about the "world of facts" which is our collective property and concern. Ludwig Wittgenstein wanted none of this historicism. To him, historical variety and change possessed no more philosophical relevance than they had done for Plato, for Descartes, or for his much-admired Frege. In one of the surviving pre-*Tractatus* notebooks, we find him jotting down the curious remark, "What is history to me? Mine is the first and only world."[3] And although for him this entry was apparently connected with the problem of solipsism, it is surely not the remark of an historically sensitive or discriminating thinker.

In this context, indeed, it is interesting to view the whole philosophical debate about the relations between facts and values—from Kant, through Schopenhauer and Kierkegaard, to Tolstoy and Wittgenstein—as an episode in the history of *political* thought. Writing in the late eighteenth century, Immanuel Kant had few serious moral expectations about history; but his own obsessively moderate political liberalism took care not to rule out such hopes on principle, and for a brief moment he was even tempted to acclaim the French Revolution as a triumph for rational morality—as the eschatological breakthrough of the noumenal world of values into the phenomenal realm of political facts.[4] Moving on by way of Schopenhauer to Wittgenstein, we see this political attitude of unhopeful moderation turning, by way of pessimism, into outright desperation. Collective morality is an illusion. The only hope for the individual is to find, and save, his own soul; and even this he can do only by avoiding worldly entanglements. One of the few pieces of authentic moral advice Wittgenstein was heard to give in his later years is the maxim, "One must travel light."[5]

Did Wittgenstein acquire this antihistoricism from Gottlob Frege? Was he converted to this view in part by Frege's denunciation of the "psychologistic" and "genetic" fallacies, and his insistence that conceptual analysis must be pursued in formal, logical and timeless terms? This could be so. But, given the tenacity of Wittgenstein's moral attitudes, it is more plausible to assume that this particular view antedated his acquaintance with Frege, and that previous moral and intellectual inclinations predisposed him to find Frege's logicism congenial. Here again, Wittgenstein's views stand in clear contrast with Mauthner's views, which he rejected. Mauthner's feeling for historical and cultural diversity may have driven him to the extreme of relativism, but at any rate it kept his sense of historical relevance alive. Even when Wittgenstein had abandoned his earlier Russellian belief in a universal structure of real logical forms, in his own later phase, in favor of a more Mauthnerian or Loosian analysis of language as a functional reflection of forms of life, he never followed up the historical implications of his new approach. His Krausian counterpart in music, Arnold Schönberg, had taught quite explicitly that a proper grasp of composition can come only through a detailed study of the logic of musical ideas, as it has developed historically, from Bach by way of Beethoven to Wagner and the new twelve-tone system. Wittgenstein's close associate, Friedrich Waismann, could similarly write an *Introduction to Mathematical Thinking* expounding the internal complexities of the concept *number* with a historico-critical fidelity reminiscent of Mach.[6] But, while Wittgenstein's later philosophical teaching displayed a clear—almost anthropological—recognition of cultural diversity, and of the relativity of language games to the modes of human life within which they are operative, he showed no feeling at all for the question, whether the course of human history has in any meaningful sense seen any rational improvement, either in our forms of life themselves, or in the linguistic procedures developed in response to their demands.[7]

If Wittgenstein was already drawn toward an extreme Kierkegaardian individualism in the years before 1914, his experience in the next few years did nothing to remove this alienation. The comradeship of active service of the Eastern Front might stimulate his human fellow feeling for the soldiers alongside whom he fought; but, by itself, it did no more to dismantle the social and intellectual barriers that separated him from the general run of these Austro-Hungarian peasants and mechanics than Konstantin Levin's fellow feeling for his estate workers could transform him into being a Russian peasant himself. So Wittgenstein's conviction that the sphere of facts is set off from the sphere of values absolutely was reflected, within his own personality, in a divorce between the reflective life of music and the intellect, in which he was a virtuoso, and the affective life of emotional warmth and relaxation, with which he dealt less easily; and this psychological division in its turn had social—not to say sociological—origins in the Austria of his youth.

To repeat, however : these sociological origins lay, if anywhere, in pre-1914 Vienna. For the pragmatical-minded men of 1920, on the other hand, the absolute moral individualism which represented the unspoken point of the *Tractatus* was, quite simply, *useless.* For their purpose, all that appeared important in the book was the parts that could be put to constructive use—its formal techniques, its theoretical model of language as a system of *Bilder,* its method of truth tables. The sweeping away of the old

Central European dynasties had left a new world waiting to be built—on the scientific and cultural, as much as on the social and political plane. Positivism, one might say, is the utilitarianism of the philosophical rationalist—the metaphysical, or dogmatically antimetaphysical, justification of an empirical pragmatism that other men "accept upon instinct." So, the Austria and Germany of the 1920s saw a natural turning toward positivism and toward questions of technique. All areas of life, thought and art called for a new instauration. The important thing was to bring the most up-to-date, effective and scientific techniques available to this great work of construction and reformation. And it was here—at the very central core of theory and intellectual life—that Wittgenstein's *Tractatus* exerted its incongruous appeal, as the bible of logical positivism. For there, it seemed, the fundamental network of intellectual tie rods had been laid down, on the basis of which one could now hope to rear a single, integrated, ferroconcrete edifice, comprising the whole of logic, mathematics, physics and positive knowledge.

This, then, was the time for construction. But it was also a time for self-determination: for the dispersal of a previously centralized authority to a score of newly independent, self-governing groups and communities. This is most obviously true, in the case of the hitherto-intractable nationalities. The Czechs under Thomas Masaryk had campaigned most actively and ingeniously to win the support of the victorious Allies for the establishment of an autonomous, sovereign Czechoslovak state. But, when the peace treaty finally dismantled the political fabric of the Austro-Hungarian Empire, most of the constituent peoples of the Empire found themselves either (like the Magyars) with a self-governing state of their own, or at least (like the Bosnians and the Slovaks) with a share in some new and ethnically more nearly homogeneous nation. The men who drafted the peace treaty could never, of course, have satisfied all the conflicting nationalist claims current in the ethnic *macédoine* of the Balkans. Not only in Macedonia itself but throughout Southeast Europe, languages, cultures and national loyalties were scrambled together, then as now, in an inextricable manner. Still, the principle of self-determination, with the consequent dispersal of sovereignty, was one on which the peace settlement of 1919–20 set considerable store. (If the resulting situation soon proved unstable, it was most directly vulnerable to further invocations of that same principle, on behalf of, say, the German minorities in Czechoslovakia and Poland, and the Hungarians in Rumania.) For the moment, the postwar settlement foresaw a period of constructive development, not just in the creation of the new Austrian Republic, but of all the other sovereign states called into being by the new "principle of nationality."

The right to autonomy, independence and self-government was, however, extended not just to the nationalities of the former Empire in the political sphere, but also to the different arts, sciences and professions, in the intellectual and cultural sphere. Under the Habsburg system, cultural and artistic life had long been organized around an elaborate system of patronage. Throughout the high classical period, every noble house or prelate maintained an organist, a composer, even a complete orchestra, having part-time duties in the family chapel or cathedral which left substantial scope for the artist's own originality and enterprise. (Similarly, to some degree, with painters and sculptors, architects and others.) Naturally enough, the imperial house itself made a major contribution of its own, which was channeled largely through the Imperial Academies; and the resulting place which these institutions held in the social establishment lent added weight to their academic standards and judgments. Many of the rising bourgeoisie were also drawn, as we saw, into the patronage of music and the arts, either on an individual basis or else collectively, through such societies as the *Musikfreunde.* The rise of aestheticism in the 1890s was reflected in the formation of café circles like *Jung Wien,* but before 1914 there was little sign of the type of organization that we have learned to take for granted by now—namely, professional institutions of, say, portrait painters or composers, organized by themselves and for themselves as the custodians of their own professional ideals, standards and techniques.

With the crumbling of the dynastic system and the construction of a new and more democratic society, cultural life too had to take a new direction. So, the liberation from earlier tastes and conventions in the 1920s stimulated a great burst of technical innovation in all the arts, as well as in the natural sciences and other intellectual spheres. Wherever the older autocracies lost power, in Germany and Russia quite as much as the former Habsburg territories, poetry and literature, painting and film

making, music and architecture—to say nothing of philosophy—
plunged into a phase of intense technical experimentation, during which artists and writers had a greater degree of liberty than
they ever enjoyed either before or (especially in Russia) since
that time. In all the arts it was the moment for a new beginning.
All those critical doubts of the prewar years—about whether
poetic language, and music, and painting, were capable of expression or representation at all—were set aside. Positivist attitudes bred action. The thing to do was just to get on with it. Let
a hundred styles bloom; and let the artists involved decide for
themselves which of the resulting experiments had paid off and
which were unsuccessful.

From this time on, aesthetic judgment was to be the prime concern, not of an individual patron (be he bishop or archduke) nor
of the great bourgeois public. Instead, artists would have the opportunity to organize their own affairs on a professional basis,
and they would have the responsibility of passing professional
judgment on the achievements of their fellows. The dispersal of
cultural authority thus followed a pattern very similar to the dispersal of social and political authority. During an initial transitional period, circles of like-minded artists, philosophers or
others gathered together, for lack of more formal professional
institutions, into coteries, which still had a strong air of patronage about them.

The Freudian circle of psychoanalysts and the philosophical
Wiener Kreis are the most familiar examples of a larger phenomenon. Such circles helped to end the ''authority gap'' in a
society most of whose legitimating institutions had ceased to
exist. More than that, however, they provided a bridge from the
stifling nineteenth-century institutions that had hitherto excluded the would-be ''modernist'' rebels to a new kind of professional identity. Thus before long the new arts of the 1920s
developed their own characteristic institutions. In some cases, as
with the Bauhaus in architecture, the primary function of these
organizations was teaching; in other cases, it was a modified
form of sponsorship or patronage, as with the International Society for Contemporary Music. Either way, this development
went along with a much greater professionalization of the arts,
as painters and architects, musicians and poets, set up shop on
their own.

The consequences of this dispersal of authority were not entirely what had been foreseen by those who denounced the earlier tyranny of individual patronage and conventional "good taste." Nor were they entirely what men like Karl Kraus hoped that they would be. To some extent, of course, this revolutionary change in the social organization of culture encouraged a liberation of the creative fantasy of the kind that Kraus had demanded and helped to remove some of the major obstacles that had stood in the way of creative innovation. To this liberation, we owe much of the richness and variety of invention—not to mention the rough energy and occasional downright ugliness—of interwar literature and artistic production. Before long, however, familiar social mechanisms began to operate, and the power vacuum created by the removal of authoritative "external" patrons began to be filled from within the newly created professions themselves.

Culture, in a word, had been Balkanized; and in the process it had been bureaucratized as well. The old conventional orthodoxies were dead and gone. But, instead of giving a place to a cultural democracy of Krausian "integral men," with each of them free to let his creative fantasy work through whatever media and procedures his own judgment chose, the professionalization of the arts too often ended by imposing new orthodoxies in place of old. The times being what they were, of course, these new professional orthodoxies were defined in terms of particular *sets of techniques.* The professionally respectable thing to do was now to display one's mastery of a particular style or method—for example, to display skill in composing string quartets around "tone rows" constructed on the twelve-tone system. So in a very different setting, and with very different epistemological foundations, the aestheticism of the 1890s became sociologically established in the artistic professions some thirty years later. ("A painter is a painter is a painter: while a musician is a musician is a musician.") From now on, there would be little scope for the emergence of further versatile, self-taught geniuses, with fingers in many pies, like Arnold Schönberg. The guild structure of the artists' trade-unions would see to that.

Against this background, it is interesting to see what has happened since 1920 to all those revolutionary movements in art and letters that, in the years before 1914, had been associated with the comprehensive Viennese critique of communication in all fields of thought and art. In each case, we find a similar pattern, as we pass in succession from one generation to another. The men of the first generation, comprising the great critical reformers themselves, came to appear in retrospect to consist of highly reluctant revolutionaries. (A recent study of Arnold Schönberg, for instance, has explicitly called him "the conservative revolutionary.")[9] For, as we saw earlier, Schönberg refused to call himself an atonalist, and insisted on being regarded as a teacher of "twelve-tone *composition,* not *twelve-tone* composition." True, he believed that the twelve-tone system offered twentieth-century composers a much richer vein of musical ideas, capable of developing according to their own inner logic, than the older classical harmony, whose resources had been exhausted. But the virtues of the new system were not, as he saw it, self-evident, nor were they entirely "internal." One could appreciate them only by considering the twelve-tone system as a natural extension of the classical seven-tone system, and so as its "legitimate heir." But one could never accuse Schönberg of idolizing these novel techniques. For him, they were never more than a promising means to carry forward the enduring missions of musical composition; never an end in themselves, to the product of an aesthetic ideology, as they were for their inventor, Josef Hauer.

Schönberg's own theory of harmony may, perhaps, have been open to serious criticism; half a century later, his insistence that "how the music sounds" has no aesthetic significance at all, and all that is important is the internal logic of its development (which can equally well be appreciated by the instructed eye, from simply studying the score) looks like a radical counter-exaggeration. The late Romantics had no doubt carried their search for "musical effects" to absurd lengths. But, as Schönberg himself acknowledged, composers like Gustav Mahler could still find ways of giving their ideas musical expression which changed the older classical system, without entirely breaking with it. And these new post-Romantic styles created modes of expression which "sounded right" to the instructed ear instead of merely conforming to popular bourgeois expectations. (Perceptively enough, the study of Mahler in the same series of books about modern composers calls him the "contemporary of the future.")[10]

It is with the next generation that we find the products and techniques of the earlier revolution becoming bureaucratized, and being made the basis for a new orthodoxy. Musical theory found its positivist ideology in the doctrine of *Gebrauchsmusik*. Like the "physicalistic" form of philosophical positivism, which accepted Mach's program for "logical construction," while abandoning his theory of sensations for a more down-to-earth view of the basic data of science, the theory of *Gebrauchsmusik* took a hardheaded and practical (even an "instrumental") view of musical composition. Composing was, after all, just another manufacturing process, aimed at satisfying external demands. So the composer should give up all highfalutin claims to "self-expression"—why should the listener have any interest in the composer's "inner psychic state"?—and view himself once again as an honest craftsman, with a market to supply. Bach, Haydn and Beethoven had not been too proud to turn out table music, or church cantatas, or incidental music for other men's plays. So why should the twentieth-century composer claim any different function? Just what craft techniques the composer made use of in his work was, of course, a matter for himself and his fellow musicians; a decent sense of professional self-respect demanded proper autonomy on the technical side. So those who wished to organize their music around twelve-tone techniques might do so; so long as they were ready to cast the results of their work into forms for which there was a genuine demand.

Alongside Paul Hindemith and the advocates of *Gebrauchs-musik,* accordingly, were those of Schönberg's followers who ignored his conservatism and made it a matter of principle to compose in accordance with the technical rules for the formation and transformation of "tone rows." Either way, a new set of functionaries ended by imposing on the music of this second generation an orthodoxy, or set of conventions, as demanding in its own way as that which the earlier, revolutionary generation had set out to displace. So, in a period of professionals working under the leadership of artistic bureaucrats, there was less scope for a few independent "loners" whose fantasy demanded forms of expression free to develop in response to new situations. And the constraints of this neo-orthodoxy have been rejected as intolerable only during the last ten or fifteen years, when a new generation of composers has appeared who are more ready and willing to accept Mahler as their "contemporary."

Given the pre-1914 situation, the revolutionary and critical moves then made in music, as elsewhere, were legitimate and brilliant; but when, in the aftermath, the novel techniques so introduced became in turn idolized and established—when the musicians concerned began thinking of themselves as *"twelve-tone* composers," rather than as "twelve-tone *composers"*—the movement lost its capacity for sustained development. In this, Arnold Schönberg himself was wiser than his own followers—not just in seeing that his technical innovations must justify themselves in the light of the whole musical tradition from Monteverdi and Bach on, but equally in understanding that music itself should not be a self-contained and full-time activity, to which a man must commit himself with monastic dedication to the exclusion of all else.

Looking at other fields, also, we find similar sequences of development. In architecture too, the modern movement had its Old Testament Prophet, in the shape of Adolf Loos; and Loos, like Schönberg, rejected the title of "revolutionary." The principles of architectural design, as Loos himself taught them, were entirely open to the future. The architect could not prescribe in advance the future forms of life or forms of culture; changes in those external forms would call for new creative responses from the architect himself; and, in this sense, the theory of design which Loos taught—and exemplified in his buildings—was directed at a truly *functional* architecture. ("If you want to understand the significance of, for example, the system of water piping in a house, look at the *use* to which that system is put. The meaning *is* the use.") In his buildings, Loos's concentration on "functional necessities" at once led to the elimination of that meaningless detail and decoration that had been a feature, both of conventional bourgeois Viennese architecture, and of its *art nouveau* successor. Stylistically, as a result, Loos's principles imposed on his designs a radical simplification, involving the sacrifice of all nonessentials; yet in his work, as in his theory, style remained the servant of use.

It was the generation that followed Loos and built upon his work that created the modern style in architecture, as such—that is, that took the first products of Loos's technical simplification and stylized them, so producing the familiar concrete-and-glass slabs or shoe boxes to which the name "modern architecture" became attached from the late 1920s on. Here, the influence of Gropius and the Bauhaus school was dominant. While basing their own slogans on Loos's principles, and presenting their own architectural style as highly functional, the younger Bauhaus generation in fact turned Loos's architecture into something quite different. Lacking Loos's own highly sensitive adaptation of every design to its own specific use, they imposed on their buildings a generalized, multipurpose structural design, capable of lending itself to *any* function.

Ironically enough, the outcome of this development was a stylized mode of design whose operative principles were almost exclusively *structural*, rather than functional. Rather than have its form determined in detail by function during the initial design, a typical Bauhaus building provided only a generalized "logical space," defining an ensemble of architectural possibilities that were realized in a specific form only subsequently, after the occupation of the building. (Recall the much-quoted notion of "dividing up the living space.") Far from being functional, the resulting structures have been, one might say, the nearest thing yet seen to the physical realization of a pure Cartesian system of geometrical coordinates. The architect defines merely the structural axes of reference, and within these the occupier is free to pursue an effectively unlimited range of lives or occupations. Functionally speaking, indeed, these buildings have been as anonymous as those of any architectural period: instead of displaying the uses to which they are put, the Cartesian style of these buildings has totally concealed it. As with the transition from Arnold Schönberg to the self-consciously twelve-tone composers of the interwar years, this change inverted Loos's principles, and substituted an atemporal, stylized structuralism for the historically sensitive and varied functionalism at which he had been aiming.

There were, no doubt, economic reasons why this Cartesian style had a certain commercial success: flexible, multipurpose buildings, like those which line Park Avenue in New York City, promised a higher rental and resale value than the more tightly designed, and specifically functional, buildings that Loos himself would have designed. And it is only when we get to the 1950s that we find this anonymous style losing its hold, and large-scale modern buildings being constructed which can be regarded as fully functional, in Loos's sense of the term. One might instance Eero Saarinen's Trans-World Airlines terminal at John F. Kennedy International Airport, a building for which the older rectangular shell has been entirely laid aside, and a new range of exterior and interior forms has been developed that are determined by the actual *use* of the building—as an instrument for channeling passengers between aircraft and surface transportation. (The resulting building has more in common with an organic cell than with a shoe box: the building is notable, in particular, for having introduced those telescopic ramps, since adopted very widely, which reach out like pseudopodia to connect with the exterior doors of the aircraft.) It is accordingly interesting to see how the name of Adolf Loos (like that of Mahler in music)is at last coming back into public attention in the 1970s as a man whose full originality we are only just beginning to recognize.

In architecture as in music, then, the technical innovations worked out before 1914 by the "critical" generation of Schönberg and Loos were formalized in the 1920s and 1930s, so becoming the basis for a compulsory antidecorative style which eventually became as conventional as the overdecorative style which it displaced. And we might pursue these parallels still further if we pleased—into poetry and literature, painting and sculpture, and even into physics and pure mathematics. In each case, novel techniques of axiomatization or sprung rhythm, operationalism or nonrepresentational art, were first introduced in order to deal with artistic or intellectual problems left over from the late nineteenth century—so having the status of interesting and legitimate new *means*—only to acquire after a few years the status of *ends,* through becoming the stock in trade of a newly professionalized school of modern poets, abstract artists or philosophical analysts. In this way, the professionalization of culture bred a new race of functionaries who have been ready to impose a novel orthodoxy, based on the idolization of new abstract techniques and structures, in place of the discredited canons of bourgeois taste and nineteenth-century academicism. In the process, the deeper human purposes that it was the function of those novel techniques to serve have too often been ignored, if not forgotten. So, poetic techniques and forms have become more important than poetic expression, the construction of quasi-mathematical systems of inductive logic more important than the rationality of scientific procedures, and—in general—form and style more important than use and function. The resulting academicization of novel professional techniques would, of course, have been as repugnant in its own way to the Karl Krauses of the world as the things against which they and the modernists were theoretically rebelling. For *self-imposed* constraints, in conformance with the scholastic conventions of an artistic or intellectual profession, can be just as inhibiting and damaging to the individual fantasy as *external* constraints, such as those imposed by the older patronage system.

With a curious unanimity, the barrenness of this professionally imposed scholasticism came to be acknowledged during the 1960s, in a wide range and variety of creative activities. Over the last few years we have seen men taking up once again threads which had apparently been broken in 1918, not only in music and architecture but in many other fields also; and there has been something approaching a comprehensive rediscovery of late Habsburg cultural potentialities and achievements, which intervening generations either overlooked or rejected outright. From John Osborne's play about the Redl Affair, *A Patriot for Me,* to the film of Thomas Mann's *Death in Venice,* from the success of *Hello, Dolly!* and *La Ronde* (both of them adaptations of Viennese originals) to the historicization of the philosophy of science, we have been rediscovering for ourselves how far artistic and intellectual tasks set aside between 1900 and 1920 are still our own.

And it is not only the cultural tasks of Habsburg Vienna that we are rediscovering; along with the Viennese Secession Exhibition at the Royal Academy in London in 1970 and the new enthusiasm for Gustav Mahler's dynamic lyricism, men like John Galsworthy and Edward Elgar—whose names were anathema to professionals a generation ago—are nowadays spoken of once again with affection and respect. And perhaps, before long, we shall be ready to appreciate fully once again the deeper creative fantasies which led the first, critical generation (whether James Joyce or Arnold Schönberg, Adolf Loos or Oskar Kokoschka) to devise, for their own legitimate purposes, those novel techniques which the professional bureaucrats of neo-orthodoxy subsequently froze into the modern style.

With this general point in mind, let us go back and look again at Wittgenstein's philosophical intentions. The ambiguities that surrounded his views and methods, from the 1920s right on up until the mid-1960s, had a professional, as well as an intellectual aspect. After 1920, the philosophical techniques introduced in the *Tractatus Logico-Philosophicus* were taken over by the logical positivists of Vienna and the philosophical analysts of Cambridge; and those techniques acquired a central place in the corpus of technical skills and doctrines around which the new and specialized academic enterprises of "professional philosophy" was growing up.

At this point, it is necessary to emphasize just how new this professional conception of philosophy was. Ever since the Middle Ages, of course, the teaching and discussion of philosophy has had a significant place in the university curriculum; but the scope of the subject has usually been seen as overlapping with those of the natural and human sciences, so that philosophy has been studied alongside, and in conjunction with, those other subjects. Even today the idea of a set of philosophical technicalities that justify the creation of a tightly knit, self-governing group of professional philosophers like the scholarly organizations of, say, topologists, microbiologists and Romance grammarians, is little more than fifty years old. And the attitude of Wittgenstein himself to this idea was in just as sharp a contrast to that of his philosophical successors—even those who saw themselves as his followers—as the attitudes of Schönberg and Loos to those of their respective followers.

Suppose we put the question, What did Wittgenstein see himself as having achieved in the *Tractatus?* Suppose we ask, that is, Was Wittgenstein consciously pioneering *novel* philosophical techniques, intended to undercut and displace earlier philosophical techniques; or was his intention rather to liberate men from subservience to the conventions of *any* technical view of philosophy? If we do so, the answer is clear. For Wittgenstein as for Kraus, the whole point of his polemical critique was one of intellectual liberation. Of course, the Vienna Circle philosophers also presented themselves in this same emancipatory role, but theirs was the liberation so characteristic of "progressive" thought, in politics and elsewhere: the kind that fights old dogmas with new, rather than free itself from dogma as such. The Viennese positivists were antimetaphysical, to be sure; but their opposition to metaphysics was buttressed, like that of Hume, by general philosophical principles as arbitrary as those of their opponents. Wittgenstein's antimetaphysical approach, on the other hand, was genuinely *nondoctrinal*. However much else changed in his actual methods of philosophizing, between 1918 and 1948, the fundamental propaedeutic never changed—

To say nothing except what can be said . . . and then, whenever someone else wants to say something metaphysical, to demonstrate to him that he had failed to give a meaning to certain signs in his propositions.[11]

In his later phase, Wittgenstein certainly changed his ideas about what was *involved* in demonstrating that a linguistic expression had not been "given a meaning"; yet the underlying philosophical task, of supervising *die Grenze der Sprache* at points where men are tempted into pointless confusion, was unaltered. And the reason why it was *important* to keep this boundary line respected was still the same. This was, to guard against the imposition of needless constraints on clear thought and right feeling, in areas where these genuinely matter—namely, in the sincere expression of human emotions, and in the free exercise of the creative fantasy. In this respect, indeed, philosophical liberation was a precondition for any proper understanding of the life of fantasy, in Kraus's sense of the term. After reading what a Cambridge colleague had written about William Blake, Wittgenstein was heard to remark: "How does so-and-so think he can understand Blake? Why, he doesn't even understand philosophy!"[12]

If, on their first meeting, Wittgenstein insisted on reading the Vienna Circle philosophers the poetry of Tagore, this then was a highly Krausian action with a genuine polemical point. For it amounted to a declaration that philosophical technicalities are, at best, a means to an end—namely, the liberation of a man's mind, so that he can face the truly profound and significant issues dealt with by writers like Tolstoy and Tagore. In this way, Wittgenstein openly dissociated himself from the "technical" or "professional" conception of philosophy, which valued the novel methods of the *Tractatus* as providing the basis for an autonomous, self-respecting academic discipline.[13] At this point, his disagreement with the logical positivists was not merely intellectual but sociological as well. Like the atonalist composers and the Bauhaus architects, the positivists were simply exchanging an old orthodoxy for a new one, and transforming ideas which had been put forward as the means of philosophical liberation into a new and quasi-mathematical set of philosophical principles.

Given his training as an engineer, of course, Wittgenstein was not opposed to mathematical calculation, in its proper place. But applied mathematics had to be applied *to* something; it had to be shown not only that the computations involved were *formally* impeccable, but also that they *did a job,* over and beyond their own formal elaboration. Too often, the modernistic style of Viennese philosophizing apparently developed sophisticated formalisms entirely for their own sake, without regard to the demands of any external relevance or application. In this way, they became like idle wheels added to a gear train without mechanical effect, paper crowns placed on a chess queen without affecting the rules for moving the piece.

Nor did Wittgenstein have any more use for the analytical philosophy developed by G. E. Moore and his Cambridge colleagues during the 1930s, or the "linguistic" philosophy cultivated at Oxford after the Second World War. In course of time, he came to respect G. E. Moore as an individual, both for his personal simplicity and single-mindedness and for the integrity of his later intellectual questioning. If we can see a progressive increase in subtlety and discrimination in Wittgenstein's writings during his last years at Cambridge, indeed, much of this can arguably be credited to the influence of the long conversations he had with Moore.[14] But it would be quite wrong to suggest that Wittgenstein shared the analytical philosophers' view of philosophical problems and methods. Seeing philosophy as they did, the analysts assumed that a clearly recognizable collection of technical issues existed, which represented, so to say, the basic "phenomena" of philosophy; and they made it their task to show how, by improved technical methods, one could offer more constructive and comprehensive solutions, or "theories," for dealing with these issues. (Wittgenstein remarked about C. D. Broad, his colleague at Trinity College, Cambridge: "Poor Broad thinks of philosophy as the physics of the abstract.")[15]

This whole business—of contriving more and more sophisticated "theories" about (for example) other minds or scientific entities or the logical construction of material objects out of sense data—represented, in Wittgenstein's eyes, a misguided collection of pseudo-technicalities, which once again confused the means of philosophy with its ends. The difference in priorities that divided Wittgenstein from so many of his fellow philosophers in Britain after 1945 is well captured in a remark by the Oxford analyst J. L. Austin. In the course of rebutting objections to the supposed triviality of his own laborious explanations of linguistic usage, Austin replied that he had never been convinced that the question, whether a philosophical question was an important question, was *itself* an important question.[16] Like any pure scientist, the professional philosopher should begin by tackling problems which were technically "sweet" and ripe for solution, whatever their extrinsic importance or unimportance. Pure philosophy must have priority; there would be time enough to apply its results to practical problems later. So, to go from Wittgenstein's Cambridge to the linguistic analysts of Oxford at the end of the 1940s was to feel that philosophy had somehow or other lost its mainspring. Anyone who listened to Wittgenstein in person was conscious of a deeply philosophical thinker struggling to clear away intellectual obstacles to the free movement of the mind. At Oxford, meanwhile, similar-looking techniques were being employed with the greatest skill, but without any deeper, or clearly philosophical purpose. It was like exchanging a real clock for a child's clock-face—which looks just the same at first sight, but does not tell time.

In one respect, above all, Wittgenstein dissociated himself from the modern movement in philosophical analysis. A good deal was said, in the Oxford of the 1950s, about the *revolutionary* character of twentieth-century British philosophy. A well-known and highly successful collection of popular talks on the subject, for instance, had as its explicit title, *The Revolution in Philosophy*.[17] Looking back at that collection from the present day, however, we can see how far the "revolution" it was proclaiming was sociological rather than intellectual—insisting on the right of academic philosophers to operate as an autonomous subprofession, with a specialized set of problems, methods and techniques. Thanks to Moore, Russell and Wittgenstein, the authors were saying, we are now "real professionals" and can look scientists in the face; and, having discredited older styles of philosophizing in favor of linguistic analysis, we have given ourselves a respectable academic job, on which we can embark with confidence and industry. For his own part, Wittgenstein was no more of a revolutionary than Schönberg. Just as Schön-

berg claimed only that his novel twelve-tone *Harmonielehre* provided the most effective way of continuing the exploration of
"musical logic" begun by (for example) Bach and Beethoven,
so Wittgenstein insisted only that his methods of philosophizing
represented "the legitimate heir to what has previously been
called philosophy." And, for all the poverty of his own reading
in the classical literature of the subject, Wittgenstein would
refer to such men as Augustine, Schopenhauer and Kierkegaard
with admiration and respect, at a time when more self-consciously revolutionary analysts could still ignore the whole
previous history of philosophy, as resting on nothing better
than an egregious sequence of intellectual blunders.[18]

If Wittgenstein dissociated his views from the analytical
philosophy of postwar Britain, he did so even more sharply from
the "logical empiricism" which dominated so much of academic
philosophy in the United States of the 1940s and 1950s. After all,
he had never been seriously drawn toward an empiricist epistemology himself, whether it came from Mach and Schlick, or from
Moore and Russell; he had always been too much of a transcendental philosopher for that. And the arguments of men like
Carl Hempel and Ernest Nagel were, in his eyes, as much a
transplantation and continuation of the formalist technicalities
of interwar Vienna Circle positivism as the shoe-box office blocks
of postwar Park Avenue were of the conventional structuralism
of Gropius and the Bauhaus. Idle symbolism and pseudo-techni-
cal jargon were being used as an excuse to substitute a set of
abstract formal conundrums, lacking any roots in real life, for
the true problems of philosophy, which we are to feel "on our
pulses" and in our own experience. (It is very important in
philosophy, he used to explain, not to be clever *all* the time.[19] For
the "clever" philosopher risks losing touch with the grass-roots
problems on which his ideas are supposed to throw light, and
becoming preoccupied with secondary problems of his own making. Only the occasional touch of honest stupidity will help us to
see where the arguments of professional academic philosophy
are failing to answer our true intellectual needs.)

To say this is not, of course, to claim that Wittgenstein's own
philosophical position was necessarily a final or definitive one,
any more than Schönberg's in music. By now we have reached a
point at which Schönberg's musical innovations and theories
can at last be seen in some perspective; and it is already begin-

ning to appear as though, in certain respects, he may have pointed his pupils toward a dead end. At the time, his critical rejection of traditional diatonic tonality was, of course, a thoroughly worthwhile innovation. Yet it would be quite consistent with Schönberg's own historical sense to argue, now, that this innovation has exhausted its own value during the subsequent half century. Schönberg himself preferred Gustav Mahler to Josef Matthias Hauer any day; it was better to break out from the conventionality of the older diatonic modalities, as Mahler did, than to sell oneself like Hauer to novel techniques of an equally conventional and stylized kind. And we may ask ourselves whether the most fruitful way ahead in music now does not itself bypass twelve-tone systems almost entirely, by moving ahead from the classical tradition—as Schönberg did, however—in a direction closer to Mahler's own. More ways existed, after all, of softening up the conventional crust of nineteenth-century counterpoint and harmony than the revolutionary modernists were prepared to allow; and as a result, there may now be available more ways of developing forms of musical expression adaptable to our actual human purposes by working ahead from Mahler and his present-day successors than from, say, Hauer or Hindemith.

Given the state of philosophical debate in the Vienna of the early 1900s, likewise, the philosophical steps that Wittgenstein took in both his major works were certainly legitimate, and probably indispensable. Yet once again we must be prepared to look at his work, not merely as a *terminus ad quem,* but also a possible *terminus a quo.* In more than one respect, Wittgenstein's work has definitively closed off lines of thought and questioning which dominated the entire post-Kantian "transcendental" tradition for more than a century; his work has made it clear beyond doubt, for instance, that, except where the forms of life from which they derive their meaning make them *functionally* indispensable, the "regulative principles" and "synthetic a priori truths" of the Kantian scheme can claim no more than a tautologous "necessity." (Recall, at this point, the sympathy between Loos and Wittgenstein.) And we are now entitled to pursue, further than Wittgenstein himself ever did, the functional considerations underlying the *historical* development of our rational methods and modes of thought, in different fields of life or inquiry. If we do this, indeed, we may well find ourselves seeing in, say, a man like Ernst Cassirer, who shared Wittgenstein's admiration for Hertz's work and used it as one of the starting points for his own *Philosophy of Symbolic Forms,* a kind of Mahler of philosophy—that is to say, a writer whose more conservative-looking arguments can perhaps provide as many clues to the way ahead in philosophy as the writings and teachings of Wittgenstein himself.[20]

Given the Viennese situation in the years 1900–14, given the systematic corruptions, distortions and falsifications of political, cultural and intellectual life that the Krausians denounced, it is probably true that the *only* effective way ahead was, for the time being, a *polemical* one. At any rate, the work of a Schönberg, say, compelled men to face the serious intellectual problems involved in developing new means of musical expression, and new ways of developing the "logic" of musical ideas, in a way that the continued secretion of mere *Schmalz* did not. At this point in cultural history, indeed, the indispensable reaction against aesthetic sloppiness and intellectual self-indulgence in all fields was an artistic and intellectual Puritanism which brought back to the task of creation the intellectual concentration and purity of vision that men had been in danger of losing.

Yet polemical Puritanism is always in danger of overreaching itself in turn and, so, lapsing into a new fanaticism. It may therefore be just as important to recognize when the Puritan reformation has completed its necessary work and brought men back to a proper balance as it was to initiate it in the first place. When that time comes, we shall find that ideas, methods and procedures which carried legitimate weight and authority during this Puritan period, have themselves become no more than a fresh starting point from which men must move ahead to meet the novel demands of a later historical situation. And one of the virtues of seeing the ideas of a Schönberg, a Loos or a Wittgenstein against the background of the historical situation from which they originally grew is just this. It helps to reconcile us to a thought that will, in the long run, be inescapable: the thought that other kinds of musical composition, architectural design and philosophical argument will in due course become as much the legitimate heirs of theirs, as those were the proper heirs of the *fin-de-siècle* traditions against which they were themselves reacting.

9

Postscript:
THE LANGUAGE OF ALIENATION

One has only learnt to get the better of words
For the thing one no longer has to say, or the way in which
One is no longer disposed to say it.

—T. S. ELIOT,
East Coker

If, in retrospect, we find the world of Kakania more familiar and intelligible than the Europe of the interwar years, this is in part for reasons of nostalgia, but there is more to it also. The thought of all that plush solidity and comfortable complacency, that frank enjoyment of money and apparent forgetfulness of social inequalities, may comfort us by its very contrast with our own modern guilts and preoccupations; but the similarities between Kakania and our contemporary world ring a bell in us quite as much as the differences. We ourselves live in a world dominated by superpowers that have become conscious of the limits to their authority; we ourselves know all the shuffles, subterfuges and dishonesties by which Imperial power seeks to justify its own continuation, long after the bonds of natural loyalty or ideological sympathy have been overstrained; and we ourselves have had repeated occasion to observe how failures in national leadership not only create a credibility gap between politicians and the citizens whose affairs they control, but act like an external ferment on the rest of culture and society, turning the milk of human relationships into a sour whey.

The results of the present inquiry thus have a wider relevance and application, which springs from the fact that Austria was only an extreme case of a more general phenomenon; its characteristic distortions and artificialities, as we have studied them here, are reproduced in miniature wherever similar conditions and relationships exist. It takes the consciously reactionary policy of an Emperor Francis, perpetuated over a hundred and twenty years by a Metternich and a Francis Joseph, to bring about a situation of such extreme ill-adaptedness as had developed in Austria-Hungary by the first years of the twentieth century; but to some extent the development of political institutions always lags behind the objective needs of any society. In this sense, late Habsburg Vienna was a social pressure cooker; the things that happened in Kakania—social and cultural, as well as political—only illustrate the ways in which familiar processes of communal life manifest themselves, so to say, under conditions of abnormal temperature and pressure.

It is not just in *fin-de siècle* Vienna that sudden wealth breeds conspicuous consumption and all the vulgarities of bourgeois taste. Thus, Raymond Chandler can describe a Southern California apartment in terms that recall Loos and Musil:

The place was old-fashioned. It had a false fireplace with gas logs and a marble mantel, cracks in the plaster, a couple of vigorously colored daubs on the walls that looked lousy enough to have cost money, an old black chipped Steinway and for once no Spanish shawl on it. There was a lot of new-looking books in bright jackets scattered around and a double-barreled shotgun with a handsomely carved stock stood in the corner with a white satin bow tie around the barrels. Hollywood wit.[1]

Nowadays as much as in 1910, again, attempts to impose conventional standards of sexual morality by legal or political means, in the name of "public decency," have a class, as much as an ethical, basis. (It was not a mere slip of the tongue that led Mr. Mervyn Griffith-Jones, prosecuting Penguin Books for their unexpurgated version of *Lady Chatterley's Lover,* to ask the question, "Is this the kind of book that you would put into the hands of your *maidservant?*") As for Karl Kraus's campaign against the feuilleton and the *Neue Freie Presse,* few would have the courage to assert that the intellectual and artistic standards of the daily and weekly press have risen substantially since 1914, or that the literary essays and art criticism published in regular periodicals today—even including the cultural and book supplements of the leading New York and London Sunday papers—are markedly more serious, honest, or capable of distinguishing between the obligations of objective reporting and personal judgment, than their counterparts in pre-1914 Vienna.

If anything, present-day confusion about the problems of artistic expression and communication, and the blurring of the lines between art and commerce, are even worse than they were when Kraus denounced the press and art of pre-1914 Vienna. Kraus's contemporaries were understandably perplexed about the conditions on which any medium is capable of conveying its corresponding message; but that perplexity at any rate reflected a genuine determination to maintain or restore standards of creative authenticity and judgment about which the artist himself could feel proper self-respect. The world of McLuhan, in which the very distinction between *medium* and *message* has itself been called into doubt, by contrast, is one in which it has become doubtful, also, how far artists are even prepared to impose severe standards on themselves any longer.[2]

As every natural scientist knows, extreme cases can bring to light, in clear and undeniable form, relationships that remain blurred in more normal, ambiguous situations. So it is worth attempting to extract one or two more general conclusions from our present inquiry, which may help us to recognize how it is that societies and cultures, philosophical doctrines and individual men, interact and respond to one another: not just as a local particular phenomenon of *fin-de-siècle* Vienna, but in the nature of things.

To bring out the central and most significant point, it is convenient to use the terminology of Wittgenstein's own later philosophy. The language of values and value judgments is learned and given its standard uses in the context of real-life problems and situations; and, in the ordinary way, men acquire their grasp of what the task of "valuation" involves—and what it requires in the way of supporting justification—by recognizing how the corresponding language games are played through within the communal framework of forms of life into which those men grow up. Naturally enough, the examples from which they learn are of varying merit and authenticity. In coming to understand what a truly honest valuation is and ought to be, when arrived at with an eye to the very highest standards, we learn also to distinguish it from those other, more slipshod, insincere, or thoughtless expressions of approval or disgust which so often pass for value judgments. Still, a man can commonly accumulate a sufficient variety of experience, in the course of a normal childhood and youth, to end by *recognizing* the highest when he sees it, whether or no he succeeds in *loving* it.

Yet what—we may now ask—if the *Lebensformen* of a particular society are so structured that they consistently frustrate the expression of honest, high-principled judgments? What if no effective occasion or mechanism exists for political change, social reform or personal morality to be collectively discussed in terms that allow men to bring to bear all the considerations which should truly be operative, given the objective demands of their real-life problems? The creation of such a situation, we could argue, is a perfect recipe for intellectual and moral alienation of an extreme kind—like the individualistic alienation we have here seen developing in the Kakanian milieu. The Krausian refrain, that the sphere of facts and the sphere of values cannot be mixed without corrupting them both, has a sociological as well as a philosophical dimension. As the Viennese situation had developed, scope no longer existed, within the actual world of political, social and cultural life, for raising moral and aesthetic issues in a way that came to grips with the actual facts of the current situation.

In the communal situation as it actually existed, genuine moral principles and aesthetic values could be arrived at only by an idealized abstraction; and they could be given an actual realization, if at all, only in the lives of those few single-minded, Puritan individuals who were capable of this abstraction. There was thus a strict sense in which—failing any occasion for the corresponding language games—these abstract, idealized values were "unsayable." The accepted communal language games really gave the term "good" no use more rigorous than its use in the phrase "good taste," while, for the strictly loyal Austrian, the question whether Francis Joseph's political decisions were correct or mistaken was meaningless. (What else did the divine right of the Habsburg *Hausmacht* imply?) So a situation developed from which, as a by-product of conscious social policies, the normal language games of valuation had been eliminated. Questions of principle and morality were, quite simply, foreign to the social and political situation thus established; correspondingly, men who conceived an overriding loyalty to considerations of principle and morality were *ipso facto* ''alienated'' from the established society and polity.

The Habsburgs had, in fact, finally attempted to abolish history, just when the social and political consequences of industrialization had begun to set a premium on constitutional and institutional *adaptability*. Even in more pragmatically run societies, such as Britain and the United States, the second half of the nineteenth century was a period of change and stress, which broke out at time into violence and even civil war. But, however much men in those countries may have lacked the capacity to recognize their own social problems, in all their complexity and urgency, they rarely denied the very existence of those problems or suggested that they could be merely willed away without major institutional adaptation. That is just what the Habsburgs did. Whenever possible, Francis Joseph pretended that change was not really inevitable; when the existence of change was undeniable, he shut his eyes to the resulting problems; when problems became overpowering, he did his best to deal with them by minor political sleight of hand; and whatever else happened, the military power and diplomatic control of the Palace, with its oil lamps and eighteenth-century sanitation, were preserved untouched.

Yet, however much one may attempt to ''abolish history,'' it will not stay abolished. Beyond a certain point, the reality of historical change, and the grave and genuine problems to which it gives rise, cannot be denied without risk of disaster. Given the Habsburg constitution, which made it impossible to cope with real-life problems in a realistic manner, these could manifest themselves only, so to say, pathologically; hence the recurrent rash of ''affairs,'' which dotted the later history of the Austro-Hungarian Empire. Thus, Stefan Zweig was quite right to feel alarm at the Redl Affair, for that episode had demonstrated just how false and artificial the ostensible state of affairs—the ''appearances'' which always had to be ''kept up''—had by this time become. And to a greater or lesser extent, all those other ''affairs'' of the years from 1870 on—the Cilli Affair, the Friedjung Affair, and the rest—illustrated the same incapacity of the Habsburg establishment to cope with the authentic problems of nationalism, industrialization and social change. Every society, of course, has its own scandals and *causes célèbres* which throw light on the points at which social tradition and prejudice have lost touch with the actual situation. The distinguishing mark of Kakania was the deliberate attempt by the Habsburg dynasty to preserve, into the twentieth century, an institutional and constitutional stasis that had elsewhere proved unenforceable by 1848 at the latest.

At the outset of our inquiry, we raised certain questions which cannot be fully answered by confining oneself to the orthodox academic divisions, for example, between constitutional and political history, between the history of music and the history of philosophy, between social theory and individual biography. Why, among all the European powers, was Austria-Hungary so uniquely incapable of overcoming the strains imposed by the First World War? (One has to say the "European" powers, having in mind the similar fate that befell the Ottoman Empire at the same time.) And how was it that, having once lost power, the House of Habsburg retained no serious body of royalist support to call for its restoration? Again, what is it that explains the extraordinary parallels among the respective ways in which different branches of fine art, music and literature developed between the 1880s and the 1930s? Or, for that matter, the similarities, in personality and ideas, of a man like Ludwig Wittgenstein and a Karl Kraus or an Adolf Loos?

By this point, we have provided ourselves with material in terms of which such questions can largely answer themselves. By 1900, Habsburg power and authority had been transformed into a mere shell, or carapace, within which the Austrians, Hungarians and other nationalities lived their real lives and coped with their real problems, in ways that had lost all real organic connection with the Habsburg establishment. Politics as it was officially practiced was one thing; the practical solution of authentic social and political problems was something quite different, though convention demanded that the resulting solutions be presented in forms that respected the appearances of the Habsburg situation. If this meant that political discussion had to be carried on in a kind of double talk, so be it. The ability to dress up substantive discussions in formalistic fancy dress was no doubt one which the average mayor or provincial governor acquired without difficulty. Yet its very lack of any organic significance meant that the disappearance of the monarchy brought, for the most part, only a sense of relief that one was no longer compelled to *pretend.*

Given a society committed to ignoring this basic falsity, it is no wonder if "communication" became a problem, or if, over questions of morality, judgment and taste, men had difficulty in distinguishing appearance from realities. In this situation, the corruption of standards had gone so deep that the only effective response was an equally extreme Puritanism. So far as Kraus and the Krausians were concerned, direct political means were out. At the center, demands for political change had crystallized around nationalism, at the periphery around working-class aspirations, and neither of these was the kind of cause to which a man of Kraus's individual integrity could warm. There remained only two possible courses of action. One could stand on the sidelines and play the part of a Greek chorus, as Kraus did in *Die Fackel,* so that those of his contemporaries who had any standards of judgment left could see for themselves how language, social attitudes and cultural values alike had become debased in a society built upon artificialities and falsehoods. Alternatively, one could wash one's hands of communal affairs entirely. Society would go to hell in its own way. All the individual could do was try, like Wittgenstein, to live in his own high-minded way, maintaining and exemplifying in his life his own exacting standards of humanity, intellectual honesty, craftsmanship and personal integrity.

If the experience of our own times gives us a new feeling for the Habsburg situation, so too—conversely—a greater familiarity with the life and times of men like Kraus and Wittgenstein can help us to see our own situation more clearly. Nowadays as much as in the years before 1914, political dishonesty and deviousness quickly find expression in debased language, which blunts the sensitivity of the political agent himself to the character of his own actions and policies. So the intention to deceive others ends by generating self-deceit. Counterargument is no weapon against this tactic, since the issues are always blurred by translation into officialese. The only effective response, as Kraus himself showed, is to quote a politician's own words straight back at him, so that everyone—or, at any rate, everyone else—has the chance of understanding what the true situation is and how it is falsified by slovenly misdescription. This is a procedure which some American commentators—for example, the editors of *The New Yorker*—have in fact rediscovered for themselves during the Vietnam and Watergate years.

In other respects too, the Krausian problems about communication have counterparts in contemporary America. However much the United States set out to be a melting pot in which the children of former Europeans—and, to a lesser extent, Asians and Africans—would learn to live together as a single American nation, this idealistic hope has been realized in practice only in part. The ethnic rivalries of Central Europe, the social exclusiveness of the Anglo-Saxons, Germanic feelings of superiority over Latins and Slavs, and the prejudices of Europeans toward "yellow men" and "black men"—all of these have been muted rather than forgotten, and every economic setback has the power to revive ethnic bitterness and racial feeling. So, in the United States today, we often seem to be watching, while only half understanding, a bungled remake of some political drama originally played out in the last days of the Habsburg Empire.

The degree of sheerly linguistic incomprehension that exists between, say, American blacks or Puerto Ricans and the official authorities with which they have to deal poses problems of communication that bear examination in the light of the Austro-Hungarian experience. For the constitutional theories of the new American republic, as set up in the year 1776, presupposed a community of interests and a consensus over national goals, which has since then been canceled out, firstly by the great immigrations after 1848, secondly by the emancipation and enfranchisement of the slaves, and finally by the sheer territorial expansion of the Republic, westward and southward from the Appalachians to Mexico, the Pacific Ocean and beyond. And, to the extent that the constitutional arrangements of 1776 have since become unrealistic, the institutions and procedures then set up may well need to be made more adaptable, if they are to serve adequately the legitimate human purposes of all the individuals and groups that now play a part in the life of the Republic. Otherwise, one may be in danger of creating and intensifying artificialities and false values of the kind that were eventually endemic in the Habsburg Empire; and, however enlightened and well intentioned, politicians and administrators compelled to operate within this unrealistic situation will find themselves unable to speak to the real needs of their fellow citizens and constituents, for lack of ideas and institutions—and even of language—capable of reflecting the actual character of those needs.

The Russian superpower has, meanwhile, developed into a condition even closer to that of Habsburg Kakania. On top of a vast internal diversity of nationalities and religions, aspirations and interests, is superimposed a constitutional system based on ideological principles which claim an authority as permanent and immutable as the divinely guaranteed *Hausmacht*. By its claim to the "leading role" as historic spokesman for the international proletariat, the Communist Party of the Soviet Union confers on itself the same cosmic right to govern, and grants itself the same immunity from criticism and judgment, that the claim to divine right implied on behalf of the Habsburg emperors. As a result, the constitutional machinery of state and party power is prevented from identifying, reflecting or responding to, the authentic needs, interests and conflicts, as they emerge out of the real lives of its subjects and citizens, except where these conform beforehand to preconceived administrative or ideological categories.

The consequences of this divergence between constitutional appearances and political realities are, once again, what the Austrian experience suggests. Those people who live in outlying, non-Russian republics and "autonomous regions" are in a dual situation—as Soviet citizens of non-Russian race—which makes possible a working compromise similar to that existing in, say, the Slavic provinces of the Habsburg Empire. A Georgian or an Armenian, for instance, is no less conscious than anyone else that the "official" pattern of Soviet life, around which he must structure his legal status, formal career and public activities, often has little to do with the real life within which he falls unhappily in love, wangles himself an apartment, or makes a little money on the side in order to pay for *Samizdat* literature. But for him, as for a Habsburg Czech, nationalism provides a natural and easy way out. Real life and its problems can be equated with, say, Georgian life and its problems—something to be faced and discussed by Georgians in their own language, written in its own script, and dealt with locally on as realistic a basis as "those bureaucrats in Moscow" will allow. Correspondingly, the artificialities of official Soviet life appear arbitrary, external impositions by a stupid, Russian-speaking officialdom which does not understand the effects of its policies on the actual lives and problems of "us Georgians."

As with the *fin-de-siècle* Viennese, the real weight of the situation bears on the Great Russians themselves. They do not have the escape route of nationalism. They cannot project the divorce between the official interpretation of any situation, in terms acceptable to ideologues and bureaucrats, and the real-life problems which they face every day for themselves, into a remote body of uncomprehending foreigners. For them this divorce is manifestly built into the actual operations of the state and party machinery. So any thoroughgoing attempt they make to deal with these actual realities in public, instead of tolerating the Soviet establishment's insistence on "keeping up appearances," is once again liable to erupt into an "affair." Where Austria-Hungary had its Friedjung and Redl Affairs, the Soviet Union has been afflicted similarly by its Pasternak and Solzhenitsyn Affairs, its Medvedev and Sakharov Affairs. Contemporary Russia has distinguished itself merely by creating a situation so totally artificial and ill-adapted to the real problems of life, that its most talented and internationally respected authors and scientists— men who are as much good Marxists as Galileo was a good Catholic—can do their own proper work, only at the risk of seeing themselves labeled "enemies of the state" or "betrayers of the party," "schizophrenics" or "enemy agents." Meanwhile, the men who operate the state and party machinery apparently fail to see how their own reflex reactions to a Solzhenitsyn or a Medvedev make them look even more ridiculous in the eyes of all outsiders than their own worst enemies could possibly do.[8]

If our examination of the social and cultural paradoxes of the last Habsburg years has any general lessons, accordingly, they are perhaps the following:

In the first place, we have seen how a culture which erects insuperable barriers to the meaningful discussion of real and urgent problems becomes, in a certain sense, "pathological." The pretense that things are other than they are cannot be kept up indefinitely; the compromise solutions which are all that the appearances permit are not indefinitely effective; and the resulting sequence of scandals or "affairs" is only one surface symptom of this continuing divergence. In Austria-Hungary, many signs and symptoms were linked into a single, larger syndrome. Anti-Semitism, suicide, rigid sexual conventions, artistic sentimentality, political "double think," the rise of an underground press, divisive nationalisms, and the alienation of serious-minded intellectuals—all of these, we have argued, either sprang from, or were enhanced by, the basic divorce of political and social realities from the appearances which were acceptable in the eyes of the Habsburg autocracy, as founded by the Emperor Francis and continued by Metternich and Francis Joseph. And, wherever constitutional theory and political practice part company for long enough from the realities of an actual situation, similar pathological syndromes can be expected.

In the second place, our study of the Kakanian syndrome—in which political, social, artistic and philosophical elements were all present—allows us to use some characteristically Wittgensteinian ideas to throw light on the processes of intellectual and social history. Philosophical arguments, as Wittgenstein taught, illustrate the stereotypes in terms of which philosophers understand—or misunderstand—certain particularly problematic terms or notions; the actual practical meaning of these notions derives from the language games within which they are given a use in real life; and those language games have a genuine force and application, only to the extent that they are themselves rooted in authentic forms of life. Given the complex sociocultural syndromes that we have studied here, there need be no surprise that the same corruption of thought and standards was capable of manifesting itself at one and the same time on every level of social and cultural life, from philosophical theory to political practice.

Nor do we need, in this case, to invoke any *Zeitgeist* to explain how, for once, the conceptual problems of philosophy mirrored in microcosm the same problems of expression and communication that were dominant in art and literature, or how these artistic problems reflected, in turn, corresponding institutional problems in the society. It was the consistent attempt to evade the social and political problems of Austria by the debasement of language—by the invention of "bogus language games," based on the pretense that the existing forms of life were other than they really were—that created the underlying occasion for men's universal confusions about the problems of expression and communication. This confusion found an outlet, both in the particular aesthetic critiques characteristic of all the different arts in late Habsburg Vienna, and also in the general philosophical critique of language as initiated by Mauthner and subsequently taken up by Wittgenstein himself. (Indeed, the phenomenon of "bogus language games" might even be regarded as a linguistic aspect of the Marxian concept of "false consciousness." In Marxian terms, the results of our inquiries have helped to show just how comprehensively such a "false consciousness" can permeate and distort the operations of any society and its culture.)

Finally: by carrying our inquiries beyond 1920, we have put ourselves in a position to reappraise one notion that covers the whole gamut of human activities, from practical politics to philosophical theory—namely, that of revolutions. Hitherto, we have been encouraged by a somewhat narrow-minded reading of Marx to think of "revolutionary situations" in excessively economic terms. Yet, while poverty and economic inequality can undoubtedly be the final spur provoking a rebellion against tyrannies or injustices of other kinds, the origins of a revolutionary situation lie in something more than economic inequalities between classes. The Habsburg Empire in its last decades was certainly a promising candidate for revolution, and the years following the 1918 defeat saw, in Budapest, Bela Kun's short-lived attempt to establish a Hungarian Communist regime. Yet the fatal weaknesses of the Habsburg regime lay not so much in its economic base—which was, after all, very different in 1910 from what it had been in 1790—as in its sheer constitutional inflexibility. Every reform that Francis Joseph introduced took the form of a minimal concession, made only when the internal pressure became unbearable, at some point and in some direction carefully chosen to do least damage to the *Hausmacht*. Apart from the 1914–18 war, there is no knowing how fanatically determined Francis Joseph's successors would have been to protect their absolute power over defense and foreign affairs; so there is no knowing whether, under other circumstances, Austria might not have evolved into a constitutional monarchy, capable of responding creatively to the political, economic and social demands of the twentieth century.

What we have come to recognize here about revolutions—and this is true, equally, of revolutions in social, cultural and intellectual life—is just how easily their results can become self-frustrating. Where an old system of political institutions (or artistic procedures or philosophical ideas) is entrenched in authority, insuperably inflexible, and fanatically determined to protect its authority against all challenge, there may be no alternative to overturning that authority in a comprehensive or *revolutionary* way. Yet how little, as we have seen, is achieved by mere revolution alone! The most likely effect of revolution for revolution's sake is always to install a new centralism, or orthodoxy, no less restrictive and inflexible than its predecessor. Failing better institutional controls, for instance, the effect of replacing an autocratic monarchy with a bureaucracy—however admirable its slogans—is too often to replace a single-headed despotism by a Hydra-headed one. On the other hand, if the older system of institutions, standards or ideas is not insuperably inflexible and its defenders are not too fanatically determined to preserve its undiminished authority at all costs, there may well prove to be unsuspected scope for increasing this adaptability—thus, introducing fresh safeguards into the human activities concerned and keeping the official operations of the relevant institutions more nearly in line with the real-life human needs toward which their activities are directed.

Just when any particular situation still shows scope for internal improvements, or is so hopeless that it has become truly revolutionary, is inevitably a matter for judgment in each case. Yet, if twentieth-century experience should have taught us anything, it is this. In a period of increasingly rapid historical change, on the political, economic, social, cultural, scientific and intellectual levels alike, anyone who embarks on a revolution takes upon himself a fresh and grave responsibility. For the prime, and most difficult, task of the modern revolutionary is to ensure that something more is achieved, as a result of his *coup,* than the mere substitution of one static, inflexible system for another. It would be a tragedy if the verdict of later historians on the twentieth century were that the outcome of all our criticisms, agonies and revolutions—whether in politics, art or thought—had simply been to replace King Log with King Stork.

Notes

Chapter 1.

1. For source references, see the Select Bibliography at the end of this book.

2. Wittgenstein, *Tractatus*, Author's Preface.

3. See H. Stuart Hughes, *Consciousness and Society*, p. 399.

4. See Stephen Toulmin, title essay in H. H. Rhys, *Seventeenth-Century Science and the Arts*.

5. This is the title Kraus gave to his own play about the First World War. See also Frank Field, *The Last Days of Mankind*.

6. Even Norman Malcolm's personal memoir of Wittgenstein, for all its merits, leaves the connections between Wittgenstein the man and his philosophical position obscure.

7. As I (S.E.T.) discovered during a trip through Kosovo-Metohija and Macedonia in 1968, more than 20 years after the Second World War, even young men in their teens and twenties are fluent in Turkish.

8. Bruno Walter, *Theme and Variations*, p. 86.

9. On Schönberg and Kraus, see Chapter 4.

10. The phrase is that of Kraus; see Chapter 3.

11. Perhaps the best picture of this circle and its concerns is that by John Maynard Keynes, in his essay, "My Early Beliefs," published in *Two Memoirs*.

12. See B. Russell, *Autobiography*, Vols. I and II, and the letters reprinted with these memoirs. There are other valuable unpublished letters between Russell and Wittgenstein among the Russell papers at Macmaster University, Hamilton, Ontario.

13. I recall in particular Russell's remarks about Wittgenstein's later philosophical work in conversations at the Moral Sciences Club, Cambridge University, in the year 1946–47; and again at a discussion-meeting at Oxford University, early in the 1950s. (S.E.T.)

14. Personal communication from Richard Braithwaite; the wording may not be exact, since the report is a confidential document, but the paraphrase is a close one. (S.E.T.)

15. Personal recollections from the period January 1946 to June 1947, after which Wittgenstein resigned from the professorship and returned to a completely private mode of life. (S.E.T.)

16. Wittgenstein, *Tractatus*, Author's Preface.

17. This has been true of all the major commentaries on the *Tractatus*, particularly those which have formed what we call the "received interpretation"—e.g. those of Max Black and Elizabeth Anscombe.

18. Conversations in Vienna, winter–spring, 1969 (A.S.J.). See also Ludwig Haensel, *Begegnungen und Auseinandersetzungen*, p. 357.

19. Paul Engelmann, *Letters from Ludwig Wittgenstein, with a Memoir*; and G. H. von Wright, "Ludwig Wittgenstein, a Biographical Sketch," in *Philosophical Review*, Vol. 64.

20. See the correspondence with Engelmann.

21. G. E. M. Anscombe, *An In-*

troduction to *Wittgenstein's Tractatus,* p. 12.

22. Engelmann, *op. cit.,* pp. 123–132.

23. M. O'C. Drury, "A Symposium," in K. T. Fann, ed., *Ludwig Wittgenstein: The Man and His Philosophy,* p. 70.

24. Anscombe, *loc. cit.*

25. See Patrick Gardiner, *Schopenhauer,* pp. 275–82; Anscombe, *op. cit.,* pp. 11 f, 168 f; Janik, "Schopenhauer and the Early Wittgenstein," in *Philosophical Studies,* Vol. 15.

26. Erich Heller, "Ludwig Wittgenstein: Unphilosophical Notes," in Fann, *op. cit.,* pp. 89–106; see also pp. 64–66. Wenner Kraft, "Ludwig Wittgenstein und Karl Kraus," *Neue Deutsche Rundschau,* Vol. 72.

27. Erik Stenius, *Wittgenstein's Tractatus: A Critical Exposition,* pp. 214–26; see also S. Morris Engel, *Wittgenstein's Doctrine of the Tyranny of Language.*

28. See Stephen Toulmin, "From Logical Analysis to Conceptual History," in Achinstein and Barker, *The Legacy of Logical Positivism.*

29. D. F. Pears, *Wittgenstein.*

30. *Tractatus,* Author's Preface.

31. Personal conversations with Professor von Wright, by S.E.T. and A.S.J. independently. Though this comment may here be quoted out of context, its sense is clearly applicable to our present argument.

32. Heinrich Hertz, *The Principles of Mechanics,* esp. Introduction. See *Gesammelte Werke;* see also the useful English edition by Robert S. Cohen.

33. See Josef Rufer, *The Works of Arnold Schoenberg: A Catalog of His Compositions, Writings and Paintings.*

Chapter 2.

1. Arthur May, *Vienna in the Age of Franz Josef,* pp. 74–75.

2. Henry Schnitzler, "Gay Vienna

—Myth and Reality," *Journal of the History of Ideas,* Vol. 15, p. 115.

3. Quoted by Henry Schnitzler, *op. cit.,* p. 112.

4. May, *Vienna* . . . , p. 23.

5. See the essay of Ernst Křenek in Bruno Walter, *Gustav Mahler.*

6. See Henry Pleasants' Preface to his edition of Hanslick's essays entitled *Eduard Hanslick: Music Criticisms 1846–99.* An abridged edition was published under the title *Vienna's Golden Years 1850–1900.*

7. May, *Vienna* . . . , p. 56.

8. May, *Vienna* . . . , p. 54.

9. Quoted by Burton Pike in *Robert Musil: An Introduction to His Work,* p. 40.

10. Robert Musil, *The Man Without Qualities,* Vol. I, pp. 32–33.

11. C. A. Macartney, *The Habsburg Empire 1790–1918,* p. 190.

12. *Ibid.,* p. 151.

13. Oscar Jászi, *The Dissolution of the Habsburg Monarchy,* p. 81 *et passim.*

14. Macartney, *op. cit.,* p. 211 n.

15. Arthur May, *The Habsburg Monarchy 1867–1914,* p. 22.

16. *Ibid.,* p. 22.

17. Jászi, *op. cit.,* p. 92.

18. May, *Habsburg Monarchy,* p. 358.

19. Macartney, *op. cit.,* p. 667.

20. Jászi, *op. cit.,* 70 ff.

21. Macartney, *op. cit.,* p. 104; see also Jászi, *op. cit.,* pp. 61 f.

22. Macartney, *op. cit.,* pp. 661 ff; see also A. J. P. Taylor, *The Habsburg Monarchy 1809–1918: A History of the Austrian Empire and Austria-Hungary,* pp. 184 ff.

23. A. J. P. Taylor, *op. cit.,* p. 184.

24. Jászi, *op. cit.,* pp. 33–34 *et passim.*

25. Robert Musil, *The Man Without Qualities,* Vol. I, p. 32.

26. Macartney, *op. cit.,* p. 603 *et passim.*

27. Musil, *The Man Without Qualities,* Vol. I, p. 93.

28. *Ibid.*, p. 97.

29. May, *Vienna* . . . , pp. 79 ff.

30. May, *Habsburg Monarchy*, p. 145.

31. Ernest Jones, *The Life and Work of Sigmund Freud*, Vol. I, p. 25.

32. Karl Marx and Friedrich Engels, *The Communist Manifesto*, p. 62.

33. Stefan Zweig, *The World of Yesterday: An Autobiography*, p. vii.

34. Musil, *The Man Without Qualities*, Vol. I, p. 330.

35. Carl E. Schorske, "The Transformation of the Garden: Ideal and Society in Austrian Literature," *American Historical Review*, Vol. 72, No. 4, pp. 1304–5, Our description of the Viennese middle-class family owes much to Schorske's article "Politics and the Psyche in *fin-de-siècle* Vienna: Schnitzler and Hofmannsthal," *American Historical Review*, Vol. 66, No. 4, and to Zweig's autobiography, to mention the most important among many sources.

36. Zweig, *op. cit.*, p. 15.

37. *Ibid.*, p. 99.

38. Schorske, "Politics and the Psyche," p. 935.

39. Zweig, *op. cit.*, p. 36.

40. *Ibid.*, pp. 74 ff.

41. *Ibid.*, pp. 71 ff.

42. Wilma Abeles Iggers, *Karl Kraus: A Viennese Critic of the Twentieth Century*, p. 155.

43. Zweig, *op. cit.*, p. 79.

44. *Ibid.*, p. 83.

45. Schorske, "Politics and the Psyche," p. 932.

46. Macartney, *op. cit.*, pp. 519 ff.

47. A. J. P. Taylor, *op. cit.*, p. 27.

48. May, *Habsburg Monarchy*, pp. 3 f.

49. *Ibid.*, p. 204.

50. Carl E. Schorske, "Politics in a New Key: An Austrian Triptych," *Journal of Modern History*, Vol. 39, No. 4, pp. 350–51.

51. See Charles O. Hardy, *The Housing Program of the City of Vienna*, Chapter One, for a discussion of the prewar situation in Vienna.

52. Macartney, *op. cit.*, p. 718.

53. For a discussion of working-class living and working conditions in early twentieth-century Vienna, see May, *Vienna* . . . , pp. 40–45.

54. See Chapter Seven of William A. Jenks, *Vienna and the Young Hitler*; see also Albert Fuchs, *Geistige Strömungen in Oesterreich 1867–1918*, pp. 85–129.

55. May, *Vienna* . . . , pp. 59–60; see also Fuchs, *op. cit.*, pp. 25–30.

56. For discussions of Lueger see P. G. Pulzer, *The Rise of Political Anti-Semitism in Germany and Austria*, pp. 162–70; Jenks, *op. cit.*, Chapter 4; Fuchs, *op. cit.*, pp. 58–63; Schorske, "Politics in a New Key," pp. 355–65.

57. Fuchs, *op. cit.*, p. 51.

58. H. von Poschinger, quoted by Hans Rosenberg in "Political and Social Consequences of the Great Depression of 1873–1896," *Economic History Review*, Vol. 13, p. 63 n. 2.

59. Quoted by Field, *op. cit.*, p. 62.

60. For discussions of Schönerer see Pulzer, *op. cit.*, pp. 148–61; 177–189; 199–218; Jenks, *op. cit.*, Chapter 5; Fuchs, *op. cit.*, pp. 176–86; Schorske, "Politics in a New Key," pp. 346–55.

61. Pulzer, *op. cit.*, p. 152.

62. *Ibid.*, p. 153. The other eleven points are cited on p. 151.

63. *Ibid.*, p. 151.

64. Schorske, "Politics in a New Key," p. 355.

65. Andrew Gladding Whiteside, *Austrian National Socialism before 1918*.

66. Quoted in Pulzer, *op. cit.*, p. 269.

67. Our interpretation of Herzl is largely, but not exclusively, drawn from Schorske, "Politics in a New Key," pp. 365–68; see also Alex Bein, *Theodore Herzl: A Biography;* and Solomon Liptzin, *Germany's Stepchildren*, pp. 113–23.

68. Quoted by Schorske in "Politics in a New Key," p. 378.

69. Zweig, *op. cit.*, pp. 26, 192 ff.

70. For a reconstruction of the career of Redl see Robert B. Asprey, *The Panther's Feast*. John Osborne's play *A Patriot for Me* is based on Asprey's account of the Redl affair.

71. Zweig, *op. cit.*, p. 208.

72. Schnitzler's life has been chronicled in Solomon Liptzin's *Arthur Schnitzler*.

73. Schorske, "Politics and the Psyche," p. 936. We owe much of the following to Schorske's insightful analysis as well as Robert A. Kann's excellent article, "The Image of the Austrian in the Writings of Arthur Schnitzler," *Studies in Arthur Schnitzler*, pp. 45–70.

74. Musil, *The Man Without Qualities*, Vol. III, p. 188.

75. Iggers, *op. cit.*, p. 33.

76. Field, *op. cit.*, p. 56.

77. Emile Durkheim, *Suicide: A Study in Sociology*, p. 299.

78. Musil, *The Man Without Qualities*, Vol. III, p. 236.

Chapter 3.

1. Karl Kraus, in *Die Fackel*, No. 400, Summer 1914, p. 2.

2. Adolf Hitler, *Mein Kampf*, p. 162.

3. May, *Vienna in the Age of Franz Josef*, p. 114.

4. For biographical information on Kraus see Field, *The Last Days of Mankind;* Iggers, *Karl Kraus;* and Paul Schick, *Karl Kraus in Selbstzeugnissen und Bilddokumenten.*

5. Schick, *op. cit.*, p. 43.

6. Iggers, *op. cit.*, p. 42.

7. Theodor Haecker, *Søren Kierkegaard und die Philosophie der Innerlichkeit*, p. 57.

8. For a biography of Weininger see David Abrahamsen, *The Mind and Death of a Genius.*

9. Otto Weininger, *Sex and Character*, p. 14.

10. *Ibid.*, pp. 1–10; 78–84.

11. *Ibid.*, pp. 46–52.

12. *Ibid.*, pp. 301–30.

13. Field, *op. cit.*, p. 66.

14. Carl Dallago, *Otto Weininger und sein Werk*, p. 3.

15. *Ibid.*, p. 6.

16. *Ibid.*, p. 38.

17. For Kraus's views on woman see *Werke*, Vol. III, pp. 13–56; see also Iggers, *op. cit.*, Chapter 7, pp. 155–70.

18. Kraus, *Werke*, Vol. III, p. 293. The translation is from Paul Engelmann, *Letters from Wittgenstein, with a Memoir*, p. x.

19. *Ibid.*, p. 351.

20. Fritz Wittels, "The Fackel Neurosis," *Minutes of the Vienna Psychoanalytic Society 1908–1910*, pp. 382–93.

21. Kraus, *Werke*, Vol. III, p. 55.

22. Quoted by Field, *op. cit.*, p. 59.

23. Kraus, *Werke*, Vol. III, p. 82. Translated in Iggers, *op. cit.*, p. 218 n.

24. Iggers, *op. cit.*, p. 94.

25. May, *Vienna . . .* , pp. 48–49; see also Field, *op. cit.*, p. 44.

26. Iggers, *op. cit.*, p. 113.

27. *Ibid.*, p. 95.

28. Field, *op. cit.*, p. 58.

29. See above, pp. 45–46.

30. See above, p. 44.

31. Iggers, *op. cit.*, p. 110.

32. Kraus, *Werke*, Vol. III, p. 103.

33. See below, pp. 103 ff.

34. Barbara Tuchman, *The Proud Tower*, p. 390.

35. Iggers, *op. cit.*, p. 86.

36. Kraus, *Werke*, Vol. III, p. 131.

37. Quoted in Iggers, *op. cit.*, p. 85.

38. *Ibid.*, pp. 87–88.

39. Field, *op. cit.*, p. 10.

40. Translator's Introduction to Johann Nestroy, *Three Comedies*, p. 21.

41. Egon Friedell, *A Cultural History of the Modern Age*, Vol. III, p. 139.

42. Engelmann, *Memoir*, p. 131.

43. Kraus, *Werke,* Vol. III, p. 326.

44. Field, *op. cit.,* pp. 3–4.

45. Iggers, *op. cit.,* p. 99. "Grubenhund" is in fact a play upon words; it signifies a type of cart used to transport the raw ore from the mines.

46. *Ibid.,* p. 100.

47. Kraus, *Werke,* Vol. III, p. 341.

48. J. P. Stern, "Karl Kraus's Vision of Language," *Modern Language Review,* January 1966, pp. 73–74.

49. G. C. Lichtenberg, *The Lichtenberg Reader,* p. 85.

50. Iggers, *op. cit.,* p. 26.

51. Rainer Maria Rilke, *Duino Elegies with English Translations,* p. 69. For the impact of the young Buber upon Rilke's Ninth Elegy see Maurice Friedman's introduction to his translation of Martin Buber, *Daniel: Dialogues on Realization.*

52. Quoted by Field, *op. cit.,* p. 51.

Chapter 4.

1. Engelbert Broda, *Ludwig Boltzmann: Mensch, Physiker, Philosoph,* p. 15.

2. Ernest Jones, *The Life and Work of Sigmund Freud,* Vol. II, p. 80.

3. *Ibid.,* p. 56.

4. May, *The Habsburg Monarchy,* pp. 183–84.

5. Fuchs, *Geistige Strömungen in Oesterreich,* p. 99.

6. Adolf Loos, *Sämtliche Schriften,* Vol. I, p. 277.

7. Peter Selz, *German Expressionist Painting,* p. 149.

8. May, *Habsburg Monarchy,* p. 321.

9. Selz, *op. cit.,* pp. 48–64, 147–160.

10. *Ibid.,* p. 60.

11. *Ibid.,* pp. 150–51.

12. Friedell, *A Cultural History of the Modern Age,* Vol. III, pp. 299–300.

13. *Ibid.,* p. 300.

14. Loos, *op. cit.,* Vol. I, p. 276. This influential essay is translated in Ludwig Munz and Gustav Kunstler, *Adolf Loos: Pioneer of Modern Architecture.*

15. Loos, *op. cit.,* Vol. I, p. 277.

16. *Ibid., passim.*

17. *Ibid.,* p. 283.

18. Quoted in Paul Engelmann's unpublished collection *Bei der Lampe.*

19. Loos, *op. cit.,* pp. 314–15.

20. May, *Vienna in the Age of Franz Josef,* p. 111.

21. Selz, *op. cit.,* p. 164.

22. *Ibid.,* p. 165.

23. Quoted in Schick, *Karl Kraus,* p. 151.

24. Willi Reich, *Schöenberg: A Critical Biography,* pp. 81 ff.

25. Selz, *op. cit.,* p. 209.

26. Barbara Tuchman, *The Proud Tower,* p. 347.

27. Edward Hanslick, *The Beautiful in Music,* Chapter 2, "Does Music Represent Feelings?"

28. Henry Pleasants' essay "Edward Hanslick," in Hanslick, *Music Criticisms.*

29. *Ibid.,* p. 17.

30. *Ibid.,* p. 206.

31. *Ibid.,* p. 121.

32. Hanslick, *The Beautiful in Music,* p. 30.

33. *Ibid.,* p. 29.

34. *Ibid.,* p. 125.

35. *Ibid.,* p. 51.

36. *Loc. cit.*

37. *Ibid.,* p. 50.

38. Arnold Schönberg, *Style and Idea,* p. 143.

39. Quoted in H. H. Stuckenschmidt, *Arnold Schoenberg,* p. 66.

40. Josef Rufer, *The Works of Arnold Schoenberg,* p. 140.

41. *Ibid.,* p. 151.

42. *Ibid.,* p. 142.

43. For information about Hauer see Reich, *op. cit.,* pp. 136–38.

44. Rufer, *op. cit.,* p. 151.

45. Reich, *op. cit.,* p. 45.

46. Quoted by Field, *The Last Days of Mankind,* p. 8.

Notes

47. Ernst Křenek in Bruno Walter, *Gustav Mahler*, pp. 128–29.
48. Schönberg, *Style and Idea*, p. 109.
49. *Ibid.*, p. 47.
50. Reich, *op. cit.*, pp. 202–3.
51. Hanslick, *Music Criticisms*, pp. 270–74.
52. Rufer, *op. cit.*, p. 143.
53. Quoted by Egon Wellesz, *Arnold Schoenberg*, p. 54.
54. Quoted by Wolfram Mauser, *Bild und Gebärde in der Sprache Hofmannsthals*, p. 5.
55. Ernst Mach, *The Analysis of Sensations*, p. 12.
56. Quoted in Hans Hammelmann, *Hugo von Hofmannsthal*, p. 14.
57. Hugo von Hofmannsthal, *Selected Prose*, p. 133.
58. *Ibid.*, p. 138.
59. Gerhard Masur, *Prophets of Yesterday: Studies in European Culture 1890–1914*, p. 132.
60. Mauser, *op. cit.*, p. 58.
61. Musil, *Young Törless*, pp. 178–85.
62. Musil, *The Man Without Qualities*, Foreword to Capricorn Books edition, Vol. I, pp. iii-iv.

Chapter 5.

1. Fritz Mauthner, *Wörterbuch der Philosophie: Neue Beiträge zu einer Kritik der Sprache*, p. xi. Conversations with Professor R. H. Popkin in 1968 were of much assistance in enabling me to approach Mauthner. (A.S.J.)
2. Mauthner, *Beiträge zu einer Kritik der Sprache*, Vol. I, p. 25.
3. Mauthner, *Beiträge*, Vol. III, p. 646.
4. Mauthner, *Die Sprache*, p. 109.
5. Mauthner, *Beiträge*, Vol. I, pp. 86–92.
6. *Ibid.*, Vol. I, p. 92.
7. *Ibid.*, Vol. I, p. 34.
8. *Ibid.*, Vol. I, p. 159.
9. *Ibid.*, Vol. III, p. 397.
10. *Ibid.*, Vol. II, p. 66.
11. *Ibid.*, Vol. I, p. 640.
12. *Ibid.*, Vol. I, p. 649.
13. Mauthner, *Die Sprache*, p. 114.
14. Mauthner, *Beiträge*, Vol. I, p. 111.
15. Mauthner, *Wörterbuch*, p. xi.
16. Werner Volke, *Hugo von Hofmannsthal in Selbstzeugnissen und Bilddokumenten*, p. 52.
17. Field, *Last Days of Mankind*, p. 245, n. 43.
18. Robert S. Cohen, "Ernst Mach: Physics, Perception and the Philosophy of Science," *Synthèse*, Vol. 18, No. 2/3, p. 162. Field, *op. cit.*, reports that Friedrich Adler, son of the molder of Austrian Social Democracy, spent the time he was in prison for the assassination of Count Sturgh in composing a book on Mach.
19. Cohen, "Ernst Mach," p. 162.
20. *Ibid.*, p. 168, n. 42.
21. Albert Einstein, "Autobiographical Notes," in P. A. Schilpp, ed., *Albert Einstein: Philosopher-Scientist*, Vol. I, p. 21.
22. Gerald Holton, "Mach, Einstein, and the Search for Reality," *Daedalus*, Vol. 97 (Spring, 1968), pp. 640 ff.
23. Holton, *op. cit.*, p. 646 n.
24. Ernst Mach, *The History and Root of the Principle of Conservation of Energy*, pp. 91–92.
25. Mach, "Mein Verhältniss zu R. Avenarius," *Die Analyse der Empfindungen und das Verhältniss des Physischen zum Psychischen*, p. 25. The translation is from *The Analysis of Sensations and the Relation of the Physical to the Psychical*, p. 46.
26. John Passmore, *A Hundred Years of Philosophy*, p. 213.
27. Wendell D. Bush, "Avenarius and the Standpoint of Pure Experience," *Archives of Philosophy, Psychology and Scientific Method*, Vol. 2 (1905), p. 26.
28. I. M. Bochenski, *Contemporary European Philosophy*, pp. 137–138.
29. Bush, *loc. cit.*
30. Richard Avenarius, *Philoso-*

phie als Denken der Welt gemäss dem Prinzip des Kleinsten Kraftmasses: Prolegomena zu einer Kritik der reinen Erfahrung.

31. Mach, *Die Mechanik in ihrer Entwicklung Historisch-Kritisch Dargestellt*, p. 521. The translation is from *The Science of Mechanics*, p. 577.

32. Mach, *Mechanik*, p. 238 (translation, p. 273).

33. *Ibid.*, p. 493 (translation, p. 546).

34. *Ibid.*, pp. 278–79 (translation, p. 316).

35. Cohen, "Ernst Mach," pp. 149 f.

36. Mach, *Mechanik*, p. 523 (translation, p. 578).

37. Max Planck, "The Unity of the Scientific World Picture." (This lecture was originally delivered at Leiden in December, 1908; it is available in English translation along with Mach's reply and Planck's own subsequent rejoinder, in the collection *Physical Reality*, pp. 1 ff). Robert Musil's Ph.D. dissertation for the University of Berlin, *Beitrag zur Beurteilung der Lehren Machs*, is a critique of Mach which is, if anything, more penetrating than that of Planck. This work came to our attention too late for full discussion in this chapter.

38. *Ibid.*

39. Holton, *loc. cit.*

40. H. von Helmholtz, in Hertz, *The Principles of Mechanics*, Preface.

41. Mach, *Analysis of Sensations*, p. 368.

42. Mach, *Science of Mechanics*, p. 318 n.

43. R. B. Braithwaite, *Scientific Explanation*, p. 90.

44. Avenarius, *op. cit.*, p. 5.

45. Hertz, *Principles of Mechanics*, p. 2. (We follow the standard English translation except that the term *Bild* and its cognates are rendered as "model," "modeling," etc.)

46. *Ibid.*, p. 40.

47. *Ibid.*, p. 38.

48. *Ibid.*, Introduction by Robert S. Cohen.

49. A. d'Abro, *The Rise of the New Physics*, Vol. I, pp. 388–94.

50. Planck, *op. cit.*

51. Wittgenstein, *Tractatus*, Props. 1.13, 1.2, 1.21, 2.1, 2.201, 2.202, 3.4, 3.411.

52. Toulmin, *Physical Reality*, Introduction.

53. E. Cassirer, *The Problem of Knowledge*, pp. 103 ff.

54. Immanuel Kant, *Kritik der Reinen Vernunft*, Vol. I, A7. The pagination throughout is that of the Berlin Academy edition.

55. Kant, *Prolegomena*, Vol. II, p. 353.

56. *Ibid.*, p. 353.

57. *Ibid.*, p. 350.

58. *Ibid.*, p. 352.

59. *Ibid.*, p. 352.

60. Kant, *Grundlegung zur Metaphysik der Sitten*, Vol. II, p. 463.

61. Kant, *Kritik der Reinen Vernunft*, B8.

62. *Ibid.*, B8.

63. Arthur Schopenhauer, *Sämtliche Werke*, Vol. I, *Die Welt als Wille und Vorstellung*, pp. 542–54 (translation by E. F. J. Payne, *The World as Will and Representation*, Vol. I, p. 46).

64. *Ibid.*, pp. 563–64 (translation, pp. 433–34).

65. Schopenhauer, *Ibid.*, Vol. III, pp. 19–20 (translation by Mme. K. Hildebrand, *On the Fourfold Root of the Principle of Sufficient Reason and on the Will in Nature*, p. 4).

66. *Ibid.*, p. 44 (translation, pp. 32–33).

67. *Ibid.*, Vol. I, p. 72 (translation, p. 34).

68. *Ibid.*, p. 47 (translation, p. 15).

69. *Ibid.*, p. 67 (translation, pp. 30–31).

70. *Ibid.*, p. 166 (translation, p. 110).

71. *Ibid.*, Vol. III, p. 513 (translation by A. B. Bullock, *The Basis of Morality*, p. 32).

72. *Ibid.*, p. 597 (translation, p. 163).

73. *Ibid.*, Vol. I, p. 489 (translation, p. 372).

74. *Ibid.*, p. 511 (translation, p. 390).

75. Søren Kierkegaard, *The Journals of Kierkegaard*, p. 234.

76. Kierkegaard, *The Point of View for My Work as an Author: A Report to History*, p. 43.

77. Kierkegaard, *The Present Age*, p. 40.

78. *Ibid.*, p. 59.

79. *Ibid.*, p. 60.

80. Kierkegaard, *The Point of View*, p. 24.

81. Kierkegaard, *The Present Age*, p. 75.

82. Kierkegaard, *The Point of View*, p. 35.

83. *Ibid.*, p. 38.

84. Kierkegaard, *Concluding Unscientific Postscript*, p. 182.

85. *Ibid.*, p. 191.

86. *Ibid.*, p. 197.

87. Leo Tolstoy, *My Confession, My Religion and the Gospel in Brief*, p. 76.

88. *Ibid.*, p. 22.

89. These passages come from *Anna Karenina* (Garnett translation), Part VIII, Chapters X–XIII.

90. The story "Two Old Men" illustrates this well; among the best of Tolstoy's fables illustrating his understanding of Christianity are "Ivan the Fool" and "How Much Land Does a Man Need?" See Leo Tolstoy, *Twenty-Three Tales*.

91. Tolstoy, *What Is Art?*, p. 61.

92. See Toulmin, "From Logical Analysis to Conceptual History."

Chapter 6.

1. The sketch of Wittgenstein's personal background and upbringing given in this section is based chiefly on conversations of A.S.J. in Vienna in winter–spring, 1969, with Thomas Stonborough and other members of Ludwig Wittgenstein's immediate family, and with others familiar with the milieu in which the family lived. On some points, see also the memoirs by Paul Engelmann and G. H. von Wright. Information about Karl Wittgenstein's spectacular business career can be found in Hans Melzacher, *Begegnungen auf meinen Lebensweg*. This volume was brought to my attention too late for use in preparing this chapter. (A.S.J.)

2. Karl Wittgenstein, *Zeitungsartikel und Vorträge*.

3. Engelmann, *Letters from Wittgenstein, with a Memoir*, pp. 31–33.

4. See Einstein's intellectual autobiography in P. A. Schilpp, ed., *Albert Einstein: Philosopher-Scientist*.

5. Friedrich Waismann, *Ludwig Wittgenstein und der Wiener Kreis*, p. 46.

6. *Ibid.*, pp. 41–43.

7. See G. H. von Wright, "Ludwig Wittgenstein, A Biographical Sketch," *Philosophical Review*, Vol. 64.

8. See Ludwig Wittgenstein, *Lectures and Conversations on Aesthetics, Psychology and Religious Belief*.

9. Personal communications from Philip Radcliffe, Timothy Moore and Mrs. G. E. Moore in 1946–48 (S.E.T.).

10. See Mach's intellectual autobiography, "My Scientific Theory of Knowledge and Its Reception by My Contemporaries," in S. Toulmin, ed., *Physical Reality*.

11. Von Wright, *op. cit.*

12. The use of this term by Wittgenstein himself (as well as by Lichtenberg, W. H. Watson, N. R. Hanson and other philosophers of language and philosophers of science) differs significantly from that made familiar recently by T. S. Kuhn in his much-discussed book, *The Structure of Scientific Revolutions*; see Stephen Toulmin, *Foresight and Understanding*, and especially Toulmin, *Human Understanding*, Part I, Sec. 1.4.

13. See J. M. Keynes, "My Early Beliefs," in *Two Memoirs;* also Bertrand Russell's essay on his friendship with D. H. Lawrence in *Portraits from Memory*.

14. Theodor Haecker, *Søren*

Notes

Kierkegaard und die Philosophie der Innerlichkeit, p. 29.

15. *Ibid.*, p. 57.

16. Heinrich Hertz, *The Principles of Mechanics*, Introduction by Robert S. Cohen.

17. Wittgenstein, *Tractatus*, 4.0031.

18. This refers to the edition of the *Tractatus* by D. F. Pears and B. F. McGuinness, especially propositions 2.1 ff.

19. Wittgenstein, *Tractatus*, 2.182.

20. *Ibid.*, 2.1.

21. *Ibid.*, 2.1512.

22. Wittgenstein, *Notebooks 1914–16*, pp. 14, 14e.

23. Wittgenstein, *Tractatus*, 2.15.

24. *Ibid.*, 2.15121.

25. *Ibid.*, 2.221.

26. *Ibid.*, 2.223.

27. *Ibid.*, 2.11.

28. *Ibid.*, 3.42.

29. For a discussion of "phase spaces" in statistical mechanics, see A. d'Abro, *The Rise of the New Physics*, Vol. I, pp. 388–94; also E. H. Kennard, *The Kinetic Theory of Gases*, pp. 338–92.

30. As remarked above, Wittgenstein expressed a desire to study physics with Boltzmann in Vienna in 1906, the year of Boltzmann's suicide; see Wright, *op. cit.*, p. 3.

31. Wittgenstein, *Tractatus*, 3.3.

32. Waismann, *op. cit.*, p. 46.

33. Wittgenstein, *Tractatus*, 2.022.

34. *Ibid.*, 3.031.

35. *Ibid.*, 2.17.

36. *Ibid.*, 2.172.

37. *Ibid.*, 4.1212.

38. *Ibid.*, 1.1.

39. *Ibid.*, 2.03.

40. This is the point of the final passages in the *Tractatus*, in which Wittgenstein speaks of using the whole argument as a "ladder," which one has to throw away after climbing up and over it; 6.54–7.

41. Wittgenstein, *Tractatus*, 6.42.

42. *Ibid.*, 6.421.

43. Engelmann, *Letters from Wittgenstein*, p. 97.

44. Iggers, *Karl Kraus*, p. 114.

45. Ludwig Wittgenstein, *Briefe an Ludwig von Ficker*, in *Brenner Studien*, Vol. I, contains the letters and postcards Wittgenstein sent to Ficker, as well as an essay by Methlagl on the relationship between Ficker and Wittgenstein and one by von Wright on the publication history of the *Tractatus*. (Our account of this history is based on Wright's essay.)

46. *Ibid.*, p. 32.

47. *Ibid.*, p. 33.

48. *Ibid.*, p. 38.

49. *Ibid.*, p. 35.

50. Wittgenstein, *Tractatus*, 6.421.

51. *Ibid.*, 6.421.

52. *Ibid.*, 6.432.

53. *Ibid.*, 4.014.

54. *Ibid.*, 6.41.

55. *Ibid.*, 6.5.

56. Karl Kraus, *Werke*, Vol. III, p. 338.

57. Waismann, *op. cit.*, p. 115.

58. *Ibid.*, p. 118.

59. *Ibid.*, pp. 68–69.

60. Wittgenstein, *Notebooks*, p. 76.

61. Wittgenstein, *Tractatus*, 6.43.

62. Engelmann, *Letters from Wittgenstein*, pp. 79–81.

63. *Ibid.*, pp. 92–93.

64. Paul Engelmann, "Über den *Tractatus Logico-Philosophicus* von Ludwig Wittgenstein," in *Bei der Lampe*, p. 15.

65. Wittgenstein, *Tractatus*, 6.53.

66. *Ibid.*, 6.54.

67. Kraus, *op. cit.*, p. 161.

68. Wittgenstein, *Tractatus*, Author's Preface, pp. 1–2.

69. Kraus, *op. cit.*, p. 124.

Chapter 7

1. See Keynes, *Two Memoirs*, and Russell, *Portraits from Memory* (Chapter 6, n. 13).

2. Tolstoy, *Anna Karenina*, Part VIII, Chapters X–XIII.

3. I am indebted to Hans Hess, of the University of Sussex, for helpful conversations on this subject. (S.E.T.)

4. The foregoing account is based partly on the memoirs of Engelmann and Wright, partly on A.S.J.'s conversations in Vienna.

5. Personal communication from Richard Braithwaite (S.E.T.).

6. There was some doubt about the authenticity of this visit, which was set at rest by the discovery of a picture postcard sent by Wittgenstein to G. E. Moore.

7. My attention was drawn to the significance of Gordon by Eric Lucas, of Tel Aviv, who explained to me the Tolstoyan associations of the *kibbutz* movement in Palestine. (S.E.T.)

8. I met Dorothy Moore immediately after this encounter, and she told me of it with great glee. (S.E.T.)

9. Drury and Watson were only two particularly notable examples of brilliant young philosophers who were powerfully discouraged by Wittgenstein from pursuing the subject professionally; this was still Wittgenstein's orally expressed attitude from 1946 on. (S.E.T.)

10. See Stanley Rosen, *Nihilism: a Philosophical Essay*, pp. 5–8.

11. Wittgenstein, *Zettel*, p. 82.

12. Waismann, *Ludwig Wittgenstein*, p. 69.

13. Remark noted down at the time, in the academic year 1946–47 (S.E.T.).

14. Told to me by Rudolf Koder in Vienna in 1969. (A.S.J.).

15. On Loos, see above, Chapter 4, pp. 93–102.

16. Bernhard Leitner, "Wittgenstein's Architecture," *Art Forum*, February, 1970, includes some interesting photographs of the house.

17. The end result of this inversion is well represented by such books as H. Reichenbach, *The Rise of Scientific Philosophy*, and A. J. Ayer, *Language, Truth and Logic*, with their insistence on the need to "set philosophy on the sure path of a science."

18. Schiller's so-called "Christmas" issue, entitled *Mind!*, was largely given over to a sustained ridiculing of later idealist philosophy in all its different manifestations.

19. See G. E. Moore's famous essay "The Refutation of Idealism," *Mind*, Vol. 12, which nowhere attacks the points actually being argued by idealists, but rather takes their words with deadpan literalness, and contradicts what they then *seem* to be saying.

20. Mr. John Macfarland drew my attention to the close resemblances between the logical arguments of Bradley and those of Russell in a paper for a graduate seminar at Brandeis University in 1967–68. (S.E.T.)

21. Mr. William Stockton demonstrated the affiliations between MacTaggart's and Moore's ethical arguments in the same seminar (S.E.T.).

22. Roy Harrod, *Life of John Maynard Keynes*, p. 78.

23. Keynes, "My Early Beliefs," in *Two Memoirs*.

24. From the large and growing literature on this group, one may particularly recommend the volumes of Leonard Woolf's autobiography.

25. John Locke, *An Essay Concerning Human Understanding*, "Epistle to the Reader."

26. As represented in such publications as the *International Encyclopaedia of Unified Science*, published by the University of Chicago Press from the 1930s on.

27. Wittgenstein, *Tractatus*, 5 ff.

28. This is the view well represented in such books as C. K. Ogden and I. A. Richards, *The Meaning of Meaning*, C. L. Stevenson, *Ethics and Language* and R. M. Hare, *The Language of Morals*.

29. As quoted above—Chapter 5, pp. 143–44.

30. B. A. W. Russell, *Our Knowledge of the External World as a Field for Scientific Method in Philosophy* (London and New York, 1914).

31. See the account in Engelmann's memoir, as confirmed in notes on the conversations between Schlick

Notes

and Wittgenstein, in Waismann, *op. cit.*

32. Waismann, *op. cit.*, pp. 65–67, 85–87.

33. Wittgenstein, *Tractatus*, 6.54.

34. See R. Carnap, *Logical Foundations of Probability*, C. G. Hempel, *Aspects of Scientific Explanation*, and E. Nagel, *The Structure of Science.*

35. Contrast the arguments of Hempel about "the theoretician's dilemma" in *Aspects*, with those of D. S. Shapere in Achinstein and Barker, eds., *The Legacy of Logical Positivism.*

36. Wittgenstein, *Tractatus*, 6.342, ff.

37. H. Stuart Hughes, *Consciousness and Society*, Chapter 10.

38. Brian Farrell, "An Appraisal of Therapeutic Positivism," in *Mind*, Vol. 55.

39. See the arguments of John Wisdom in his collection, *Philosophy and Psychoanalysis;* the term "cerebroses" is, however, my own coining (S.E.T.). It is worth noticing that some orthodox Freudian analysts in Britain also view the task of unraveling neuroses as concerned largely with the bringing to light of such "misconceptions," as became apparent in discussions with Roger Money-Kyrle and others in the early 1950s.

40. Engelmann, *Letters from Wittgenstein*, p. 97.

41. Quoted by Morris Lazerowitz, "Wittgenstein on the Nature of Philosophy," in K. T. Fann (ed.), *Ludwig Wittgenstein: the Man and His Philosophy*, pp. 139–40.

42. *Ibid.*, pp. 182–86.

43. *Ibid.*, pp. 209–10. In an earlier essay about Wittgenstein (*Encounter*, Jan. 1969), I got myself into difficulties over the exact rendering of the phrase *hinweisende Erklärung* in this remark; several correspondents wrote to the magazine claiming that my words "consequential clarification" should be replaced by "ostensive definition." It may be that Wittgenstein's positivist followers took the phrase in this sense; but Wittgenstein himself insists that such *Erklärung* is *not* a kind of "definition." Despite the arguments of Michael Lipton and others, I accordingly use the rendering "ostensive *demonstration*" here, as best capturing the sense of Wittgenstein's words *in their philosophical context.* (S.E.T.)

44. Wittgenstein, *Philosophical Investigations*, p. 125.

45. *Ibid.*, pp. 11–12.

46. Hertz, *The Principles of Mechanics*, Introduction, p. 8.

47. Recall Frank Ramsey's remark to Wittgenstein, commenting on the ambiguous status of the whole *Tractatus* argument: "If you can't say it, you can't say it, and you can't whistle it either!" Recall also the parallel difficulties that Kant gets into when he attempts to say anything about the *Ding-an-sich*, which is (on his own principles) incapable of being talked about meaningfully.

48. See *The Philosophy of G. E. Moore*, P. A. Schilpp, ed., pp. 661 ff.

49. "Two Dogmas of Empiricism," in W. V. O. Quine, *From a Logical Point of View.*

50. Several such examples appear in my own unpublished notes of Wittgenstein's lectures at Cambridge University in the period 1946–47. (S.E.T.)

51. Waismann, *op. cit.*, p. 115.

52. *Ibid.*, p. 117.

53. Wittgenstein, *Lectures and Conversations*, pp. 59–64.

54. Wittgenstein, *Philosophical Investigations*, p. 116.

55. See Paul L. Holmer, "Indirect Communication," in *Perkins Journal*, Spring 1971, pp. 14–24.

56. Engelmann, *Letters from Wittgenstein*, p. 39.

57. *Ibid.*, p. 50.

58. *Ibid.*, p. 59.

59. *Ibid.*, p. 55.

Chapter 8

1. W. W. Bartley III has done some particularly useful work on this period; he has brought to light the

part played by Bühler's ideas about "imageless thought" and "rule awareness" in the theories of education underlying curriculum reform in Austria from 1919 on. As he points out, both Karl Popper and Ludwig Wittgenstein enrolled in the resulting teacher-training courses.

2. See Mach's autobiographical essay reprinted in the collection *Physical Reality,* S. Toulmin, ed.

3. Quoted from Wittgenstein's *Notebooks 1914–1916,* p. 82, by John Passmore in his essay on "The Idea of a History of Philosophy," *History and Theory,* Beiheft 5, p. 4.

4. Mr. J. J. Shapiro has drawn my attention to certain crucial passages in Kant's late essay *Die Ende aller Dinge,* which is often dismissed as "senile" but makes clear on a careful reading the historical implications of Kant's "liberal ideology." (S.E.T.)

5. Quoted to me by a fellow research student at Cambridge in the period 1946–47. (S.E.T.)

6. F. Waismann, *An Introduction to Mathematical Thinking.*

7. I have myself attempted to pursue this "historico-rational" direction further in *Human Understanding,* Vol. I. (S.E.T.)

8. C. A. Macartney, *The Habsburg Empire 1790–1918,* p. 88.

9. Willi Reich, *Schönberg oder der konservativ Revolutionar.*

10. Kurt Blaukopf, *Mahler oder der Zeitgenosse der Zukunft.*

11. Wittgenstein, *Tractatus,* 6.53.

12. Noted down at the time, in 1946–47. (S.E.T.)

13. When the Aristotelian Society and Mind Association held their Joint Session at Cambridge in the summer of 1946, Wittgenstein gave deep offense by ostentatiously leaving town on the very day the session was due to begin.

14. He used to spend at least one period of two to three hours each week in conversation with Moore in his study, at 86 Chesterton Road, Cambridge, during which times Dorothy Moore had strict instructions not to let them be disturbed. (S.E.T.)

15. Quoted by John Wisdom in conversation, 1946–47. (S.E.T.)

16. Personal conversations, around 1953. (S.E.T.)

17. Introduction by G. Ryle to A. J. Ayer *et al., The Revolution in Philosophy.*

18. For Wittgenstein's positive appreciation of such writers as Augustine, Schopenhauer, Kierkegaard, even Heidegger, see the reports of Waismann, Drury, Wright, Malcolm and others, already cited.

19. Wittgenstein's words about A. J. Ayer were, in fact, "The trouble about Ayer is, he's clever *all* the time." Noted down at the time, in 1946–47. (S.E.T.)

20. Cassirer has, of course, had considerable—and healthy—influence on the cognitive psychology of Werner, Kaplan and others. Besides Cassirer, one might point to R. G. Collingwood as another philosopher who seemed more "conservative" than Wittgenstein during their lifetimes, but whose greater *historical* sense gives his arguments an added interest to a later generation.

Chapter 9

1. Raymond Chandler, *The Little Sister,* p. 67.

2. Andy Warhol's film *Sleep* is perhaps the extreme illustration of this tendency.

3. See Roy and Zhores Medvedev, *The Medvedev Papers;* and Andrei Amalrik, *Involuntary Journey to Siberia.*

Select Bibliography

[NOTE: We regret that William Johnstone's *The Austrian Mind*, a work which will be indispensable for all future students of Austrian culture, appeared too late for us to use it in preparing this book.]

Abrahamsen, David, *The Mind and Death of a Genius*. New York: Columbia University Press, 1946.

Abro, A. d', *The Rise of the New Physics*, 2 vols. New York: Dover, 1952.

Achinstein, Peter, and Barker, S. F., eds., *The Legacy of Logical Positivism*. Baltimore: Johns Hopkins Press, 1969.

Amalrik, Andrei, *Involuntary Journey to Siberia*, trans. by Manya Harari and Max Hayward. New York: Harcourt, Brace, Jovanovich, 1970.

Anscombe, G. E. M., *An Introduction to Wittgenstein's Tractatus*. London: Hutchinson University Library, 1959.

Asprey, Robert B., *The Panther's Feast*. New York: Bantam Books, 1969.

Avenarius, Richard, *Kritik der reinen Erfahrung*, 2 vols. Leipzig: Füs, 1888–1890.

———, *Philosophie als Denken der Welt gemäss dem Prinzip des Kleinsten Kraftmasses: Prolegomena zu einer Kritik der reinen Erfahrung*. Leipzig: Füs, 1876.

Ayer, Alfred Jules, *Language, Truth and Logic*, 2d ed. New York: Dover, 1946.

Bein, Alex, *Theodore Herzl: A Biography*, trans. by Maurice Samuel. Philadelphia: Jewish Publication Society of America, 1940.

Black, Max, *A Companion to Wittgenstein's Tractatus*. Ithaca, N.Y.: Cornell University Press, 1964.

Blaukopf, Kurt, *Mahler oder der Zeitgenosse der Zukunft*. Vienna: Fritz Molden, 1968.

Bochenski, I. M., *Contemporary European Philosophy*, trans. by Donald Nicholl and Karl Aschenbrenner. Berkeley and Los Angeles: University of California Press, 1961.

Boltzmann, Ludwig, *Lectures on Gas Theory*, trans. by Stephen G. Brush. Berkeley and Los Angeles: University of California Press, 1964.

———, *Populäre Schriften*. Leipzig: Johann Ambrosius Barth, 1905.

Braithwaite, Richard B., *Scientific Explanation*. Cambridge: Cambridge University Press, 1953.

Braunthal, Julius, *In Search of the Millennium*. London: Victor Gollancz, 1945.

Breicha, Otto, and Fritsch, Gerhard, *Finale und Auftakt: Wien, 1898–1914*. Salzburg: Otto Müller, 1964.

Broch, Hermann, *Hofmannsthal und seine Zeit*. Munich: R. Piper, 1964.

Select Bibliography

Broda, Engelbert, *Ludwig Boltzmann, Mensch, Physiker, Philosoph.* Vienna: Franz Deutike, 1955.

Buber, Martin, *Daniel: Dialogues on Realization,* trans., with an introductory essay, by Maurice Friedman. New York: Holt, Rinehart and Winston, 1964.

Carnap, Rudolf, *The Logical Foundations of Probability.* Chicago: University of Chicago Press, 1950.

Cassirer, Ernst, *The Problem of Knowledge: Philosophy, Science and History since Hegel,* trans. by William H. Woglom, M.D., and Charles W. Hendel. New Haven and London: Yale University Press, 1950.

Chandler, Raymond, *The Little Sister.* Boston: Houghton, 1949.

Copi, Irving M., and Beard, Robert W., eds., *Essays on Wittgenstein's Tractatus.* London: Routledge and Kegan Paul, 1966.

Copleston, Frederick, S. J., *A History of Philosophy;* Vol. VII, Part II, *Schopenhauer to Nietzsche.* Garden City, N.Y.: Doubleday Image Books, 1965.

Crankshaw, Edward, *Vienna: The Image of a City in Decline.* New York: Macmillan, 1938.

Dallago, Carl, *Otto Weininger und sein Werk.* Innsbruck: Brenner Verlag, 1912.

Dugas, René, *La Théorie physique au sens de Boltzmann et ses prolongements modernes.* Bibliothèque Scientifique. Neuchatel: Le Griffon, 1959.

Durkheim, Emile, *Suicide: A Study in Sociology,* trans. by John A. Spaulding and George Simpson. New York: Free Press of Glencoe, 1951.

Engel, S. Morris, *Wittgenstein's Doctrine of the Tyranny of Language.* The Hague: Martinus Nijhoff, 1971.

Engelmann, Paul, *Dem Andenken an Karl Kraus.* Vienna: Otto Kerry, 1967.

———, *Bei der Lampe.* Unpublished manuscript.

———, *Letters from Ludwig Wittgenstein, With a Memoir,* B. F. McGuinness, ed., trans. by L. Furtmüller. Oxford: Basil Blackwell, 1967.

Fann, K. T., ed., *Ludwig Wittgenstein: The Man and His Philosophy.* New York: Dell, 1967.

Favrholdt, David, *An Interpretation and Critique of Wittgenstein's Tractatus.* Copenhagen: Munksgaard, 1964.

Field, Frank, *The Last Days of Mankind: Karl Kraus.* London: Macmillan, 1967; New York: St. Martin's Press, 1967.

Fraenkel, Josef, ed., *The Jews of Austria: Essays on Their Life, History and Destruction.* London: Valentine Mitchell, 1967.

Frege, Gottlob, *The Basic Laws of Arithmetic: Exposition of the System,* trans. and ed., with an Introduction, by Montgomery Furth. Berkeley and Los Angeles: University of California Press, 1967.

———, *The Foundations of Arithmetic: A Logico-Mathematical Enquiry into the Concept of Number,* trans. by J. L. Austin. Oxford: Basil Blackwell, 1968.

Friedell, Egon, *A Cultural History of the Modern Age,* trans. by Charles Francis Atkinson; 3 vols. New York: Knopf, 1954.

Friedman, Maurice S., *Martin Buber: The Life of the Dialogue.* New York: Harper and Row, 1960.

Fuchs, Albert, *Geistige Strömungen in Österreich 1867–1918.* Vienna: Globus Verlag, 1949.

Select Bibliography

Gardiner, Patrick, *Schopenhauer*. Baltimore: Penguin Books, 1963.

Geach, Peter, and Black, Max, eds., *Translations from the Philosophical Writings of Gottlob Frege*. Oxford: Basil Blackwell, 1960.

Gould, Glenn, *Arnold Schoenberg: A Perspective*. University of Cincinnati Occasional Papers, No. 3, University of Cincinnati, 1964.

Griffin, James, *Wittgenstein's Logical Atomism*. Oxford: Oxford University Press, 1965.

Gurney, Ronald W., *Introduction to Statistical Mechanics*. New York: McGraw-Hill, 1949.

Gustav Klimt, Egon Schiele Graphische Sammlung Albertina. Vienna: Rosenbaum, 1968.

Haecker, Theodor, *Søren Kierkegaard und die Philosophie der Innerlichkeit*. Munich: J. F. Schreiber; Innsbruck: Brenner Verlag, 1913.

Hammelmann, Hans, *Hugo von Hofmannsthal. Studies in Modern European Literature and Thought*. New Haven: Yale University Press, 1957.

Haensel, Ludwig, *Begegnungen und Auseinandersetzungen mit Denkern und Dichtern der Neuzeit*. Vienna: Österreichischer Bundesverlag für Unterricht, Wissenschaft und Kunst, 1957.

Hanslick, Edward, *The Beautiful in Music;* trans. by Gustav Cohen. Library of Liberal Arts. Indianapolis and New York: Bobbs-Merrill, 1957.

———, *Music Criticisms 1846–99;* trans. and ed. by Henry Pleasants. Peregrine Books. Baltimore: Penguin Books, 1963. A revised edition of *Vienna's Golden Years 1850–1900* (New York, 1950).

Hardy, Charles O., *The Housing Program of the City of Vienna*. Washington, D.C.: Brookings Institution, 1934.

Hare, R. M., *The Language of Morals*. Oxford: Clarendon Press, 1961.

Harrod, Roy, *The Life of John Maynard Keynes*. New York: Harcourt, Brace, 1951.

Heller, Erich, *The Disinherited Mind: Essays in Modern German Literature and Thought*. New York: Farrar, Straus and Cudahy, 1957.

Helmholtz, Hermann von, *Popular Scientific Lectures*, Morris Kline, ed., trans. by H. W. Eve *et al.* New York: Dover, 1962.

Hempel, Carl, *Aspects of Scientific Explanation*. New York: Free Press, 1965.

Hertz, Heinrich, *Gesammelte Werke*, 3 vols. Leipzig: Johann Ambrosius Barth, 1804.

———, *The Principles of Mechanics Presented in a New Form*, trans. by D. E. Jones and J. T. Walley, with Preface by H. von Helmholtz and Introduction by Robert S. Cohen. New York: Dover, 1956.

Hitler, Adolf, *Mein Kampf*, trans. by Alvin Johnson. New York: Reynal & Hitchcock, 1939.

Höffding, Harald, *Modern Philosophy*, trans. by Alfred C. Mason. London: Macmillan, 1915.

Hoffmann, Edith, *Kokoschka: Life and Work*. Boston: Boston Book and Arts Shop, 1946.

Hofmannsthal, Hugo von, *Gesammelte Werke*, 3 vols. Berlin: S. Fischer Verlag, 1924.

———, *Selected Plays and Libretti*, edited with an Introduction by Michael Hamburger. Bollingen Series XXXIII. New York: Pantheon Books, 1963.

————, *Selected Prose*, trans. by Mary Hattinger *et al.*, with an Introduction by Herman Broch. Bollingen Series XXXIII. New York: Pantheon Books, 1952.

Hughes, H. Stuart, *Consciousness and Society: The Reorientation of European Social Thought 1890–1930*. New York: Vintage Books, 1958.

Iggers, Wilma Abeles, *Karl Kraus: A Viennese Critic of the Twentieth Century*. The Hague: Martinus Nijhoff, 1967.

Jászi, Oscar, *The Dissolution of the Hapsburg Monarchy*. Chicago: University of Chicago Press; London: Phoenix Books, 1961.

Jenks, William A., *Vienna and the Young Hitler*. New York: Columbia University Press, 1960.

Jones, Ernest, *The Life and Work of Sigmund Freud*, 3 vols. New York: Basic Books, 1953–57.

Kant, Immanuel. *Werke*, 3 vols. Berlin: Th. Knauer, n.d.

————, *Critique of Practical Reason and Other Works on the Theory of Ethics*, trans. by Thomas Kingsmill Abbott, 6th ed. London: Longmans, 1909.

————, *Critique of Pure Reason*, trans. by Norman Kemp Smith. London: Macmillan, 1964.

————, *Prolegomena to Any Future Metaphysics*, trans. with an Introduction by Lewis White Beck. The Library of Liberal Arts. Indianapolis: Bobbs-Merrill, 1950.

Kappstein, Theodor, *Fritz Mauthner: Der Mann und sein Werk*. Berlin and Leipzig, 1926.

Kennard, Earle H., *Kinetic Theory of Gases with an Introduction to Statistical Mechanics*. New York: McGraw-Hill, 1938.

Keynes, John Maynard, *Two Memoirs*. London: A. M. Kelley, 1949.

Kierkegaard, Søren, *Concluding Unscientific Postscript*, trans. by David F. Swenson, and completed after his death with an Introduction and Notes by Walter Lowrie. Princeton: Princeton University Press, 1941.

————, *The Journals of Kierkegaard*, trans. by Alexander Dru. New York: Harper and Row, 1959.

————, *The Point of View for My Work as an Author: A Report to History*, trans. with Introduction and Notes by Walter Lowrie; newly edited with a Preface by Benjamin Nelson. New York: Harper and Row, 1962.

————, *The Present Age and Of the Difference Between a Genius and an Apostle*, trans. by Alexander Dru. New York: Harper and Row, 1962.

Kneale, William and Martha, *The Development of Logic*. Oxford: Clarendon Press, 1962.

Kohn, Caroline, *Karl Kraus*. Stuttgart: J. B. Metzlersche Verlagsbuchhandlung, 1966.

Kohn, Hans, *Living in a World Revolution: My Encounters with History*. The Credo Series. New York: Pocket Books, 1965.

Kraft, Werner, *Karl Kraus: Beiträge zum Verstandnis seines Werkes*. Salzburg: Otto Müller, 1956.

————, *Rebellen des Geistes*. Stuttgart: Kohlhammer, 1968.

Kraus, Karl, *Werke*, Heinrich Fischer, ed., 14 vols. Munich: Kösel Verlag, 1952–1966.

Křenek, Ernst, *Exploring Music: Essays by Ernst Křenek,* trans. by Margaret Shenfield and Geoffrey Skeleton. London: Calder and Boyars, 1966.

Kroner, Richard, *Kant's Weltanschauung,* trans. by John Smith. Chicago: University of Chicago Press, 1956.

Kuhn, Thomas. *The Structure of Scientific Revolutions.* Chicago: University of Chicago Press, 1963.

Landauer, Gustav, *Skepsis und Mystik: Versuche ins Anschluss an Mauthners Sprachkritik.* Berlin: Egon Fleischel, 1903.

Lichtenberg Reader: Selected Writings of Georg Christoph Lichtenberg, trans. and ed. with an Introduction by Franz Mauthner and Henry Hatfield. Boston: Beacon Hill Press, 1959.

Liptzin, Solomon, *Arthur Schnitzler.* New York: Prentice-Hall, 1932.

———, *Germany's Stepchildren.* Philadelphia: Jewish Publication Society of America, 1944.

Locke, John. *An Essay Concerning Human Understanding.* New York: Dover, 1959.

Loos, Adolf, *Sämtliche Schriften,* Vol. I. Vienna: Verlag Herald, 1962.

Macartney, C. A., *The Habsburg Empire 1790–1918.* London: Weidenfeld and Nicholson, 1968.

Mach, Ernst, *The Analysis of Sensations and the Relation of the Physical to the Psychical,* trans. from the 1st German edition by C. M. Williams; revised and supplemented from the 5th German edition by Sydney Waterlow. New York: Dover, 1959.

———, *The History and Root of the Principle of Conservation of Energy,* trans. by Philip E. B. Jourdain. Chicago: Open Court Press; London: Kegan Paul, Trench, Trübner, 1911.

———, *Die Mechanik in ihrer Entwicklung, Historisch-Kritisch Dargestellt,* 5th ed. Leipzig: F. A. Brockhaus, 1904.

———, *The Science of Mechanics: A Critical and Historical Account of Its Development,* trans. by Thomas J. McCormack, 6th edition with revisions through the 9th German edition. La Salle, Ill.: Open Court, 1960.

Malcolm, Norman, *Ludwig Wittgenstein: A Memoir,* with a bibliographical sketch by G. H. von Wright. London: Oxford University Press, 1958.

Marx, Karl, and Engels, Friedrich, *The Communist Manifesto,* trans. by Samuel Moore. New York: Washington Square Press, 1964.

Maslow, Alexander, *A Study in Wittgenstein's Tractatus.* Berkeley and Los Angeles: University of California Press, 1961.

Masur, Gerhard, *Prophets of Yesterday: Studies in European Culture 1890–1914.* New York: Harper and Row, 1961.

Mauser, Wolfram, *Bild und Gebärde in der Sprache Hofmannsthals. Österreichische Akademie der Wissenschaften, Philosophisch-Historische Klasse, Sitzungsberichte* 238. Vienna: Hermann Bohlaus, 1961.

Mauthner, Fritz, *Beiträge zu einer Kritik der Sprache,* 3 vols. Stuttgart: J. G. Cotta, 1901–3.

———, *Die Sprache.* Die Gesellschaft: Sammlung Sozial-Psychologischer Monographien. Herausgegeben von Martin Buber. Vol. 9. Frankfurt a/M: Ruetten & Loening, 1906.

Select Bibliography

———, *Wörterbuch der philosophie: Neue Beiträge zu einer Kritik der Sprache.* Munich: Georg Müller, 1910.

May, Arthur J., *The Habsburg Monarchy 1867–1914.* Norton Library. New York: W. W. Norton, 1968.

———, *Vienna in the Age of Franz Josef.* Norman, Okla.: University of Oklahoma Press, 1966.

Medvedev, Zhores, *The Medvedev Papers,* trans. by Vera Rich. London: Macmillan, 1971.

Mehta, Ved, *Fly and the Fly-Bottle: Encounters with British Intellectuals.* London: Weidenfeld and Nicholson, 1963.

Munz, Ludwig, and Kunstler, Gustav, *Adolf Loos: Pioneer of Modern Architecture.* New York: Praeger, 1966.

Musil, Robert, *Beitrag zur Beurteilung der Lehren Machs.* Ph.D. Dissertation, University of Berlin, 1908.

———, *The Man Without Qualities,* trans. by Eithne Wilkins and Ernst Kaiser; 3 vols. London: Secker and Warburg, 1953–60.

———, *The Man Without Qualities,* trans. by Eithne Wilkins and Ernst Kaiser, Vol. 1. New York: Capricorn Books, 1965.

———, *Young Törless,* trans. by Eithne Wilkins and Ernst Kaiser. New York: New American Library, 1964.

Nagel, Ernest, *The Structure of Science.* New York: Harcourt, Brace, 1961.

Nestroy, Johann, *Gesammelte Werke.* Herausgegeben von Otto Rommel; 6 vols. Vienna: Anton Schroll, 1948–49.

———, *Three Comedies,* trans. ("and fondly tampered with") by Max Knight and Joseph Fabry. New York: Frederick Ungar, 1967.

Norman, F. ed., *Hofmannsthal: Studies in Commemoration.* University of London Institute of Germanic Studies, No. 5. London, 1963.

Ogden, E. K., and Richards, I. A., *The Meaning of Meaning.* New York: Harcourt, Brace and World, 1946.

Osborne, John, *A Patriot for Me.* New York: Random House, 1970.

Passmore, John, *A Hundred Years of Philosophy.* London: Gerald Duckworth, 1957.

Pears, D. F., *Wittgenstein.* London: Fontana, 1969.

Peters, H. F., *My Sister, My Spouse: A Biography of Lou Andreas-Salomé.* New York: Norton, 1962.

Peursen, C. A. van, *Ludwig Wittgenstein: An Introduction to His Philosophy,* trans. by Rex Ambler. London: Faber and Faber, 1969.

Pike, Burton, *Robert Musil: An Introduction to His Work.* Ithaca, N.Y.: Cornell University Press, 1961.

Pitcher, George, *The Philosophy of Wittgenstein.* Englewood Cliffs, N.J.: Prentice-Hall, 1964.

Planck, Max, *Heinrich Rudolf Hertz: Rede zu seinen Gedächtniss.* Leipzig: Johann Ambrosius Barth, 1897.

Plockman, George Kimball, and Lawson, Jack B., *Terms in Their Propositional Contexts in Wittgenstein's Tractatus: An Index.* Carbondale, Ill.: Southern Illinois University, 1962.

Pulzer, Peter G. J., *The Rise of Political Anti-Semitism in Germany and Aus-*

tria. New Dimensions in History: Essays in Comparative History. New York, London, Sydney: John Wiley & Sons, 1964.

Quine, W. V. O., *From a Logical Point of View.* Cambridge, Mass.: Harvard University Press, 1961.

Ramsey, Frank P., *Foundations of Mathematics and Other Logical Essays.* London: Kegan Paul, Trench, Trübner, 1931; New York: Harcourt, Brace, 1931.

Reich, W., *Schoenberg: a Critical Biography,* trans. by Leo Black. London: Longmans, 1971.

Reichenbach, Hans, *The Rise of Scientific Philosophy.* Berkeley: University of California Press, 1951.

Rhys, H. H., ed., *Seventeenth Century Science and the Arts.* Princeton, N.J.: Princeton University Press, 1961.

Rilke, Rainer Maria, *The Duino Elegies, with an English Translation,* trans. by C. F. MacIntyre. Berkeley and Los Angeles: University of California Press, 1965.

Rosen, Stanley, *Nihilism: A Philosophical Essay.* New Haven and London: Yale University Press, 1969.

Rufer, Josef, *The Works of Arnold Schoenberg: a Catalog of his Compositions, Writings and Paintings,* trans. by Dika Newlin. New York: Free Press of Glencoe, 1963.

Russell, Bertrand. *The Autobiography of Bertrand Russell,* 3 vols. Boston: Little, Brown, 1968–70.

———, *Mysticism and Logic.* Garden City, N.Y.: Doubleday, 1957.

———, *Our Knowledge of the External World.* London: Allen and Unwin, 1926.

———, *Portraits From Memory.* London: Allen and Unwin, 1956.

———, *Principles of Mathematics.* New York: Norton, 1964.

Schachter, Josef, *Prolegomena zu einer kritischen Grammatik. Schriften zur Wissenschaftlichen Weltauffassung.* Vienna: Julius Springer Verlag, 1935.

Schick, Paul, *Karl Kraus in Selbstzeugnissen und Bilddokumenten.* Reinbeck bei Hamburg: Rowohlt, 1965.

Schilpp, Paul Arthur, ed., *Albert Einstein Philosopher-Scientist,* 2 vols. Library of Living Philosophers. New York: Harper and Row, 1959.

———, ed., *The Philosophy of G. E. Moore.* Library of Living Philosophers. La Salle, Ill.: Open Court Press, 1945.

———, ed., *The Philosophy of Rudolf Carnap.* Library of Living Philosophers. La Salle, Ill.: Open Court Press, 1963.

Schmalenbach, Fritz, *Oskar Kokoschka,* trans. by Violet M. Macdonald. Greenwich, Conn.: New York Graphic Society, 1967.

Schnitzler, Arthur, *Anatol: Living Hours: The Green Cockatoo,* trans. by Grace Isabel Colbron. New York: Modern Library, 1925.

———, *Hands Around: A Roundelay in Ten Dialogues,* trans. by Keene Wallis. New York: Julian Press, 1929.

———, *Professor Bernhardi,* trans. by Louis Borell and Ronald Adam. London: Victor Gollancz, 1936.

Schönberg, Arnold, *Style and Idea,* ed. and trans. by Dika Newlin. New York: Philosophical Library, 1950.

Select Bibliography

———, *The Theory of Harmony*, trans. by Robert D. W. Adams. New York: Philosophical Library, 1948.

Schopenhauer, Arthur. *Sämtliche Werke*, 5 vols. Leipzig: Insel Verlag, n. d.

———, *The Basis of Morality*, trans. by Arthur Broderick Bullock, 2d ed. London: Allen & Unwin, 1915.

———, *Die beiden Grundprobleme der Ethik*, 5th ed. Leipzig: F. A. Brockhaus, 1908.

———, *On the Fourfold Root of the Principle of Sufficient Reason and On the Will in Nature*, trans. by Mme. Karl Hillebrand. London: George Bell and Sons, 1881.

———, *The Will to Live: Selected Writings of Arthur Schopenhauer*, trans. by R. B. Haldane, J. Kemp *et al*, ed. by Richard Taylor. New York: Doubleday Anchor, 1962.

———, *The World as Will and Representation*, trans. by E. F. J. Payne, 2 vols. New York: Dover, 1966.

Sedgwick, Henry Dwight, *Vienna: The Biography of a Bygone City*. Indianapolis: Bobbs-Merrill, 1939.

Selz, Peter, *German Expressionist Painting*. Berkeley and Los Angeles: University of California Press, 1957.

Shakespeare, William, *The Life of Timon of Athens*. Folger Library General Reader's Shakespeare. New York: Washington Square Press, 1967.

Spranger, Eduard, *Lebensformen: Geisteswissenschaftliche Psychologie und Ethik der Persönlichkeit*. Halle: M. Niemeyer, 1922. Trans. by Paul J. Pigors as *Types of Men*. Halle: M. Niemeyer; New York: Hafner Publishing Co., 1928.

Stenius, Erik, *Wittgenstein's Tractatus: A Critical Exposition of Its Main Lines of Thought*. Oxford: Basil Blackwell, 1960.

Stern, J. P. *Lichtenberg, A Doctrine of Scattered Occasions*. Bloomington: University of Indiana Press, 1959.

Stevenson, C. L., *Ethics and Language*. New Haven: Yale University Press, 1960.

Stuckenschmidt, H. H., *Arnold Schoenberg*, trans. by Edith Temple Roberts and Humphrey Searle. New York: Grove Press, 1959.

Taylor, A. J. P., *The Hapsburg Monarchy: a History of the Austrian Empire and Austria–Hungary*. Harmondsworth: Penguin Books, 1948.

Taylor, Ona, *Maurice Maeterlinck: A Critical Study*. Port Washington, N.Y.: Kennikat Press, 1968.

Tolstoy, Leo, *Anna Karenina*, trans. by Constance Garnett. New York: Grosset and Dunlap, 1931.

———, *Hadji Murat: A Tale of the Caucasus*, trans. by W. G. Carey. New York, Toronto, San Francisco: McGraw-Hill, 1965.

———, *Twenty-Three Tales*, trans. by Louise and Aylmer Maude. The World's Classics. London: Oxford University Press, 1965.

———, *What Is Art?* trans. by Aylmer Maude. Library of Liberal Arts. Indianapolis: Bobbs-Merrill, 1960.

———, *My Confession: The Complete Works of Lyof Tolstoï*, translator anonymous. New York: Thomas Y. Crowell, 1889.

Select Bibliography

Toulmin, S. E., *Foresight and Understanding*. New York: Harper and Row, 1961.

——, *Human Understanding*. Oxford: Oxford University Press; Princeton, N.J.: Princeton University Press, 1972.

——, ed., *Physical Reality: Philosophical Essays on Twentieth Century Physics*. New York: Harper and Row, 1970.

Tuchman, Barbara, *The Proud Tower: a Portrait of the World Before the War, 1914–18*. New York: Bantam Books, 1967.

Urmson, J. O., *Philosophical Analysis: Its Development Between the Two World Wars*. Oxford: Clarendon Press, 1956.

Volke, Werner, *Hugo von Hofmannsthal in Selbstzeugnissen und Bilddokumenten*. Reinbeck bei Hamburg: Rowohlt, 1965.

Waismann, Friedrich, *Ludwig Wittgenstein und der Wiener Kreis*, B. F. McGuinness, ed. Oxford: Basil Blackwell, 1967.

Walter, Bruno, *Gustav Mahler*, trans. by James Galston, with a biographical essay by Ernst Křenek. New York: Greystone Press, 1941.

——, *Theme and Variations: An Autobiography*, trans. by James A. Galston. New York: Knopf, 1946.

Warnock, G. J., *English Philosophy Since 1900*. London: Oxford University Press, 1958.

Weiler, Gershon, *Mauthner's Critique of Language*. Cambridge: Cambridge University Press, 1970.

Weininger, Otto, *Sex and Character*, translator anonymous. London: William Heinemann, 1906; New York: G. P. Putnam's Sons, 1906.

Wellesz, Egon. *Arnold Schoenberg*, trans. by W. H. Kerridge. New York: Da Capo Press, 1969.

Whitehead, Alfred North, and Russell, Bertrand, *Principia Mathematica*. Cambridge: Cambridge University Press, 1962.

Whiteside, Andrew Gladding, *Austrian National Socialism Before 1918*. The Hague: Martinus Nijhoff, 1962.

Wien am 1900. Exhibition Catalogue. Vienna: Rosenbaum, 1964.

Wisdom, John. *Philosophy and Psychoanalysis*. Oxford: Basil Blackwell, 1953.

Wiskemann, Elizabeth, *Czechs and Germans: A Study of the Struggle in the Historic Provinces of Bohemia and Moravia*. London: Oxford University Press, 1938.

Wittgenstein, Karl, *Zeitungsartikel und Vorträge*. Vienna, 1913.

Wittgenstein, Ludwig, *Briefe an Ludwig von Ficker*, G. H. von Wright ed., in collaboration with Walter Methlagl. Brenner Studien Vol. I. Salzburg: Otto Müller, 1969.

——, *Lectures and Conversations on Aesthetics, Psychology and Religious Belief*. Berkeley: University of California Press, 1967.

——, *Notebooks 1914–1916*, G. H. von Wright and G. E. M. Anscombe eds., trans. by G. E. M. Anscombe. Oxford: Basil Blackwell, 1961.

——, *Philosophical Investigations*, G. H. von Wright and G. E. M. Anscombe eds., trans. by G. E. M. Anscombe. Oxford: Basil Blackwell, 1953.

——, *Tractatus Logico-Philosophicus*. Trans. by C. K. Ogden, with an Introduction by Bertrand Russell. London: Kegan Paul, Trench, Trübner, 1922; New York: Harcourt, Brace, 1922.

Select Bibliography

———, *Tractatus Logico-Philosophicus*, trans. by D. F. Pears and B. F. Mc-Guinness, with an Introduction by Bertrand Russell. International Library of Philosophy and Scientific Method. London: Routledge and Kegan Paul, 1961; New York: Humanities Press, 1961.

———, *Zettel*, G. H. von Wright and G. E. M. Anscombe eds., trans. by G. E. M. Anscombe. Oxford: Basil Blackwell, 1967.

Wood, Frank. *Rainer Maria Rilke: The Ring of Forms*. Minneapolis: University of Minnesota Press, 1958.

Ziolkowski, Theodore, *Hermann Broch*. Columbia Essays on Modern Writers, No. 3. New York: Columbia University Press, 1964.

Zohn, Harry, ed., *Der farbenvolle Untergang: Österreichisches Lesebuch*. Englewood Cliffs, N.J.: Prentice-Hall, 1971.

———, *Karl Kraus*. Twayne's World Author Series. New York: Twayne Publishers Inc., 1972.

Zweig, Stefan, *The World of Yesterday: An Autobiography*, translator anonymous. New York: Viking Press, 1943.

ARTICLES

Ableitinger, Alfred, "The Movement Toward Parliamentary Government in Austria Since 1900: Rudolf Sieghart's Memoir of June 28, 1903," *Austrian History Yearbook II* (1966), pp. 111–35.

Boltzmann, Ludwig, "Theories as Representations," *The Philosophy of Science*, Arthur Danto and Sidney Morgenbesser, eds. Cleveland and New York: Meridian Books, 1960, pp. 245–52.

———, "Über die Methoden der theoretischen Physik," *Katalog mathematischer und mathematisch-physikalischer Modelle, Apparate und Instrument*. Munich, 1892, pp. 89–97.

Bush, Wendell D., "Avenarius and the Standpoint of Pure Experience," *Archives of Philosophy, Psychology and Scientific Method*, II (1905).

Čapek, Milič, "Ernst Mach's Biological Theory of Knowledge," *Synthèse*, XVIII, No. 2/3 (April, 1968), pp. 171–91.

Carstanjen, Friedrich, "Richard Avenarius and His General Theory of Knowledge: Empiriocriticism," *Mind*, VI (1897), pp. 449–75.

Cohen, Robert S., "Ernst Mach: Physics, Perception, and Philosophy of Science," *Synthèse*, XVIII, No. 2/3 (April 1968), pp. 132–70.

Cowan, Joseph L., "Wittgenstein's Philosophy of Logic," *Philosophical Review*, LXX (July, 1961), pp. 362–75.

Daly, C. B., "New Light on Wittgenstein," *Philosophical Studies*, X (1960), pp. 5–48; XI (1961–1962), pp. 28–62.

Daviau, Donald G., "The Heritage of Karl Kraus," *Books Abroad*, 1964.

———, "Language and Morality in Karl Kraus's *Die Letzten Tage der Menschheit*," *Modern Language Quarterly*, XXII, No. 1 (March, 1961).

Dummett, Michael, "Wittgenstein's Philosophy of Mathematics," *Philosophical Review*, LXVIII (July, 1959).

Engel, S. Morris, "Schopenhauer's Impact upon Wittgenstein," *Journal of the History of Philosophy*, VII, No. 3 (July, 1969), pp. 285–302.

Select Bibliography

Fann, K. T., "A Wittgenstein Bibliography," *International Philosophical Quarterly*, VII (August, 1967), pp. 317–39.

Farrell, Brian, "An Appraisal of Therapeutic Positivism," *Mind*, LV (1946), pp. 25–48, 133–50.

Favrholdt, David, *"Tractatus 5.542,"* *Mind*, LXXIII (January, 1965), pp. 557–562.

Fischer, Heinrich, "The Other Austria and Karl Kraus," *In Tyrannos: Four Centuries of Struggle Against Tyranny in Germany*, Hans J. Rehfisch, ed. London: Lindsay Drummond, 1944.

Frege, Gottlob, "On Herr Peano's Begriffsschrift and My Own," *Australasian Journal of Philosophy*, XLVII, No. 3 (May, 1969).

Geach, P. T., "Review of G. Colombo's Translation of the *Tractatus* into Italian," *Philosophical Review*, LXVI (December, 1957), pp. 556–59.

Hall, Roland, "Review of *Schopenhauer* by Patrick Gardiner," *Philosophical Quarterly*, XIV (April, 1964), pp. 174–75.

Hamburg, Carl, "Whereof One Cannot Speak," *Journal of Philosophy*, L (October 22, 1953), pp. 662–64.

Heller, Erich, "Ludwig Wittgenstein: Unphilosophical Notes," *Encounter*, XIII (September, 1959), pp. 40–48.

—— et al., "Ludwig Wittgenstein: A Symposium, Assessments of the Man and the Philosopher," *The Listener*, LXIII (January 8 and February 4, 1964), pp. 163–65, 207–9.

Hintikka, Jaakko, "On Wittgenstein's Solipsism," *Mind*, LXVII (January, 1958), pp. 88–91.

Holmer, Paul L., "Indirect Communication," *Perkins Journal*, Spring 1971, pp. 14–24.

Holton, Gerald, "Mach, Einstein, and the Search for Reality," *Daedalus*, XCVII (Spring, 1968), pp. 636–73.

Janik, Allan S. "Schopenhauer and the Early Wittgenstein," *Philosophical Studies*, XV (1966), pp. 76–95.

Jenks, William A., "The Later Habsburg Concept of Statecraft," *Austrian History Yearbook II* (1966), pp. 92–110.

Johnson, W. E., "The Logical Calculus," *Mind*, I (1892), pp. 1–30, 235–50, 340–58.

Kann, Robert A., "The Image of the Austrian in the Writings of Arthur Schnitzler," *Studies in Arthur Schnitzler*, Herbert Reichert and Herman Salinger, eds. Chapel Hill: University of North Carolina Press, 1963, pp. 45–70.

Keyt, David, "Wittgenstein's Notion of an Object," *Philosophical Quarterly*, XIII (January, 1963), pp. 13–25.

Kraft, Werner, "Ludwig Wittgenstein und Karl Kraus," *Die Neue Deutsche Rundschau*, LXXII, No. 4 (1961), pp. 812–44.

Kraus, Karl. *Die Fackel*, No. 400 (Summer, 1914).

Leitner, Bernhard, "Wittgenstein's Architecture," *Art Forum*, February 1970, pp. 59–61.

Levi, Albert William, "Wittgenstein as Dialectician," *Journal of Philosophy*, LXI (February 13, 1964), pp. 127–39.

Select Bibliography

McGuinness, B. F., "The Mysticism of the *Tractatus*," *Philosophical Review*, LXXV (July, 1966), pp. 305–28.

Methlagl, Walter, and Rochelt, Hans, "Das Porträt: Ludwig Wittgenstein zur 80 Wiederkehr seines Geburtstags." Unpublished radio broadcast of April 19, 1969.

Moore, G. E., "The Refutation of Idealism," *Mind*, XII (1903), pp. 433–53.

Munson, Thomas, "Wittgenstein's Phenomenology," *Philosophy and Phenomenological Research*, XXIII (September, 1962), pp. 37–50.

"Passionate Philosopher, The," *The Times Literary Supplement*, Friday, May 1, 1959, pp. 249–50.

Passmore, John, "The Idea of the History of Philosophy," *History and Theory*, Beiheft 5 (1965), pp. 1–32.

Payne, E. F. J., "Schopenhauer in English: A Critical Survey of Existing Translations," *Schopenhauer Jahrbuch*, XXXIII (1949–50), pp. 95–102.

Peursen, C. A. van, "Edmund Husserl and Ludwig Wittgenstein," *Journal of Philosophy and Phenomenological Research*, XX (September, 1959), pp. 181–95.

Plochman, George Kimball, "Review of *An Introduction to Wittgenstein's Tractatus* by G. E. M. Anscombe," *The Modern Schoolman*, XXXVII (March, 1960), pp. 242–46.

Ramsey, Frank P., "Review of the *Tractatus Logico-Philosophicus* by Ludwig Wittgenstein," *Mind*, XXXII (October, 1923), pp. 465–78.

Rhees, Rush, "Miss Anscombe on the *Tractatus*," *Philosophical Quarterly*, X (January, 1960), pp. 21–31.

———, "*The Tractatus*: Seeds of Some Misunderstandings," *Philosophical Review*, LXXII (April, 1963), pp. 213–20.

Rochelt, Hans, "Das Creditiv der Sprache," *Literatur und Kritik*, XXXIII (April, 1969), pp. 169–76.

———, "Vom ethischen Sinn des Wittgensteinischen *Tractatus*." Unpublished manuscript.

Rosenberg, Hans. "Political and Social Consequences of the Great Depression of 1873–1896 in Central Europe," *Economic History Review*, XIII (1943), 58–73.

S., "A Logical Mystic," *The Nation and Athenaeum* (January 27, 1923).

Schaper, Eva, "Kant's Schematism Reconsidered," *Review of Metaphics*, XVIII (December, 1964), pp. 267–92.

Schick, Paul, "Die Beiden Sphären," *Der Alleingang*, I, No. 1 (February, 1964), pp. 28–36.

Schnitzler, Henry, "Gay Vienna—Myth and Reality," *Journal of the History of Ideas*, XV, No. 1 (January, 1954), pp. 94–118.

Schorske, Carl E., "Politics and the Psyche in *fin-de-siècle* Vienna: Schnitzler and Hofmannsthal," *American Historical Review*, LXVI, No. 4 (July, 1961), pp. 930–46.

———, "Politics in a New Key: An Austrian Triptych," *Journal of Modern History*, XXXIV, No. 4 (December, 1967), pp. 343–86.

———, "The Transformation of the Garden: Ideal and Society in Austrian Literature," *American Historical Review*, LXXII, No. 4 (July, 1967), pp. 1283–1320.

Select Bibliography

Schwayder, David, "Review of *Wittgenstein's Tractatus: A Critical Exposition of its Main Lines of Thought*," *Mind*, LXXII (April, 1963), pp. 275–88.

Smith, Norman, "Avenarius' Philosophy of Pure Experience," *Mind*, XV (1906), pp. 13–31, 149–60.

Stern, J. P., "Karl Kraus's Vision of Language," *Modern Language Review*, (January, 1966), pp. 71–84.

Toulmin, Stephen, "Criticism in the History of Science: Newton, Time and Motion," *Philosophical Review*, LXVIII (1959), pp. 1–29, 203–27.

——, "Ludwig Wittgenstein," *Encounter*, XXXII, No. 1 (January, 1969), pp. 58–71.

Weiler, Gershon, "Fritz Mauthner," *Encyclopedia of Philosophy*, Paul Edwards, ed., 8 vols. New York: Macmillan, and The Free Press, 1967.

——, "Fritz Mauthner as an Historian," *History and Theory*, IV, No. 1 (1964), pp. 57–71.

——, "Fritz Mauthner: A Study in Jewish Self-Rejection," *Leo Baeck Yearbook*, VIII (1963), pp. 136–48.

——, "On Fritz Mauthner's Critique of Language," *Mind*, LXVII (January, 1958), pp. 80–87.

Wittels, Fritz, "The Fackel Neurosis," *Minutes of the Vienna Psychoanalytical Society 1908–1910*. Edited by H. Nunberg and E. Federn. New York: International Universities Press, 1967, pp. 382–93.

Wittgenstein, Ludwig, "Logisch-Philosophische Abhandlung," *Annalen der Naturphilosophie*, XIV (1921), pp. 185–262.

——, "Wittgenstein's Lecture on Ethics," *The Philosophical Review*, LXXIV (January, 1965), pp. 3–27.

Wright, Georg Henrik von, "Georg Christoph Lichtenberg," *Encyclopedia of Philosophy*, Paul Edwards, ed., 8 vols. New York: Macmillan and The Free Press, 1967.

——, "Ludwig Wittgenstein, a Biographical Sketch," *Philosophical Review*, LXIV (October, 1955), pp. 527–44.

Zemach, Eddy, "Wittgenstein's Philosophy of the Mystical," *Review of Metaphysics*, XVIII (September, 1964), pp. 38–57.

Index

Index

Index

Index

Index

Index

Index

Index

Index

A NOTE ON THE AUTHORS

Allan Janik was born in Chicopee, Massachusetts, and studied at St. Anselm's College, Villanova University, and Brandeis University. He has taught philosophy and the history of ideas at La Salle College and at Wellesley College, and is now a fellow at the Research Institute of the Brenner Archives at the University of Innsbruck in Austria. His other books include *Style, Politics and the Future of Philosophy*.

Stephen Toulmin was born in London and studied at Cambridge University. He has taught philosophy and the history of ideas at Oxford University, the University of Melbourne, the University of Leeds, Brandeis University, Michigan State University, and the University of Chicago, and is now professor of philosophy at the University of Southern California. His other books include *Human Understanding* and *Knowing and Acting*.

ELEPHANT PAPERBACKS

European and World History
Mark Frankland, *The Patriots' Revolution,* EL201
Lloyd C. Gardner, *Spheres of Influence,* EL131
Gertrude Himmelfarb, *Darwin and the Darwinian Revolution,* EL207
Gertrude Himmelfarb, *Victorian Minds,* EL205
Thomas A. Idinopulos, *Jerusalem,* EL204
Allan Janik and Stephen Toulmin, *Wittgenstein's Vienna,* EL208
Ronnie S. Landau, *The Nazi Holocaust,* EL203
Clive Ponting, *1940: Myth and Reality,* EL202
Scott Shane, *Dismantling Utopia,* EL206

American History and American Studies
Stephen Vincent Benét, *John Brown's Body,* EL10
Henry W. Berger, ed., *A William Appleman Williams Reader,* EL126
Andrew Bergman, *We're in the Money,* EL124
Paul Boyer, ed., *Reagan as President,* EL117
Robert V. Bruce, *1877: Year of Violence,* EL102
Philip Callow, *From Noon to Starry Night,* EL37
George Dangerfield, *The Era of Good Feelings,* EL110
Clarence Darrow, *Verdicts Out of Court,* EL2
Floyd Dell, *Intellectual Vagabondage,* EL13
Elisha P. Douglass, *Rebels and Democrats,* EL108
Theodore Draper, *The Roots of American Communism,* EL105
Joseph Epstein, *Ambition,* EL7
Lloyd C. Gardner, *Spheres of Influence,* EL131
Paul W. Glad, *McKinley, Bryan, and the People,* EL119
Daniel Horowitz, *The Morality of Spending,* EL122
Kenneth T. Jackson, *The Ku Klux Klan in the City, 1915–1930,* EL123
Edward Chase Kirkland, *Dream and Thought in the Business Community,*
    1860–1900, EL114
Herbert S Klein, *Slavery in the Americas,* EL103
Aileen S. Kraditor, *Means and Ends in American Abolitionism,* EL111
Leonard W. Levy, *Jefferson and Civil Liberties: The Darker Side,* EL107
Thomas J. McCormick, *China Market,* EL115
Walter Millis, *The Martial Spirit,* EL104
Nicolaus Mills, ed., *Culture in an Age of Money,* EL302
Nicolaus Mills, *Like a Holy Crusade,* EL129
Roderick Nash, *The Nervous Generation,* EL113
William L. O'Neill, ed., *Echoes of Revolt: The Masses, 1911–1917,* EL5
Gilbert Osofsky, *Harlem: The Making of a Ghetto,* EL133
Edward Pessen, *Losing Our Souls,* EL132
Glenn Porter and Harold C. Livesay, *Merchants and Manufacturers,* EL106
John Prados, *Presidents' Secret Wars,* EL134
Edward Reynolds, *Stand the Storm,* EL128
Edward A. Shils, *The Torment of Secrecy,* EL303
Geoffrey S. Smith, *To Save a Nation,* EL125
Bernard Sternsher, ed., *Hitting Home: The Great Depression in Town and*
    Country, EL109
Athan Theoharis, *From the Secret Files of J. Edgar Hoover,* EL127
Nicholas von Hoffman, *We Are the People Our Parents Warned Us Against,*
    EL301
Norman Ware, *The Industrial Worker, 1840–1860,* EL116
Tom Wicker, *JFK and LBJ: The Influence of Personality upon Politics,* EL120
Robert H. Wiebe, *Businessmen and Reform,* EL101
T. Harry Williams, *McClellan, Sherman and Grant,* EL121
Miles Wolff, *Lunch at the 5 & 10,* EL118
Randall B. Woods and Howard Jones, *Dawning of the Cold War,* EL130

ELEPHANT PAPERBACKS

Literature and Letters
Stephen Vincent Benét, *John Brown's Body*, EL10
Isaiah Berlin, *The Hedgehog and the Fox*, EL21
Robert Brustein, *Dumbocracy in America*, EL421
Anthony Burgess, *Shakespeare*, EL27
Philip Callow, *From Noon to Starry Night*, EL37
Philip Callow, *Son and Lover: The Young D. H. Lawrence*, EL14
Philip Callow, *Vincent Van Gogh*, EL38
James Gould Cozzens, *Castaway*, EL6
James Gould Cozzens, *Men and Brethren*, EL3
Clarence Darrow, *Verdicts Out of Court*, EL2
Floyd Dell, *Intellectual Vagabondage*, EL13
Theodore Dreiser, *Best Short Stories*, EL1
Joseph Epstein, *Ambition*, EL7
André Gide, *Madeleine*, EL8
Gerald Graff, *Literature Against Itself*, EL35
John Gross, *The Rise and Fall of the Man of Letters*, EL18
Irving Howe, *William Faulkner*, EL15
Aldous Huxley, *After Many a Summer Dies the Swan*, EL20
Aldous Huxley, *Ape and Essence*, EL19
Aldous Huxley, *Collected Short Stories*, EL17
Sinclair Lewis, *Selected Short Stories*, EL9
William L. O'Neill, ed., *Echoes of Revolt: The Masses, 1911–1917*, EL5
Budd Schulberg, *The Harder They Fall*, EL36
Ramón J. Sender, *Seven Red Sundays*, EL11
Peter Shaw, *Recovering American Literature*, EL34
Wilfrid Sheed, *Office Politics*, EL4
Tess Slesinger, *On Being Told That Her Second Husband Has Taken His First
  Lover, and Other Stories*, EL12
B. Traven, *The Bridge in the Jungle*, EL28
B. Traven, *The Carreta*, EL25
B. Traven, *The Cotton-Pickers*, EL32
B. Traven, *General from the Jungle*, EL33
B. Traven, *Government*, EL23
B. Traven, *March to the Montería*, EL26
B. Traven, *The Night Visitor and Other Stories*, EL24
B. Traven, *The Rebellion of the Hanged*, EL29
Anthony Trollope, *Trollope the Traveller*, EL31
Rex Warner, *The Aerodrome*, EL22
Thomas Wolfe, *The Hills Beyond*, EL16

ELEPHANT PAPERBACKS

Theatre and Drama
Robert Brustein, *Dumbocracy in America,* EL421
Robert Brustein, *Reimagining American Theatre,* EL410
Robert Brustein, *The Theatre of Revolt,* EL407
Irina and Igor Levin, *Working on the Play and the Role,* EL411
Plays for Performance:
    Aristophanes, *Lysistrata,* EL405
    Pierre Augustin de Beaumarchais, *The Marriage of Figaro,* EL418
    Anton Chekhov, *The Cherry Orchard,* EL420
    Anton Chekhov, *The Seagull,* EL407
    Euripides, *The Bacchae,* EL419
    Euripides, *Iphigenia in Aulis,* EL423
    Euripides, *Iphigenia Among the Taurians,* EL424
    Georges Feydeau, *Paradise Hotel,* EL403
    Henrik Ibsen, *Ghosts,* EL401
    Henrik Ibsen, *Hedda Gabler,* EL413
    Henrik Ibsen, *The Master Builder,* EL417
    Henrik Ibsen, *When We Dead Awaken,* EL408
    Heinrich von Kleist, *The Prince of Homburg,* EL402
    Christopher Marlowe, *Doctor Faustus,* EL404
    The Mysteries: Creation, EL412
    The Mysteries: The Passion, EL414
    Sophocles, *Electra,* EL415
    August Strindberg, *The Father,* EL406
    August Strindberg, *Miss Julie,* EL422